LLOYD'S OF LONDON

ALSO BY GODFREY HODGSON

An American Melodrama:
The Presidential Campaign of 1968
(with Lewis Chester and Bruce Page)

Do You Sincerely Want to Be Rich?
(with Charles Row and Bruce Page)

America in Our Time

All Things to All Men:
The False Promise of the Modern American Presidency

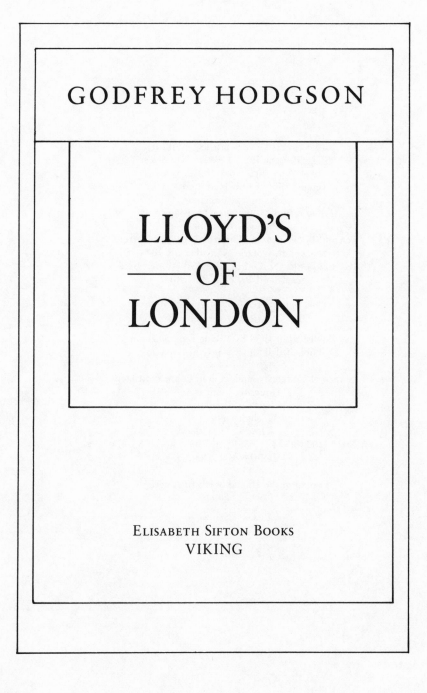

GODFREY HODGSON

LLOYD'S
—OF—
LONDON

ELISABETH SIFTON BOOKS
VIKING

ELISABETH SIFTON BOOKS • VIKING
Viking Penguin Inc., 40 West 23rd Street,
New York, New York 10010, U.S.A.
Penguin Books Ltd, Harmondsworth,
Middlesex, England
Penguin Books Australia Ltd, Ringwood,
Victoria, Australia
Penguin Books Canada Limited, 2801 John Street,
Markham, Ontario, Canada L3R 1B4
Penguin Books (N.Z.) Ltd, 182–190 Wairau Road,
Auckland 10, New Zealand

Published in 1984 by Viking Penguin Inc.
Published simultaneously in Canada

Library of Congress Cataloging in Publication Data
Hodgson, Godfrey.
Lloyd's of London.
Includes index.
1. Lloyd's. I. Title.
HG8039.H62   1984   368'.102'094212   83-47926
ISBN 0-670-43595-3

Printed in the United States of America
Set in Sabon

CONTENTS

· I ·

THE LINER IN LIME STREET   7

· 2 ·

THE RINGING OF THE LUTINE BELL   33

· 3 ·

THE VOYAGE   45

· 4 ·

PASSENGERS AND CREW   76

· 5 ·

OFFICERS AND TRAVEL AGENTS   119

· 6 ·

THE STORM   151

· 7 ·

FIRE ON BOARD   195

· 8 ·

MAN OVERBOARD!   220

· 9 ·

A MUTINY IN FIRST CLASS   242

· 10 ·

CALM SEA AND PROSPEROUS VOYAGE?   284

· 11 ·

DRY DOCK   301

· 12 ·

ICEBERGS!   320

EPILOGUE   362

INDEX   365

CHAPTER 1

THE LINER IN LIME STREET

Lloyd's is a market for the transaction of insurance business between Lloyd's Brokers, acting for Assureds, and Underwriters accepting risks on behalf of Syndicates of Names.

Report of a working party
under the chairmanship of Sir Henry Fisher
into *Self-Regulation at Lloyd's*, May 1980

Quinquereme of Nineveh from distant Ophir
Rowing home to haven in sunny Palestine,
With a cargo of ivory,
And apes and peacocks,
Sandalwood, cedarwood, and sweet white wine . . .
Dirty British coaster with a salt-caked smoke stack
Butting through the Channel in the mad March days,
With a cargo of Tyne coal,
Road-rail, pig-lead,
Firewood, iron-ware, and cheap tin trays.

John Masefield, *Cargoes*

The first news that the *Bill Crosbie* was about to be transformed from a living freighter into a loss payable by underwriters at Lloyd's was an SOS on the morning of 4 January 1980. It was picked up by a passing ship and relayed to the Lloyd's intelligence department, at Colchester, fifty miles north-east of London, in the form of a telex from the marine radio station at Valentia Island, off the south-western tip of County Kerry, in Ireland. Before noon, Lloyd's had confirmation that the *Bill Crosbie* was in trouble from the Canadian coastguard's rescue co-ordination centre in Halifax, Nova Scotia, and from the ship's owners, Crosbie & Co. Ltd, in St John's, Newfoundland. By 2.30 that after-noon, the casualty reporting officer at Colchester, Roger Lowes, had passed the message back to the half-dozen salvage tug companies of various nationalities that patrol the North Atlantic looking for profit-able acts of knight errantry to perform on vessels in distress.

Colchester then reported what had happened to those responsible for insuring the *Bill Crosbie* at Lloyd's: to Crosbie & Co.'s marine insurance brokers, Holmwood & Crawfurd, an old-established company with offices in the Minories, near the Tower of London; and to the leading underwriters, Henry G. Chester & Co., which had accepted the risk on behalf of a syndicate of around a thousand wealthy individuals. That acceptance had been signified by a rubber stamp thumped on to a slip of paper, and by initials scrawled thereon by the present Henry Chester, nephew and namesake of the firm's founder, at his wooden 'box' in the underwriting Room at Lloyd's, half a mile west of the Tower in the heart of the shipping, insurance and financial district of the City of London.

If the *Bill Crosbie* was lost, the Chester syndicate and all the other Lloyd's syndicates and London insurance companies that had signed Holmwood & Crawfurd's slip and so accepted a share of the risk would be liable to pay the owners her insured value. But she was not lost yet. She was a small vessel, 2,500 tons deadweight and 307 feet long overall, built in Sweden fifteen years before. After a couple of years in British ownership she had been bought by the Canadians and put to work in the Far North trade. It is a dangerous calling, and shipowners pay an extra premium to insure vessels in it.

On this particular voyage the *Bill Crosbie* sailed from Halifax and picked up a cargo of steel beams and grinding-balls in Montreal, then headed for Ireland. The weather was atrocious, with waves between twenty and twenty-five feet high. Five hundred and fifty miles east of her home port, St John's, the cargo in number 1 hold shifted, canting the *Bill Crosbie* over in a thirty-degree list to port. The crew were lucky. When a lumpy cargo shifts suddenly, it can send a ship straight to the bottom. But as it was, the *Bill Crosbie* limped on, and help was at hand. The *Atlantic Saga*, a modern container ship that had passed on her first distress signals, was soon standing by. And a big salvage tug, the *Hirtenturm*, out of Bremen in West Germany, was a day's sailing away and hurrying to the scene.

As soon as she came up, the *Hirtenturm* took off fourteen of the crew, leaving only a skeleton crew of three on board as she took the *Bill Crosbie* in tow. The weather and the *Bill Crosbie*'s list worsened, however, and on 7 January the *Bill Crosbie*'s master took off the last of the crew. The *Hirtenturm* made St John's at half past one in the afternoon of 9 January, with the *Bill Crosbie*'s port gunwale now under water. She was moored alongside the quay at Harvey's wharf in St John's harbour. But at nine o'clock that night she rolled to port and sank in forty-five feet of water with only the tip of her superstructure poking above the surface.

For the crew of the *Bill Crosbie* and for her rescuers, those five days and nights in the January storms on the Grand Banks must have been a terrifying ordeal. At Lloyd's, they were routine. A very modest marine casualty. A few lines teletyped on a strip of paper and tacked up on a notice-board in the Room. So much paperwork in a broker's office, so much to be dealt with by an underwriter's claims man. So much money to be paid out. Elemental fury, tamed into laconic entries in books of account.

That is Lloyd's. It is a place where all the perils of this world, its storms and fires and floods and earthquakes, and every possible man-made calamity are systematically reduced to manageable routine. These perils are chopped up and spread around and shared out so that instead of being an unbearable risk for a few, they are a small risk for many and thus lose their terror.

That is the fundamental idea of insurance: to make risks bearable by sharing them around, at a price; or, as an Elizabethan Act of Parliament pithily put it, 'the losse lighteth rather easilie upon many, than heavilie upon few'. It was not invented at Lloyd's, of course. The quinquereme of Nineveh in the first verse of Masefield's poem, as a matter of established historical fact, is just as likely to have carried marine insurance, written by a Phoenician merchant, as the dirty British coaster in the last verse. Still, Lloyd's is a place where marine insurance has been written for three hundred years. Around that primal function, other insurance markets have grown up. And Lloyd's has come to provide many other services besides insurance to the world's maritime industry. Most of them derive from that second highly valuable commodity which the founder of Lloyd's coffee house dispensed, along with refreshment, to his customers, the merchants in Tower Street: accurate information about ships and their cargoes. Lloyd's intelligence department at Colchester, with its computer that tracks the comings and goings of more than 20,000 ships active in international maritime trade in every significant port outside the Soviet-dominated countries, from Aarhus to Yokohama, is the brain at the centre of a whole system of services to shipping.

So there is Lloyd's the private international organization, providing information and many other services to the maritime industry, and there is Lloyd's the insurance market, where brokers come to buy marine, non-marine, aviation and motor insurance from syndicates of underwriters. A very large share of that business – more than half

overall, and as much as two-thirds in certain specialist markets – is sold
to the United States. Proportionally, only a tiny share of the insurance
premium paid in the United States every year comes to Lloyd's. Still,
Lloyd's is very important to the American insurance industry, for two
reasons. First, Lloyd's specializes in arranging insurances that no one
else either can or will do, and that includes some of the very biggest
and most dangerous risks – to take a single example, oil-drilling rigs.
Second, Lloyd's will arrange insurances that no one has undertaken
before. Lloyd's, in other words, plays the role of the specialist and the
innovator in an American industry that is highly regulated and also
dedicated to a high volume of repetitive business. Lloyd's can do this
because it is limited in the United States to what is called 'surplus lines'
business – that is, business that no one else wants. And Lloyd's has also
specialized in reinsurance: the insider's branch of the insurance industry that consists of professionals laying off part of their risks to
other professionals.

So, paradoxically, there is Lloyd's, ultra-British and ultra-
conservative, deeply involved in the American insurance business, and
involved moreover as the high-risk innovative gunslinger in the American marketplace. And then there is Lloyd's the ingenious mechanism
of syndicates, in which individuals venture their whole fortune, to the
last penny, with no limited liability, and yet which by another paradox
has had the effect of preserving the old-established private fortunes
of several hundred of Britain's wealthiest families, besides the lesser
stakes of thousands of more modestly affluent folk, through decades
of economic recession and high taxation.

This book will look at all those aspects of a truly extraordinary
institution. It will examine how the machinery is supposed to work,
and investigate what happened when, on a number of occasions in the
past few years, things went spectacularly wrong. It will follow the
thread of Lloyd's own efforts to put its own house in order, and it will
show how that may be harder than most Lloyd's people think. In the
process, it will wander a long way from the underwriting Room in Lime
Street and a long way, too, from the sober probity of its best traditions.
Under its worsted-suit, silk-tied exterior, in fact, Lloyd's can be an
arena for gladiatorial conflict where the rewards are still high for those
with brains and nerve, and where the devil still takes the hindmost.

The original business of Lloyd's was marine insurance, and well over
a third of Lloyd's aggregate premium income of some $5 billion a year
still comes from marine insurance. Although it can give rise to disputes
of quite mind-numbing complexity, in general the marine market

conforms to a relatively simple pattern that illustrates the basic principles of Lloyd's operation. We could do worse than follow through
the fate of the *Bill Crosbie*, and see exactly how her estate was wound
up after her mortal remains were towed out of St John's harbour,
bottom up, by a tug called the *Irving Birch*, and sent to their last resting
place twelve miles out in the Atlantic.

It fell to Lloyd's to act as her executors as a consequence of certain
historical and geographical facts, notably the fact that the St Lawrence
River freezes over every winter while the North Atlantic, at that
latitude, does not. As a result, the British colony of Newfoundland
(which did not become a part of Canada until after the Second World
War) traditionally looked eastward to Britain, not up the river to Montreal. One of the old-established Newfoundland firms that has kept
some of this orientation towards Britain is the family firm of the
Crosbies, which has been coasting in the Maritimes and adventuring
in the Far North trade for more than a hundred years. The Crosbie fleet
has never been large, no more than half a dozen tough, smallish ships.
The *Bill Crosbie* belonged to a Crosbie subsidiary called Chimo Shipping and, like the rest of the fleet, was insured at Lloyd's.

For the underwriter, this was a fairly simple claim. Henry Chester
has been insuring Crosbie ships for many years. His recollection is that
only two individual brokers from Holmwood & Crawfurd have shown
him the Crosbie account in twenty years. The whole fleet of three or
four vessels would be insured on a single 'slip'. A slip is the piece of
paper containing a summary of the proposed insurance that is physically taken round the Room at Lloyd's to be initialled by underwriters
on behalf of their syndicates. The actual Lloyd's policy, which until the
First World War was signed by underwriters in the Room, is now
signed and recorded on a computer at the Lloyd's Policy Signing Office.
An underwriter who is willing to accept a given risk puts his syndicate's
stamp and his initials on the slip, and he may add any special terms or
alterations in the conditions of the policy that he insists on. He also
writes in the proportion of the risk he is prepared to accept. Any
number of Lloyd's underwriters or insurance companies outside
Lloyd's may write a 'line' – that is, take a share in a given risk. But the
first to initial it, the leading underwriter, takes responsibility for
settling claims and for any negotiations with the broker that may arise.

The Crosbie insurance came up for renewal on 1 February every
year, and Chester himself dealt with it. He would ask a few questions,
and the broker would go back to his client and get the answers. Mostly
his questions would be about differences between one year's figures and

the next. There might be an odd case where an outstanding claim for a repair to one of the fleet had been increased, and Chester would want to know why. But, in general, it was straightforward business, dealt with in a few polite exchanges at the Chester 'box' on the ground floor of the underwriting Room at Lloyd's and quickly disposed of for another year. A box is an underwriter's place of work; it is a big desk, with a superstructure for telephones, records and reference books, and two high-backed wooden benches on either side, where the 'active' underwriters for the syndicates and their key staff spend their working hours. All members of the syndicates are underwriters; the professionals who actually spend their days in the Room doing the business are called active underwriters to distinguish them from the syndicate members who merely provide a share of the working capital and take a share of the profits.

For Henry Chester, a gravely courteous man of about sixty with a slight limp, the Crosbie account was a nice piece of business: no big deal, certainly, for a man who is accustomed to accept tens of millions of dollars in premium every year; still, something he would be sorry to lose, and over the years he expected to break even or do a little better than even on it. Chester was the leading underwriter for the hull of the *Bill Crosbie*. (The cargo was separately insured by a Canadian broker with the Insurance Company of North America in New York.) The insured value of the hull was Canadian $850,000. Of this the Chester box, as the leading underwriter, had taken 3·2 per cent for the major syndicate it manages, and another 0·5 per cent on behalf of another smaller syndicate managed by the firm. Henry Chester's decision to sign the slip meant that all the individual members of his two syndicates between them had accepted responsibility for 3·7 per cent of the ship's value. The rate was healthy. On top of the basic rate for insuring the hull, there was the additional premium for insuring a ship trading in the dangerous waters of the Far North. If the *Bill Crosbie* had ventured farther up the St Lawrence than Montreal, that too would have added to the premium.

There was no difficulty in agreeing to treat the *Bill Crosbie* as a 'constructive total loss'. The term means simply that, although the ship could perhaps have been salvaged and repaired, the cost of the operation would have come to more than the insured value. A salvage company did in fact cut into the hull and rescue the cargo, and the hull was raised in order to be towed out to sea and sunk in a safer place, and 23,000 gallons of diesel fuel were pumped out and auctioned off. The brokers contacted the Lloyd's Underwriters Claims and Recoveries Office, which is housed in a new ten-storey office building a few hundred yards from Lloyd's. LUCRO instructed the St John's office of the Salvage Association (an organization closely connected with Lloyd's), which sent a surveyor to look at her before she was sunk. He carried out his survey and contacted the owners. In this instance it was a simple matter to establish the documentation, get repair estimates and show to the satisfaction of all parties that the costs would exceed the insured value. 'In a case like that,' Chester says, 'you would expect to pay the claim promptly.'

As far as the Chester box was concerned, that was the end of the *Bill Crosbie* business: a fairly uncomplicated casualty, of modest size, and promptly paid. The Lloyd's system had worked smoothly. On 1 February 1980, Henry Chester signed a new slip to cover Crosbie & Co.'s new fleet. Forty per cent of the risk was placed in Lloyd's, with Chester as the leader as usual; the rest was taken by London insurance companies. The rate of premium, as a result of the demise of the *Bill Crosbie*, was up. On 5 March 1980, just two months after the casualty and eight months before the vessel was physically disposed of, the Chester box sent a cheque for $850,000 to Chimo Shipping. That was not quite the end of the story, however.

While the *Bill Crosbie* was still listing in twenty-foot waves and before the *Hirtenturm* had taken her in tow, her owners signed a salvage agreement with the tug company under what is known as 'Lloyd's open form'. This is a generally accepted form of agreement – so common that a master in difficulties will 'sign' it over the radio knowing exactly what he is agreeing to – under which responsibility for the cost of salvage, awards of financial reward for salvage, and any other disputes that may arise must be settled by arbitration in London. Individual members drawn from a panel of Queen's Counsel – eminent lawyers, in this case ones who specialize in maritime and commercial law – resolve some 150 cases a year from all parts of the world. There is an appeals procedure, which goes to another QC, but once you sign a Lloyd's open form, anywhere in the world, you must accept arbitration in London. So the loose ends of the story that began with the *Bill Crosbie* wallowing towards the stormy coast of Newfoundland will eventually be tidied up in quiet chambers in the Temple or one of the other Inns of Court where London lawyers have their chambers. Long before that, the Crosbies have had their money, and have been able to spend it on buying or chartering another tough little ship to send venturing through the dangerous waters of the Far North.

The two Chester syndicates' share of that money came to Canadian

$31,875. Dividing that sum by the thousand or so individual members, or 'Names' as they are called, who belong to the syndicates would mean that the average Name was some $32 poorer by the death of the *Bill Crosbie*. The system had worked its simple magic. The loss had lighted 'rather easily upon the many than heavily upon the few'.

The possibility of making this happen for shipowners and for the owners of every other kind of industrial and commercial property is more important than is apparent at first sight. It is not just that it makes many activities less risky and therefore more profitable, but that some activities become possible that would be impossible without insurance. It is not simply that shipowners who have already decided to trade in the North Atlantic do a little better than they might otherwise do because they can insure their ships. For if they could not insure their ships, they would never be able to raise the money to buy them in the first place. And what is true of such a relatively traditional and un-complicated asset as a ship is far more true of such an incomparably more complex, expensive and dangerous thing as a nuclear power station.

The accident to one of the two nuclear power reactors at Three Mile Island, near Harrisburg, Pennsylvania, in March 1979, has been called 'the most important sociotechnical event of the decade'. Because a valve failed, the reactor overheated, releasing substantial quantities of radio-active material into the atmosphere. It was more than the worst acci-dent in the nuclear industry's history (outside the Soviet Union). It was its worst political crisis. It led to a radical reassessment of plant safety and therefore of investment plans in the nuclear sector of the power-generating industry around the world. And it whipped up a storm of political opposition that will delay the construction of nuclear plants for many years.

Against such a dramatic canvas, the insurance implications of Three Mile Island might seem tame. However, they were not trivial for the nuclear power industry. If nuclear power plants could not be insured, they could hardly be built or operated. Special arrangements existed for insuring the seventy-six nuclear plants in the United States, but the accident at Three Mile Island showed that these arrangements might fall short, by many hundreds of millions of dollars per plant, of covering the full potential cost of a nuclear accident. This is a far cry from the simplicities of the loss of the *Bill Crosbie*. It is not just that a nuclear plant is infinitely more sophisticated than a freighter, nor even that the sums of money involved are more than a thousand times greater. The insurance of nuclear plant is a highly complicated system in itself.

As for the two plants at Three Mile Island, after the accident they were totally uninsured. Quite apart from the damaged reactor itself, there were hundreds of millions of dollars' worth of turbines, generators, computers and other plant at risk. The way in which cover was ultimately arranged for the stricken plant and its undamaged twin illustrates how vital insurance is in modern high-technology industry and how Lloyd's fits into the international insurance system.

Lloyd's has been involved in insuring nuclear plants from the start. The two nations that pioneered the use of nuclear reactors for generating electric power in the 1950s were Britain and the United States, both with highly developed insurance industries. But in both countries insurance men were wary of this new, dangerous, expensive and largely secret technology. They were frightened by the possible aggregations of liability. And they were afraid that they might be doubly exposed, because risks which they were covering directly could also come back to them through reinsurance arrangements.

So it was agreed from the start that nuclear risks would be written not by individual insurance companies but by 'pools' of companies, sharing the premium as well as the cost of any losses. And secondly it was agreed that anyone who underwrote a nuclear risk must do so as a 'net line' – in other words, he would specifically exclude it from any arrangements he might have for reinsuring* his business. (There was a precedent for this net-line rule in the so-called 'target risks agreement'. At the approach of the Second World War, the American insurance industry had agreed with its partners at Lloyd's that such potential 'target risks' as the mid-town Manhattan tunnels, the Golden Gate bridge or the Mellon family's art collection would not be covered by reinsurance contracts, for the same reason: the industry was afraid of unpredictable aggregations of risk and of double exposure through reinsurance.) Other basic rules of the nuclear insurance game were laid down in the 1950s. One was that nuclear risks were defined as being those requiring special licensing by the controlling authority. A second was that all properties on a nuclear *site* (and there might be more than

---

* Most underwriters cover themselves with reinsurance, in one form or another. The two commonest are 'quota-share' and 'excess-of-loss' reinsurances. In a quota-share reinsurance, the underwriter pays a reinsurer a premium to accept a certain proportion, or quota share, of all the losses he may have to pay on the whole of his book of business. Alternatively, he can pay premium to a reinsurer to pay any loss in excess of a named figure.

one nuclear plant on a site, as there was at Three Mile Island) would be insured by the nuclear pool as a single package.

There were separate pools for insuring nuclear power plants as they were built in different countries: first in Britain, then in the United States, then in Canada, West Germany, Switzerland, Belgium and so on. Lloyd's underwriters took a big share in most of these pools, and Lloyd's brokers played a big part in placing the risks. In the United States, Lloyd's share of the nuclear business was originally as high as 33 per cent: as more and more American insurers came in, it was whittled away, but it was still as high as 7 per cent at the time of the Three Mile Island accident in 1979.

Back in the 1950s, the United States Congress was eager to encourage the building of nuclear power plants. So under the Price–Anderson Act of 1956 (valid for ten years, but renewed in 1966 and 1976) a nuclear plant operator's maximum third-party liability was limited to $560 million. The first $60 million of that was to be provided by the pool; the remaining $500 million would be made available by the federal government.

The history of the American nuclear insurance pools is complicated. There were separate arrangements for insuring the power plant itself as property and for covering the utility company against liability to third parties. In the beginning, the rivalry between stockholder-owned insurance companies and mutual companies led to the creation of four separate pools: the stock companies and the mutuals each had one pool for property insurance and another for liability. The amount of cover available increased gradually over the years, then spurted sharply forward after the Three Mile Island crisis. (In this spurt, too, Lloyd's was involved.)

By 1973, the stock companies had merged their property and liability pools into one, named American Nuclear Insurers (ANI). Three years later another rivalry, this time in the utility industry, further complicated the picture. This was the ideological rivalry between the public power utilities belonging to the American Public Power Association, and the private enterprise utilities grouped in the Edison Electric Institute. Some of the private Edison companies formed a breakaway pool with a 'captive' mutual insurance company, called Nuclear Mutual Limited, owned by a group of utility companies and established in Bermuda to avoid American taxes and regulation.

The two plants at Three Mile Island belonged to Metropolitan Edison, a Pennsylvania subsidiary of General Public Utilities Corporation (GPU). In spite of the Edison connection, the plants were insured with A N I for a maximum of $300 million for physical damage. Fortunately, third-party liability was not – at least immediately – as appalling as it might have been. There were families to be compensated for being relocated from the immediate vicinity of the plant, but radioactivity had not escaped in massive quantities, as was feared at the time of the accident. It was some time, however, before the full potential cost of the physical damage was appreciated. As late as January 1980, nine months after the accident, it was still assessed at no more than $210 million, but this was no more than a guess. There were still half a million gallons of radioactive water slopping around in the damaged reactor, T M I 2, and no one could get close enough to estimate the cost of repairs with any accuracy. The Nuclear Regulatory Commission, the federal government's licensing authority, had withdrawn its licence from both plants. So, on top of the physical-damage bill for clearing up the mess left by the accident, there was the little matter of lost revenue and the cost of replacing the power which the two big plants had once produced. Revenue loss alone was running at $25 million a month, $300 million a year. To date, the accident has cost about $1 billion in clean-up costs, and more than another $1 billion in lost revenue.

Under the Price–Anderson law, nuclear operators are obliged to buy only third-party liability insurance. But there was another reason why G P U desperately needed to insure its plants. The utility was not allowed to increase its rates in order to pay for all these new costs. All it could do was to go to the bond market, where it succeeded in floating $400 million of bonds on fairly stringent terms. But it was a condition of those bonds that the plants, on which the bonds were secured, be insured. G P U, not to put too fine a point on it, found themselves the proud possessors of not one but two nuclear plants, each worth more than a billion dollars, sitting at the mercy of the elements on an island in the Susquehanna River, which might turn out to be completely uncovered by insurance. Moreover, since insurance was a condition of the bonds, even their possession might not be certain. There had not been any stockholder or bond-holder suits, but the G P U management could not dismiss those possibilities. With the greatest possible urgency, therefore, Harry Gerrety, G P U's experienced risks manager, set about trying to find new insurance cover.

A N I did not know to what extent the existing policy was exhausted; no one could be sure what the cost of the accident would ultimately turn out to be. G P U asked A N I to reinstate the policy, but A N I refused to do this. And it raised another awkward question: when did the cost of the original accident end? When it was finally possible to get back into the damaged plant to do repair work, what if more damage to the other plant resulted, either from radioactivity or from any other cause? Was that covered under the existing policy?

So GPU turned to the other pool, NML, to see whether it was willing to insure the undamaged plant, TMI 1. NML agreed, subject to various conditions. The policy was attached on 19 July 1979, with a limit of $225 million, shortly increased to $300 million. Lloyd's underwriters were the leading reinsurers of this policy.

But that still left GPU needing insurance on the damaged plant, TMI 2. Significantly, it turned to Lloyd's. American brokers made approaches on behalf of GPU to two of the biggest firms of Lloyd's brokers: Marsh & McLennan, the biggest insurance broker in the United States consulted C. T. Bowring (Marsh acquired Bowring later in 1980); Frank B. Hall, the third-biggest American broker, consulted the Sedgwick Group. Both British brokers said that it could not be done, that no meaningful amount of cover could be placed at Lloyd's or anywhere else – and for a specific reason. All nuclear policies are written on a site basis, so the two plants could not be separately insured. The two big London brokers said that no new insurance could be placed on what remained unmistakably a single nuclear site.

One of the two American brokers did not take no for an answer. Frank B. Hall turned to a new, comparatively small firm of Lloyd's brokers, Fenchurch International Group. It had been formed only a couple of years before by three young brokers – Roger Earle, Michael Small and Peter Bedford – who had recently quit the long-established firm of Bland Payne when it merged with Sedgwick Forbes to form the giant Sedgwick Group. They were aggressively looking for business, and they were itching to get their hands on any business that Sedgwick said could not be done.

It was Michael Small who thought of a way of doing it. Everyone at Lloyd's has a nickname, and Small is known as 'Mission Impossible'. He thought he saw his opportunity in a technical point. The Nuclear Regulatory Commission had withdrawn the nuclear-power production licences from both the Three Mile Island plants. Therefore, Small argued, they need no longer be classified as nuclear plants. There could be no objection to insuring them against named *non*-nuclear perils – fire, windstorm and the rest – just as if they were so many warehouses full of valuable computers and heavy generating plant.

Fenchurch International planned a layered programme of insurance in the approved fashion. On one slip, insurers would be asked to accept the risk of the first $10 million of any non-nuclear loss. On another slip, underwriters would be asked to take the next $15 million in excess of $10 million, a third would take the slice of potential loss from $25 million to $50 million, and a fourth the risks from $50 million to $100 million.

But the key to the whole operation was getting it underwritten at Lloyd's. Michael Small broked it first to a leading underwriter, Dick Hazell, who writes non-marine insurance and reinsurance for the F. R. White syndicate. Small had itemized the values that were to be covered, including the control room with its computers and the turbine house with its generating plant, all properly depreciated. He was asking Hazell to underwrite it for 'five cents' – that meant five cents for every hundred dollars of insured value, or 0·05 per cent. That may not sound like much, but it would work out at $600,000 in premium over the three years of the contract for all the underwriters who signed the slip. The brokers, in return for 'placing' the slip, could expect a brokerage commission of 20 per cent, split 15 per cent to Frank B. Hall, who had produced the client, and 5 per cent to Fenchurch as the 'wholesale' broker. (Hall, as an American broker, would not have been allowed to approach Lloyd's underwriters except through a Lloyd's broker like Fenchurch. Later, Hall acquired a Lloyd's broker of its own.)

Roger Earle and Michael Small knew what they were doing when they showed the slips with this set of propositions on them to Dick Hazell at his box in the Room at Lloyd's. For one thing, Hazell is an experienced underwriter who is known and trusted in the market and is not unwilling to take a sensible sort of risk if he can see some money to be made out of it. But there was an additional reason. Hazell had never underwritten any of the American nuclear pools, either as a member of them or as one of their reinsurers. He had therefore not been called on to pay any of the Three Mile Island losses. More to the point, because he was a member of the pools, he was not bound by the agreement to write 'net lines', uncovered by reinsurance. He could write the slip and be covered by his existing reinsurance arrangements.

Small carefully explained his proposition. Hazell listened and read the slips. Then he put his syndicate stamp carefully in the place of honour allotted to the leading underwriter at the top of the space provided, and wrote in '15%' before adding his initials in green ink.

That was the big, confident line the Fenchurch boys wanted to start the ball rolling. It meant they could get support for their slips from the other underwriters to whom they broked the risk around the gallery of the Room (where the non-marine syndicates, as the junior market, have their boxes). Without too much difficulty, they placed 70 per cent of the different layers of the insurance at Lloyd's, and the rest with various insurance companies in the London market.

'All went swimmingly for a year', Roger Earle reminisced later. 'GPU were tickled pink. Then things began to go wrong.' The trouble was that powerful people at Lloyd's thought the concept of the 'non-nuclear' insurance had been wrong from the start. The second syndicate with its name on the slip, just below Hazell's, was that of Harvey Bowring & Others, the main non-marine syndicate owned by the second-biggest of the Lloyd's brokers, C. T. Bowring. The chief underwriter for that syndicate is Murray Lawrence, a calm, powerfully built man in his middle forties who played both cricket and golf for Oxford. He was already one of the shrewdest and most respected underwriters in the non-marine market, and was to become one of the two deputy chairmen of Lloyd's a couple of years later. Although Harvey Bowring & Others were committed to the Three Mile Island slips, Lawrence had not personally initialled them. That had been done by his deputy in his absence. Many other underwriters, too, had initialled the slip not knowing that on a nuclear insurance they could not be covered by their reinsurance and not fully aware that the insurance was nuclear. The agreement not to be covered by reinsurance on nuclear insurances, after all, was more than twenty years old, and there had been virtually no significant losses on American nuclear pool insurances before Three Mile Island. Murray Lawrence understood all too well, however, that though Fenchurch had had a perfect right to broke the risks and underwriters a right to accept them, his syndicate was committed to a possible £4 million share of any future loss, and it would not be covered by reinsurance.

It was a potentially embarrassing situation, to put it mildly. The man in the most delicate spot was John Pryke, the underwriter for the C. E. Heath syndicate and chairman of the Lloyd's nuclear subcommittee, which had guided Lloyd's underwriters on nuclear matters since the 1950s. He was quite certain that the policy broked by Fenchurch International was misconceived. For one thing, technically the NRC had *not* withdrawn its licence from the Three Mile Island site, but merely withdrawn its authorization to generate electricity there. There could be no doubt, Pryke believed, that it was a nuclear site. The language of the policy specified that any site where there were substantial quantities of radioactive material was a nuclear site. Half a million gallons clearly qualified as a substantial quantity of radioactive water.

Pryke could and did warn underwriters that they would not be able to count on reinsurance, but he could not order them not to underwrite the business if they wanted to. After all, Dick Hazell knew perfectly well what he was doing and accepted the risk as a sound piece of business, and rather a profitable one at that.

In the end, a highly amicable solution was worked out. John Pryke drew Fenchurch's attention to the fact that their own 'errors and omissions' policy might not cover them in the circumstances (all brokers cover themselves with errors and omissions insurance). Murray Lawrence made it plain that he might think he ought to cancel his syndicate's support for the Fenchurch policies. In any event, it became clear that they could probably not be renewed. On 10 January 1980 A N I issued cover for the undamaged T M I 1 in the amount of $300 million. The N M L policy covered T M I 2. Between them, these policies eliminated the need for the Fenchurch 'named peril' cover on T M I 2 as a non-nuclear risk. Just over a year later, on 1 April 1981, A N I issued a new policy covering both plants. Since then, the American nuclear polls have pressed forward with new insurances to cover nuclear plants. A total of up to $1 billion in cover for each plant is now available. Lloyd's brokers and underwriters played their part in placing and writing most of these big new insurances.

The complex history of the Three Mile Island insurances reveals a side of the Lloyd's reality very different from the story of the *Bill Crosbie*. Whereas most marine casualties are essentially simple, the arranging of a major non-marine cover is apt to be complicated. Whereas in traditional marine insurance Lloyd's underwriters work essentially on their own, in modern non-marine insurance they often fit in as a comparatively small though important piece in an intricate mechanism. In a major non-marine insurance, several big American brokers and several Lloyd's brokers represent different interests; one or more governments and half a dozen different industry associations or consortia may help to set the rules of the game; and insurance is likely to be only one of many considerations in the competing strategies of giant corporate groups manoeuvring to avoid catastrophic losses and keep their long-term investment plans on course.

In the rather rarefied atmosphere of major non-marine insurance business, the individual underwriter is apt to find himself with re-stricted freedom of choice. The dominant figure is the broker, and especially the big Lloyd's broker, with a staff of many hundreds of specialists adept at coping with the technological, legal and political implications of billion-dollar investments and high-technology systems. Even the biggest of these Lloyd's brokers, moreover, are being drawn into a largely subsidiary position in an international system in which the queens of the battlefield are the giant American mega-brokers, with access to the corporate accounts of the largest multi-national corporations. In this international insurance world, Lloyd's plays a vital specialist role, highly profitable to both its brokers and underwriters; yet it is increasingly hard to avoid the conclusion that it is essentially a subordinate role. So that is the first paradox, when you look at it closely: the ultra-British Lloyd's of London is heavily dependent on fitting into the interstices of the American insurance industry.

The Three Mile Island story also hints at another paradox in the workings of the modern Lloyd's. Lloyd's is a place where, on the one hand, individualism and initiative of the sort that produced Michael Small's ingenious scheme are both praised and – possibly to a lesser degree – practised. On the other hand, it is a system where individual initiative has to a considerable extent been superseded. It is the market as a whole, rather than the individual underwriter, that must organize insurance cover for a vast and potentially hazardous new industry in an age of high technology, multinational enterprise and exploding insurable values. The market, accordingly, organizes itself with com-mittees and subcommittees and market agreements – some of them, like the international agreements on nuclear plants or on oil pollution, far transcending Lloyd's. There hovers around much of this a flavour of convention, concordat, even cartel.

Yet in spite of this tendency, Lloyd's remains a *market* – not an entity, still less an organization. Powerful forces can intervene – as John Pryke and Murray Lawrence did – to use their influence to prevent the market behaving in what they saw as a rash and dangerous way. But it remains a market. No one can be certain of controlling it. There is an Establishment at Lloyd's, and it has great influence, but it does not have absolute power. Indeed, as we shall see, the Committee, which is the institutional representation of the Establishment, proved to have too little power to control events. In a marketplace, many follow the crowd, content to take home a steady income by avoiding any depar-ture from the beaten track. Individuals like Roger Earle and Michael Small, or Dick Hazell, can still chart their own path. If they can meet a need, even a passing need, there will be money to be made, and no one will hold it against them that they moved in swiftly to grasp an opportunity.

It is hard to think of any event significant enough to be reported in the news media (including those that are significant but unknown to the media) that does not have an impact somewhere in the Room at Lloyd's. If there is a war between Iran and Iraq and ships are marooned in the Shatt-al-Arab waterway, then Lloyd's underwriters will be called on to pay up on blocking-and-trapping policies. If a painting sells for a record price at Sotheby Parke Bernet, that will directly affect the premium charged by the specialist underwriters who insure art exhibitions and art treasures in transit. If a foreign businessman is kidnapped in Italy or Argentina, Lloyd's underwriters will be at risk, and specially trained former British Secret Intelligence Service officers may well move in, as a condition of the Lloyd's policy, to advise the client how to handle the ransom negotiations. If a deep-sea diving team raises gold bullion from a wreck, or a tanker pollutes the beaches of Brittany, or a hurricane sweeps the oil rigs in the Gulf of Mexico, or two jetliners collide over Chicago, Lloyd's is affected. People at Lloyd's will have to pay up at least a share of the cost. And the Lloyd's system, reaching far beyond the underwriting Room or even the City of London, begins to operate, deciding what claims should be settled, and for how much. I have myself heard a Lloyd's broker discuss in the most unexcited way how to place insurance cover for an offshore oil and gas field off the northern coast of Australia valued at more than $10 billion. I have also been present when an underwriter declined to accept the risk of death, permanent total disability and temporary total disability on the earthly life of His Holiness the Pope. (The policy was sought by a Los Angeles film-maker who was under contract to cover a papal journey and did not want to be out of pocket if disaster deprived him of his subject.) It is a world inhabited by people of the greatest imaginable diversity: by people of the most stifling conventionality and respectability and also by buccaneers without a scruple to their name.

It is time to meet some of these people, to present our credentials to the red-robed waiter at the main entrance and to claim our privilege, as imaginary members, to walk through the heavy glass doors into the controlled tension, the routine excitement, of the Room.

For more than three centuries London has been drifting to the west. There is good reason for this. The prevailing wind is from the west. From the reign of Queen Elizabeth I to that of Queen Elizabeth II, people in London burned coal in their homes and workshops and, for more than a century, in countless ships, locomotives and factories as well. To escape the resulting smoke, grime and fog, anyone who could afford to moved out to the west.

That is why the seats of power and government are not, strictly speaking, in London at all. Buckingham Palace, Downing Street and the Houses of Parliament are all in the neighbouring city of West-minster. The theatre, shopping and entertainments districts of Mayfair and Soho are in the eighteenth- and nineteenth-century suburb that is still known as the West End, and the smartest sections of the city for modern Londoners are even farther to the west in what were once the outlying villages of Knightsbridge, Kensington and Chelsea. But, just as in New York the financial community has stayed downtown, close to the wharves and counting houses where the first merchants and shippers did their business, so the business heart of London is still huddled in the ancient City of London, a self-governing enclave where more than half a million people work every day and fewer than twenty thousand sleep every night.

Even within the square mile of this city within a city, the farther you go to the east, the more you move back in time, unpeeling layer after layer of London's historical sources of wealth, until you come to the most fundamental of them all: shipping. First, west of St Paul's Cathedral, come the lawyers and the newspapers in the Temple and Fleet Street. Then, east of the Cathedral, clustered around the Palladian façade of the Lord Mayor's Mansion House, the classical portico of the Bank of England and the Royal Exchange, with the new tower of the Stock Exchange across the street, come the bankers and the brokers, the discount market and the foreign banks that make London the centre of the Eurodollar business, and the great names of the merchant bankers – Rothschilds, Barings, Lazards, Warburgs. At last, between London Bridge and the Tower, you come to the oldest part of the City, the bit that still metaphorically smells of the sea. In a few yards you will come across the head offices of half a dozen shipping lines whose names and flags were once household words all over the world: Shaw Savill, Peninsular & Oriental, Cunard. In the middle of this eastern third of the City, from Tower Hill in the south to Leadenhall Street in the north, and from Gracechurch Street to the Minories, you are in the insurance capital of the world.

For the time being, you can still walk along Fenchurch Street, through the heart of this district and within fifty yards of Lloyd's, and not be aware that it is there. (That will soon change. Work has already begun on the new Lloyd's building, designed by the architect Richard Rogers, who does not believe in hiding either his or his client's light under a bushel.) Only if you cut up any one of half a dozen alleys to your right will you understand why every insurance enterprise of any size in the world has its offices here. You will find your way blocked by the long, low bulk of the Lloyd's building.

It may have something to do with the shape of the building, six storeys high and over a hundred yards long and with rounded prow jutting into Lime Street, or it may be because of the internal design of the vast oblong underwriting Room with its superstructure of offices above. It may be because of a certain obsolete elegance about the marble-faced columns, the light wood panelling and other touches that suggest the workaday opulence of the luxurious ships that raced for the Blue Riband in the North Atlantic in the 1930s. Most of all, no doubt, it is because of the subconscious associations of the fact that in this building, built in the 1950s, and in its half-dozen predecessors, men have made and lost money gambling on the perils of the sea. Whatever the precise origin of the symbolism, the comparison seems inescapable. Lloyd's is a liner, moored in Lime Street, the constant flux of activity round its doors, like the throb of powerful diesel engines, a reminder of perils and adventures in less sheltered corners of the world.

Like a liner, Lloyd's accommodates passengers, officers and crew, who come together under one roof for a common purpose. (She is not, emphatically, that modern invention the one-class ship.) Life on board has a certain grace and style. Still, this is not a voyage of pleasure. This is a place where people come together for business – specifically, for a highly specialized version of what is perhaps the oldest of all human commercial institutions. Lloyd's is a market.

If you push through the heavy glass doors any weekday between the hours of ten and five, into the underwriting Room, you will see, endlessly repeated and with infinite variations, the very simple transaction around which the whole system revolves.

A man – and it is almost always a man – sits at the receipt of custom in one of several hundred peculiar wooden structures, half office, half market-stall, arranged in long rows with aisles between them on the floor and in the galleries of the Room. The man is an underwriter – more precisely, an 'active underwriter'. The structure is his 'box'. It consists of two parallel benches separated by a desk. On the desk, there are more or less elaborate additions to accommodate records, telephones, card indexes, references, sometimes now computer terminals.

Another man – or, increasingly often in the last five years, a woman – slides into the seat next to the underwriter. 'Let me broke you on this,' he will say. And he will put in front of the underwriter a piece of paper summarizing a proposal of insurance on behalf of his client.

The piece of paper is the 'slip'. It spells out the broker's name and that of his client (unless for some reason, as for example in a kidnap and ransom policy, the client wishes to keep his name secret). It will specify the kind of insurance that is sought, and how much. The first underwriter to accept the risk, the 'leading underwriter', sets the rate of premium and the broker's commission, or brokerage, which comes out of the premium. If the underwriter is willing to insure the risk, he takes a rubber stamp and stamps on the slip the name and number of one or more of the syndicates he represents. And then he takes his pen and carefully traces his initials over the stamp. Many brokers do this with an elaborate flourish with an old-fashioned fountain pen. It is, after all, an act of a certain significance, both symbolic and practical. And lastly he commits himself and those he is writing for to a certain specified percentage of the risk, which could be as much as 100 per cent or, in the case of some vast venture like an offshore oil field or a supertanker, as little as one half of one per cent.

The broker will do his best to get the underwriter to take a 'line', as this commitment to a given share of a risk is called. And the underwriter will question the broker, sometimes sharply, about the nature of the cover required and the record and reputation of the broker's client. Both of them must act, by the sacrosanct tradition of the market, 'in utmost good faith'. The Latin version of that phrase, which is the motto of Lloyd's, is *uberrima fides*, which means 'good faith overflowing'. If the parties do not live up to that high standard, then, in theory at least, their bargain is invalid. The broker is bound by it to reveal to the underwriter any information known to him that could be relevant to the transaction. And once the bargain has been struck, the underwriter has committed himself and every member of the syndicate he represents to the last penny.

Behind each of the parties who thus come together in an agreement initialled in the Room there stand whole structures of other interests.

The active underwriter – Henry Chester, Dick Hazell or Murray Lawrence, among many others, in the two examples we followed – is there to insure risks on behalf of himself or of one or more syndicates of underwriters, some of which have several thousand members. All members of these syndicates must be underwriting members of Lloyd's, or 'Names'. Most of them are 'outside Names' who never come anywhere near the Room at Lloyd's except perhaps once or twice a year to lunch with their active underwriter or with the agent who handles their business. In order to be accepted as a member of Lloyd's, each of these Names has had to convince the Committee of Lloyd's that he or she was independently wealthy at the time to the tune of about

£100,000 (roughly $150,000) in unencumbered assets. There are variations and exceptions to that requirement. Working Names have to 'show' less wealth. Foreign Names have to show more. The principle, however, is the same. All Names put their wealth unreservedly at the disposal of the active underwriter, without limited liability. He makes bargains on their behalf. If the insurance contracts he accepts lose money, then the Names on his syndicate (including himself) are liable to the extent of every penny and every piece of property they own, down to their bed linen.

The premiums that are paid for the insurances that the underwriter writes, on the other hand, go to his syndicate. Its members have to deposit some of their investments with Lloyd's, but in general they are not obliged to sell income-earning assets, only to lodge them with the syndicate in trust. They continue to earn income on their capital, therefore, and at the same time they can hope to earn a second income on the same assets. If times are good for the insurance market, and if the underwriter is prudent and skilful, that second income can be handsome, perhaps 10 per cent or more on their capital – on top of what it is already earning.

As well as this underwriting profit, there is also investment profit to be made. Underwriters and their syndicates may collect more money in premium on a particular insurance contract than they ever have to pay out in losses. And even if they don't, they may still make a profit. There is the dimension of time to consider. Even if the losses on a given contract eventually add up to more than the premium that was paid, the underwriter may still profit because in the meantime he has had the use of the premium money.

Underwriters must accumulate reserves against possible losses in the future. And the profit from investing those reserves may be very substantial – $100 million or more for the bigger Lloyd's syndicates. And of course those reserves offer tax advantages to the syndicate members who own them: turning current income into capital gains can be very advantageous for wealthy individuals in Britain, for one can set off these gains against losses incurred elsewhere or, if the gains are liable for taxation in the United Kingdom, they are taxed at a far lower rate than investment income.

Once upon a time, most underwriting members of Lloyd's were just what they sound like: they wrote insurances on their own behalf, and there are still some who do that today. Again, there are outside Names who do not write their own business in the Room, but who in other respects manage their own Lloyd's business. For most members today, the chain between their ultimate responsibility and the man who transacts business with a broker in their name is longer and more complicated. Most likely, these days, the outside Name's business, including the management of his trust funds, reserves and accounts, are looked after for him by what is officially, but confusingly, called an 'underwriting agent', but is known colloquially as a 'members' agent'. This is quite a distinct kind of firm from what is called an 'agency company' or 'managing agent', which looks after the accounts, the investments and the administration of a syndicate or small group of syndicates written by one particular 'active underwriter' or by a small team of them. To give a concrete example, an individual Name, let us call him Lord Bareacres, lives in Herefordshire and runs three farms, but is a member of Lloyd's. His Lloyd's business is managed by R. F. Kershaw Ltd, members' agents. Kershaw may arrange for Lord Bare-acres to become a Name on Syndicate 128, whose legendarily successful underwriter is Ian Posgate, known throughout the Room as 'Gold-finger'. Syndicate 128, in turn, is managed by Posgate & Denby (Agen-cies) Ltd, managing agents. We shall look in greater detail at how these relationships on the underwriting side of the market work, and in particular at certain alleged conflicts of interest that arise in them. For the moment, the point is that when underwriter meets broker in the Room, and contracts to receive a certain amount of premium in return for accepting certain risks, that premium is already going to be divided several ways.

On the broker's side of the deal, there are similar complexities. The individual broker who waits patiently in line at a box for the chance to broke a risk to the underwriter may not himself be a member of Lloyd's in his or her own right. If the slip deals with fairly routine business, or with the annual renewal even of quite an important insurance, it is likely to be broked in the Room by an employee of one of the big firms of Lloyd's brokers, whose directors do most of their business in their own office buildings in the surrounding streets and only descend on to the floor of the Room at relatively infrequent intervals. The firm of Lloyd's brokers, in turn, may not be directly representing a client, but acting on behalf of another firm of brokers, anywhere in the world, who produced the business originally and who agree to share the brokerage commission with the Lloyd's broker for the privilege (and the advantages) of placing it at Lloyd's. For most of the big Lloyd's brokers, again, though the Lloyd's market is very important, it takes only a fraction, and in most case less than half, of their business. The same broker who is showing a slip to underwriters in the Room at Lloyd's may be counting on placing another large share of the same business elsewhere in the London market (with London insurance companies or the London offices of companies from the United States, Western Europe or elsewhere), or even outside London.

The variations on the quintessential coming together of the broker, representing someone who wants something insured, and the underwriter, who is willing to risk his own and other people's money to insure it, are almost infinite. Until the early part of the twentieth century, Lloyd's was overwhelmingly a marine insurance market. Now the non-marine market is substantially bigger, and there are two other markets, motor and aviation, each with its specialists, traditions, problems and way of doing business. Those are the four chief divisions of the market, but there are countless subdivisions. Marine risks may cover hulls or cargoes. Non-marine may involve property, casualty or personal accident. A bargain may have to do with direct insurance or with reinsurance. That reinsurance, in turn, may be on either a quota-share or excess-of-loss basis, or it may be facultative. An underwriter might accept all losses, in excess of $50 million, say, each and every risk, on behalf of a giant American or Japanese insurance company, and then reinsure all losses over $60 million in the reinsurance market, like a bookie laying off his bets, retaining just that share of both premium and risks on which he thinks he can make a profit.

Round the simple market meeting between broker and underwriter, then, a whole machinery of gigantic interlocking structures wheels profitably. There is the structure of Lloyd's itself. There is the world shipping intelligence service and the network of agents, and the empire of specialist periodicals that depend on its computerized data base. Then there is the structure of the market and its ancillary services: Lloyd's employs a bureaucracy to 'keep the coffee house' – that is, to provide the market's administration back-up. It more than fills an eleven-storey office building a couple of streets away until the new building is ready, as well as the Policy Signing Office at Chatham, also computerized, which keeps track of Lloyd's records, policies and claims.

Then there is the overlapping structure of the dozen big firms of Lloyd's brokers, which pull in business from all over the world; some of it goes into the Lloyd's market, some to other markets. The marine insurance of the whole world comes to Lloyd's. The non-marine business comes overwhelmingly from the English-speaking world: roughly, half from the United States, a quarter from Britain, and half the rest from Britain's former dominions. Lloyd's brokers, who are great travellers, characteristically feel more at home where they can talk English and find a gin and tonic. Several of them have helped Third World countries to set up their own insurance industries – far-sighted, because the reinsurance premiums from such national corporations find their way to Lloyd's in the end. Over the past twenty years, the big Lloyd's brokers have expanded their brokerage income and their profits. They have also become an integral part of a world economy, providing specialist services to multinational corporations, especially in such high-risk, high-technology, capital-heavy industries as oil and gas drilling and refining, supertankers and bulk carriers, aviation, and major civil and plant engineering and construction.

At the same time Lloyd's underwriters have pioneered all sorts of new kinds of insurances, including kidnap and ransom policies, livestock insurance, computer and other plant leasing insurance, product liability and professional indemnity, some of which have proved quietly profitable, others spectacularly not.

Altogether it is calculated that the presence of the Lloyd's market in the City of London supports more than 70,000 jobs. Insurance is by far the largest component of the City of London's 'invisible exports', amounting in 1980 to £974 million (about $1·5 billion), and two-thirds of that came from Lloyd's underwriters and brokers. (The contribution in some recent years has been enough to make the difference between a positive and a negative balance on Great Britain's trading accounts. But, to put the matter in perspective, it should be remembered that Britain's trading exports are now running at well over $100 billion a year.) Altogether, in 1978 (which because of Lloyd's three-year accounting system is the latest for which figures are available) Lloyd's earned premiums worth £2,163 million, or $3·3 billion.

Great fortunes have been made at Lloyd's since the Napoleonic wars and even earlier. In late Victorian times, while new fortunes continued to be made there, the emphasis shifted subtly: Lloyd's became a place where fortunes made elsewhere could be protected and enlarged in a congenial and gentlemanly environment. To be a non-working member of Lloyd's was not only highly profitable in most years, but also avoided the stigma polite society attached in those days to 'trade'. Money made in Welsh coalmines, Clyde shipyards, Midland foundries, colonial plantations and goldfields, as well as in shipping and insurance, could be gilded by the historical antiquity and elegant associations of Lloyd's.

Throughout, the fortunes of Lloyd's reflected the prosperity or adversity of the world economy and, increasingly as the twentieth century went by, of the American economy. They were little affected by the long Calvary of the British economy between 1918 and 1939, or by its more recent woes. The great liner sailed serenely on. In the mid-1960s it was buffeted by the unusually severe hurricanes in the Gulf of Mexico. Underwriters, for the first time in living memory, lost money on two consecutive years' accounts. But the stabilizers worked, and the great ship righted itself.

For more than a quarter of a century after the Second World War, in fact, while the men on the bridge kept a weather eye on the horizon, and necessary modifications were made from time to time in the engine-room, Lloyd's remained for most of the passengers and the crew alike a snug and in some ways a smug place. People worked hard there. They also generally earned considerably more than the same efforts could have earned in most other departments of British life. They took real risks, yet they hardly seemed to threaten an essentially stable future. For the average working member of Lloyd's, that meant an interesting life with congenial society, a good income and financial security, and departure at a gentlemanly hour in the evening to a comfortable home in the commuter belts of the Home Counties. For an inner group of big brokers and leading underwriters – most, if not quite all, descendants of men who had been notables at Lloyd's before them – it meant all the restrained splendours of the best life that England has to offer: sailing on the Solent or the Crouch, hunting in the shires, shooting and salmon fishing in Scotland, and weekends with good wine and good company in mellow East Anglian farmhouses or Cotswold manors. There was the psychological comfort, too, of reflecting that their sons would follow them to Eton or Harrow or Winchester and, in the fullness of time, after learning to play a good game of cricket and behave like a gentleman, follow their fathers into the Room.

Just because Lloyd's was a workaday place that really had made itself useful to half the world, in fact, and was therefore conscious that it had earned its money, its inhabitants were sheltered, longer than almost any other section of the British professional and management class, from the harsh realities of a world that was changing at dangerous speed.

Because Lloyd's was organized as a sort of club, with the means of excluding those who refused to accept, even on the surface, a code of ethics, it was protected from the knowledge that standards of business behaviour everywhere were changing. Because Lloyd's employed no industrial workers, it was sheltered from the bitterness of industrial politics and class consciousness. Because it was plugged into the world economy, it was protected against the decline of the British economy. Because it was a world where almost everyone accepted conservative social and political ideas, it was possible to persevere in the naïve belief that, as long as Lloyd's earned a lot of foreign exchange for the British economy, it would be spared criticism in the press or Parliament. Above all, perhaps, life had simply gone on so busily at Lloyd's that people there had forgotten that the world is an indifferent place, with no more commitment to maintaining the way of life of the English upper-middle class than to preserving that of the Amazonian Indians. It was not until the middle of the 1970s that these unpalatable realities crashed into the bows of the liner in Lime Street with the impartial violence of the iceberg that stove in the *Titanic*.

CHAPTER 2

THE RINGING OF THE LUTINE BELL

When sorrows come, they come not single spies,
But in battalions.

William Shakespeare, *Hamlet*

In October 1799 the British frigate *Lutine* foundered off the Dutch coast on the sands at the mouth of what is now known as the Ijsselmeer but was called for generations the Zuider Zee. It was the time of the Napoleonic wars. Like the ancient war between Athens and Sparta, the contest between France and Britain was a fight between an elephant and a whale. France was militarily supreme on the continent of Europe. Britain could only use her fleet to blockade European ports and her wealth to subsidize Napoleon's enemies. The French ironically called those subsidies, because of the mounted figure on the gold sovereign, 'the cavalry of St George'; and Her Majesty's Ship *Lutine* was a transport for those metaphorical horsemen. She was carrying a huge treasure in gold and silver bullion and coin, sent by London bankers to shore up the credit of their allies in Hamburg.

She was at the time one of the worst losses Lloyd's underwriters had ever paid. So *Lutine* became something of a mascot at Lloyd's. Of repeated attempts to raise her treasure (most recently in the summer of 1980), the most successful were made by local Dutch fishermen in the first two seasons after the wreck. From time to time since then, a handful of coins, a cannon-ball or some other relic has been rescued from the shifting sands. In 1857 freak storms temporarily made the approach to the wreck much easier, and divers were able to raise, as well as the usual handful of coins and some shot, the frigate's massive wooden rudder and her ship's bell, which weighs eighty pounds. A table and an elaborately carved chair were made from the rudder for the Chairman of Lloyd's. And the bell now hangs in state over the Caller's rostrum at the very centre of the Room.

For many years the Lutine bell was rung whenever, somewhere in the world, a ship sank. Recently that custom has been in abeyance.

Nowadays the bell is rung for various ceremonial announcements, and after a ship is reported overdue. Then whenever definite news – either that she is safe, or that there is no hope – arrives, the bell is rung as a signal that dealings in the overdue market must stop, so that no underwriter in the market gets an unfair advantage over another. But for generations of Lloyd's men, the symbolism of the Lutine bell was more clear-cut. It meant bad news.

In the spring of 1978, it must have felt for many Lloyd's veterans as if they could hear the constant ghostly chiming of the Lutine bell as one piece of bad news chased another across the floor. The entire year of 1978, in fact, was one that the collective memory of Lloyd's would prefer to suppress: a page in the log that deserved to be torn out. Each month brought worse news than the last: news of crushing financial losses and of the danger of even greater losses to come; worse, intimations that the traditional character of the institution must soon be irreversibly changed, and in such a way that its cherished autonomy might be threatened; worst of all, bitter recriminations that forcibly suggested that the gentlemen (and newly admitted ladies) of the Society could no longer confidently rely, as they and their predecessors had relied to their mutual profit for three centuries, on the certainty that their dealings in the Room would be conducted 'in utmost good faith'.

On 3 February of that unhappy year Robert Kiln, a prominent member of the Committee of Lloyd's and a man with something of a reputation in the market as a philosopher, warned a symposium in the City of London that the flush times might be coming to an end for the world insurance industry. 'I have a feeling,' Kiln said,

that the next few years' results are not going to be as good as the last three years'. In fact I would be very surprised if quite a number of people don't pull out of this business in the next few years. There will be certain Lloyd's Names who are going to have sizeable losses in the next few years – not all Lloyd's Names, but some of them. I am sure, too, that there are some companies operating in the London market and the overseas market who will also be faced with sizeable losses. It is going to be very interesting to see who best survives the next three years.

Kiln hastened to add that he thought it would be Lloyd's and London that would survive best, and would deserve to, and that it would be their new competitors who would pull out first. Still, the overall implication of Kiln's talk was undeniably ominous, and it was picked up by some of the more wide-awake London financial journalists. Here was a man with intimate knowledge of the market acquired as a canny underwriter over many years, and a member of the Committee, predicting losses to come. As in Pharaoh's dream, Kiln was saying plainly enough, the seven good years were over, and the lean years were coming to eat them up.

For rather more than seven years, in fact, things had gone remarkably well at Lloyd's. For most of British business, the 1970s were one long misery of raging inflation, endless strikes and labour disputes, falling shares of world markets, and vanishing profits. The insurance industry, in contrast, had ventured boldly into world markets, and had reaped a rich reward.

Insurance is a cyclical industry, but it has its own biorhythm: its fluctuations do not coincide with those of the world economy. The late 1960s, a time of prosperity elsewhere, were threadbare years at Lloyd's. The market was hard hit by Hurricane Betsy, which ravaged the Gulf of Mexico and the offshore oil rigs there in 1965. There were overall losses averaging £6,000 per Name in that year, and in the two years 1967 and 1968 the number of Names, which had been rising steadily since the Second World War, slightly fell. Then came the 1970s. By 1978 the number of Names had grown by two-and-a-half times to more than 15,000. Premium income and profit more than doubled.

It did not take long for Robert Kiln's prophecy to come true. Suddenly, even the inattentive newspaper reader was aware that Lloyd's had run into choppy seas.

On 16 March the supertanker *Amoco Cadiz*, carrying more than 200,000 tons of crude oil, was wrecked off the coast of Brittany. The result was the worst oil spill in history and insurance claims amounting to more than $2 billion, many of which found their way, directly or on reinsurance, to Lloyd's. That seemed to be the signal for a long series of marine disasters of every kind. One of them, a fire that destroyed the French oil tanker *Betelgeuse* and the oil terminal at Bantry Bay, in the west of Ireland, with the loss of fifty lives, less than nine months later, could ultimately cost insurers, many of them at Lloyd's, as much as the wreck of the *Amoco Cadiz*. That was only one of more than thirty supertankers lost in fifteen months. At the same time there was a rash of scuttling and an epidemic of marine fraud of every kind, and even an outbreak of piracy in the Mediterranean, not to mention war in the Persian Gulf. And all this rained down on underwriters' heads at a time when competition and overcapacity in the market were keeping the rates of premium low.

Less than a week after the loss of the *Amoco Cadiz*, rumours of trouble of a very different kind began to percolate out of the Room. On 22 March the *Guardian* reported that the F. H. Sasse syndicate was suing to recover more than $3 million from a Brazilian reinsurance company, the IRB. The dispute arose out of insurances placed at Lloyd's on slum property in the United States, it seemed, and the authorities in New York had ordered an investigation. 'Fears are growing,' the *Guardian* reported, 'that the British insurance market may have been a victim of a big American arson swindle.'

It was not long before more detail began to appear in the papers. The United States Attorney for the Southern District of New York was indeed looking into fire-raising on properties in the South Bronx insured at Lloyd's. The chain of liability, it emerged, ran through insurance men in New Jersey and Miami with apparent ties to organized crime, through a Lloyd's broker to the underwriter, Sasse, with the effect that the members of his syndicate were burdened with enormous losses. The British papers dwelled lovingly on the fact that these included, among a good sprinkling of lords and ladies, Princess Margaret's private secretary and a former equerry to the Queen Mother. It was titillating enough that these noble Names theoretically stood to lose everything down to their heraldic cuff-links. What gave the story an extra edge was that the members of the Sasse syndicate did not intend to take their misfortune with a stiff upper lip. They decided to sue. The disputes that arose out of the Sasse affair involved some $40 million in losses. They also threatened to snap the essential taproot of the market, the necessary trust between syndicate, underwriter, broker and insured.

Lloyd's was not accustomed to being written about in the newspapers. It was even less used to being criticized in the House of Commons. Yet the very day after that first intriguing reference to the Sasse affair in the *Guardian*, a Conservative Member of Parliament, Jonathan Aitken, demanded a brief debate about another festering Lloyd's row. (In Britain, because the law of defamation makes no allowance for the media's right or duty to report matters of public interest, as it has done in the United States since the *New York Times* v. *Sullivan* case in the early 1960s, matters can be raised under parliamentary privilege in the House of Commons when and even because they cannot be aired in the press.) As in the Sasse case, the ethical standards of Lloyd's were at issue. The circumstances were these: 301 Fiat cars, bound for Wilmington, Delaware, and New York, were reported as a 'constructive total loss' after a fire had broken out on the ship taking them from Italy, the *Savonita*. The broker who had reinsured the Italian insurer at Lloyd's refused to claim the loss from underwriters. An investigator found that many of the cars claimed for as total losses were driving happily round Italy. The biggest marine broker at Lloyd's, Willis Faber, took the business anyway and eventually collected the claim from underwriters, but not before a nasty, protracted dispute. Once again, the principle of utmost good faith was called into question, and so was Lloyd's reputation for fairness.

At the same time, Lloyd's was coming under pressure from another direction. Roughly half of all Lloyd's premium comes from the United States. In specific markets, the proportion is far higher than that. Much of this American business came from the big American brokers, and they were getting tired of seeing up to half of the commission on the business they drummed up for Lloyd's go to British brokers. Moreover, after a period of rapid growth in which they established a national network by acquisitions, they were looking to the international market, where the London brokers had been quicker to see the opportunities. So each of the three biggest brokers in the United States – Marsh & McLennan, Alexander & Alexander and Frank B. Hall – was actively looking for a London partner.

Alexander & Alexander had been talking for years about a merger with Alexander Howden in London. In 1978 it renewed its offer of a merger, but the Howden management declined. It then turned to the biggest of the British brokers, the Sedgwick Group, itself recently created by a merger between Sedgwick Forbes and Bland Payne, and now roughly the same size as Alexander & Alexander. Marsh & McLennan, not to be outdone, was also looking around in London. In 1980 they bid successfully for C. T. Bowring, one of the four biggest London brokers. Neither of these deals had yet matured in the spring of 1978. (In the end, the talks between Sedgwick and Alexander & Alexander broke down, and Alexander & Alexander went back to their old friends at Alexander Howden.) But in April the Committee was faced with a firm bid from Frank B. Hall for a medium-sized Lloyd's broker, Leslie & Godwin. Committee members believed that within months, in all probability, at least three major forces in the Lloyd's market would be under American control.

On 19 April the Committee announced that henceforth shareholdings in any Lloyd's broker by any non-Lloyd's insurance interests must be limited to 20 per cent. The Committee was at pains to explain that the rule did not discriminate against American or foreign interests, and would apply equally to any British firm that might be thinking of taking over a Lloyd's broker, but the explanation was not convincing.

In public relations terms, the decision was a blunder. No one could think of any British interests outside Lloyd's that were threatening to take over a major Lloyd's broker. The new rule looked to be aimed fairly and squarely at the big American brokers who had produced so much of Lloyd's business, and hard as the Committee tried to maintain the semblance of even-handedness, it was in truth aimed to prevent the big London brokers coming under American control. The result was a considerable explosion of anger from the United States, in which the voice of John Regan, chairman of Marsh & McLennan, was distinctly heard.

In May a bill was introduced in the New York State legislature that seemed to offer the American brokers a devastating revenge on Lloyd's. New York was to have its own reinsurance exchange, in direct competition with one of the most important parts of Lloyd's business. As we shall see, the New York exchange (and others in Illinois and Florida) constitutes a long-term future challenge to Lloyd's and certainly not a mere petulant reaction to the Committee's 20 per cent rule. Understandably, however, press coverage lumped the two issues together. 'American bid for Lloyd's' was the headline in the London *Sunday Times* on a story about the 20 per cent rule. 'New York May Soon Challenge Lloyd's' headlined the *Financial Times* of London on a story about the New York reinsurance exchange. 'That will teach the proud and insular men of Lloyd's to discriminate against Americans!' That was the tone of much American press comment, echoing the irritation of many American insurance men at what they saw as clumsy and ungrateful British protectionism, and it was picked up in Britain too. There was no love lost for Lloyd's in Fleet Street, it seemed. Commentators revealed their own impatience with the apparent arrogance and disingenuousness of the way the Committee of Lloyd's had handled the issue of American shareholdings.

All the rest of the year, the bad news kept on pouring down on Lloyd's. Applications for membership were now 12 per cent off. Bahrain and New Zealand were among the nations that threatened to follow New York by setting up reinsurance exchanges of their own. The Arab nations vehemently denounced Lloyd's for unilaterally increasing war-risk premiums on insurance of shipping in the Persian Gulf. Four firms of Lloyd's brokers were suspended in the course of the year, and the City of London Fraud Squad investigated another, Christopher Moran. Then, at the end of November, the news broke of what were thought at the time to be the most catastrophic losses in the entire history of Lloyd's. This was the computer leasing affair. Lloyd's underwriters had written $1 billion or so of cover on a brand new book of business: computer leases held by numerous American banks and finance houses. Now IBM had brought out a new line of mainframe computers that were both more powerful and cheaper than the machines covered by the leases. Customers broke their leases and traded up to the new series. The computer leasing companies stood in line to collect the unpaid value of their leases under their Lloyd's policies. At first the prophecies of woe were apocalyptic. Even when the market's nerves had steadied and it was possible to make a cool estimate of what underwriters stood to lose, the best estimate was that computer leasing would wipe out something over half the market's collective profits for the year.

The Lloyd's community was still reeling from the computer leasing claims when the Committee issued a report from the board of inquiry that had been sitting all summer on the *Savonita* affair. Big brokers were well represented on the board, set up by a committee of which the same was equally true. It was harshly critical of the conduct and motives of Malcolm Pearson, the comparatively small broker who refused to pay the *Savonita* claim because he suspected fraud, and it almost wholly exonerated Willis Faber, the brokerage firm that took over collecting the claim.

The London press exploded in virtually unanimous indignation. The report itself did not read like a truly impartial inquiry, said the editorials, and the way the Committee made it available made things incomparably worse. Acting on legal advice, Lloyd's refused to let newspapers so much as collect a copy of the report unless they were willing to sign an indemnity, promising in advance to reimburse Lloyd's for any libel damages that might result from publishing the report! 'The way in which Lloyd's has mishandled the *Savonita* affair,' commented the *Sunday Telegraph,* normally sympathetic to Lloyd's, 'has dealt its reputation the worst blow in living memory . . . not to put too fine a point on it, Lloyd's has succeeded in making itself appear both incompetent and cowardly.'

When the report appeared, the head of information and publicity at Lloyd's, a normally relaxed character called David Larner, happened to be in Chicago. On Saturday morning, 9 December, he climbed aboard a plane to fly back to London and found with pleasure that there was a stack of English papers in the rack. With no more than mild curiosity, he pulled out a *Daily Telegraph* and a *Financial Times* to see what they might have to say about the *Savonita* report. He went through the *FT* first and found nothing. That was a damp squib, he thought. Then he found the editorial in the *Telegraph*. 'It was so bad that I tried to get off the plane,' he remembers. 'But by that time it had started to roll.' Larner got back home just in time to read the *Sunday Telegraph*'s even harsher comments.

Over the weekend, the immediate past Chairman of Lloyd's, Sir Havelock Hudson, called publicly for a searching investigation into the whole system of supervision of the market. In fact, the instrument for such an investigation already lay to hand. The Committee had already agreed to set up a working party to review its own self-regulatory power. That decision had been ratified at a general meeting of Lloyd's members on 8 November. On 12 December, the Committee announced this earlier decision and promised to set forth its exact terms of reference and the name of its chairman before long. Early in the New Year, the chairman's name was announced. He was Sir Henry Fisher, a former High Court judge and former director of the merchant bank Schroder Wagg, and now the head of Wolfson College, Oxford. Incidentally, he is a son of Geoffrey the former Archbishop of Canterbury. Of the six members of his 'working party', four were Lloyd's men – two underwriters, one broker, one members' agent – and two were distinguished outsiders, one a banker, Robin Broadley of Barings, the other a journalist, David Watt, formerly of the *Financial Times* and now director of the Royal Institute of International Affairs. The terms of reference were broad: to inquire into self-regulation at Lloyd's and to review the constitution of Lloyd's, the powers of the Committee, and any other relevant matters. The Committee had set a process in motion which would be very hard to stop.

So far this narrative has been confined to what a reasonably assiduous newspaper-reader might have learned of what was happening at Lloyd's. And it is worth noting that most of the 'outside Names', those who do not work in or around the Lloyd's market, would have learned little more. Instead, they would have been richly nourished on gossip and rumour, two commodities that Lloyd's, like any other market, generates in profusion. To public opinion generally, then, and to many members of the Lloyd's community itself, it looked as if the Committee had reacted precipitately, even with a touch of panic, to the threat of outside interference in its affairs.

When you ascend in the Chairman's elevator to the Committee's suite on the second floor, you enter a world that is both physically and psychologically very different from the purposeful, self-interested commercial bustle of the Room. The Committee room itself was brought up in the 1950s, lock, stock and barrel, from the Marquis of Lansdowne's palace at Bowood, in Wiltshire, when the building was being fitted out. It was designed by Robert Adam, and the rest of the Committee's quarters were decorated in harmony with these graceful splendours of an eighteenth-century grandee. There are pillars, ornate plasterwork, mahogany furniture. The staff of 'waiters' who serve the Committee work with the quiet efficiency you would find in the admiral's quarters on an aircraft carrier. It is a calm world, a place for the long view. Here the criterion is no more, as it is in the Room below, 'Will it make money?' but rather, 'Is it good for Lloyd's?'

Once men are elected to the Committee, and even more when by some mysterious process of peer-group acceptance they take their place in an undefined inner oligarchy of potential chairmen, their point of view changes. A chance incident suggested the revealing parallel. Once I was sitting in a waiting room in the Committee suite when a broker I know came by on his way to see the Chairman. A waiter called to show him in. 'Right,' he said, 'I've got the blotting paper down the seat of my pants.' It was a joke. He was going not to be rebuked by the Chairman, but to negotiate with him, more or less on equal terms, yet he instinctively thought in terms of a boy at an English boarding school going to see the head prefect for a whacking. That is what being elected to the Committee means for Lloyd's men, virtually all of whom once came from public schools, and many of whom still do. It means they have been made prefects. Like Tom and East at the end of *Tom Brown's Schooldays*, they have taken on responsibility. The time for bird's-nesting and fights behind the chapel is over. It is time to start listening to the Doctor's sermons.

In 1978 the Committee did see things differently from the ordinary outside Names and the rank-and-file who worked in the Room. It was thinking further ahead. It had access to more precise information. It was relatively undismayed by some of the big losses that were being discussed in the press as if they meant the end of Lloyd's. 'Spectacular losses,' Sir Peter Green, later Chairman, once muttered to me, 'are just marvellous free advertising.'

On the other hand, the Committee was more worried than outsiders by other dangers. For one thing, it knew more about them. Since late 1977 the grim facts had been trickling through about the Sasse affair. Yet oddly enough the incident that most shook the leadership at Lloyd's and led, more than any other sequence of events, to the setting up of the Fisher inquiry was one that was little noticed inside the market and hardly commented on outside it. 'The first one that started me thinking about the need for an inquiry,' said Ian Findlay, who took over from Sir Havelock Hudson as Chairman of Lloyd's in November 1977, 'was the butter mountain.'

The amount at stake was not large by the standards of modern insurance claims: about $15 million. What happened was that brokers Lyon de Falbe broked to Lloyd's underwriters, led by the Chester box, cover for an assured called Wijffels, a Dutch shipper, on shipments made under the European Economic Community's Common Agricultural Policy. The upper limit on the value of any one shipment was £1 million ($1·5 million). What the brokers did not tell the underwriters was that there was any chance of the shipments being 'aggregated' – that is, of several of them being at risk from the same incident. But that is just what happened: several shipments ended up in the same warehouse at Elst, in Holland, which caught fire.

The underwriters were understandably annoyed. They said the brokers should have told them there was a risk of more than one shipment being lost at the same time. The brokers argued that it was not a fact they should have informed underwriters about. Many complex issues became involved, among them the question of whether the standard 'errors and omissions' policy with which most Lloyd's brokers protect themselves was adequate.

Underwriters refused to pay the claim for the lost butter unless the broker agreed to accept arbitration. (Lloyd's had always gone to great lengths to insist that members submit their disputes to arbitration, not least because that avoided publicity.) Lyon de Falbe consulted its lawyer, who advised that the brokerage firm could argue that it was the agent of the assured, not of the underwriters, and that since it owed no duty of care to the underwriters, it could not be held guilty of negligence towards them. That might be a reassuring line of argument for the broker, but for Lloyd's it opened up terrifying vistas. What if – instead of relying on 'utmost good faith' – brokers in general took to going to their lawyers and arguing that they owed no duty to underwriters to give them the fullest possible information?

Months went by, and there was the danger of an action being fought in open court (as opposed to an arbitration) between a Lloyd's broker and Lloyd's underwriters. The potential damage to Lloyd's was enormous. In the end, the worst did not come to the worst. Findlay and his predecessor, Hudson, managed to persuade the parties to accept arbitration. But both men felt that it had been an uncomfortably close thing. Yet that was not the worst of it, from Findlay's point of view. It became clear that neither the Chairman nor the Committee had the power to compel a broker to accept arbitration, might no longer be able to rely on their moral authority, and that in modern conditions the Committee's powers were wildly inadequate.

It was this feeling – that the Chairman and the Committee neither had the formal power to police disputes, nor could rely on the old moral authority – that explained the blundering 20 per cent rule, intended to keep American brokers from taking over Lloyd's brokerage firms. If the American brokers each owned their own subsidiary at Lloyd's, the Committee would face new boys who would not be amenable to being asked to drop by for a little chat in the prefects' room. Leading members of the Committee, and not least Findlay himself, liked the United States too well, had too many friends there, to feel any anti-American resentment of a merely chauvinist kind. But if the Committee could no longer control Englishmen, it would find it impossible to impose its rules on American brokers, who in sheer power and money terms could well afford to ignore the Committee if they chose to.

Ian Findlay personally opposed the 20 per cent rule on principle, considering it undue interference with free enterprise. But he was outvoted. 'Everyone was terrified of the Americans,' one member of the Committee told me.

So the pressures on the Committee mounted. There was the fear, brought home by the butter-mountain case, that the Committee did not have the powers it needed to do its job. There was a sense that ethical standards in the market had fallen; the Sasse and Moran affairs reinforced nervousness on that score. There was the uncomfortable prospect of Lloyd's being invaded by huge, foreign-based financial powers. All of this added up to a crisis, a conviction that things were slipping out of control. But there was something else. There was the fear that, if Lloyd's did not act, someone else would.

More than any other, the *Savonita* case marked the turning-point. It revealed a hidden chasm between Lloyd's values and those of outsiders. To outsiders, it appeared that Lloyd's did not much care whether or not there had been fraud, so long as the customs of the market were followed. To Lloyd's people, on the contrary, it seemed that the media did not care about the facts of the case, but only wanted to knock Lloyd's. The *Savonita*, like the Sasse affair, conjured up for Ian Findlay and the Committee the disagreeable prospect of litigation, in open court, both between members of the Lloyd's community and against the Society of Lloyd's itself. And Jonathan Aitken's parliamentary intervention raised the even more alarming spectre of interference by the House of Commons. Successive Lloyd's acts had given the Committee and Society of Lloyd's almost unlimited freedom from the sort of regulation to which insurance companies are subject in Britain and elsewhere. Parliament has left it to Lloyd's to regulate itself. The gravest of the dangers raised by the events of 1978 was that Parliament might retract or abridge this proud autonomy.

Rather than allow that to happen, Findlay and his Committee took the step, itself by no means free from danger, of calling in a working party with broad powers to propose changes to the constitution of Lloyd's. Parliament would have to ratify any changes that Fisher did propose, so the Fisher inquiry led to Lloyd's asking Parliament to pass a new Lloyd's bill. Thus did the bad news of 1978 lead to a constitutional crisis for Lloyd's. We shall trace that chain of consequences. But first we must go back to see how Lloyd's has evolved. We must learn how the system works, and unearth the subterranean truth behind the angry headlines of 1978.

CHAPTER 3

THE VOYAGE

... Upon the losse or perishinge of any shippe there followeth not the undoinge of any man, but the losse lighteth rather easilie upon many, than heavilie upon fewe ...

Act 'for the hearing and determining of causes
arising from policies of assurance', 1601

Distance, in time as in space, lends enchantment. The descendant of an ancient family will proudly tell you that the founders of his house's fortunes were moss-troopers, pirates or gigolos; he will be less happy to discuss the details of his own tax and business affairs with you. So it is with Lloyd's. It likes nothing better than to boast of its ancient history and traditions; it is noticeably less interested in analysing the more recent past. But the truth is that the links with the first two centuries of its history – with coffee-house waiters and East India merchants and master mariners swaggering up from the river in their bag-wigs and silver-buckled shoes – are somewhat tenuous. Like other ostensibly immemorial British institutions – like Parliament, or the Bank of England or the ancient universities – Lloyd's in its present form is essentially an invention of the eminently practical Victorians, who took good care to dress their innovations in costume; and their creation has in turn been radically transformed in the twentieth century.

The solemn trappings of the Georgian past, in fact, the red-robed waiters and the legends of the Lutine bell, serve as graceful distractions to take the potentially envious public's eye off the central proposition: that Lloyd's is and always has been about *money*. It is not only a place where a great deal of money is made and a great deal more is protected from loss, but an integral, smoothly running part of that intricate machinery of international capitalist industry and trade which grew up, essentially as an Anglo-American joint enterprise, in the last quarter of the nineteenth and the first half of the twentieth centuries. Many of the question marks that must now be attached to Lloyd's future are consequences of the relative shrinking of that Anglo-American domination of the world economy. At the same time, the period costume should not be allowed to conceal the market's remarkable adaptability. Again and again, as we shall see, it has been able to change its practice swiftly, even ruthlessly, but in such a way that the comforting forms of the old ways were preserved.

That contrast between conservatism and adaptability is a very British trait. Lloyd's is an institution, essentially created in the past hundred years and very substantially changed over the past twenty years, which takes care to disguise this adaptability behind carefully preserved traces of its embryonic past. It is as if Exxon or Shell had chosen to build facsimiles of the *Mayflower* or Nelson's HMS *Victory* to hide the pragmatic utilitarianism and sheer size of their super-tankers. Such antiquarianism might be charming and even reassuring. But it would be a naïve observer who was misled into supposing that the purpose of the vessels was essentially commemorative. So by all means let us enjoy the carefully preserved patina of tradition at Lloyd's, but let us not make the mistake of overlooking the unsentimental energy with which its members pursue profits.

The modern English are not great coffee drinkers, and the coffee they drink is for the most part anything but great too. Beer has been the Englishman's tipple since time immemorial, and for more than a century the public house has been the Englishman's club. Tea reigns in private. First imported from China in the reign of the first Queen Elizabeth, it became the pre-eminent social beverage by the beginning of the eighteenth century. 'Here thou, great Anna! whom three realms obey,' wrote Alexander Pope of Queen Anne, 'Dost sometimes counsel take – and sometimes Tea.' Tea was, and still is, the drink in England for private occasions: for the intimate gathering, the family circle, the heart-to-heart. But for two vital generations in the late seventeenth and early eighteenth centuries, it was not beer, or tea, but coffee that played the crucial part in the story of English social, intellectual and business life.

Coffee was first drunk in England just before the outbreak of the Civil War between King Charles I and Parliament, at Balliol College, Oxford. It is said to have been introduced by the King's loyal Archbishop of Canterbury, William Laud, who brought an émigré Cretan scholar with him to Balliol who knew how to prepare the 'soote colour' drink as well as how to expound medieval Greek texts. But it was after both Laud and his master Charles had been beheaded, when the Puritan 'Saints' ruled and the theatres and the bear-baiting and other more dissipated entertainments of the town were forbidden, that the craze for coffee houses first caught on.

The first of them was opened in London in 1652 in St Michael's Alley, Cornhill, in the heart of the ancient City, by Pasqua Rosee from Ragusa, apparently the Italian servant of an English Turkey merchant who had learned the habit of sociable coffee drinking in the Levant, and had noticed how popular with his friends was the coffee his servant Pasqua brewed for them every morning. Thirty years later, 'foreigners remarked that the coffee house was that which specially distinguished London from all other cities', as Lord Macaulay put it in his classic portrait of the state of England in 1685; 'that the coffee house was the Londoner's home, and that those who wished to find a gentleman commonly asked, not whether he lived in Fleet Street or Chancery Lane, but whether he frequented the Grecian or the Rainbow'. There were coffee houses for all purses and all tastes in all parts of the town. By the early years of the eighteenth century there are said to have been 3,000 of them; if that is an exaggeration, the names of more than 500 have been traced – and that in a city with no more than 750,000 inhabitants.

The coffee house was more than a place where a man could put down his penny at the bar and have a cup of coffee, a seat and his share of the warmth from the fire. It was the place where you went to talk, to idle, to gossip, to play cards, to learn the news, to play politics ... and to do business. There were literary coffee houses, like Will's, in Bow Street, Covent Garden, where the great Dryden held court. And there were coffee houses in the older, eastern part of the town, especially in the crowded alleys round the Royal Exchange, where the merchants gathered to do their varied business. Such were Garraway's and Jonathan's. There you could exchange foreign currency, buy and sell cargoes of textiles or arms, tobacco or spices, auction a ship before the candle burned all the way down, discount a bill, buy and sell stock in the East India Company and the other joint-stock ventures, or negotiate a loan. And there, too, no doubt, you could insure a bottom or a cargo.

At the end of the seventeenth century, marine insurance was already hundreds of years old in London. Both the ancient Greeks and the ancient Phoenicians understood the practice and the principle of it, and in AD 533 the Byzantine emperor Justinian exempted 'nautical usury' from the general law that interest could not go above 6 per cent. It is probable that this early marine insurance took the form of what is known as 'bottomry'. This was a loan against a ship's voyage: if the ship was lost, the loan was lost with it; but if the ship came in, the loan was repayable, together with a 'premium', which simply means 're-ward', for the lender. Bottomry was well known to the Hanseatic merchants of north Germany, the Baltic and Scandinavia, and is mentioned in the laws of Wisby, one of the chief Hansa ports, at the beginning of the fourteenth century. For several centuries in London, the Hanseatic merchants in their fortress-trading post, the 'Steelyard' (where Cannon Street railway station now stands), insured ships and cargoes. So did the 'Lombard' merchants, as the English called them, who came from all over northern Italy and had operated as bankers in Lombard Street since the reign of Edward I in the thirteenth century.

The age of Elizabeth I was a time of economic as well as political nationalism in England. That was when the Royal Exchange and the first great trading companies were founded. As early as 1574 Englishmen were involved in marine insurance, because in that year a man called Richard Candler tried to get a monopoly. He was indignantly opposed by the Company of Notaries, who claimed they had a right to register insurance policies, and by the company of brokers, described by a contemporary chronicler as 'assistants to the merchants in buying and selling and in their contracts, concerned also in the writing of insurance and policies and suchlike'.

In 1601, two years before the great Queen's death, an Act of Parliament sought to establish a court 'for the hearing and determining of causes arising from policies of assurance'. The court did not catch on. But the act has left us, in the grandiloquent periods of Elizabethan English, a definition which shows that the principle of insurance was already perfectly understood:

And whereas it has been tyme out of mynde an usage amongste merchantes, both of this realme and of forraine nacyons, when they make any great adventure (speciallie into remote parts) to give some consideracion of money to other persons (which commonlie are in noe small number) to have from them assurance made of their goodes, merchandizes, ships and other things adventured ... which course of dealinge is commonlie termed a policie of assurance; by means of which policie of assurance it comethe to passe that upon the losse or perishinge of any shippe there followeth not the undoinge of any man, but the losse lighteth rather easilie upon many, than heavilie upon few ...

Throughout the seventeenth century, there was marine insurance in London (fire insurance came along towards the end of the century, and all the other forms of insurance later still), but no marine insurers as such. Those who were merchants also underwrote risks; and their assistants the brokers took their risks round to other merchants to underwrite them in return. As a contemporary pamphlet put it: 'The business of Insurance as a distinct Employment, is in itself an Innovation, the knowing and wary Traders themselves being formerly the only Insurers.'

One of the coffee houses where these merchant-broker-underwriters were to be found in the business district was the one opened by Edward Lloyd some time shortly before 1687. Lloyd was originally, like his father, a journeyman framework stocking knitter – a respected trade, but not one where a man was likely to make his fortune. He opened his first coffee house in Tower Street, near the river. The very first reference to Lloyd's coffee house is what we would now call a small ad placed in the *London Gazette* for 18–21 February 1689 by one Edward Bransby of Derby. Bransby had been robbed of five valuable watches, he said, by a 'middle sized Man, having black curled Hair, Pockholes in his face, wearing an old brown Riding Coat and a black Beaver hat'. Anyone who gave information about the missing watches to Mr Bransby in Derby, or 'at Mr Edward Lloyd's Coffee-House in Tower-street', was to have a reward of one guinea.

In 1691 Lloyd moved to a more spacious house in a better neighbourhood – on Lombard Street, which had been synonymous with banking and still is today. ('It's all Lombard Street to a china orange,' Victorian sporting gents would say, meaning the next thing to a dead cert.) The coffee room in this second Lloyd's was reached down a narrow passage along the side of a shop and up a flight of stairs. It was a big, bare room, forty feet by fifty, with a sanded floor dotted with rough tables, like a tavern. It was an immediate success. Within a year Lloyd was paying the poll tax on three waiters and two waitresses, as many as the long-established Jonathan's or Garraway's. By 1696 Lloyd was consciously trying to attract shipping men, because he started a not very successful and shortlived shipping news-sheet, like many others that were beginning to appear. Soon his coffee house became one of the chief commercial sale rooms in London, where ships, wine, brandy and even books were sold at auction, the bids coming furiously as the candle guttered down to its end. As early as 1710 the great journalist Richard Steele described a custom peculiar to Lloyd's coffee house, which survives today in the functions of the Caller in the Room. A waiter, known to habitués as 'the Kidney', climbed into 'a sort of pulpit and read every paper with a loud, distinct voice while the whole audience are sipping their respective liquors'.

It is pleasant – and reasonable – to think of marine insurance being written in this cosy atmosphere from the start. Lloyd's coffee house was frequented by just the sort of men who wrote insurances on ships and cargoes as a sideline. (The category, incidentally, included both the diarist Samuel Pepys and Daniel Defoe.) But unfortunately there is not a shred of evidence to prove that marine insurance was written there until the mid eighteenth century.

Edward Lloyd died in 1713. Just before his death his daughter married the head waiter at the coffee house, William Newton, who took over the business but died almost immediately. The ownership of the coffee house passed several times, by inheritance or marriage, before settling in the hands of a partnership of 'masters' in the early eighteenth century. It was clearly a valuable property. The last decade of the seventeenth and the first two decades of the eighteenth centuries were a time of expansion for British maritime trade, and in these dangerous times the growth of marine insurance naturally more than kept pace with the growth of trade. Lloyd's coffee house shared in the prosperity of both shipping and insurance.

Like other boom times, this was also a period of speculative fever and a time of opportunity for sharks, crooks and rogues or – as they were called at the time – 'brokers'. So disreputable were the connotations of the word that the men who performed what we would now call the broker's function insisted on being called 'office keepers' instead. Both the speculative boom and the rascality of the brokers were to have their effect on the development of Lloyd's, though, as we shall see, in a perverse and paradoxical way.

There was a series of scandals. One of the most malodorous involved the insurance of a vessel called the *Vansittart*. Desperate for names to complete his cover on the ship, the broker forged imaginary ones. When the *Vansittart* was lost, part of the cover was found to be non-existent. These scandals lent support to the case for regulating insurance, and took place against the backdrop of one of the craziest booms in history.

It began in the shares of a newly formed enterprise called the South Sea Company, worked up by excitement at the always dubious prospect that the fabulous trade of the Spanish Main would be thrown open to British vessels. That was why it was called the South Sea Bubble. It soon overflowed, however, and inflated the infant stock market as a whole. The price of securities of companies of all sorts were driven up to wildly unjustifiable levels, and in 1720 the Bubble inevitably burst. There were, it was said, only three survivors: Guy's Hospital, still one of London's greatest teaching hospitals, which was founded by a Bible seller, Thomas Guy, who had been lucky enough to invest £45,000 in the South Sea Company and saw his money grow to more than half a million; and the two great insurance companies founded by royal charter, the Royal Exchange and the London Assurance.

After the Bubble burst, the House of Commons legislated swiftly to prevent a recurrence of speculative excesses. While the House was debating, it received a message from King George I: His Majesty had accepted princely gifts of stock from other companies during the market boom, in return for his royal charter. Now, his royal palm greased with £300,000 from each of the two companies, the King signified his gracious wish that charters should be granted to the Royal Exchange and the London Assurance. But George I was not an absolute monarch. He needed the assent of Parliament, and there were already clever lawyers in the House of Commons in 1720. The Bubble Act, as it was called, not only established the two insurance companies but also, paradoxically, ensured the fortunes of Lloyd's coffee house and the independent underwriters who gathered there.

What lay behind the intrigues, the bribery, the impassioned oratory in the House, and the far from dignified wrangling before the government's law officers who had been appointed to report on the question, was the conflict between the advocates of insurance monopoly, and the independent underwriters. On the one side, a powerful group of merchants, known as the 'Mercers' Hall men', wanted a monopoly of marine insurance for the companies they had set up. The individual underwriters, who stood to lose what was becoming for some an important part of their livelihood, naturally resisted stubbornly. The upshot was that the House of Commons sharply criticized the companies, but gave them their monopoly. Or rather – they must have been clever lawyers! – it gave them what looked like a monopoly and in the absolutely crucial respect was not. No corporation, society or partnership, said the Act, other than the Royal Exchange or the London Assurance, might assure ships or merchandise at sea. But any private underwriter or individual might underwrite policies 'as if this Act had never been made'.

In practice, the result allowed the private underwriters to stay in business and indeed actually favoured them, by removing competition from partnerships and firms. The two chartered companies quickly ran into trouble, had to be bailed out by a second Act of Parliament and turned increasingly to fire insurance, leaving marine insurance to the private underwriters. The latter, now protected by Parliament against competition from partnerships, firms or companies, increasingly gathered at Lloyd's coffee house. Almost a hundred years later, there were still private underwriters to be found at other coffee houses or writing insurances in their own offices. But the insurers, and their agents the 'office keepers', increasingly found it convenient to go to Lloyd's coffee house and find all the underwriters they needed to back their policy in one place.

For the next fifty years, through the long peace while Sir Robert Walpole was prime minister, and through the victorious wars of mid-century, Britain's maritime trade, with the East India Company and the sugar islands of the West Indies, and especially with the North American colonies, expanded and prospered steadily; and marine insurance grew and prospered with it. But Lloyd's coffee house, though it was emerging as the unchallenged centre for this profitable business, was not in all respects a dignified or respectable place. It became the centre for gambling, and in particular for unpleasant forms of gambling – on the prospects of people on trial for their life, for example, and on the chances of recovery of prominent people reported in the newspapers to be sick.

Some of the solider and more serious underwriters were so shocked by these practices, and at the same time so concerned by the disrepute they threatened to bring to the market, that they decided to secede. Early in 1769, they persuaded Thomas Fielding, one of the waiters at Lloyd's, to set up on his own. Probably they backed him when Fielding took a lease on a house in Pope's Head Alley, one of the best addresses in the City. Fielding also managed to get the Post Office to transfer the monopoly of shipping news to his rival venture. For a few years, there were two Lloyd's coffee houses, and relations between them were naturally venomous. It was the breakaway New Lloyd's that was to be the winner.

Before the secession to Pope's Head Alley, the first stage in the history of Lloyd's had been accomplished. A body of independent, specialist marine underwriters had come into existence, had beaten off the competition of officially sponsored monopolies and was associated with the name of Lloyd's coffee house. For this eighteenth-century embryo to grow into the modern market, however, the history of Lloyd's had to pass through three more stages: the coffee house had to grow into an autonomous institution; it had to take responsibility for its own collective reputation (and it would be drawn into elaborate commitments before that job was finished); and the market had to expand far beyond the boundaries of its original concern with marine insurance.

On 13 December 1771, seventy-nine merchants, underwriters and brokers who had decided to branch out on their own signed what has been called 'the most important document in the history of Lloyd's': 'We the Underwritten,' it said, 'do agree to pay our several subscriptions into the Bank of England in the Names of a Committee to be chosen by Ballot for the Building a New Lloyd's Coffee House.' It was certainly a decisive move. Lloyd's as a market, from that moment on, no longer existed on the sufferance of the owners of a coffee house. Henceforth, those who practised their business in the market would take responsibility for its fortunes and therefore for its reputation, even if for a long time to come there was only the vaguest comprehension of what that responsibility implied. And the instrument they chose to govern themselves by has lasted for more than two hundred years. They elected a committee.

The first committee was not conspicuously effective. The immediate priority was to find a permanent home for the market. For two years the committee failed to find a suitable one, and when a home was found, it was not the committee's doing. It was thanks to the 'exertion and personal influence' of one of the handful of men whose names are still remembered at Lloyd's: of the man, indeed, who is commemorated under his portrait in the Royal Exchange as the 'Father of Lloyd's' – John Julius Angerstein.

He was to become one of the great merchant princes of the age, a man who was on terms of equality with the greatest figures of his time, the friend of Pitt and of Nelson. His face, in Sir Thomas Lawrence's wonderful portrait, is that of the man of the world incarnate: shrewd, experienced, with the formidable confidence, even arrogance, masked by urbanity, of one who has commanded success. It is the face of the man who, when Lawrence painted him in 1795, had been Chairman of Lloyd's for five difficult years of war and blockade; who, two years before, had staved off a financial panic singlehanded by personally persuading Pitt to shore up credit by issuing a government loan; who told a parliamentary committee in 1810 that of some thousand underwriters at Lloyd's he only bothered to show his account as a broker to some two hundred, and as to the rest, he added superbly, 'I do not know their names!' It is the face of a man who had the audacity to accept the biggest single risk ever showed to Lloyd's up to his time, or for a long time afterwards: the insured value was £656,800 on the voyage of the frigate *Diana*, bound from Vera Cruz in Mexico with a cargo of treasure. His benefactions were on the same princely scale as his strokes of business: the greatest of them was the collection of pictures he acquired with the advice of Lawrence, Sir Joshua Reynolds and the gifted American painter Benjamin West which after his death became the nucleus of the National Gallery.

In 1771, however, all this lay a quarter of a century ahead. Angerstein was a relatively young immigrant with his name and his fortune to make. He was born in Russia in 1735 into a long-established family of German merchants in St Petersburg. He came to England at the age of fourteen and got a job as a junior clerk in the counting house of a 'Russia merchant' who frequented Lloyd's coffee house, and by the age of twenty-one he was underwriting there on his own account. His judgement and honesty were so valued that policies he had signed were known as 'Julians' and specially regarded. While the committee dithered over a new home for the market, Angerstein acted. He approached the Mercers' Company, who still owned the Royal Exchange, and inquired whether there might be any suitable space over the exchange trading floor. He was shown two rooms to let for £160 a year, and took them on behalf of 'the gentlemen who attend new Lloyd's coffee house'. The committee ratified his action, and the rooms over the Royal Exchange became the home of Lloyd's for more than half a century.

They saw great changes. The last quarter of the eighteenth century and the first fifteen years of the nineteenth were a time of almost uninterrupted war. They were also the heyday of Britain's industrial revolution. British manufactures and British exports grew explosively, but so did the dangers of trade by sea. For much of the period, ships could neither leave Britain nor return except in convoy, and sometimes even that did not save them. One of the worst months in the history of Lloyd's was August 1780, at the height of the American war, when the combined fleets of Spain and France fell on the East India and West Indies convoy and captured fifty-five out of sixty-three ships. The loss was estimated at £1·5 million. In the Napoleonic wars, more than 3,000 British ships were lost by enemy action in just nine years from 1793 to 1802. High risks brought high rates, and high rates in turn meant high profits for the lucky and the skilful. High risks and high profits led to the emergence of the professional underwriter; and in the long period from the outbreak of the American War of Independence to Waterloo, the professionals finally ousted the merchants who underwrote risks as a sideline.

The prestige of Lloyd's as an institution was enhanced, too, by the war. Lloyd's worked closely with the British Admiralty in such matters as the organization of convoys and the exchange of shipping intelligence. Lloyd's underwriters contributed munificently to the Patriotic Fund for the widows and orphans of sailors killed in the wars and to other funds to commemorate famous victories with gifts of money and silver and gold plate to the victorious admirals.

Ever since 1771, in a general sense, the committee had taken charge of the fortunes of Lloyd's. From 1804 on, the Committee (this is a good moment to give it a capital C) was helped by a secretary, John Bennett. (The reason for the appointment of the first secretary is amusing: Earl Camden, then Secretary of State for War, refused to correspond with the Masters, then still officially the proprietors of Lloyd's, on the pompous grounds that it was beneath his dignity as a nobleman 'to enter into epistolary intercourse with the waiters of Lloyd's Coffee House'!) But the Committee had not yet gained control of the membership, or even of who could come and go in the rooms above the Royal Exchange.

For the rest of the century they swarmed with gatecrashers of every kind. There were seventy-nine original subscribers to the 'new Lloyd's' in 1771. By the height of the Napoleonic wars, the old Lloyd's coffee house having long faded away, between 1,000 and 1,500 men regularly frequented the market. Ambitious young clerks on the way up, writing risks without the capital to pay if they had a casualty, rubbed shoulders with broken old underwriters who had taken one risk too many. Lawyers and stockbrokers wrote a few risks in the hope of easy money, and some underwriters disappeared from the market in the winter months to avoid the risks of storm losses. The Committee was powerless to collect subscriptions from a whole regiment of hustlers and hangers-on who thronged the rooms, or even from professional underwriters too mean to pay their subscriptions. All these miscellaneous gatecrashers and freeloaders jostled men of as great distinction and substance, perhaps, as have ever worked in the Room at Lloyd's: men like Angerstein himself; like Brook Watson, who succeeded him as Chairman of Lloyd's and was Lord Mayor of London and Member of Parliament for the City into the bargain; like Zachary Macaulay, the father of the historian, who gave up a great business in the West African trade to throw himself into the fight for the abolition of slavery; like Dicky Thornton, who left £4 million when he died and once put up £250,000 himself on a single risk; or like Sir Francis Baring, founder of what has always been second only to Rothschild's among the great merchant banks of the City, and who was described in his day as 'the first merchant in Europe'.

The problem was not solved until a group of these weighty underwriters announced that they would propose, at a general meeting of subscribers, that the right of subscribing, and therefore of using the underwriting rooms, should be restricted to merchants, underwriters and brokers 'recommended by two or more members'. (The word 'members' was in itself a new usage at Lloyd's.) The decision to accept this resolution, taken by a general meeting in April 1800, was important. From that turning-point on, those who were later called members could choose, through the agency of the Committee they themselves elected, who was, and who was not, to be of their number.

The next step was to provide Lloyd's with its first written constitution. As was to happen again more than once, the impulse for an important change came from a row of no great significance in itself.

In 1810 the House of Commons appointed a select committee to inquire into the monopoly of the two chartered insurance companies. The committee's hearings turned into a searching investigation of Lloyd's, in which the considerable envy and malice of Lloyd's rivals was vented at great length. The record of the hearings provides a fascinating body of information about the workings of marine insurance and international trade at the time. But Lloyd's, ably defended by Joseph Marryat in the House of Commons, and by Angerstein before the select committee, emerged triumphantly from the test.

It was not this public ordeal, but an ugly domestic row, that led to constitutional change. John Bennett, the secretary, had been given confidential intelligence by the Royal Navy about dangers to shipping from Napoleon's blockade in the Baltic. There was no question of Bennett using this information for his own profit (as Pepys, more than a century earlier, had unashamedly used information he acquired as Secretary to the Navy to make money for himself underwriting marine insurance). But losses had been high, and underwriters were furious when they found out that Bennett had had information in his possession all along which, if he had published it in the Room, might have made them think twice about writing certain risks. Bennett had in fact given his news to the Committee; but he had not thought it right to publish it. The result was a vote of censure on the Committee passed by a meeting of subscribers. More important, a special committee of twenty-one subscribers was appointed, its recommendations accepted and incorporated into a Trust Deed.

This Trust Deed of 1811 was Lloyd's first formal constitution. It lasted as such until it was replaced by the first Lloyd's Act of Parliament in 1871. The Deed bound the subscribers to duly observe perform fulfil and keep all the singular rules and regulations for the time being which have been heretofore passed and confirmed and also all such further rules as shall or may at any time hereafter be duly passed and confirmed by a majority of the subscribers for the time being present at two general meetings to be convened for that purpose.

The Trust Deed set up rules for electing subscribers and for electing the Committee and for appointing firms of Lloyd's agents in ports around Britain and abroad; most important of all, it gave the Committee power to act on behalf of the subscribers. Now Lloyd's had a formal, corporate legal existence. Its institutional development was far from complete, but with the end of the French wars the focus of its history shifts to the second task: safeguarding the collective reputation of Lloyd's.

'Individually,' goes the old Lloyd's saying, 'we are underwriters; collectively we are Lloyd's.' Each man writes his risks as an individual. But even in an age of rampant individualism, and the late eighteenth and early nineteenth centuries were certainly that, it became clear that the individual still stood or fell by the collective reputation of the market. Lloyd's gradually, and often reluctantly, came to accept that its prosperity ultimately depended on its reputation. The story of the development of Lloyd's as an institution is the story of ever greater protection for the commercial public; it is also the story of how the rules of a private club have been gradually given the sanction of law by the authority of Parliament.

The first golden age of Lloyd's, the age of the American and French revolutions, was the age of the romantic passion for liberty. The men who wrote marine insurance at Lloyd's in those years looked forward to the economic liberalism of the age of *laissez-faire*. The rights of property were all but absolute to them, and they seem to have thought of the rights of a subscriber at Lloyd's as a sort of freehold property.

The first task for the Committee then was a very elementary one. It was to establish just who was a member of Lloyd's, and who could be excluded from membership. But gradually the Committee, wanting to protect the security of the policy, greatly circumscribed the liberties of the freeholder.

First, it took steps to exclude those who were actually guilty of fraud. Even that minimum protection took time to achieve. Then, insureds must be protected against the insolvency of underwriters. That, too, was a slow business. Initially, the Committee took care that under-writers should be solvent when they joined the market. It took something close to a revolution before the members accepted that the Committee must constantly monitor every member's solvency.

Only comparatively recently, and tentatively, was the attention of reformers turned from protecting the interests of the insured to protecting the interests of insurers. The doctrine still is that underwriting members run their own risks with unlimited liability. But in the twentieth century there has been a start in the direction of protecting at least the non-professional Names against fraud. It is no accident that the first move in that direction, in the Harrison fraud case (1923), did not come until after the outside Names had come into existence, and the second substantial move, in the Sasse case (1978–80), came after their number had sharply increased.

After Waterloo, the first golden age of Lloyd's came to an end. With the end of the war, rates fell sharply too, from an average of from 5 to 8 per cent to 1 or 1·5 per cent. As profits ebbed away, so slowly did the subscribers. Their numbers fell steadily for almost thirty years, from a peak of 2,150 in 1814 to under 1,000 in 1843.

On the night of 10 January 1838, the Royal Exchange burned to the ground. The accident might have been a catastrophe for Lloyd's. In the event it was a blessing. The Chairman, George Richard Robinson, behaved with great energy. The very next morning Lloyd's was back at work in the Jerusalem coffee house. Robinson threw a grand banquet to announce his determination that Lloyd's would survive, and a special committee opened negotiations immediately for new accommodation for Lloyd's in a new Royal Exchange. This was opened in 1844 with plethoric feasting and appropriate pomp by Queen Victoria in the presence of the Duke of Wellington, Sir Robert Peel and the young William Ewart Gladstone.

By that time the special committee had grappled with the question of membership. It created four different categories of membership: 'underwriting members', who had the run of the rooms and who alone could sign a Lloyd's policy; annual subscribers, who were the brokers; 'Merchants' Room subscribers'; and 'Captains' Room subscribers'. The first two categories are self-explanatory. The fourth was shortlived – the idea was that sea-captains should continue to visit the rooms in search of news and good cheer – and survives only in the sense that the members' restaurant in the modern Lloyd's is called the 'Captains' Room'. But the brilliant stroke was the 'Merchants' Room' subscription. This brought in a prestigious and influential group of members, with valuable business, yet kept the underwriting room from being swamped with sightseers and amateurs. The

Merchants' Room subscription lasted only ten years, but it did the trick.

The years of the revival of Lloyd's – from the opening of the new rooms until 1870 – were the years of recovery from the Hungry Forties' economic misery and near-revolutionary political ferment to the high-Victorian prosperity and confidence. Virtue and seriousness came into fashion, and the devil-may-care attitudes of the Regency and the Corinthian 1820s gave way to earnestness. In 1828, when a pair of rogues called Hoskin and Russell conned underwriters into returning premium with false information and then pocketed it, the Committee threw them out; almost certainly it was exceeding its powers in doing so. Fifteen years later, in 1843, the Committee was given the power to decline renewal of subscription. In 1851 it was resolved that insolvent members should lose their membership. And in 1853 two subscribers called Bell forged the names of real underwriters to a false policy: the doorkeepers were ordered to exclude them from the Room. The Committee, again, had no power to do this, but did it anyway, and the membership approved.

Already in the 1850s the Committee began to ask for guarantees from new members, but selectively at first. In 1857 one new member paid a deposit of £5,000 instead of giving a guarantee, simply because his father had moral objections against giving a guarantee. For a good many years new members were asked to give either a guarantee or a deposit, or neither, at the whim of the Committee. Gradually it became usual to demand a deposit, and after 1882 this became an inflexible rule. From 1866 onwards a standard trust deed devised by lawyers was used to secure the deposit, and the amount continued for many decades to be £5,000.

With the new concern for commercial morality, new problems and practices occurred. In 1869, for example, a broker called Farrar was ordered to reinsure lines on three overdue vessels. Unable to reinsure them with underwriters, he did so with a clerk called Morris, who had no money and couldn't pay when the ships failed to appear. The Committee sent for Farrar and accused him of breaking the by-laws by doing business with a man who was not an underwriting member. Farrar excused himself by saying the by-laws only forbade him to do that *in the Room*. He got away with this (though Morris was barred) because on legal advice the Committee decided there was nothing they could do. This was only one example that encouraged a general feeling that the Committee must be given the power to tighten up the rules. This feeling hardened into resolve with the case of the *Venezuelan*.

A. B. Forwood was a Liverpool shipping man who was both an underwriting member of Lloyd's and the managing director of a company that owned a steamer called the *Venezuelan*, which was damaged by a storm in mid-Atlantic. A passing ship brought the news to New York, where the newspaper headlined the story as a 'Mid-Ocean Horror'. Forwood, however, had solid information in a wire from the purser, who had been rescued and taken to the United States, that the damage was slight. So Forwood was able to make £500 by writing £1,000 at £50 per cent in the overdue market. In other words, he accepted £500 of premium, knowing that there was no danger of paying a claim. The market was furious, and the Committee excluded Forwood without hearing his side of the story. It had no power to do so. Forwood therefore was able to get an injunction from the Lord Chancellor, who in the end delivered a severe judgement against the Committee of Lloyd's. But long before the case was heard, the Committee had realized its mistake and also realized that in effect once a man was a member, the Committee had no control over him unless he did something indefensibly dishonest. It set about drafting what became the Lloyd's Act of 1871.

If the Trust Deed of 1811 was Lloyd's first written constitution, the Act of 1871 was the first detailed constitution sanctioned by the power of Parliament. It gave the Committee power over members of Lloyd's, but it also controlled people outside Lloyd's, because it made it a criminal offence for any non-member to sign a Lloyd's policy. Without this necessary provision, none of the other reforms intended to protect the insured public – the deposits and later the audit and the central funds – would have achieved their purpose. Still, Parliament thus stiffened with the authority of the criminal law the privileges of what had been a private body, and what remained a body which could choose or refuse members at will.

The Act makes both bankruptcy and conviction for fraud grounds for expelling members, but at the same time it goes to great lengths to protect members from what might seem, and what was about to be deemed by the law, high-handed treatment. The Act made Lloyd's a legal entity. It confirmed the existing distinction between underwriting and non-underwriting members, and forbade underwriting members to write a policy in the name of a partnership or a company in the City of London – though they might do so elsewhere. It forbade non-underwriting members to write policies at Lloyd's, though again they were free to do so elsewhere. It settled what offences a member could be expelled for, and established an elaborate machinery for doing so after his rights had been carefully protected. It specifically recognized the provision of shipping intelligence as one of the objects of Lloyd's, and it made it a criminal offence for non-members to use or to imitate the 'stamp mark' of Lloyd's on policies. (Lloyd's thereupon chose the mark that still distinguishes all Lloyd's policies: the anchor.)

Recognizably, this Victorian statute was legislating for something essentially like the Lloyd's market of today, as far as marine insurance is concerned. But there is no mention in it of Lloyd's brokers, not even in their formal status as 'annual subscribers', and there is no mention of any but marine insurance. Much of the history of Lloyd's in our own century has concerned the rise of non-marine insurance and the growth of broker power.

In 1872 a gentleman from Liverpool called J. T. Danson wrote a furious diatribe against Lloyd's in a pamphlet. His rhetoric is amusing if overblown: 'You are living on your past, you are effete ... you are hucksters, you are walking in shackles and mistaking your awkwardness for dignity.' His motives do not matter now, nor his proposals for reform, but on one point Danson was uncomfortably accurate. 'Your premium income,' he wrote, 'compared to the companies is almost trivial.' Until 1844, liability for an insurance company's policies had fallen on the trustees or directors who actually signed them. Nothing could have been better calculated to discourage men from becoming trustees or directors of insurance companies. But Gladstone's great Company Act changed this, and there was a rush to float insurance companies: well over 300 were formed in the next nine years. By the mid-1870s, Lloyd's was feeling this new competition acutely in its marine business. (With the exception of a very little fire business from about 1874 on, all Lloyd's underwriting was then marine underwriting.) It was a time of technological revolution at sea, too. Steamships were growing in size, and insurable values were rising steeply. At that time it was exceptional for an underwriter to write on behalf of as many as six Names. Most wrote for syndicates of only two or three, and one out of every five policies was written not by a syndicate at all but by an individual underwriter for himself alone. The danger was that, as the value of individual ships and of their cargoes rose, Lloyd's underwriters would no longer be able to compete with the companies. Many of the ablest Lloyd's underwriters recognized the possibility that Lloyd's might just fade away, and went to work for the companies.

One of them found a way to fight back, however, and just in time.

His name was Frederick William Marten, and his bold idea was extremely simple. Marten invented the big syndicate. The Lloyd's market, even in the 1870s, had many advantages over the companies: it was concentrated in one place; and it had access to vital services, like the register and the network of shipping intelligence (these were being energetically expanded in these same years). But the one thing the companies had, and Lloyd's did not, was financial capacity, and that was what Marten's big syndicate provided. It was not big by modern standards, of course. A successful marine underwriter today may write for 2,000 Names. Marten never wrote for more than twelve, but that was enough. By the 1880s the volume of business his syndicate was writing exceeded that of even a big company, and he was pulling the marine business back to Lloyd's.

While Marten was making it possible for Lloyd's to survive, a tall young man in the very next box in the Room was beginning what can only be called a revolution in the scope of Lloyd's business. Cuthbert Eden Heath was the son of an admiral. He came from one of those English families that keeps one foot in the landowning aristocracy and the other in solid upper-middle-class business. His family destined him for the navy or, failing that, the Indian Civil Service. He went into Lloyd's, and at first this was a bitter private humiliation, only because he was too deaf to be accepted by more prestigious professions.

Heath has been called, indeed had to be called, the father of the modern Lloyd's. He left it a market in which non-marine competed with marine on equal terms both in status and in volume of business. It was essentially as a result of this revolution wrought by Heath that in 1911 Parliament, in a new Lloyd's Act, extended the purposes of the Society to include 'the business of insurance of every description', instead of merely 'the business of marine insurance'.

Heath did not, of course, invent non-marine insurance. When he became a member of Lloyd's in 1880, the oldest English fire-insurance office, the Phoenix, was just two hundred years old. (For those intrigued by the connection between Puritanism and capitalism, it was founded by Nicholas Barbon, also one of the first great London real-estate speculators, whose father was the Puritan divine Praise-God Barebones, a name his son changed when he went into exile in the Low Countries.) But he did invent the non-marine reinsurance treaty, now an important part of the business of Lloyd's, and the excess-of-loss reinsurance, which made Lloyd's so valuable to some of the biggest insurance companies in the world.

He was the first Lloyd's underwriter to concern himself with what might be called the retail end of the insurance business. Ceaselessly inventive, he was always on the lookout for new kinds of business which the general public, as well as the business community, needed. There is a famous story about him being asked whether he would give a certain kind of cover and answering simply: 'Why not?' Cuthbert Heath was always a 'Why not?' man. It is an attitude commoner in business in North America than in Britain, and it is no accident that Heath played such an important part in bringing American business to Lloyd's. Heath, and to a considerable extent Heath alone, made Lloyd's what it has become in a non-marine, as well as a marine, market: an innovative and experimental, not a conservative and traditionalist, community; a specialized working component of the machinery of a *world* insurance system.

The fire-insurance companies were badly caught by the great Tooley Street fire of 1861 in the warehouses lining the south bank of the Thames in the Pool of London, and by a succession of other major fires in the next twenty years. In the early 1870s, a small fire-market revived at Lloyd's. In 1885 Cuthbert Heath's father, the by now retired admiral, who was a director of one of the oldest fire-insurance offices, the Hand-in-Hand, proposed to his son to reinsure part of the Hand-in-Hand's book of risks, and Cuthbert Heath took it.

Almost immediately, Heath introduced a characteristic innovation into his growing book of fire business. When a business lost premises or stock in a fire, Heath reasoned, he needed to be insured not only against the physical losses, but also against the loss of profit until he could replace his stock and reopen his business. So Heath introduced a loss-of-profits insurance into his fire policies. The established fire-insurance companies were aghast. Heath was summoned before the Fire Offices Committee and told that his new-fangled policy was nothing less than an invitation to fraud. Heath went right on writing loss-of-profits policies, though, and most fire companies followed in his footsteps.

Just as New York was terrified of mugging in the 1960s, London in the 1880s was in a panic about burglary. The panic seems to have begun with the exploits of Charles Peace, a burglar and murderer who was hanged in 1879; the number of burglaries is said to have doubled between 1885 and 1888. A broker asked Heath whether he would cover a house against burglary as well as fire. 'Why not?' was Heath's answer. Heath and the broker, W. H. Wood, were lucky. The novel policy was reported in a monthly magazine, the *Oracle*, and later in a popular evening newspaper, the *Pall Mall Gazette*. Burglary policies, at two shillings and six pence per £100 (0·125 per cent) to cover the contents of a house, caught on. By the end of the century, no middle-class home was thought safe without a burglary insurance. Heath was reinsuring many of them at Lloyd's.

A direct result of the burglary cover was a new 'all risks' policy for jewellery. A relative of Heath's lost a piece of jewellery that was covered under a burglary policy. She sent in a claim, but because the loss was accidental she was not covered. Again Heath's instinct was to ask: 'Why not?' At a higher rate, ten shillings (0·5) per cent, he would cover jewellery against all risks. That in turn led naturally to another form of cover, which has now become standard all over the world: the 'block policy' for jewellers. The diamond merchants of Hatton Garden, in the 1880s as today, are in the habit of carrying their stock round in their pockets and in the palms of their hands, and buying and selling stones in each other's offices and even on street corners. A book-keeper working for one of them was aghast at the risks his employer was running. He got the boss's permission to approach Heath through a broker. Heath quoted a premium to insure the gems wherever they might be.

Those are only some examples of the stream of innovative covers that came from the Heath box. It was Heath who introduced workmen's compensation insurance, blanket policies for bankers, and many other forms of insurance which are now standard. Perhaps the most important of all was excess of loss.

The big American insurance companies had been badly hit by the Chicago fire of 1871 and other big city fires. But none of them compared in magnitude as a source of loss for insurers with the San Francisco earthquake of 18 April 1906, when 30,000 houses were destroyed and the total loss to underwriters was some $180 million, $40 million of which fell to British insurers. The Heath syndicate had been the leader of earthquake policies at Lloyd's. Cuthbert Heath had personally pioneered earthquake insurance, painstakingly working out the history of earthquakes and other natural disasters from what records he could find and entering the rates in his own hand in the earthquake book. The rate for San Francisco was fifteen shillings per cent (0·75 per cent) for steel and concrete buildings, and twenty shillings per cent (1 per cent) for the wooden houses. Now all his careful research was irrelevant. The worst-imaginable disaster had happened. A whole city had been destroyed. But were underwriters liable? After all, some of the damage had been done by fire, some by seismic shocks. Some of the policies covered only fire. Heath saw that he must cut through all such quibbling. He sent to his agent in San Francisco the famous cable that sealed his reputation, and that of Lloyd's, in the United States: 'Pay all our policy-holders in full irrespective of the terms of their policies.'

There was to be an immediate and rewarding consequence in addition to the lasting glory of that gesture. Not long after the San Francisco earthquake, the Hartford, already one of the leading insurance companies in the United States, sent representatives to London to see if Cuthbert Heath could think of a way of protecting them against a recurrence on the scale of what had happened in San Francisco. Small losses the Hartford could afford to pay, better than any Lloyd's syndicate, because it was bigger than any *one* of them. What it wanted cover against was the catastrophic loss from an earthquake, a major fire or a windstorm that might destroy an entire city neighbourhood. Heath's answer was what he called excess-of-loss cover. That meant that the direct insurer would not bother to reinsure routine losses, and would pay reinsurance premiums only for losses above an agreed figure, up to an upper limit. In this way huge risks could be spread not only 'horizontally', among the different underwriters, each with several Names behind them, but also 'vertically', by 'layering' the risk so that neither the direct insurer nor any reinsurer stood exposed to intolerably great losses.

In the same years when the courteous Cuthbert Heath was revolutionizing the techniques of Lloyd's business and extending its potential for reaching new markets, an equally remarkable but far stormier figure was physically extending Lloyd's presence, first along the coastlines of the world and then across new frontiers of twentieth-century technology.

Lloyd's as an underwriting market was often saved at crucial moments by the services which Lloyd's as an institution provided for the seafaring community. The habit of posting the latest shipping intelligence in the coffee house, and of having it read out by 'the Kidney', had helped to make Lloyd's *the* centre of marine business. From 1734, shipping news was published in *Lloyd's List*, and in 1760 *Lloyd's Register* began to appear, with vital factual information about vessels that underwriters might be asked to insure: present and former owners, ports, voyages, tonnage. In the Napoleonic Wars, Lloyd's began to build up what was to grow into a worldwide network of agents, able to carry out surveys of vessels and cargoes and in many other ways represent underwriters in every significant foreign port. The *List*, the *Register* and the agents helped Lloyd's to survive in the thirty

unprofitable years after Napoleon was banished to St Helena. After
1856 the Lloyd's agents were supplemented by the Salvage Association,
established jointly by Lloyd's underwriters and the marine insurance
companies in London. Its purpose was to minimize loss to underwriters
by salving and repairing ships and recovering their cargoes wherever
possible. Even that virulent enemy of Lloyd's, J. T. Danson, conceded
the value of these ancillary services.

In the early 1870s there was serious discussion of a scheme that
would have had the effect of removing the Salvage Association, the
Lloyd's agents, the intelligence-gathering operations, the *List* and the
Register from Lloyd's exclusive control and handing them over to a
new body on which Lloyd's representatives would be in a minority. It
was immediately after this dangerous moment that a new strong man
appeared at Lloyd's. This was not an underwriter, or even a member
of Lloyd's, but the new Secretary, Henry Hozier. In 1874, when he
applied for the job, Hozier was an obscure thirty-year-old army officer.
When he resigned in 1906, he was one of the notable figures of Edwardian England, a man with an ambitious yet practical vision of how
Britain might dominate the sea trade of the world. Quite appropriately
he was to become the father-in-law of Sir Winston Churchill, who
married his daughter Clementine in 1908. Hozier possessed many of the
less attractive characteristics that were common among the servants of
Empire: he was pompous, vain, domineering, quarrelsome and ex-
travagant. He was also energetic, determined and intelligent. 'Before
long,' one historian says simply, 'Hozier was the ruler of Lloyd's.'

He won that position not only by the efficient and autocratic way
in which he ran things in the City, but even more by the energy with
which he travelled the world to make life more profitable for underwriters. First, he turned his attention to the difficulties they faced
paying claims in distant ports in an age before the invention of modern
communications and air travel. If claims had to be sent by sea mail to
London and payments had to travel by the same means, months could
elapse between a casualty and full payment. So, first in Australia, India
and China, and later worldwide, Hozier arranged for claims to be paid
by the local Lloyd's agents. He built up the network of agents energetically. But his great life work was the creation of a world system of signal
stations owned by, or in communication with, Lloyd's.

Shortly before Hozier became Secretary, a firm at Falmouth, in
Cornwall, offered to run a signal station for Lloyd's. Hozier's predecessor did not even trouble to answer their letter. When a row broke
out between this first enterprising firm and their rival, the local Lloyd's

agent, Hozier took the train down to Cornwall and saw his opportunity. He conceived his grand design of a system of signal stations on islands or headlands commanding the approaches to ports, linked to Lloyd's by telegraph. 'Their information,' he wrote proudly in a 1901 report, 'is not of value to underwriters and others interested in marine insurance alone; but is also of great importance to owners of vessels and cargoes. It is frequently of much pecuniary advantage that a vessel which may be making for some particular point may be intercepted before she reaches harbour, and ordered to some other port where her cargo can be dealt with to greater advantage.' Hozier was unconsciously foreseeing the seaborne trade of the late twentieth century, when supertankers are controlled by computers in New York, London or Houston and redirected to the port where their cargo will fetch marginally the highest price.

Not one vessel in ten, Hozier boasted, arrived at a British port without being first sighted and reported by one of his stations. And he was not shy about claiming that it was to them that Lloyd's underwriters owed their great prosperity. 'After the close of the Napoleonic wars,' he wrote accurately, 'the position that Lloyd's held with regard to maritime intelligence appears to have sunk; but within the last quarter of a century Lloyd's has again risen; and at the moment holds practically the monopoly of the collection and distribution of shipping intelligence throughout the world.'

This was the high point of Lloyd's in the maritime world, and the zenith of Britain's dominance as a maritime power. In 1901, Britain had 346 vessels of more than 5,000 gross tonnage, out of a world total of 596. (Germany came second with 124, the United States third with 36, France fourth with 23, Japan fifth with 19.)

This largely British-owned, British-built fleet traced a pattern of trade that reflected Britain's primacy not only as an exporter – a position in which she was increasingly challenged by the United States and Germany – but also as an importer of food and raw materials. Hozier sprinkled the late Victorian trade routes – radiating out from London and the other great north European ports, to the east coast of the United States and Canada, to the River Plate, the Cape, India, China and Australia – with signal stations. 'Report me to Lloyd's,' signalled the liners and the dirty British coasters, and Hozier's signalmen did. Only one of his stations survives, at Gibraltar. But in their day they had the humdrum romance of a Kipling ballad. By 1884, only ten years after Hozier came to Lloyd's there were seventeen of them round the British and Irish coasts and six abroad. By 1891 there were forty in Britain and 118 scattered elsewhere. The system did not extend to the United States. 'An excellent system of life-saving stations has been established by the United States,' Hozier reported, 'but these stations have not been equipped with a view to reporting passing vessels. There is thus no official system of semaphore as in Europe.' However, the great east coast ports did set up stations at their approaches: New York at Sandy Hook and Fire Island, Philadelphia at the mouth of the Delaware River, and Baltimore at the mouth of Chesapeake Bay. Most important of all, because it was the first landfall of the great North Atlantic liners, was the light-vessel at Nantucket Island.

Elsewhere the long arm of Lloyd's reached out to desolate headlands at the western approaches to the English Channel, like the Old Head of Kinsale, on the Irish coast, and Ushant, in Brittany; to Brunsbüttel-koog, at the entrance to the Kiel Canal, and Hamlet's Elsinore, on Öresund between Denmark and Sweden; to the hill of Kom-el-Nadura behind the harbour of Alexandria, and Sandheads at the flat mouth of the Hooghly below Calcutta; to lonely island stations like Ascension and St Helena; to Morro Castle, in Havana Bay, and foggy Belle Isle at the approach to the St Lawrence River; and at all the corners of the Pacific from the Straits of Magellan by way of Honolulu to Tasmania.

Hozier's imagination did not stop at this world system of stations for physical signalling with semaphores, linked to London by the telegraph. He saw ahead to the coming age of wireless telegraphy. In the 1890s, researchers in several countries were experimenting with the new technology. It was not until 1896 that Marconi made good his claim to be the most successful of them, and his eventual triumph was not certain for some years later still. Hozier not only saw how essential it was for Lloyd's to be in on what was happening, but was involved in the research personally. He studied the principles of early radio and, with the famous conjuror Maskelyne, succeeded in producing apparatus that was able to transmit and receive messages over substantial distances.

Gradually, however, Marconi pulled ahead. Hozier was on the board of one of the Marconi companies, and he persuaded the British government to give Lloyd's a licence to operate wireless telegraphy from half a dozen stations to ships at sea. Under a 1901 agreement between Lloyd's and the Marconi enterprise, these stations began to send and receive private messages to crew and passengers as well as recording ships' locations and sending messages from owners. For a moment, it was conceivable that Lloyd's of London might develop into a worldwide communications conglomerate.

It did not happen. In 1906, after the agreement had been in force for five years, Marconi brought an action under it on the grounds that the service Lloyd's was providing was insufficient. Marconi won, and although for a while Lloyd's was allowed to keep four wireless telegraphy transmitting stations, Marconi was awarded the two most important ones at the approaches to Europe – at Malin Head, on the north coast of Ireland, and at Crookhaven, at the entrance to Cork harbour, in the south. (For some years, Marconi had been operating a radio station at Nantucket at the other end of the Atlantic trade route.)

The lawsuit was hardly a catastrophe for Lloyd's. For Hozier, however, it was the end of a dream, and it led to the end of a career. Shortly after Marconi's victory in the courts, the British government, through the Postmaster-General, Sydney Buxton, who had responsibility for communications, withdrew Lloyd's licence to operate wireless telegraphy. In the process, in the House of Commons Buxton challenged the accuracy of figures Hozier had cited on Lloyd's behalf. Hozier was beside himself. Buxton spoke in the House of Commons under privilege, and therefore could not be sued for libel. But he could be punished for his insult in another way. Hozier dictated a letter challenging Buxton to a duel. Whatever hold the *code duello* might have had among touchy Frenchmen or hot-blooded Louisiana planters, in the City of London in 1906 it was as obsolete as the pigeon post – and indisputably illegal.

Hozier was under attack in any case for his extravagance on Lloyd's behalf. It transpired that he had spent more than £25,000 of the Society's money – a huge sum – in his endless but also extremely comfortable journeyings through the world of palace hotels and first-class saloons in search of signal stations. In the end, he had to resign. Shortly afterwards, he died in Panama, and with his boots on: he was prospecting for a site for a signal station near the new Canal. Hozier had been a great Secretary of Lloyd's; perhaps the greatest. He had been greater still as a servant of the maritime world as a whole, and of the dream of worldwide Anglo-Saxon empire that thrilled his generation.

By 1906, Hozier was already in certain respects a man of the past. Not that marine insurance declined rapidly in the early years of the century. Even today, it maintains something close to parity with non-marine in the volume of Lloyd's business. Rather, in Hozier's last years, the most innovative minds in the market had turned towards the new non-marine market. And it was there that the most urgent problems for the Committee and the Society had already arisen.

Hozier's nemesis inside Lloyd's was a young and serious underwriter called Sidney Boulton, who had been elected to the Committee in 1902.

Together with Cuthbert Heath, Boulton played the leading part in the next major series of reforms of the procedures of Lloyd's. In the end, two major reforms were effected two years after Hozier's death. One made it compulsory to put premiums paid to underwriters into a trust fund for greater safety until all claims against them had been paid. The other was strict auditing of underwriters' accounts.

Again, the impetus for reform arose from a scandal. A certain Percy George Calvert Burnand, elected an underwriting member of Lloyd's in 1885, deposited £5,000 in what had become the usual way, and wrote a profitable book of marine business for several years without incident. He then joined the board of a travel agency called Gaze & Sons which was apparently never solvent. This was the time of Queen Victoria's death and the accession of her elderly, cigar-smoking son, Edward VII. The Coronation was to be the great event of the year in 1902, as spectacular a ceremony for the masses and the classes as the old queen's Diamond Jubilee. Gaze & Sons invested heavily in buying up seats to watch the procession. Then the king fell ill with appendicitis and the Coronation had to be postponed. Although they had an underwriter on the board, Gaze & Sons had not insured against that contingency, and they stood to be wiped out. They tried to raise money on bills, but without security the banks refused to lend money on them.

Burnand obligingly provided the security by insuring the bills. He bound his syndicate of five Names to pay if the bills were not met within thirty days. They were not met. They were renewed several times. The banks became nervous. Burnand found an insurance company to guarantee his guarantee. In the end, the crazy card house collapsed. Burnand had let his syndicate in for more than £100,000 of liabilities, had not bothered to charge a single penny of premium and never told the Names what he had done. There was a lawsuit, everything came out, three of the Names were ruined and one merely impoverished, and Burnand joined the list of those who have used and betrayed the name of Lloyd's.

A number of other insolvencies occurred in the market in those same years, and the general feeling of unease grew. It had become the custom for underwriters to insure their own business with each other. In 1906 Cuthbert Heath decided that he would not sign a guarantee policy on behalf of a fellow member unless that member would agree to submit his underwriting accounts to a strict audit. Some members thought this was a sensible reform to protect the security of the Lloyd's policy and, therefore, the reputation of Lloyd's. Others regarded it as an outrageous trespass on their privacy. Matters came to a head in

1908. A journalist called Harcourt Kitchin used to write about the Lloyd's market from time to time in *The Times*, which in those days used no by-lines, so that Kitchin's contributions were anonymous. On 17 July *The Times* published a powerful editorial calling for a 'semi-private audit' of Lloyd's underwriters; it was written by Kitchin, almost certainly inspired by Sidney Boulton and, possibly, known in advance to the Committee. Five days earlier, the Committee had procured a legal opinion to the effect that it was not within the powers of the Corporation of Lloyd's to guarantee its own members, and that new laws would be needed if that were desired. But the Committee was fiercely divided on this issue, as were Lloyd's members, who held the ultimate power to accept or to reject the principle of an audit.

A special committee was appointed to consider the question. Things dragged on. Finally, there was a full meeting of members on 3 November 1908. But before the meeting, Cuthbert Heath took a simple and decisive action. He took a piece of ordinary foolscap scratch paper, and scribbled on it two sentences:

We, the undersigned underwriting members, would agree to hand to the Committee of Lloyd's annually a statement, signed by an approved accountant, that we were in possession of assets reasonably sufficient to wind up our underwriting accounts. We suggest that a Committee should be appointed to consider the best method of carrying out the above proposal.

It was a clever stroke. Any underwriter who refused to sign must raise at least the suspicion that he was not in a position to withstand the audit, in which case his business would simply melt away.

There were still a few diehards at the meeting, but they were routed by a speech from a respected member, F. A. White, who remarked that the editorial from *The Times* had been reprinted with approval 'from Canada to China'. He then joined to the mounting pressure for the audit another idea that had been kicking around the Room for even longer: the idea of putting premiums in trust. This safeguard had been suggested by a writer in the *Economist* as early as 1890: 'Let the deposit remain as at present,' the paper wrote then, 'but in front of it place all the premium received. Put the premiums in joint names of themselves and an officer of Lloyd's. Profits would be payable as ascertained.' In 1908, some underwriters were already following this prudent practice, but it was not general or mandatory, so it could be presumed that those who most needed to put their premiums in trust were those who were least likely to have done so. White's proposal swept the meeting. By the end of 1908, all syndicates had been ordered by the Committee to return audit certificates within three months, and premiums were to be held in trust and kept for the payment of claims.

These reforms powerfully improved the security of a Lloyd's policy. They only incidentally protected the Lloyd's underwriter. When Burnand failed, the Committee did nothing to reimburse those who had insured with him. His failure led to the introduction of the audit, but it took another, even bigger, even more preposterous scandal to convince the Committee and the members to take the next step. Not even the audit, strict as it was to be, could protect those who held Lloyd's policies against deliberate fraud, and in that case all the members of Lloyd's stood to lose, because the reputation of Lloyd's as a whole was threatened. It took the self-destructively lunatic behaviour of an underwriter named Stanley Bruce Knowles Harrison to teach those hard lessons. Fortunately, if that is the right word, he did so in a fashion which the collective memory of Lloyd's has not yet forgotten.

When the mass car market came along after the First World War, it brought with it 'never-never' hire-purchase finance. The finance companies were paid by the purchaser in bills which they then took to discount houses in the City for ready cash. Because the discount houses were wary of this type of paper, the new finance houses – and they were springing up like mushrooms – began to go to insurance companies to guarantee their customers' credit. Then they turned their attention to Lloyd's, and one of the Lloyd's underwriters who started doing this business was Harrison.

Up to that point Harrison had been writing mixed business – marine, non-marine and motor – for a syndicate of five Names. He also had a small brokerage business. In 1921 he started writing credit insurance for the Industrial Guarantee Corporation, a dubiously solvent but undeniably aggressive finance house. In return for premium income of only £20,000, he wrote insurance on no less than £2 million.

Next, Harrison fell into the clutches of a bold Swedish schnorrer called Holsteinson. His dodge was to draw bills secured on imaginary cabs and buses; insure the bills with Harrison; and discount the worthless bills, turned to gold by the magic of the Lloyd's policy and Harrison's signature, for good hard cash. Early in 1923, the ingenious Scandinavian departed for his northern home, leaving Harrison lumbered with worthless paper that would have stood him in for a nasty loss of £17,000. By the end of the year, Harrison would have taken that medicine with a sigh of relief, but now he flinched from it. He had been in trouble with the Committee already, and so had foolishly hidden his credit business from the audit by keeping double books. He dare not go to the Committee and make a clean breast of his troubles. Instead of quitting, he doubled – or much more than doubled. What he did was to borrow money on bills made acceptable by his signature. He was known to be in trouble, perhaps desperate, and he was fleeced accordingly. Some of his bills, even with the credit insurance to make them negotiable, changed hands at discounts of 50 per cent and above. In his last agonies, it was discovered later, he raised a nominal £10,000 on bills covered by his insurance. The bookmaker who bought the bills paid £4,500 for them, and the intermediary who arranged the deal took £2,000 for himself, leaving the wretched Harrison with just £2,500!

Nevertheless, it wasn't until he bounced a cheque that the Committee realized what had been going on. It is easy to say that it ought to have known that such maggoty dealings were going on under the banner of the anchor mark. It is reasonable to criticize the Committee and Arthur Lloyd Sturge, who was unlucky enough to be the Chairman of the day, for not spotting the trouble sooner. But as soon as they did learn what had happened, Sturge and the Committee rose superbly to the occasion.

Within a week of Harrison's confession, Sturge had ferreted out the appalling magnitude of the possible losses. He called a general meeting, and told it bluntly that the amount owing was at least £100,000 and might be as much as £300,000. The underwriting members, Sturge admitted, had no legal obligation to pay these debts, and he had no power to make them do so. But if they did not volunteer to make Harrison's liabilities good, he told them, then 'the name of Lloyd's will be seriously injured and will never recover in our lifetime'.

Not a single member rose to disagree in principle with what Sturge was proposing. However, there were naturally some who wanted to wait and see before paying up. Sturge simply refused to end the meeting until it had agreed to do what he clearly saw must be done. In the end, for some reason, the money was raised on one of the strangest insurance slips ever signed at Lloyd's. Every single underwriting member signed it. Even more unusual was the fact that the loss had occurred *before* the slip was signed: the loss was £200,000, and the premium was just two shillings and sixpence, or about nineteen cents. The burden was distributed among the underwriting membership in proportion. The biggest syndicate had to pay more than £10,000; the oldest member had to find just eightpence, or roughly a nickel.

The Committee did not pay every claim in full. It reserved the right to adjust what it considered dubious or dishonest claims; after all, many of those who had claims on Harrison had bought them at a discount knowing full well that he must be in desperate trouble. But in the end it paid out £367,000, the balance above the £200,000 subscribed by members coming from the Corporation's own funds. It was, as Sturge had clearly seen, cheap at the price. Genuinely enlightened self-interest is almost as rare as altruism.

There have been other smashes and scandals at Lloyd's in the twentieth century – though not very many of them, considering the number of members and the volume of money. There was the Roylance affair in the 1920s, and the Piggot smash, which cost the Names on the syndicate affected more than £100,000 each – a considerable amount of money in those days. But undoubtedly the most interesting and potentially significant was the scandal concerning an underwriter named Alec Wilcox, which came to light in 1954.

Sensitive members of Lloyd's might take umbrage at the extent to which I have presented the Society's history as a series of rows and scandals. But there is a solid reason for this. The members of Lloyd's, by and large, as befits men busily and on the whole successfully occupied in making money, are both pragmatic and conservative. In normal times, few of them spare much thought for extracting general principles from the mass of detail in which their lives are immersed. Fewer still, perhaps, spend much time concocting schemes for reform. It takes a thundering good scandal to bring home to the membership that new safeguards may be needed.

So it took the Forwood affair to make the Committee realize that its authority over members needed to be defined by Act of Parliament. It took the Burnand failure to make the more conservative members accept the need for the audit, and for safeguarding premium income in a trust fund. It took the Harrison crash to drive home that the whole credit of Lloyd's could be fatally damaged by fraud. The Wilcox case carried the Committee's conception of enlightened self-interest one step further. In the Harrison case, the members paid up so that the *insureds* should not suffer. The precedent established by the Wilcox case was that, at least in certain highly unusual circumstances, the Committee was prepared to relieve Names of their liability.

The Wilcox case was a straightforward story of fraud (insofar as fraud is ever straightforward). A dishonest underwriter had managed to find a dishonest accountant to sign his annual certificates of audit. A syndicate's books, as a result, were systematically cooked for years. Premium income was hidden. The trust fund was raided. Profits were invented and paid out. The Committee took the view that the Names, who were ruined by these operations, could not have known what was going on, and that the credit and fair name of Lloyd's demanded that they should be protected. Even in such a citadel of rugged individualism as Lloyd's, the mentality of the welfare state has perhaps made some progress.

Very soon it will be three hundred years since Edward Lloyd, coffee man, 'citizen and framework knitter', moved from Great Tower Street to the corner of Lombard Street and Abchurch Lane. It is just over two hundred years since 'new Lloyd's' emerged from the coffee house and first acquired premises of its own. From the opening of the American War of Independence to the final defeat of Napoleon, Lloyd's lived through forty profitable years. For a quarter of a century after Waterloo it stagnated and might have disappeared altogether. As late as the 1870s there was a serious possibility that the market would wither away, unable to compete with the greater resources of the insurance companies.

In a real sense, therefore, Lloyd's is not just under three hundred years old, but just over one hundred. Its statutory being, its code of rules, its badge, date from 1871. Of the four markets, marine was rescued from the suffocating competition of the companies in the 1870s and 1880s only by Marten's invention of the modern syndicate. By 1980, moreover, the marine market accounted for little more than a third of the total premium income of Lloyd's. Of the other three markets, non-marine is less than a hundred years old, and was only officially acknowledged in legislation seventy years ago. The first Lloyd's motor policy was issued in 1904, and the first aviation policy in 1911, but the motor market did not develop to any significant size until after the First World War, and the aviation market not until after the Second. The nature of the business, its origins, the way it is handled and the character of the membership have all been radically transformed even more recently than that. So it is time to let the dead bury their dead, and make the acquaintance of the living inhabitants of the Room.

CHAPTER 4

PASSENGERS AND CREW

Individually, we are underwriters; collectively, we are Lloyd's.

Traditional definition,
said to have been first formulated by a Lloyd's underwriter
when asked what he did by a lady at a dinner party

As you approach the main entrance to Lloyd's, you are likely to be greeted by a cheerful man in a red serge robe and a top hat with a startling resemblance to Sergeant Bilko. He is the proud possessor of a signed photograph presented by Phil Silvers, the actor who made Bilko immortal, if that is the right word. His name is Len James. He will take your coat and pass you on to a more lugubrious colleague enthroned in a wooden pulpit in the middle of an entrance hall. These are the waiters, who act as messengers, receptionists and staff in the Room and its surrounding facilities. They are lineally descended from the waiters of Edward Lloyd's coffee house. Today they may be black as well as white, and women as well as men. All are resplendent in scarlet, and all are uniformly dignified, knowledgeable and polite.

As you wait to be met – those who are not members, subscribers or associates, as a sign warns you, may not enter the Room unescorted – you take in your surroundings. At one end of the entrance hall is the Lloyd's war memorial, a stained-glass window depicting a naked man holding the Lloyd's flag and surmounting the globe, between four flags: the Union Jack of Great Britain, the white ensign of the Royal Navy, the red duster of the Merchant Navy, and the red-white-and-blue roundel of the Royal Air Force. Opposite the war memorial is the heavy revolving door into the Room, flanked for some reason by the steering wheel of the aircraft carrier HMS *Ark Royal* and a framed photograph of the Queen Mother.

The third wall is partly glass, so that while you wait for your escort you can glimpse the subaqueous life inside the Room like a visitor staring into an aquarium. You can see the open end of two of the boxes, numbers 107 and 108. You idly study the nearest one and notice that it is a varnished wooden pen with room for no more than five or at most six people to sit facing one another along either side, and in some intimacy at that. People at Lloyd's are individualists in their conformist way, or are conformist in an individual way. If you are going to spend eight hours a day for the rest of your life in a space smaller than a lifeboat, you will make it comfortable in your own way, fitting it to the shape of your business and your personality. So while all boxes in the Room are generically similar, each one is different. The one you are staring at has a high superstructure to accommodate business records and reference books. Underneath, several men and a woman are busy writing and occasionally making phone calls; through the glass you can't hear what they are saying. The sharp end of the box, metaphorically speaking, the end where the active underwriter himself sits, is at the far end; a short line of brokers stand waiting to show him business.

You have just time to be conscious of the same pattern of boxes repeated with variations in the part of the Room you can see through the glass wall, and of the constant swirl of movement, like a street market. The brokers, women as well as men, carrying their business in leather slipcases, are the shoppers. The underwriters wait for them like the stallholders. Then your escort arrives to take you through the revolving door into the Room.

It is a vast space, more than a hundred metres long, two storeys high, with the marine market – the Senior Service – on the ground floor, and the non-marine market upstairs in the gallery. You are coming into it near the end of the north side. The wall on your left is a long notice-board, with telex copy from the Lloyd's intelligence services pinned up, giving news of the movements of ships, losses, collisions, casualties, air crashes, fires, earthquakes and other natural disasters, as well as political or industrial news likely to affect the market. On the same wall appear press clippings, official notices and all the other information that a purser on a liner might put up outside his office for the infor-mation of the crew and passengers.

After a few feet, you come out into the ceremonial open space at the centre of the room, in front of the rostrum where the red-robed Caller intones into a microphone the names of members who are wanted on the phone or in person. His constant drone is part of the background noise of the Room. In front of him sits the loss clerk, David Barling, whose job again strangely combines the archaic with the technological. He takes information that has arrived by radio and microwave from all over the world at the Lloyd's intelligence services computer at

Colchester, and enters it with a quill pen and a flowing copperplate hand in two enormous ledgers as big as church Bibles. One is the missing and overdue book, the other the loss book. Behind and above the Caller the bell of HMS *Lutine* hangs from an ornate cast-iron gantry.

Bell and book are reminders of an almost obsolete function of Lloyd's: the overdue market. Once there was a thriving market in reinsuring overdue vessels. Now the market has been killed by the speed of modern communications. Its only monument is the last surviving overdue broker, a tiny, ancient man called Cecil Amery. When a vessel is overdue, he will take it round the market and see what rate he can get for its reinsurance. Very occasionally, the Lutine bell is rung for an overdue vessel: two rings if she is safe, one for a loss. Nowadays the bell is rung as often for other reasons: to announce that a member of the Royal family is visiting the market, or – sadly often – for a bomb warning (always so far a false alarm).

A few feet to the west of this forum of venerable ritual is the busiest ganglion of the modern market: the Posgate box. In the autumn of 1982, at the climax of the greatest storm ever to smash into the hull of the liner in Lime Street, Ian Posgate was suspended. Whether he will be allowed back to practise his trade now depends on the outcome of multiple litigation and on the decision of the Committee of Lloyd's, of which, just to complicate matters even further, Posgate was, until 1983, a member. We shall come in due course to the events that led to Posgate's fall. Here, in the meantime, in the present tense, is a sketch of the most talented and most successful of modern underwriters before the fall.

There are plenty of corners of the Room where you can catch a whiff of greasepaint. But this is the only one where you can imagine klieg lights. Many leading underwriters have presence. They wear a rose in their buttonhole, make an entrance fashionably late, shoot a couple of inches of white poplin cuff, displaying gold links, unscrew the top of a gold fountain pen and scribble their initials with a stagy flourish. There are plenty of these leading men at Lloyd's, even a few stars. Ian Posgate is the only superstar. They call him Goldfinger in the market. It is not just that he is said to have the highest earned income in England. (He drew over £700,000, or $1·1 million, in commission in 1981.) It is not just that he has been consistently at or near the top of the unofficial league table of the most successful underwriters. Posgate has style. He competes fiercely, always ready to cut the rate of premium, in a market where the collective spirit is as evident as individualism. He writes far bigger 'lines' – percentages of a given risk – than any other underwriter in the modern market. He positively seeks out dangerous business where his competitors are nervous because there have been heavy losses. War, hijacking, political upheaval, catastrophe, have been his opportunities. He courts publicity, charms journalists and knows how to portray himself, in spite of his resonant success, as the outsider. In a way, it is true. He is a self-made man, where his closest rivals, like Sir Peter Green and Stephen Merrett, would be known at Lloyd's, if they were not known for themselves, for who their fathers were. At the same time, there is a hint of mystery, even scandal, about the Posgate myth. He has been in deep trouble in the past, and has constantly chafed against the Committee's authority. He is revered by the Names on his syndicates because he makes them so much money. He is idolized by the people who work for him. He has been elected to the Committee of Lloyd's, the highest honour his peers have to bestow. A man of his sardonic intelligence probably gets even more pleasure out of the envy he inspires. It is, after all, a sincerer form of flattery than imitation, and in his case easier.

Posgate accepts risks on behalf of more than half a dozen syndicates, some managed by the Alexander Howden group, some by his own agency, Posgate & Denby. Each managing agent has a major marine syndicate and a major non-marine syndicate. The Howden syndicates, being older, are bigger than the Posgate & Denby ones. In addition, Posgate writes specialist business – for example, aviation and livestock – for smaller syndicates. The total premium income flowing into all these syndicates was around £150 million ($375 million) in 1982, or not far short of 10 per cent of the entire income of the Lloyd's market. An insurance company with that volume of premium would inhabit a sizeable office building. But at Lloyd's all that money flows through the Posgate box, a space some fifteen feet by ten. Of course some administrative back-up is provided by Howden, and Posgate & Denby have a small office over a jeweller's shop round the corner in Fenchurch Street. But, more than most underwriters, Posgate does his business in his box on the floor of the Room.

The box is the standard size. The table, topped with blue baize, is divided down the middle by a slot full of metal-bound record and rate books. Each side of the table is the circuit for a flow of money. Posgate sits at one corner, on the aisle. His deputy, Mark Denby, sits opposite. They divide the underwriting between them on principles they can understand but can hardly explain. Denby is one of the most respected underwriters at Lloyd's in his own right, a lean, blond man with a greyhound profile and big glasses. But even the newest recruit on the box calls him 'Mark'. They call Posgate 'Mr Posgate' to his face, and behind his back 'the Boss'.

Posgate's side of the box is the channel for money flowing in: for premium. Denby's side, apart from Denby himself, deals with claims: money flowing out. The third, crucial flow is invisible at the box: reinsurance. Through brokers, either at Lloyd's or outside, a syndicate reinsures a proportion of its risks for two reasons: to limit its own exposure to claims, and to keep its premium income within the limits laid down by Lloyd's. No syndicate is allowed to write more than a certain amount of premium, determined in relation to the number of Names belonging to it and the amount of their deposits.

Andrew Bathurst, Posgate's claims man, sits next to Denby. Behind him, in a little dickey-seat, sit Kate Sliwinska Judd, a barrister, born in Poland, whom Posgate hired when she was working for the Corporation of Lloyd's, and David Burnett, her assistant, a young lawyer from her former chambers. Next to them is a large copying machine that takes up an appreciable share of the entire space on the box. Beyond that, in isolation like a tail gunner, sits Kevin, the cargo covers man. The rest of the aircrew is made up of Christine, who deals with livestock, and three young assistants: Nick is a Londoner who got the job blind through an employment agency; Adrian comes from a mining village in Durham via Durham University; Rupert, a recent Oxford graduate, was hired by Posgate while he was broking a risk to him at the box.

The day begins for them at nine o'clock. A stack of computer cards is waiting to be sorted: pink for United States dollars, white for pounds sterling, blue for Canadian dollars. They have come up overnight from the Lloyd's Policy Signing Office at Chatham. A code identifies what type of business each card represents. The assistants split them up into premium and claims, and check the coding. By early 1984, a micro-processing system will have been introduced, with a VDU in the box.

By ten o'clock the brokers begin to drift up. At first they are junior staff bringing routine business: amendments to slips signed the previous day and the like. The main business of the day does not get under way until around eleven o'clock.

Shortly before that, Ian Posgate has slipped into his seat. He is a slim man with a high forehead and brown eyes, conservatively dressed in a grey bird's-eye suit and a navy-and-white silk tie. A gold watch chain disappears into the snowy folds of a large linen handkerchief in his breastpocket, gold glasses are pushed back to the top of his head. His voice is precise, almost pedantic; his manner that of a Cambridge don, except for a higher intensity of nervous energy.

The brokers queue alongside his seat. They are mostly youngish men, smartly dressed, with an occasional young woman, usually in a dark suit with gold jewellery. The brokers show Posgate their slips: proposals for new insurances or renewals of existing policies. (The formal 'signing slips' will be made out later.) Each has the broker's name in the top left-hand corner. They are long strips of paper, folded several times, with the details of the insurance on the left, and the stamps of the Lloyd's syndicates or companies and the percentages of the risk that they are accepting on the right.

Posgate deals with them with astonishing speed and decisiveness. He picks up the right stamp – they have different-coloured handles – and whacks it down on the slip. Then he scribbles the percentage line he will take for the syndicate and its name: 'Spalding' for the Howden syndicates, 126 and 127, 'Posgate' for the newer, smaller Posgate & Denby syndicates, 700 and 701. Generally he writes a bigger line for the Spalding syndicates. Other stamps with coloured wooden handles wait to be used for the aviation, livestock and other smaller syndicates.

In a couple of hours Posgate writes millions of dollars and pounds of risks of an impressive variety. The first on this particular day is a reinsurance. The New York office of a big British insurance company wants to lay off part of its commitment to insure a British-based multinational chemical company worldwide for its third-party liability. The insurance company is willing to meet all claims up to the first £100 million, and it is proposing that Posgate makes himself responsible for the next $100 million: 'a hundred million dollars, excess of a hundred million pounds', as the broker puts it. Posgate quickly accepts 10 per cent of this line – 6 per cent for the Spalding syndicate and 4 per cent for Posgate.

The second was a 'facultative' – special – reinsurance on a fleet of ships trading with the River Plate. This is a Monday at the height of the Falkland Islands crisis. The previous Wednesday Lloyd's announced fourteen days' notice of cancellation of normal war-risk insurances for ships sailing to and from the River Plate. In effect, that meant shipowners with vessels trading with Argentina had to make their own arrangements to insure them, both against the risk of sinking due to military action, and against what is called 'blocking and trapping', meaning the loss of profit if the ship cannot be used because of a war (as happened to dozens of ships trapped in the Shatt al Arab as a result of the war between Iraq and Iran in 1980). Posgate stamped it quickly, then leaned over to me and said he had taken more than £1 million in extra war-risk premium in under a week on fleets trading with the River Plate. The special insurance is not particularly expensive: the standard rate of premium is 0·25 per cent on the value of the fleet, and Posgate is charging only 0·15 per cent for 180 days.

The next broker produced another war risk, this time on a fleet of twenty-odd American tankers trading to the Persian Gulf. Posgate renews the slip, on which he is the leader, with a little over 10 per cent of the risk split between his two syndicates. The slip has a fat file of shipping movement reports stapled to it: Posgate insists on being informed exactly when each ship in the fleet goes into the Gulf.

A diversion. A Willis Faber broker arrives selling French carriage clocks, which Posgate collects. The broker is doing a comic bazaar-trader number: 'They're all cheap,' he says in a put-on Yiddish accent. 'You know me!' After a certain amount of clowning, Posgate says he will think about buying one, and gets on with the job.

The slips are coming thick and fast now, and a dozen brokers or more are standing in line, close enough to read each other's business or listen to what is being said.

A small Swedish general cargo ship.

A shipping line in the Far East with twelve small freighters. Posgate increases their rate from 0·375 to 0·525 per cent because they have had some losses.

A romantic hint of opulence and tax avoidance: an investment company with a Spanish name in Zurich wants to insure a couple of houses in the expensive Chelsea section of London and their contents, including some valuable paintings.

A British bank, wanting to insure the personal effects of its employees in Buenos Aires. The employees have been evacuated to Uruguay, the furniture is safely in store in Buenos Aires. 'A nice risk,' says Posgate, writing 100 per cent of it.

A 'binding contract', giving authority to insurance companies in South Africa to write policies insuring shops against damage from political riots. Again Posgate writes 100 per cent.

Part of the risk on a British Petroleum oil-drilling platform in the North Sea.

War risks on the nine Boeing 707s owned by a middle-sized Middle Eastern airline.

Professional indemnity insurance for a London firm of money brokers and financial advisers.

Another reinsurance, this time of a certain proportion of the 'mineral account' of an insurance company, covering their exposure on oil, gas, sulphur and uranium drilling and mining.

A new building for an American steel corporation.

Posgate has been writing steadily for an hour and a quarter now, and for the first time since he came into the box there is a short pause. Then it begins again, though at a less hectic pace.

An insurance covering a construction company against confiscation and expropriation of their plant on a contract in Indonesia. The risk is led by Posgate's rival Stephen Merrett, who takes 50 per cent, and Posgate accepts the other half.

A steel barge.

Another reinsurance: this time 'excess of loss' on an American company's oil and gas business. For once Posgate takes a small line: 2·5 per cent of the very large account that is being offered.

A series of seven slips, each dealing with part of an insurance company's reinsurance programme protecting its North Sea oil-rig account. In other words, the company is insuring a whole book of rig business and wants Posgate to reinsure it against certain particular losses.

More South African political riot insurance, this time a reinsurance programme covering a big South African insurer on this type of risk.

IBM. The giant manufacturer wants product liability cover on its aviation business with the very high maximum of $200 million for any one occurrence. In other words, IBM wants to be covered against possible claims arising from an accident attributable to failure of electronic equipment it supplied to an aircraft. 'That is what we call long tail,' says Posgate. 'We won't know for many years whether we have made or lost money on that one.'

South Africa again. This time a crop-spraying contractor based in Cape Province but operating all over southern Africa wants cover for a fleet of small aircraft. The policy excludes liability for damage done in the course of spraying defoliant for military purposes. Posgate writes 100 per cent of the risk.

Legal liability for a ship repairer.

A string of racehorses, some in training in English stables, some in Tennessee.

A small vessel, total loss insurance only.

A Spanish fleet. 'The figures are quite bad, I'm afraid,' says the broker frankly.

A very big British container fleet. 'It's a big exposure,' says Posgate, 'but the risk is low.' He points out that the ships are mainly operating between London and Sydney, where port accidents are comparatively few.

A paper and pulp mill in Mississippi.

A tow between Nova Scotia and Spain. Posgate writes only a small line.

Reinsurance for the 'captive' insurance company owned by one of the Seven Sisters oil companies. Nowadays giant oil companies own their own captive insurance companies, usually based in Bermuda for reasons of taxation, regulation and convenience. But they reinsure a certain proportion of their risks with Lloyd's and other markets.

Just before lunch Posgate demonstrates how hungry he is still. A broker comes and asks him something. Posgate gives him an answer, and the broker says he will have to go back and check with the leader. 'Bring it to me then, and I'll write it all.' It is a joke. Posgate knows the man has a current insurance policy and that the broker will not break it. But he is planting the seed of the idea that he is ready to look at any good business.

The last broker before lunch is a specialist in bloodstock. He wants cover for the yearlings sold at Tattersall's horse sales at Newmarket. The policy goes into recondite detail about 'whistling' and 'roaring' and other symptoms of unsound wind in racehorses.

No insurer can be simultaneously expert in veterinary science, the politics of southern Africa, transatlantic towing and aviation. But an underwriter must be an expert in assessing a risk, and assessing the rate of premium that will allow him to make money on insuring that risk. There is no doubt at all that Ian Posgate is a virtuoso at that.

Every underwriter's business is different. In each of the four distinct markets at Lloyd's – marine, non-marine, aviation and motor – there are big syndicates and small, generalists and specialists, syndicates managed by agencies owned by the big brokers, and others that are fiercely independent. New syndicates are being formed all the time; but the Secretan marine syndicate, number 367, whose underwriter, Anthony Pilcher, writes for more than 1,000 Names, is thought to be more than two hundred years old. The Poland syndicate, underwriting engineering and motor finance as well as general marine and non-marine, is more than a century old, and the C. E. Heath syndicate started with three Names in 1881.

Ian Posgate testified to a House of Commons committee that he wrote for a total of more than 4,000 Names permitted to write a total of £136 million of premium income. Stephen Merrett, of Merrett

Syndicates, likewise told Parliament that he wrote for 3,300 Names. The other big names in the marine market are Sir Peter Green, the former Chairman of Lloyd's, whose Janson Green syndicate belongs to the brokers Hogg Robinson; Henry Chester, whom we have met, who is an independent; Dick Outhwaite's syndicate, number 317; and Secretan. One of the biggest syndicates is PCW, owned by the brokers J. H. Minet and named after its underwriter, Peter Cameron-Webb, who has just retired and gone to live in Switzerland: we shall hear more of him.

One of the biggest independent underwriting agencies at Lloyd's is R. W. Sturge & Co., founded by Arthur Lloyd Sturge in 1894. The company in 1981 had a premium income of £144 million. The active underwriter for its non-marine syndicates 210 and 212 is Ralph Rokeby-Johnson, and in the same parliamentary hearings he drew a map of Sturge's competition in the non-marine market. The biggest was the Merrett non-marine syndicate, whose underwriter is Robin Jackson, with a premium income capacity of £66 million ($99 million). That means that the aggregate wealth of the Names belonging to the Merrett non-marine syndicate entitled them in 1981 to authorize Robin Jackson to write business on their behalf to that total: a syndicate's premium income capacity is the handiest measure of its comparative size.

Second in order of capacity in the non-marine market came Rokeby-Johnson's own Sturge syndicates, with £58 million ($87 million). Third was the Three Quays agency, owned by the biggest Lloyd's brokers, Sedgwick. Its active underwriter is Dick Hazell, whom we met insuring Three Mile Island. His syndicate's capacity in 1981 was £42 million. Fourth was R. J. Kiln, with £37 million, an independent agency owned by the family and employees of Bob Kiln, the prophet of lean years ahead. And fifth was C. E. Heath, with £35 million. Rokeby-Johnson added that he suspected that the Bowring non-marine syndicate would be as big as those he listed, but he had not been able to acquire exact information on them.

The motor and aviation markets are smaller, though the Ariel syndicate, in the aviation market as its name would suggest, is big. These dozen or so big managing agencies, each controlling half a dozen syndicates, and each underwriting on behalf of 1,000 Names or more, some of them independent, some owned by big brokers, make up the underwriting Establishment at Lloyd's. Four or five dozen active underwriters make up the list of those who regularly act as the leading underwriter on important risks. But the short-list of the active underwriters who write for the big syndicates does not exhaust the number of those who lead interesting and sometimes highly profitable lives. Some of the most interesting boxes at Lloyd's belong to the specialists.

Bert Stratton's day, for example, can be as interesting as Ian Posgate's, though he writes for a far smaller syndicate. He is a specialist in personal accident insurance. One morning I spent in his box brought him the following slips, among many others.

A special plan known as 'Star Cover', insuring ten singers, including John Denver, Dolly Parton, Grace Slick and David Bowie, for sums between $2 million and $4 million apiece on behalf of RCA Records, to protect the recording company in case of accident to their stars.

An amateur football team in the South-east Surrey Intermediate League, to cover transport to and from matches. Stratton looked his rate up in a handwritten rating book and found it listed under 'football teams'.

A 27-year-old dancer in a Broadway musical, who earns $75,000 a year and wants to insure her legs for $500,000. Stratton persuades the Heath broker who is making the inquiry that what she really needs is an accident policy to cover temporary total disability and permanent total disability. He agrees to write the cover for two years.

He renews personal accident cover for Gulf & Western Corporation on the New York Knickerbockers, the New York Rangers ice-hockey team and the Washington Senators soccer players.

Another broker arrives waving a telex from Canada, inquiring what the premium would be to insure 550 professional cowboys for a season of seventy rodeos. Stratton is politely dubious. 'I think you'll have to leave this one with me. We do a lot of these, not Canadian, but American, and we get a lot of claims on them. Is it going to hurt you if you leave this until Monday?'

The same broker has another proposition. A professional opera singer, aged thirty-six, who has just signed a ten-year television contract in Germany, wants $1 million in personal accident cover. Again Stratton demurs. 'I'd like to see five-year average earnings before I agree to a million dollars just like that,' he says mildly, and alters the slip so that it reads, 'Sum assured not to exceed five years' earnings.'

A new broker slides into the place next to Stratton in the box.

'What's this?' Stratton asks. 'A stallion going by air?'

'No,' says the broker, deadpan. 'Loss of use.'

Stratton raises an eyebrow.

'If the stallion doesn't perform because of traceable sickness or disease, his contract is up the spout.'

'How much would the stallion's fees be?'

'This one gets a thousand Australian dollars.'

Stratton writes it.

An even stranger dialogue happened a few minutes later.

'Bert, excuse me,' said a broker, 'did you give the Pope to someone else?'

There has been a short, rather ill-tempered muddle over who is broking an insurance on the Pope's life. Stratton sorts out the muddle, and the broker who suspected he had been stitched up smiles again. It turns out that the insurance is wanted by a Californian documentary film-maker who has a contract to shoot a film about the Pope during a visit to Latin America and is covering himself in case the Holy Father falls ill and cannot make the trip. It is all in a morning's work.

Another specialist underwriter is Bob Gordon, of the G. C. de Rougemont & Others syndicate, a dapper man who wears a red rose in his buttonhole. The bread and butter of the syndicate's business is routine marine insurance, both hull and cargo, which accounts for three-quarters of its premium income. The remaining quarter is more exciting specialist business. Gordon writes bankers' indemnity: insuring banks against borrowers defaulting. He insures the transit of diamonds and securities, mostly for security and armoured-car companies. He has stopped writing the wholesale jewellers in London's Hatton Garden diamond district. 'I let Hatton Garden go,' he says. 'The rest of the market took it up, and they're losing money on it,' he says with some satisfaction. Gordon calls himself 'very commercial'. It is one of his favourite words. He likes to insure wealthy clients with major collections of jewellery. 'I'm not interested in a woman in Hampstead who has £20,000 in diamonds,' he says dismissively. 'Generally speaking, I'm interested in the woman who has £200,000 worth or more.' Perhaps the most interesting of his specialities is all the objects held for sale by Christies, one of the two big London art auction houses, under one premium. (The other big house, Sotheby's, insures part of its own stock of art through a 'captive' insurance company. The rest is underwritten at Lloyd's but not led by G. C. de Rougemont.) Much of Gordon's business comes from insuring art works in transit. Some of this is for the private dealer or collector. One of Gordon's assureds, for example, is a big London commercial gallery that sends paintings out on spec to potential buyers all over the world, and also exports paintings on behalf of collectors who have bought them in Bond Street. Another source of premium is the big travelling exhibitions sent out by governments, like the recent Italian, Egyptian, Chinese and Indian shows that have visited London, New York and Paris. Gordon laments the increasing tendency of the British and American governments to give a financial guarantee to the government that is exporting the exhibition, in place of insurance. Only the French government remains faithful to insurance. Part of the trouble is that values have gone up to the point where only limited insurance cover is available, even at Lloyd's.

One of the most mysterious classes of business written at Lloyd's is insurance on shipments of bullion. One slip covers the regular monthly shipments of gold from South Africa to the Bank of England. Another covers frequent deliveries of diamonds from the Soviet Union to the West. Lloyd's is understandably secretive about details in both cases, but both the sums insured and the premium are very substantial.

The first kidnap and ransom insurance policy at Lloyd's was written after the Lindbergh kidnapping in the United States in 1932. There was a steady trickle of demand for this kind of cover during the next forty years, much of it from the United States. Rutherford Vernon, underwriter to the Hudson syndicate, became a specialist in it. Then, in the early 1970s, kidnap and ransom ('K & R') became big business. Lloyd's underwriters are the world leaders in the field, but they are not alone. They have eager competition, especially from American insurers like Chubb and American International Underwriters. One of the secrets of Lloyd's competitive success in this field is that Lloyd's underwriters work with a close-mouthed consultancy company, largely staffed by former British Special Air Service and intelligence officers, who advise clients both before and after a kidnapping.

Some 90 per cent of the kidnap and ransom insurance written at Lloyd's is written by the Cassidy, Davis box. Tony Cassidy and Bill Davis learned their business with the Hudson syndicate and branched out on their own only in 1977. Ironically, this highly capitalist enterprise got its first boost from left-wing guerrillas: from the Tupamaros in Uruguay and the Montoneros and ERP (Ejército Revolucionario Popular) in Argentina in 1970–71. At about the same time there was a wave of abductions of bank officers' wives in small banks in those American states that do not allow branch banking; it was penny-ante stuff, and ransom demands were for correspondingly small amounts; $50,000–100,000. In 1971 K & R insurance was bringing in $1·5 million to Lloyd's.

Then, on the morning of 19 September 1974, Montoneros disguised as policemen and telephone repairmen waved two Ford Falcons into a side-street off the Avenida Libertador in downtown Buenos Aires. It was a brilliantly executed snatch. The cars contained the brothers Juan and Jorge Born, grandsons of the founder of Bunge & Born, 'the Octopus', one of the world's five biggest grain merchants, a house whose wealth and power had hitherto been matched by absolute discretion. The Born brothers disappeared into thin air in the middle of a city of 10 million people. It was not until the following June that carefully picked reporters were contacted, blindfolded and taken on a zigzagging ride around the city to a safe house in the suburbs. There they met the leader of the Montoneros . . . and Jorge Born. (His brother had been quietly released a couple of weeks earlier.) Jorge was to be freed too, but only against a ransom set at the stupendous figure of $60 million.

That same autumn Patti Hearst was kidnapped in California.

In Italy, by the mid-1970s, kidnappings, most of them not for political motives but for straight cash, were occurring at the rate of more than a hundred a year.

In Northern Ireland in 1975, a Dutch industrialist called Dr Herema was seized by Eddie Gallagher, who is said to have been on an IRA death-list for hanging on to money he had stolen on the IRA's behalf.

Worldwide, for the past ten years, there has been at least one kidnap somewhere every seven days. And while no known ransom paid has come even close to the $60 million paid out by Bunge & Born, the sums insured have risen steadily, and so for several years did the premium income to Lloyd's. It was $8 million in 1973, $32 million in 1974, and in 1979 it had reached $60 million out of a world total of $75 million in premium for this class of business. Since then, while the number of people insured has continued to grow, fierce competition from American and other insurers has brought rates of premium down. Tony Cassidy estimated in the spring of 1982 that the total of kidnap and ransom premium to Lloyd's for the full year would be around $45 million, out of a world total down to $75 million.

Kidnaps have taken place in most parts of the world, but in two they are now endemic. Each represents a market for Lloyd's, though each is entirely different.

In Italy, the kidnappers are mainly professional underworld criminals – what the Italians charmingly call *malviventi*, 'bad livers'. Their motives are generally financial. (Not always, as the kidnapping of former prime minister Aldo Moro in 1977 showed: that was a political act, mounted by the Red Brigades to expose the supposed weakness and corruption of bourgeois society.) Of course the political radicals in Italy, the Red Brigades and their various rivals, need money, and, like the early Bolsheviks or the IRA, they turn to common crime to get it. But most Italian kidnapping is *la mala vita* – gangsterism, not politics. The market in Italy therefore consists of wealthy individuals, most of them Italian. A number of Italian insurance companies began to offer K & R policies in the 1970s. This led to an outcry in the press and Parliament, denouncing kidnap insurance as encouraging kidnapping. The Italian government and the Confindustria (the powerful Italian employers' confederation) brought heavy pressure on the companies to withdraw this type of cover. Though it was never actually made illegal, the Italian authorities could make it difficult for Italian nationals to export the premium to buy cover at Lloyd's. Still, most wealthy Italians contrive to keep funds abroad somewhere. It is less than an hour's drive from Milan into Switzerland. A substantial quantity of Italian K & R business reached Lloyd's brokers somehow, and got through to Cassidy & Davis.

Tony Cassidy explained how the policies for that market are structured. His firm offers a given rate – say 3.5 per cent – for the first miliardo, or 1 billion Italian lire, which is roughly $1 million. The higher the sum insured, the higher the rate. It might be 4.5 per cent on the second miliardo, 5.5 per cent on the third. There would be a limit of five miliardi, and the client would be expected to take a high coinsurance, accepting one-third of the risk himself.

The market in Latin America is quite different, and potentially much richer. It is largely, though not entirely, with American multinational companies who have many employees, including American nationals in key executive jobs, in countries like Argentina or Uruguay, not to mention Nicaragua or El Salvador, where political kidnapping for either anti-capitalist or anti-*yanqui* reasons is common. Again, the two motives cannot be easily separated. In Guatemala, for example, during the last elections, left-wing guerrillas used extortion to raise campaign funds. They were not interested in making political demands, which they knew would not be met; they had no other means of fund-raising.

The demand for blanket cover for corporation employees rose sharply after 1973, when the Ford Motor Company paid $1 million as protection money against a repetition of the attempted kidnapping of one of its top executives in Argentina. After that, savvy American managements decided that they needed insurance. And energetic Lloyd's brokers crisscrossed the United States confirming them in that belief.

Some American multinationals, including some of the world's biggest corporations, insure all their employees in Latin America against the risk of kidnapping. Others insure only a specific list of named key executives. And others take out no insurance at all. Tony Cassidy is at pains to insist that not all multinationals take K & R insurance. 'That's absolute rubbish,' he says. He is equally vehement in his insistence that he does not make it a condition of insuring a client that the client commission Control Risks Ltd to advise it. Yet Cassidy does urge clients to hire Control Risks to do a security survey of their business. If the client agrees, he will rebate 10 per cent of their premium. And if the client adopts the advice Control Risks gives them, then Cassidy will rebate a further 10 per cent.

There was a distinctly John le Carré atmosphere about the offices of Control Risks Ltd, which I first visited when it was housed in a six-storey office building next to Ye Old Crutched Friars pub in America Square, between Lloyd's and the Tower of London: electronic locks, a document shredder in a corridor and bags of shredded paper going down in the elevator to an incinerator. (The company has since moved to an equally anonymous office in a modern multistorey building in Victoria Street.) Until recently Control Risks was a subsidiary of the Hogg Robinson broking and travel group, of which Sir Peter Green is a director. A management buy-out has now been arranged, partly beçause the directors of Control Risks feel its business will grow faster if it is not tied to one broker, and partly because Hogg Robinson, with broking and other interests in many parts of the world, including the Middle East, were nervous that Control Risks would get involved in politically controversial situations.

The idea of Control Risks was conceived in 1974 by Julian Radcliffe, a Hogg Robinson broker with an interesting background. He specialized in what are called 'political risks' – that means, among other things, insuring firms against the risks of contracts being broken or other financial losses due to sudden changes of government; something big contractors, building civil engineering works in, for example, the Middle East or Latin America or many parts of Africa, cannot afford to ignore.

Radcliffe was aware of the swelling demand, especially in the United States, for K & R insurance, and also of the amounts of premium that might be available. He was also aware of the mounting criticism of this type of insurance. He wrote a paper for Tim Royle, then chief executive officer of Hogg Robinson, analysing the whole problem rather comprehensively from three points of view: that of morality, that of public policy, and that of commerce.

Morally, was it right or wrong to bargain for someone's life? Radcliffe was clear that it was right if life could be saved.

Does paying ransom encourage crime? Does the availability of insurance increase the amount of ransom that will be demanded? Does it undermine or interfere with the police and make the position worse? Radcliffe argued that none of these criticisms was conclusive. And in commercial terms it was clear that a company had both a duty to protect its employees and an interest in protecting its budget.

Then he went on to argue that it would be in the interests of assureds, brokers and underwriters alike to set up a specialist consultancy firm to advise clients how they could minimize the risks of kidnapping and how to handle ransom demands if a kidnap did take place. He discussed the idea with Tim Royle, and there were also discussions in the Committee of Lloyd's. The result was Control Risks Ltd.

The original idea was to set the consultancy firm up as a joint subsidiary of Hogg Robinson and a major security firm. But that did not work out. Instead, Control Risks was created as a subsidiary of Hogg Robinson alone. From the start, a high proportion of the staff came from the SAS and from other intelligence and security departments of the British governments. The intriguing question is how Radcliffe, or someone else at Hogg Robinson, made the contacts that enabled these government-trained specialists to be recruited. Radcliffe himself says merely that he has been interested in terrorism and in how to combat it since he was an undergraduate at Oxford.

The present managing director of Control Risks, Arish Turle, is an intense, dark man who was a major in the elite Special Air Service regiment. He was decorated for gallantry in the Dhofar campaign in Oman, where the SAS defended the Sultan against Communist rebels in the early 1970s, and later served on the staff of General Sir Frank King, commander of the British security forces in Northern Ireland. General King is now the chairman of Control Risks. Other directors, besides Turle, incude Tim Royle of Hogg Robinson; Sir Robert Mark, former head of Scotland Yard; Dr (formerly Major-General) Richard Clutterbuck, a professional soldier turned academic who has published several books about terrorism; Simon Adams-Dale, a former SAS major; Christopher Gross, who has a background 'working for the government', I was told; and others with army, police or intelligence experience.

Radcliffe and Hogg Robinson were lucky in their ability to plug into the SAS circuit. The regiment, originally formed during the Second World War to raid behind the German lines, has long experience in what its soldiers call 'keeni-meeni' operations (the word comes from Swahili and describes the way a snake slithers through the grass). The SAS has been involved in secret undercover operations in Kenya, southern Arabia (Aden, Oman and Yemen) and Northern Ireland. The regiment has also acquired considerable expertise in training protection teams for heads of state and other important personages, and also in providing 'reaction teams' to deal with terrorist incidents such as aircraft hijacking. The quality of SAS training was universally acknowledged after SAS advisers helped West German anti-terrorist troops free a hijacked airliner at Mogadishu, Somalia, in 1977, and even more after the Iranian embassy siege in London in 1980. The regiment's expertise received less welcome publicity when it was revealed in 1970 that former SAS officers and men, working for a commercial organization called Watchguard, were offering to train bodyguards for heads of state in Africa and the Middle East, and again in the late 1970s when reports surfaced in the London *New Statesman* of similar services offered by an outfit with SAS connections called KMS Ltd – the letters standing for Keeni-Meeni Services.

As Arish Turle told me, both from a marketing point of view and operationally, Control Risks Ltd's key asset is highly trained personnel. The staff has grown from three in 1974 to more than sixty today, at least fifteen of them field men. The company has had to reach wider than the SAS to find that many people. It has taken men from the Special Branch of Scotland Yard and from what Turle called 'other branches of the government service', presumably a euphemism for the Secret Intelligence Service, the counter-espionage Security Service and military intelligence. One requirement is languages: Spanish-speaking operatives, in particular, are in great demand.

Here is how Control Risks works. A client becomes aware that he is responsible for staff who are exposed to the risk of kidnap, or that he and his family are at risk. He may or may not insure at Lloyd's. If he does, Control Risks' fees are paid out of the premium paid to Cassidy, Davis. The first thing Control Risks does is to carry out a Phase 1 survey. This means visiting the corporate client's head office and reviewing security risks and policy with top management. If as a result of those contacts management decides that the company is unacceptably exposed in a given country or countries, then Control Risks will go ahead and carry out a Phase 2 survey. It will study the place of work, residence and travel habits of executives and others who might be kidnap targets. Control Risks does not provide bodyguards, nor does it sell equipment. It does provide security instructors – for example, to train chauffeurs in how to evade road blocks. Besides kidnaps, Control Risks advises clients on how to deal with 'product extortion' – threats to poison food, for example – and 'property extortion', such as bomb threats. As with kidnaps, it advises both on how to minimize the risk of extortion, and also on how to respond to a threat when it is made.

Control Risks is proud that not a single client has been kidnapped when it has been able to organize his protection. It has nevertheless been involved in more than eighty extortion incidents to date, most of them kidnaps. (Other fashionable forms of extortion include calling up a supermarket and threatening to poison the fruit.) When news of an incident comes in to the company's communications centre in Victoria Street, key personnel are summoned by bleeper. Either Arish Turle or another top man will go to brief the corporate client's head office on what to do. A Control Risks team will head for the site of the kidnap with a director of the client company to carry out the negotiations; Control Risks personnel never actually do the negotiating on behalf of the client, though they are on hand to advise. The consultants in the field will have secure coded communications both with the corporate client's head office and with Victoria Street, where there is a computerized data base with detailed information about earlier kidnaps. If an earlier trace on kidnappers turns up, the information can be given to the consultant in the field instantly. One Control Risks man told me a high proportion of kidnaps are carried out by gangs with 'form' that can be recognized by the computer. Even so, it is often many weeks before the victim can be recovered. The longest incident Control Risks has been involved in lasted for 300 days. Consultants on the spot are rotated frequently enough to prevent them becoming too emotionally involved with the victim and his or her family.

Both Cassidy, Davis and Control Risks insist on certain basic rules to counter the accusation that they are encouraging kidnapping by enabling people to insure against it. All policies issued to cover K & R by Lloyd's underwriters carry certain conditions. One is that the existence of the insurance must be kept totally secret. Even if it is inadvertently disclosed, it is automatically invalid. With some difficulty, underwriters persuaded the Lloyd's Policy Signing Office at Chatham to accept that these are the only policies on which the name of the assured is never mentioned. Second, as soon as possible after a kidnap takes place, the local police must be informed. Control Risks encourages clients to make contact with the police even before a kidnap, making them aware that there is a kidnap possibility, for two reasons: they will get a better response from the police if a kidnap does take place, and they are more likely to get tip-offs. Last, the cover under the policy is limited to the amount a person or firm could afford to pay out if they had not been insured. They must pay the ransom out of their own resources, and only then are they refunded by underwriters.

K & R consultancy can be hairy work. During the evening rush-hour in Bogotá, Colombia, on 28 September 1976 George Curtis, vice-president of Beatrice Foods, was snatched by kidnappers. Arish Turle arrived together with two other Control Risks personnel, Joe Smith from the company's Washington office (Control Risks has offices in Washington and Bonn, and a representative in Italy) and another former SAS major, Simon Adams-Dale. The initial ransom demand was $5 million. In eight months of negotiations, Turle and his colleagues helped the Beatrice people talk that down to less than $500,000, and eventually Curtis was freed; he was thrown out of a car on a Bogotá backstreet. Turle and Adams-Dale were not so lucky. On the orders of a Colombian judge they were arrested and thrown into gaol, where they stayed for six weeks until, under heavy pressure from the British government, they were released. Not all risks, after all, can be controlled, even by the professionals!

The latest trend is for Lloyd's to broaden the cover available for companies whose executives work in politically unstable countries. Cassidy, Davis now offer a package policy covering the assured not only against kidnap and ransom and products extortion, but also, for example, against the costs of emergency repatriation, including such risks as a nasty surprise from the United States Internal Revenue Service if an executive has to return unexpectedly to United States resident status for income-tax purposes. The Iranian revolution has sharpened the perception in the boardrooms of multinational companies that we live in an unpredictable as well as a dangerous world.

Not all underwriting is as much fun as the personal accident business that Bert Stratton writes, with its showgirls and cowboys, or as exciting as Tony Cassidy's kidnap and ransom business. Most of the business of the non-marine market is more humdrum, and infinitely harder to grasp in a concrete way than a dancer's legs or a cowboy's horse. Most non-marine insurance is an exercise in the mathematics of abstract risk. But it is safe to say that, in spite of the growth in 'political' insurance, the combined premium of all the personal accident, art, bullion transit, and kidnap and ransom insurance written at Lloyd's together does not come to as much as one-tenth of the money that reaches the market in the form of premium on reinsurance treaties. And Lloyd's is about money. As the old Yorkshire and England cricketer Wilfred Rhodes used to say, 'You don't play this game for fun!'

An underwriter can write either *direct insurance* or *reinsurance*. Direct insurance means what it says: the underwriter insures the assured directly against whatever risks he may want to protect himself against. In reinsurance, another insurer is being protected: the re-insurance underwriter is sharing some part of the direct insurer's risk. Reinsurance, in turn, can be arranged in an infinity of different ways. These all fall into two generic types, however: either proportional, or 'quota-share', reinsurances; or 'excess-of-loss'. Quota-share re-insurance, in which the reinsurer agrees to take a given share of the entire risk on an insurer's book of business, in return for a given proportion of the premium, is often used when an insurer feels he is overtrading generally. Specifically, it is used by Lloyd's syndicates when they have taken in so much premium that they are in danger of breaching the premium income limits laid down for their safety by the Committee. In excess-of-loss treaties, the direct insurer accepts all the losses up to a certain figure, and the reinsurer, in return for a propor-tion of the premium to be agreed, accepts all losses over that figure. There are many variants on this basic principle, such as catastrophic reinsurance, where the direct insurer reinsures all the separate insurable risks that might be damaged by a single catastrophic event, such as a Japanese earthquake or a hurricane in Florida; or facultative re-insurance, which takes care of a single specially large risk.

Ted Nelson is the underwriter of the K. F. Alder agency, a middle-sized outfit writing for some 600 Names, specializing in reinsurance. Nelson is a burly, quiet-spoken man in his forties. Of the business he writes, 80 per cent comes from the United States, and three-quarters of that is reinsurance. For the Lloyd's non-marine market as a whole, roughly two-thirds of the business comes from the United States and Canada, one-fifth from Britain, and the remaining 15 per cent from all parts of the world, though with the 'old Commonwealth' countries, Australia, New Zealand and South Africa disproportionately repre-sented.

I asked a highly intelligent non-marine underwriter whether this distribution of the business did not reflect a pre-1914 view of the world on the part of Lloyd's. He said it might look like that, but in fact the reason was that many countries did their best to keep Lloyd's out in order to protect their own insurance industry. He went through the major insurance markets of the world one by one. Japan? Lloyd's tried and failed to get the status of a licensed insurer there. The only business Lloyd's can get is 'facultative' reinsurance on some of the biggest risks on the books of some of the huge Japanese insurance companies. 'I'd write a lot of Japanese earthquake if I could get the business, but I can't.' Europe? 'The Munich Re and the Swiss Re have got into such a strong position that they have a stranglehold on the direct writing companies; they virtually tell them how to write their business. If I were offered a German fire treaty I wouldn't take it, because I would know that if there was any money to be made on it they wouldn't be offering it to me!' Mexico is similarly dominated by the giant Munich and Swiss reinsurance companies. France, Brazil, Argentina, India – all big markets – were dominated by one or more big national reinsurance companies.

'These are the reasons,' my friend went on, 'why you keep coming back to the United States. Number one, there is the sheer size of the American market. It is about half of the world market in property and casualty insurance anyway, so it is normal that half of our reinsurance business should come from there. Two, it is more advanced than most other countries in consciousness of insurance, so reinsurance is more necessary there. And, three, the United States is very prone to natural disasters, more so than Europe: hurricanes, windstorms, floods, earthquakes, every kind of disaster known to man.'

Ted Nelson's box is highly automated. A microprocessing system with three VDUs was installed early in 1981, linked to the agency's claims office in the Minories. Whenever a claim is presented, the computer flashes up the whole history of the policy. The computer also gives the underwriters a full record of all the business they write. Perhaps the biggest boon the computer has delivered is that it enables the underwriter to know instantly whether the rates of premium he is charging are yielding a profit on each of ninety-nine classified types of business.

A broker slides into the bench next to Nelson. He is a director of Willis Faber.

'Let me broke it to you,' he begins.

His proposition is an excess-of-loss reinsurance treaty for a small mid-western insurance company that was unfortunate enough to buy an even smaller company in Louisiana just two days before a hurricane hit. Nelson's syndicate is already protecting them against any loss bigger than $800,000. The hurricane cost them that in one fell swoop. Now the broker wants Nelson to renew. Scrupulously, as the custom of the market demands, he reminds Nelson that there has been an even bigger loss from a Great Plains tornado. Nelson negotiates a slight increase in the rate of premium and agrees to the renewal.

A woman broker arrives with a renewal slip for a loss-of-profits insurance. She is blonde, wearing a velvet jacket and lots of gold jewellery. Nelson stamps the slip mechanically.

Next, another woman broker, with a Scots accent. She wants to change the terms of a 'binding authority', allowing a Belfast broker to insure property in that tormented city on Nelson's behalf. 'As you see,' she says, 'it's gone well in the past. This year it's been a disaster.' She produces a report showing there is no reason to believe that losses are the result of terrorist activity. Nelson discovers that there is a technical mistake in the documents, and the broker agrees to take them back to the office to correct them.

Then the Commonwealth of Australia wants to be protected against catastrophic claims for workmen's compensation: anything over $300,000 on any one claim would be met by Nelson's syndicate. No sale.

'He knows I won't take it,' Nelson says amicably after the broker has gone. 'We've discussed it endlessly. We've known one another for almost thirty years. It has low premium and a catastrophe risk. And it is the longest of long-tail business. If someone is badly injured in an accident now, it could be fifty years before you close your books on the claim, if you're lucky. I don't like it.'

The next conversation is less friendly. A young broker with a tooth-brush moustache upbraids Nelson for not paying a claim arising out of an air disaster. Nelson points out the broker delayed for several years before putting it in. 'Look,' he says crossly, 'you're right out of court on this!' Eventually the young broker moves off, muttering as he goes: 'Hopefully at the end of the day we can come to a reasonably amicable agreement!'

Nelson smiles ruefully after him, and says: 'Yes, that would be nice, wouldn't it?'

The next slip, broked by an American with a southern accent working for C. E. Heath, is a renewal on a simple renewal treaty for one of the biggest mid-western insurance companies. Nelson signs happily with a sigh of relief.

Once upon a time, the 'active underwriter' sat with the tails of his frock-coat carefully splayed on either side of him and his top hat on the floor next to him, and accepted risks at his box in the Room – very much as Henry Chester or Ian Posgate does today – but for his own account alone. In those days, until just about a hundred years ago, the man who wrote the risks himself *was* the 'underwriting member of Lloyd's'. Late in the nineteenth century, underwriters began to increase the capital available to them, and therefore the size of the risks they could write, by accepting risks on behalf of a syndicate of half a dozen other Names. Now underwriters like Posgate or Stephen Merrett write for more than 3,000 Names each, most of whom never come anywhere near Lloyd's from one year's end to the next. These Names may be knowledgeable about insurance, or they may be utterly ignorant. They include farmers' wives from Scotland, Nigerian chiefs, professional athletes and doctors. The outside Names are as vital to the working of the Lloyd's mechanism as the active underwriters. Lloyd's has come to depend on the complementary relationship between the professionals, who write the business, and the wealthy amateurs who make available the capital that enables them to do so: between the Crew and the Passengers.

Working Names, who go into the Room every day, and 'outside Names', who never go there, are equally at risk. They carry unlimited liability for losses the syndicates accepting business on their behalf may incur. When new members join Lloyd's, they go before a Rota committee, a subcommittee of the Committee, so called because members of the Committee take turns to attend. They are there solemnly warned that unlimited liability means what it says. If the worst comes to the worst, they will be liable for their syndicate's losses down to their collar studs. As a concession, they will be allowed to keep some of their bed linen.

The basic principles of underwriting, like its risks, are the same for the lady amateur and for the market professional. To explain them inescapably involves deploying a minimum of elementary arithmetic. Simple at the worst, it has here been even more simplified to remain within the writer's mathematical competence!

An underwriter accepts premium and, with it, the obligation to pay claims. The premium comes in either in a lump sum or in a certain number of fixed instalments. The claims come straggling in unpredictably over an unknown period of time that varies according to the class of business. The claims in what is called 'short-tail' business – say, motor insurance – will almost all fall within the first year after the premium is paid. At the other extreme, in the case of a long-tail business like product liability insurance, underwriters will be meeting claims against asbestos manufacturers from asbestosis victims for as much as fifty years after the liability was incurred.

In every year, therefore, insurers will meet a certain proportion of the claims arising against a given year's premium. A further number of claims will have been reported but not yet settled. And a third category of claims will have been 'incurred but not reported' (INBR). The prudent underwriter carries over to the next year the reserves he believes from experience he will need to meet the reported but unsettled, and the INBR, claims.

Because of the need to maintain reserves against claims remaining to be settled, the accounts of Lloyd's syndicates are kept open for three years. The underwriter does not know whether a profit or a loss has been made until the third year has elapsed. At the end of 1983, the 1981 account was closed. The 1982 and 1983 years will remain open while underwriters accept new premium for 1984.

In strictly underwriting terms, a profit is made only if the claims incurred against a given insurance come to less than the premium paid. But insurance cannot be separated from the fundamental premise of capitalism: that time is money. Because insurers must keep reserves against possible claims, they are also in a position to earn interest on those reserves. As well as making an underwriting profit, therefore, the underwriter can hope to earn two other kinds of income on his capital at the same time: interest in some form or another, and any capital appreciation on the money invested. Put the other way round, that means that the underwriter can make capital available for underwriting without forgoing the income and capital appreciation on the money.

This is one fundamental reason why, if you have got capital you can afford to risk, underwriting is an attractive proposition. You can get two different kinds of income on the same money. If you have $100,000 and you want to start a toy store, you must take the money out of the bonds or other investments where it is earning interest, before you can buy the lease of the store and the toys that will make up its stock in trade. If you set up as an underwriter, you can leave the money in the bonds, keep on earning income on it, and simultaneously start collecting premium from punters wishing to insure themselves. In due course there will be claims. But you can meet them out of accumulated premium, with luck and if your underwriting account has been written with prudence. In the meantime, you still get the income.

That means that you can turn over your money several times in a year. The profitability of your underwriting will depend on a set of variables. One is how fast you can turn your capital over. A second is how successful the underwriting is in terms of the ratio between premium and claims – that is, how long it is before claims amount to 100 per cent of premium. A third, crucial variable is the rate of interest.

A couple of examples illustrate the equation, and also suggest just how profitable underwriting can be if the numbers are meshing right.

Suppose that an insurance company sets up an underwriting subsidiary and gave it £100 to work with.

Assume that it can write three times the amount of its capital in a year as premium.

And assume that it holds premium, on average, one year before it has to be paid out in claims.

The prevailing rate of interest is 15 per cent.

But the company is writing three times as much premium as its capital.

Suppose there is no underwriting profit at all, but losses come to exactly 100 per cent of premium every year.

Here is the sum:

Capital available	£100
Premium written	£300
Investment income	£45
Claims	£300
Return on investment	£345
minus	£300
Return on £100 capital	£45

A 45 per cent return on capital is not bad.

It follows that in a time of high interest rates, like the past several years, underwriters can afford to lose money on their actual underwriting, because they are getting such a good rate of return on the reserves they hold to meet claims. The temptation in these circumstances is to 'write for premium': that is, to accept business, knowing that it will not yield an *insurance* profit, for the sake of getting your hands on the cash flow and the investment income it will generate. That is a potentially dangerous practice, since it is hard for underwriters, once they have abandoned the standard that the business they write must make a profit, to know where to draw the next line.

Another little sum illustrates the point:

Capital	£100
Premium income	£300
Investment income	£45
Claims @ 110% of premium	£330
Return	£345
minus	£330
Net return	(15%)

Suppose that several factors change for the better from the underwriter's point of view.

Assume that the new company can write not three but four times its capital in premium income every year.

Assume it is underwriting at break-even point every year.

The rate of return on investments still averages 15 per cent, but now you are paying claims on average after not twelve but eighteen months.

Then the arithmetic of underwriting improves dramatically:

Capital	£100
Premium income	£400
Investment income	£90
Claims	£400
Reserves plus income	£490
Claims	£400
Net return	£90

So in perfectly plausible circumstances underwriting can yield a return on capital employed of 90 per cent! That is how highly geared the business is. And of course the gearing works the other way round. If you are writing at a ratio of 4 : 1 between premium income and capital, and your ratio of claims to premium reaches 125 per cent, then your investment income melts away, because at the point when, underwriting at break-even, you would have 20 per cent of your premium left, and earning income, it has all gone!

This high gearing helps to explain why insurance is such a cyclical industry. When the arithmetic is right, underwriters can earn fabulous profits. That attracts new capital into the business. When Lloyd's was earning high profits in the early 1970s, all kinds of new competition came into the market, from big American insurance companies entering the reinsurance business, to fringe insurers in the Mediterranean quoting ultra-low rates of premium to win marine business away from Lloyd's. Rates in most kinds of insurance fell. So in the end marginal insurers will be forced out of business, and rates will recover.

The fortunes of every individual underwriting member of Lloyd's are governed by that same arithmetic. To cope with the underwriting ventures of what is now an army of more than 20,000 Names, a two-tier system of agencies has grown up. The nomenclature is infuriatingly confusing. The affairs of underwriting syndicates are managed by underwriting agencies, known as 'managing agents'. The affairs of individual Names are managed by what are officially called 'underwriting agents', but are known colloquially as 'members' agents'. Sometimes both types of agency are owned by the same company or group, often by a big broker. Sometimes they are quite separate.

Every syndicate writing insurance in the Room is managed by an agency company, or managing agent. The managing agent keeps the syndicate's accounts, invests the premium received until it is needed to pay out claims, and pays the claims. It is paid by underwriting commission deducted from the Names' accounts.

Every Name at Lloyd's must pay underwriting commission to some managing agent or other. Not every Name, however, has his or her affairs managed by a members' agent. Some are what are called 'direct Names'. They join a syndicate of their own accord, and thereafter manage their own affairs, do their own accounts and pay their own taxes. For most members, however, and especially for those who are not insurance professionals, that is burdensome. Increasingly, therefore, Names' underwriting is handled for them by members' agents.

Every member pays in two ways for the privilege of underwriting. There is an underwriting 'salary', a fixed amount related to the amount of business the member is writing that year. It is usually based on a £40,000 premium income limit, known as a 'share'. Typically, the salary would be 0·75–1·0 per cent of the premium income the member was writing. That is split between the managing agent and the members' agent, usually 60 per cent to the managing agent and 40 per cent to the members' agent. In addition, the Name pays profit commission – if there is a profit – typically at the rate of 20 per cent on the underwriting profit. The basis on which that is calculated varies: for example, how costs are assigned before a profit or loss is struck. Typically, out of the 20 per cent profit commission 15 per cent goes to the managing agent and 5 per cent to the members' agent.

The members' agent keeps the Names' underwriting accounts, including their tax accounts; keeps them informed; and, if need be, intervenes on their behalf with the managing agent. Perhaps the most crucial function he performs, however, is to get a Name on to profitable syndicates.

With the mushroom growth in the number of members of Lloyd's, members' agents – whose income is related to the number of Names they act for – have become big business. All the dozen big brokers own sizeable members' agents. Two of the bigger independents are Dashwood Underwriting Agencies and R. F. Kershaw. Dashwood was built up by Sir Francis Dashwood, Baronet, lineal descendant of the rake who founded the Hellfire Club in the mid eighteenth century. Ronnie Kershaw was a leading member of the Eton College rugby club in company with two other Lloyd's notables: Jeremy Peyton-Jones, chairman of the brokerage house Clarkson's, and John Weller-Poley, a man of many interesting connections, as we shall see. (Double-barrelled names, now considered pretentious and old-fashioned in most circles in Britain, still flourish at Lloyd's.) Kershaw started life as a broker. Then he began to introduce a few of his friends to Lloyd's. Seven years after coming out of the army at the end of the Second World War, he found that commission on such introductions made the greater part of his income. In 1954 he set up a members' agency which rapidly became one of the biggest at Lloyd's. In 1970–71 he sold the agency to the Vestey family, possessors of one of the largest and most mysterious fortunes in Britain. Starting out in the nineteenth century as Liverpool shopkeepers, the Vesteys have built up a business empire based on meat, food processing, refrigerated storage and shipping, and insurance, estimated to be worth at least £1,000 million ($1·5 billion). The London *Sunday Times* made them a household word in 1981 when it detailed the extraordinary lengths the family had gone to avoid paying tax, even succeeding in avoiding paying income tax on the income from one group of family trusts since 1916. A Lloyd's members' agency might seem peripheral to their other interests, but it was a shrewd buy, just in time to catch the growth in income produced by the explosion in the number of Names in the 1970s.

The big broker-owned syndicates do not need to pay to recruit Names. But for other syndicates new Names and the capital they bring with them can be lifeblood, as they are for members' agents. In the circumstances, many are willing to pay handsomely to recruit new members. There are different arrangements. Sometimes a member of Lloyd's will say to his agent: 'I can get you new Names, is there anything in it for me?' There will be a minimum of £1,000 a Name. There are stories of well-connected Names making a point of hanging round country clubs in South Africa, Bermuda and other haunts of the well-heeled to trawl for Names. It should be remembered that anyone who is a member of Lloyd's must by definition be very comfortably off himself, so professional recruiters are rare, though not perhaps quite non-existent. What is common is for agents to pay an annual commission to accountants, solicitors and other professionals who steer their clients into membership of Lloyd's.

Who can be a member of Lloyd's? The essential requirement is that a Name must be able to 'show wealth'. In theory, you have to prove that you have £100,000. In practice the minimum for Names who are United Kingdom, European Community or Commonwealth citizens domiciled or resident in the United Kingdom is £50,000. The minimum for citizens of the same country resident abroad is £100,000, while the minimum for nationals of all other countries, including the United States, is £135,000.

Each Name is given a premium income by the Committee of Lloyd's. That means the Name is allowed to accept premium, and the risks that go with the premium, up to that amount. Liability is unlimited in theory. In practice, if business is competently written, while there may well be losses, they are unlikely to eat up the Name's reserves – though it can happen! In practice, the individual non-working Name has no means of knowing whether or not his premium income limit has been exceeded. The practical safeguard is that each syndicate has a premium income limit, the aggregate of the individual limits of all its members. So long as the active underwriter stays under that global figure, he is all right. If he exceeds it, he will find himself called up to explain by the Committee of Lloyd's.

The first line of reserves is controlled not by the individual Name but by the syndicate. This is the premium trust fund, held in trust jointly by the Name and the agent. Generally, about two-thirds of this money will be held in American dollars, in bank deposits and United States government bonds. About 10 per cent will be held in Canadian dollars, also in bank deposits and bonds. Most of the balance – that is, around one-quarter – will be held in 'gilt-edged' British government stock. In many syndicates the balance will be held in other convertible currencies, according to the syndicate's business; for example, if it writes a Belgian motor account, it will keep a certain amount of its premium on trust in Belgian francs.

The Name must also make a deposit of one-quarter of the wealth shown. This must take the form either of a bank guarantee or of specified investments, usually government bonds or blue-chip fixed interest stocks. Then the Name will build up, out of profits accumulated at Lloyd's, both personal reserves and a 'special reserve', which benefits from some special taxation arrangements.

A typical Name who has proved wealth of £100,000 would be able to write £200,000 of premium income. He would probably want to split this between several syndicates to get a good spread of risks: for example, he might join two marine syndicates with a £40,000 'share' in each, two non-marine syndicates with £50,000 in each, one aviation syndicate and one motor with £10,000 in each. He would deposit £25,000, and his agent would probably try to build up his personal and special reserves to £50,000 before he took any profit out.

One of the cornerstones of Lloyd's financial stability is the three-year accounting system. To make this system work there has to be a way of carrying balances over from one year's underwriting to the next. The method used at Lloyd's, appropriately, is an imaginary insurance policy called a 'reinsurance to close'. What happens is that at the end of three open years the syndicate's entire reserve fund becomes the premium for a policy against which all future claims on the syndicate's previous years must be paid. So both reserves and valid claims against them are rolled over into the next year.

An example illustrates how this is done. At the end of 1979 a marine underwriter is closing his accounts on the 1977 year of account. Of the premium written in that year, £1 million was paid in 1977, £700,000 in 1978 and the last £100,000 in 1979. That makes a total of £1·8 million in premium received for the 1977 year. Against that must be set the claims. In 1977 £150,000 was settled in claims relating to that year's premium, in 1978 £500,000 and in 1979 £250,000, making a total of £0·9 million in claims settled out of the 1977 premium. That leaves a surplus of £0·9 million. But out of that the underwriter knows from experience that he will have to settle further IBNR claims. Lloyd's audit requires that a certain proportion of the remaining premium must be set aside to meet various categories of claims. The total reserve required came to £300,000. But the veteran underwriter wanted to be on the safe side, so he reserved an extra £300,000, making £0·6 million altogether in reserves to take care of IBNR claims attributable to the premium written in 1977. And that left a tidy underwriting profit of £300,000 to be distributed among the Names. But the 1977 account itself started out with a reserve of £0·9 million reinsured forward from earlier years to take care of remaining liabilities arising from premium written in those earlier years. So the total reinsurance to close carried forward into 1978 in this (real) example was £1·5 million.

The method is more clearly seen if it is set out as a series of steps:

1. Reinsured forward from 1976		£0·9 m
2. 1977 premium received in 1977	£1.0 m	
in 1978	£0·7 m	
in 1979	£0·1 m	
Total 1978 premium		£1·8 m
3. Less claims settled in 1977	£150,000	
1978	£500,000	
1979	£250,000	
Total 1977 claims		£0·9 m
4. Underwriting surplus		£0·9 m
5. Less reserve for IBNR		£0·6 m
6. Underwriting profit		£0·3 m
7. Reinsurance to close (No. 5 plus No. 1)		£1·5 m

No judgement an underwriter has to make is trickier or more crucial than his assessment of how much to carry forward by way of re-insurance to close. He wants to show an underwriting profit if possible, or his Names will be unhappy and perhaps eventually will drift off to more successful syndicates. (As we shall see, tax considerations can complicate this. There are some highly popular syndicates at Lloyd's that have not made an underwriting profit for years, on purpose. Still, most underwriters prefer to write at a profit.) On the other hand, the underwriter dare not leave himself under-reserved against a possible flood of IBNR claims later. Every type of insurance business has a different profile. Even in motor insurance, there will be some claims outstanding that have not been settled by the end of the year, and some that have been incurred but not reported by 31 December. That is the shortest of short-tail business. Under-reserving is especially dangerous in long-tail business, such as professional indemnity, medical malpractice or product liability. A lot of this business comes to the Lloyd's market in the form of reinsurance treaties with big American companies.

Asbestosis is a case in point. Asbestosis claims have been hanging over Lloyd's for a decade or more, ever since it was first established that there was a high rate of incidence of certain carcinomas among people who had worked in asbestos fabricating plants or with asbes-

tos – for example, in shipyards. The major American asbestos manufacturer, Johns-Manville Corporation, was so badly hit by claims that
it was forced to go into bankruptcy in 1982. And in early 1982,
asbestosis claims were causing many syndicates serious problems as
they tried to close the 1979 account. The claims relate to earlier years
when the business was written and the claims originated as a result of
employees covered by the policies reinsured at Lloyd's being exposed
to the asbestos fibre; but the claims would not have been lodged until
many years later when the sickness appeared. Similar problems have
arisen in connection with dioxin, Agent Orange and other toxic chemicals. As a result, in some classes of business Lloyd's now requires
reserves for IBNR claims as high as 95 per cent of premium.

The audit is another of the cornerstones of Lloyd's. Its requirements
are strict. Names must restate their means every four or five years. They
must maintain their deposits to cover their premium income limit. If
they want to increase that limit, or if they have overwritten it, the
deposit must be increased. (The highest premium income limit, allowed
to Ian Posgate and half a dozen other members, is £500,000. Generally
the Committee does not allow more than £450,000 in premium income
in any one year to any one Name. Some big brokers and some wealthy
outside Names get round this by making half a dozen members of their
family Names.) But the key to the audit is the insistence on adequate
reserves in syndicates' accounts.

Each year's business, as we have seen, is kept open for three years,
and closed at the end of the third. Auditing the closing year is comparatively simple. Each Name either takes a profit or pays a 'call' to top
up his Lloyd's funds. The two open years provide advance warning of
any problem. They also involve more complicated judgements, especially about the appropriate level of reserves. If the Name's deposit is not
big enough to meet the requirements of the audit, then there is an 'open
year deficiency'. This is now so common, in the current unfavourable
underwriting climate, that it is almost normal.

Most Names protect themselves against disastrous losses by taking
out a 'stop loss' policy with another Lloyd's syndicate, or a company.
You carry the first 10 per cent possible loss yourself. For example, if
your premium income is £200,000 you might get a stop loss policy for
'£100,000, excess of £20,000'. The premium you would pay for that
kind of cover would be of the order of £1,500–2,000. This is an
allowable expense against tax, but you must pay it for four years before
you can claim it back, because of the three-year accounting period. The
importance of tax in any Name's calculations is suggested by the fact

that, because the Inland Revenue in effect pays three-quarters of any losses (since they can be offset against tax at 75 per cent top rate), many Names now take stop loss insurance '£100,000 excess of tax recovery', and so pay a lower premium.

There are three stages to the audit process.

In the first stage the individual Names are audited and a report is made. If they are in default, then their funds will be used first, starting with the special reserve, to top up their deposit. If that is not enough, the personal reserve is used. And if that is not enough, the Name will be 'called' for more. That must be done in May, because in the second stage the whole syndicate is audited and must produce a 'certificate of underwriting account', showing that none of its Names is in default, by 31 May. Finally, in the third stage, Lloyd's as a whole goes to the insurance division of the Department of Trade, the responsible department of the British government, to get a certificate of audit saying that none of its syndicates is in default.

Tax is something that underwriters have constantly in the corner of their mind. It is often assumed by critics that Lloyd's is nothing more or less than a gigantic mechanism for tax avoidance. There is something in this, though not quite in the way the critics assume. After all, Lloyd's was performing its function in essentially the same way as it does today when income tax was insignificant. Members of Lloyd's enjoy few tax privileges, and those they do enjoy are logically justified, and allowed by Parliament, because of the exceptional risks underwriters accept with unlimited liability. Still, having said all that, being a member of Lloyd's does afford tax advantages to several thousand of the wealthiest people in Britain, advantages that were significant in the decision of more than ten thousand new members to come forward and start underwriting in the 1970s.

The tax position of members of Lloyd's is complicated. Four different taxes are involved:

1. Income tax in Britain is levied at the basic rate of 30 per cent. (Various allowances can be set off against that – for example, allowances for dependent children and other dependants.) Tax payers in higher brackets then pay higher rates of income tax.
2. In addition, an investment income surcharge is levied on what is called 'unearned income' – Conservative spokesmen like to insist that it may have been earned before being saved and invested – up to a top rate of 75 per cent. Under the Labour government of 1974–9 the top rate on unearned income was as high as 98 per cent.

3. A separate capital gains tax is levied on appreciation in the value of realized capital assets at the rate of 30 per cent.
4. Capital transfer tax is payable when capital assets are transferred, whether by gift or inheritance; it replaces estate duty, the old British death duty.

An underwriting member of Lloyd's may have up to nine different amounts of tax to pay – quite apart from income tax paid on salary or professional earnings or on profits or dividends from a farm or business outside Lloyd's. Syndicates do not pay tax, though they do pay some, not all, tax on behalf of their Names. First, there is income tax to be paid on underwriting profit. If you are a working Name you pay at the lower rate for earned income; if an outside Name, you pay the investment income surcharge. Then on each of four funds – premium trust fund, deposit, personal reserve and special reserve – there may be both investment income tax and capital gains tax to be paid.

One major advantage of being a member of Lloyd's is that the basic rate of income tax is payable one year and one day after the close of the account, and the higher rate for those in higher brackets (which every member of Lloyd's presumably is) six months later still. That full tax is not due until four and a half years after the start of underwriting. This helps the Name to build up reserves.

The special reserve benefits from generous tax arrangements; strangely, they were conferred by Sir Stafford Cripps, the austerely socialist Chancellor of the Exchequer in the Labour government of 1945–51, and only slightly modified in 1955. A Name is allowed to transfer into the special reserve 50 per cent of profit or £7,500 each year, whichever is the lesser. This concession is very advantageous to those who pay tax at high rates; they can accumulate reserves net of 30 per cent, instead of 75 per cent, tax. The money is withdrawable only on death or resignation. But it does enable a Name to accumulate reserves that justify writing more premium income. And there are further concessions on death. The special reserve is split into uneven amounts. The Name's estate pays tax at the basic (lower) rate on 70 per cent of the money, and on the remaining 30 per cent at the higher rate for the year in which the money was first put into the fund. When a Name dies, the government gives him another last favour: his Lloyd's assets count as business assets, and so are valued at only half their value for the purposes of capital transfer tax.

The real advantage of being a member of Lloyd's, says Ken Goddard, a former tax inspector who is head of the taxation department at

Lloyd's, does not lie in taxation, but in the fact that you make your money work twice. He is echoed by the syndicate accountant to one of the biggest broker-controlled members' agencies: 'The greatest advantage of being a member of Lloyd's is that you can write several times your stake, while continuing to earn income on it.'

No doubt. But the tax advantages are significant. A member of Lloyd's, to take a small example, must pay only the basic rate of tax on 1 January. He need not pay the higher rate tax until 1 July. Anyone else – a freelance writer, for example – is assessed at what the Revenue thinks he has earned, and must pay that whole amount straight away. The member of Lloyd's has the use of his money for another six months; the freelance writer does not.

The clearest tax advantage comes if you are lucky enough, or your underwriting agent is clever enough, to make a moderate loss on your underwriting. If you sustain losses, they are repaid by the government. If you are already paying 75 per cent of your investment income in tax, the government will therefore pay three-quarters of your losses. In fact, when the Conservative government cut the top rate of investment income tax from 98 per cent to 75 per cent there was some grumbling at Lloyd's, because the gearing had gone down. Before that, the government was repaying the lucky losers £49 for every £50 they lost. Losses are never good in themselves. But if losses meant more premium, and therefore more investment income, and the government was paying for them, they could be viewed with equanimity.

More important is the fact that it lies with underwriting agents, within limits, to arrange their reserving to make sure that their Names do show a loss on their underwriting. If a Name, for example, has premium income of £30,000, pays claims of £15,000, and reserves £20,000 for IBNR liabilities, he has a loss of £5,000, and the Inland Revenue will send him a cheque for three-quarters of that. Suppose a Name makes £5,000 in underwriting profit, £2,000 in investment income and £5,000 in capital appreciation, he has made a profit of £12,000 and pays tax on that. But suppose instead that he made a *loss* of £5,000 on underwriting. He has still made £2,000 in investment income and £5,000 in capital gain. In that case, he will get a cheque from the Inland Revenue for the difference between the tax due on his investment income and capital gain, and the recovery payable against his losses. That does not even go into the possibility for syndicates, within the limits of agreements reached between Lloyd's and the Inland Revenue, to turn investment income into capital gain at a lower rate of tax by selling securities at a higher price ('cum dividend') before the dividend is paid, and then buying them back at a discount afterwards 'ex dividend'.

'High tax payers can't lose by being members of Lloyd's,' one leading members' agent told me. He pointed out that while some syndicates, like P C W in the marine market, had not made a taxable profit for years, now – thanks to the competitive downward pressure on rates of premium – non-marine syndicates generally were moving into a period when they would be showing widespread underwriting losses. The consequence, he predicted, would be embarrassing both for Lloyd's and for the Inland Revenue, and perhaps for the Conservative government as well. In the summer of 1983, members of Lloyd's received handsome cheques from their agents, representing investment income and capital appreciation on their Lloyd's assets. Then in January 1984 they got almost equally handsome cheques, averaging perhaps some £5,000 apiece for as many as half of the 20,000-odd United Kingdom resident members of Lloyd's, from Her Majesty's Commissioners of Inland Revenue.

The money, of course – as the recipients will be quick to point out – represents a return of taxes already paid. Even so, the political symbolism of this unusual redistribution of wealth, in a country with more than 3 million people unemployed and many millions more suffering from savage cuts in public expenditure, is unfortunate to say the least.

Who are the members of Lloyd's?

It is easy to say who they used to be.

Before the great expansion of membership in the 1970s, there were four main categories of members, overlapping, and arranged concentrically, like the rings on a target, around the market itself.

1. The market professionals themselves, active underwriters and working brokers.
2. Members of 'Lloyd's families' – Bowrings, Fabers, Sturges, de Rougemonts, Pilchers, D'Ambrumenils and the like – and of families connected with shipping and insurance – Mountains of Eagle Star Insurance, Vesteys of Union International and the Blue Star Line – who were not themselves active at Lloyd's.
3. Members of the great British banking and industrial dynasties: Rothschilds and Barings, Abel-Smiths and Couttses, Tennants and Guests and Guinnesses, Samuels of Shell and Pilkingtons of the glass empire and Willses of Imperial Tobacco.

4. The wealthy landed families, some with titles, some without: men like the Duke of Marlborough, with 15,000 acres or more in Oxfordshire, or the Marquis of Salisbury, with about as much on the suburban fringes of North London; also, less prominent but still wealthy landowners like the Clives from Herefordshire, the Sykeses from Yorkshire or the Portmans from Dorset, who own a big chunk of London just behind Marble Arch.

Those were the original members of the club. The train of events that led to its rapid expansion began, strangely enough, with a hurricane in the Gulf of Mexico. In late 1965 and the New Year of 1966, Hurricane Betsy did billions of dollars' worth of damage, and in particular smashed offshore oil- and gas-drilling platforms by the dozen. There were also seven total losses of big oil-drilling barges, from different causes, in different parts of the world from West Africa to the North Sea. Largely as a result of these acts of God, coming on top of a cyclical fall in rates of premium, 1965 was the worst peacetime year at Lloyd's in living memory. And 1966 was not much better.

Hurricane Betsy was a watershed in the history of Lloyd's, though in a way that would have been hard to predict. Before 1965 the membership had been growing steadily, in line with the gradual spread of prosperity in post-war Britain. There had been 631 members in 1913, 1,882 in 1938, 2,422 in 1948 and 4,499 in 1958. By 1965 it had reached and passed 6,000. But the average loss per Name across the whole market in that year was more than £6,000, and in 1966 more than £3,000. In the money of that time, those were very heavy blows. Too heavy for some; they forced some members to give up underwriting. For the first time in more than a century, the membership actually dwindled. In the three years 1966–8, 295 members resigned, almost twice as many as had resigned in the previous eight years together. Over the two years 1967 and 1968, there was a net loss of thirty-eight members. (Remember, because of the three-year accounting period, it takes three years for losses to turn into a 'call' on members for more money.)

It was not a very big decrease, but it was enough to cause concern. The Committee of Lloyd's set up a prestigious working party, chaired by Lord Cromer, head of the Baring banking family and later British ambassador in Washington as well as Governor of the Bank of England, to see what could be done to increase the 'capacity' of the market: that is, the number of Names and the amount of capital they brought with them to back the market's underwriting. Specifically, the working party was asked to look at, among other things, 'any method of encouraging a steady flow of new members'.

One of Cromer's major recommendations, swiftly adopted by the Committee, was that the minimum 'show of wealth' required of members should be reduced from £75,000 to £50,000. In rapid succession the Committee also accepted overseas members (1969), women (1970) and finally 'mini-Names', who needed to show only £37,500. In other respects, too, it was made significantly easier to become a member of Lloyd's in the 1970s; for example, in certain circumstances it was possible for a time to count your own home as part of your show of wealth.

These measures, taken as an almost panic reaction to the losses of 1965–6 and the ensuing resignations of 1967–8, came at a moment when, unnoticed by the Committee of Lloyd's, the tide had turned. After 1969 Lloyd's enjoyed the biblical seven fat years of high profits. In 1970–73 and again in 1975, profits were more than 8 per cent of net premiums. For a Name showing £100,000 and writing £200,000 in premium income, that meant £16,000 in underwriting profit *on average*, on top of £10,000 or so of safe investment income at prevailing interest rates – not to mention capital gain. That at a time when a successful business executive in Britain might earn £15,000 a year.

This prosperity at Lloyd's coincided with a period that was in other respects deeply worrying for people in Britain with capital. The burden of taxation on 'unearned' incomes rose under the Labour governments in 1964–70 and did not fall correspondingly under the Conservative government headed by Edward Heath in 1970–74. Other economic stormclouds threatened other ways of protecting or increasing personal fortunes. The end of the long 1960s bull market on the Stock Exchange; the collapse of the property and 'fringe banking' shares many investors had shifted their money into; and finally the oil price rise and the hyperinflation it triggered – all combined to induce a mood of near-panic among people with private wealth in Britain. The coalminers' strike of 1974 and the government-ordered three-day working week were greeted with a chorus of jeremiads; this, to the established British upper-middle class, seemed to be 'the end of civilization as we know it'. This time it was not a panic at Lloyd's, driving a few hundred members to resign. It was a panic outside, and it impelled thousands of people to seek membership.

By the mid-1970s, solicitors, accountants and personal financial advisers were urging their clients to consider the advantages of joining Lloyd's. This advice was not always wholly altruistic. Members' agents were offering cash inducements to professional advisers who brought in new Names. A contributory factor may have been the growth of 'life broking' and other personal financial advice programmes; many of the firms offering these services were themselves subsidiaries of Lloyd's brokers. The brokers in turn owned members' agencies and had a direct interest in recruiting new members. At the same time the high profits to be made in the market led to overwriting, and syndicates were looking for new members to sop up excess premium income. 'Overwriting in 1976,' one members' agent commented cynically to me, 'led to the crying out for new Names. They came rushing in, just in time for the problems in 1978!'

The combined result of all these factors was that membership, after checking briefly and even sliding back a notch in 1967 and 1968, shot forward with renewed momentum, and for a while on an exponential rising curve. There were still under 6,000 Names in 1970, 7,500 in 1974, 14,000 in 1978. In that year 3,636 new members were elected, 877 of them women and 492 of them from overseas, against only 31 resignations and 133 members who died. In 1979 there were again well over 3,000 new members, and only 180 resignations and deaths. Membership of Lloyd's, like the possession of Gucci luggage or a tie from Yves St Laurent, was becoming a badge of membership not in the upper class, but in the upper-middle class.

After the storms and stresses of 1979, membership continued to increase, though more slowly. There were 1,492 new members in 1980, 880 in 1981, 1,296 in 1982. Resignations, after averaging only 43 a year between 1976 and 1979, were 143 in 1981 alone, and 124 in 1982.

As of 1 February 1984 there were 23,438 members of Lloyd's, 4,818 of them women. This was the breakdown in terms of nationality:

United Kingdom	19,986
United States	1,694
Western Europe	629
South Africa	293
Australia	284
Canada	242
New Zealand	138
Middle East (Islamic countries)	58
Israel	15
Nigeria	13

There are, therefore, plainly enough, two memberships of Lloyd's: an old, pre-Cromer membership of some 6,000 Names, and a new membership, more than twice as large (in round terms, making no precise calculation of the effect of deaths and resignations) that has joined since the Committee set out to encourage recruitment. It would be a mistake to exaggerate or caricature the change, however. Some journalists have suggested that the market's troubles in the late 1970s were caused by a 'different kind of member' joining Lloyd's, by inference a species of member with lower ethical standards than the old brigade. That does not stand close inspection. For one thing, to the extent that individuals who could be held to have 'caused' problems were members of Lloyd's, most of them had been members long before the big influx of new Names. Several of the individuals who played controversial roles, including Malcolm Pearson (not to mention Dennis Harrison, John Valentine Goepfert and Giorgio Mitolo) were never members of Lloyd's at all. And in any case, a change in the sociological character or even in the ethical standards of outside underwriting Names would not directly affect behaviour in the market.

Quite apart from that, however, if the membership of Lloyd's expanded rapidly, it did not necessarily *change* all that much. True, nearly 4,000 women and nearly 3,000 foreigners became members. It would still be wrong to portray Lloyd's as suddenly overrun by invading hordes of costermongers, women, Arabs and Americans! Lloyd's remains overwhelmingly a British institution, however dependent on overseas business. It also remains overwhelmingly an English upper-middle-class institution. The new membership ought not to be too sharply contrasted with the old in terms of class or culture. Many new members, after all, are the wives and children of the old. Many more are men who are not very different in sociological terms from those who were already members, or are their wives. It is far from unknown for men to make their wives members of Lloyd's (of course with their agreement!) without becoming members themselves, as a sort of family hedge against unlimited liability.

What happened in the 1970s seems to have been that, first, more members of those same groups, indeed often more members of the same families who had always supplied Names, were advised that it would be worth their while to become members of Lloyd's; and second, at the same time thousands of men and women from newly prosperous categories of the upper-middle class joined them: lawyers, doctors, accountants, businessmen, farmers, real-estate developers.

Lloyd's people like to stress the number of self-made people, especially the actors, sports stars and show-business people, who are members. It confers a modern, democratic image. It is true that there are people in those categories who are members: the members of the Pink Floyd rock group, for example, though neither the Beatles nor the Rolling Stones. So are boxer Henry Cooper, tennis player Virginia Wade, jockey Lester Piggot and golfer Tony Jacklin. Bestselling authors Jeffrey (*Kane and Abel*) Archer, Edward (*Lateral Thinking*) de Bono and John Julius Norwich are Names. So are gastronome Quentin Crewe, baritone Sir Geraint Evans, novelist and TV presenter Melvyn Bragg, libel lawyer Peter Carter-Ruck and photographer Patrick, Lord Lichfield.

The fact remains that hunting for names which you recognize from the newspapers in the list of members of Lloyd's is like hunting for a needle in a haystack. They are buried in sheaves of double-barrelled names like Ingleby-Mackenzie and Remington-Hobbs, and even treble-barrelled names like Alston-Roberts-West, Anstruther-Gough-Calthorpe or Montagu-Douglas-Scott. Even these Victorian Gothic embellishments are largely outnumbered by names that are neither famous nor feudal, like Smith and Brown, Cohen and Robinson.

What is unmistakable, as one browses through the list, is the tenacity of the connection in Britain between wealth and land. With rare exceptions, say the economic historians, no one made money out of land in Britain. But once you had made money, by marriage or in prize money at sea, in the law or in trade, selling slaves in the West Indies or cotton in the East, it was in land that you invested it, for a steady return and for status. In the past thirty years, there has been a new land boom in England. Land that changed hands for a few pounds per acre after the Second World War is now worth £2,000–3,000 per acre or more, and far more than that if it happens to be near a city. So the old landowning families, once proud but poor, are now rich again.

Lloyd's passenger list is, in fact, an irresistible document for anyone with historical or sociological curiosity, or even just plain financial prurience. The royal family is on board, in the persons of the Duchess of Kent, Prince Michael of Kent, Princess Alexandra and her businessman-husband Angus Ogilvie, and the Queen's first cousin Simon Bowes-Lyon. Six of the twenty-six non-royal dukes are members of Lloyd's, and so are four duchesses, with marquesses, earls, viscounts, barons, baronets and knights bachelor too many to enumerate. There are descendants of national heroes: Anson, Alanbrooke, Winston Spencer Churchill, MP. There are a dozen High Court judges, half a dozen Nigerian chiefs, Arabian sheikhs and at least one Italian *nobildonna*, as she calls herself. There is Sir Hugh Wontner, who owns the Savoy Hotel, and C. Y. Tung, who owned the biggest fleet of tankers in the world until he died recently. And there are sonorously named chieftains like Colonel Sir Owen Watkin Williams-Wynn, descended from Welsh kings, the Irish Sir Marmaduke Blennerhassett and, from Scotland, Captain Sir Rupert Moncrieffe of that Ilk.

Lloyd's is a roster of old money: Alnutt, Amory, Asquith, Barclay, Beecham, Beit, Bonham-Carter, Buxton, Cadbury, Cazalet, Cazenove, Cobbold and Coutts, down to Sebag-Montefiores, Seymours, Sitwells, Wards, Waley-Cohens and Wallop William-Powletts. And there is new money: publishers Robert Maxwell and George Weidenfeld; Rocco Forte, son of the founder of the Trust House–Forte hotel chain, the world's biggest; and five Suterwallas from Southall. Indian names, Arab names, Jewish names, Greek names and bread-and-dripping North Country English names, all testifying to the fact that, hard as it is to make a fortune in a single lifetime in Britain, it can still be done.

The list ends magniloquently: Zinkin, Zino, Zinsli, Ziskin, Zoephel, Zoutendijk, Abdulla Sassoon Zubaida, Sir Philip Francis de Zulueta, Harry David Zutz and Bonne Sietse Zylstra. What commercial odysseys have brought those names from what corners of the earth to become members of Lloyd's?

Yet the exotic are outnumbered by the prosaic. The new men are greatly exceeded by those who, if they are not old members of Lloyd's, are not different from the old members: by the billbrokers and shipbrokers, the brewers and bankers, the fresh young daughters of belted earls, and the dowager countesses: in short, by the whole cast of characters in the English social comedy from Fielding's time to P. G. Wodehouse; and in that comedy the self-made men like Mr Pickwick were always safely outnumbered by the gentlefolk. Perhaps that was what happened at Lloyd's in the 1970s, after all. Where before only shrewd serious-minded men of business in the mould of old Jos. Sedley of *Vanity Fair* and the Forsytes were to be found among the members of Lloyd's, there is no doubt that if Tom Jones were making his way in the world today, he would become a Name at Lloyd's, and so too would Bertie Wooster, and a good few of those strong-minded young women it was his fortune to encounter. Purposeful and debonair, silly or tough, the characters of the English comedy of manners can still be seen striding down Lime Street and Fenchurch Avenue towards the Room.

CHAPTER 5

OFFICERS AND TRAVEL AGENTS

The labour, the agitation, the perpetual vexation, is not to be described. I would rather begin the world again and pursue any other line. It is painful to a degree; we can hardly ever satisfy our principal. If men got their twenty or thirty thousand a year the compensation is not too great for the trouble they receive.

Broker witness,
before a parliamentary committee of 1811

Brokers have come up in the world.

The root of the word 'broke' means a spit or a spike, and to broke was originally to broach. A broker was a tapster, a fellow who retailed wine from the barrel, and so by extension it came to mean any retail trader, generally with a contemptuous connotation. 'A Houndsditch man,' explains a character in a Ben Jonson play, written around 1600, 'one of the devil's near kinsmen, a broker'. In Elizabethan times it had already come to be used for a pawnbroker and for the tribe of rogues called fripperers, who trained boy pickpockets to add to their stock of silk scarves and pocket handkerchiefs; it also meant a pimp or bawd. In the eighteenth century, sensitive brokers preferred to be known by the euphemism 'office-keepers'.

Lloyd's brokers have been ultra-respectable for a couple of centuries and more. Even so, they have recently come up in the world. Fifty years ago, it was the underwriter who was the big man, sitting at the receipt of custom and doing the broker a favour by writing his risks for him. Now it is the brokers who have the whip hand. For one thing, it is the brokers who connect Lloyd's to the world market. If underwriters in theory are sedentary and introvert, brokers are mobile and extrovert. They like to tell stories about their ubiquity, like the story about the day they opened the first through flight from London to Ulan Bator. There were only two passengers: both Lloyd's brokers. If the underwriter's badge of office is a fountain pen, the broker's is a black cowhide briefcase with the British Airways Concorde tag still dangling from the handle.

There has been a change in the relationship between Lloyd's and the rest of the world. Once Lloyd's was unique: the only place in the world where you could place marine and some other types of major insurance. Now it is only one important insurance market among many. Lloyd's needs the world as much as the world needs Lloyd's. And it is the Lloyd's brokers who make the connection.

There have been two stages to the ascension of the brokers. The first came after the Second World War, when many important underwriters, needing marketable stock to capitalize high incomes, and also to enable their heirs to pay high death duties, sold their syndicates to the broking firms they knew; tax rulings by the Inland Revenue made it cheaper for a Lloyd's broker than for any other kind of firm to acquire an underwriting syndicate.

The second stage came when the Lloyd's brokers turned themselves into international insurance conglomerates, and indeed in some instances into financial and service conglomerates with important non-insurance assets. For many of them, this was only another twist to a long story of adaptation. Many Lloyd's brokers – C. T. Bowring and Willis Faber are examples – grew out of general trading companies in the nineteenth century, which became involved in insurance because of their connection with shipping. For a couple of generations insurance was their primary interest. But they saw no reason not to diversify in any promising direction.

If the outside Names are the passengers on SS *Lloyd's* and the underwriters are the crew, brokers fulfil a strange double function: they are the travel agents who drum up the business, and at the same time the officers are, increasingly, recruited from amongst them.

Just as a travel agent does not send all his passengers on one liner, so the dozen big firms of Lloyd's brokers do only part of their work with Lloyd's itself, and place a substantial proportion of their insurance business outside Lloyd's. Virtually all of them own underwriting syndicates at Lloyd's, but many of them also own insurance companies of their own in London and elsewhere. Some, in addition, underwrite risks on behalf of big foreign insurance and reinsurance concerns. Some have interests in banking or finance: Willis Faber, for example, owns around 25 per cent of the shares in Morgan Grenfell, the London branch of the House of Morgan, and C. T. Bowring only recently disposed of the merchant bank Singer & Friedlander, as well as of Bowmaker, one of the biggest consumer credit corporations in Britain. Many retain close connections with shipping, shipowning or shipbroking. Several, including Hogg Robinson, own travel agencies. And most have recently expanded in the growing business of life insurance and pension planning.

These dozen big firms, of course, are the élite of an élite. There are approximately 3,500 insurance brokerage firms in Britain, according to the British Insurance Brokers Association, and there are 270 'Lloyd's brokers' – firms, not individuals. Those in turn were concentrated in some 167 'broker groups', according to the Fisher Report of 1980. But more than two-thirds of all the premium placed at Lloyd's was brought there by the twelve biggest broker groups.

Lloyd's brokers are supposed to be bigger and in certain respects more highly qualified than the other insurance brokers in Britain. Where the latter, for example, need to show a working capital and a margin of solvency of only £1,000 ($1,500), a Lloyd's broker must have a paid-up share capital of £50,000 and in some cases a margin of solvency of as much as £1 million ($1·5 million). Lloyd's brokers are connected to the Lloyd's market in other ways, too, unlike other insurance brokers: most of their directors are members of Lloyd's, for example. (Many of them have acquired British retail brokers from around the country, incidentally.)

Lloyd's brokers do the same things that other insurance brokers do. They *advise* a client about the kind of insurance protection the client needs. They act as the client's agent in *placing* his business with an underwriter. In so doing they *produce* the business for the market. And they act for the client in *administering* his insurances and *collecting* any claims.

Lloyd's brokers perform these functions on behalf of a special category of clients, for the most part, and in relation to a different market. They are in the business of placing what is sometimes called 'primary' insurance business, on behalf of clients that are usually other insurance companies or major corporations.

The world volume of premium income for all kinds of insurance (excluding life insurance) was running in 1981 (according to the most reliable estimate, that of the Swiss Reinsurance Group) at around $261 *billion*. Of that total, almost exactly half – $131 billion – originated in the United States, 8·7 per cent in West Germany, 7 per cent in Japan, 5·8 per cent in France and 5·3 per cent in Great Britain; another 10·7 per cent came from the next five most developed insurance markets – Canada, Italy, the Netherlands, Australia and Switzerland. Only some 12 per cent came from the whole of the rest of the world together. About one-third of the total premium income is made up of small 'personal lines' – individuals insuring their homes, cars and personal belongings. These personal lines are absorbed by local insurance markets, and in many countries laws forbid this direct business to be placed abroad. Local insurers also take part of the local share of the remaining two-thirds of the total, which is commercial insurance. But roughly half of the world total is available to be placed in the international market.

The British brokerage groups, including their overseas subsidiaries, have a healthy share of that world business and the brokerage commission on it: about 20 per cent, or £10 billion ($15 billion) in premium, and a total of some £500 million ($750 million) in brokerage commission and fees in 1980. Not all of the international business handled by 'Lloyd's brokers' goes to Lloyd's, not by a long chalk. One authoritative recent estimate is that roughly 80 per cent of the premium handled by the major British broking groups goes to insurance companies in London and around the world rather than to Lloyd's.* Lloyd's brokers, collectively, are bigger than Lloyd's.

The exact figures are hard to establish for reasons of comparability, and they vary from year to year. But the general point is that they compel one to modify the traditional picture of Lloyd's as the massive nucleus of a British and global insurance system, with the big Lloyd's 'brokers swinging in orbit around the Room.

First, Lloyd's receives only a minority of the premium income sucked out of the world system by British brokers. Second, while Lloyd's is indeed a very large insurance market, it is not the biggest. Collectively, the American market's underwriting capacity is much larger than Lloyd's. So is the London companies market. In 1980 the Swiss Reinsurance Group alone received more premium income than Lloyd's, and the Munich Re was not far behind. Third, while the big British broking groups got off the mark quicker in the search for international business in some classes of business, the American brokers are bigger, and they have been growing faster in recent years. Marsh & McLennan, the biggest American insurance broker, was roughly twice the size of C. T. Bowring when the merger between the two took place; Sedgwick, the biggest British broker (ahead of Bowring), is roughly the same size as the number two in the United States, Alexander & Alexander.

A more accurate model of the international insurance system would put the big international brokers, both American and British and some

---

* Philip Olsen, of the London stockbrokers Kitcat & Aitken, an expert on the finances of the insurance broking business, estimates that in 1979 the total premium income handled by British brokers was about £7·2 billion ($10–11 billion), and in that year, excluding 'reinsurances to close' (see Chapter 4), Lloyd's received premium incomes of £1·5 billion ($2·25 billion), or a whisker over 20 per cent of the total.

from other countries too, at the centre. These draw in premium from a great variety of sources: from local retail brokers; in the form of reinsurance on big international and smaller national insurance companies; directly from major insureds, like shipping fleets, airlines and industrial companies; and from the captive insurance companies of oil companies and other multinationals. They then place this business wherever they can find the capacity they need and at the best rate of premium. In this system, with its crisscrossing webs of money flowing in and out as premium on direct insurance and reinsurance, with subsidiary (though still very large!) flows of commission, split many ways, the big British brokers are intricately intermeshed with their American counterparts.

In a perceptive (though arguably misnamed) book entitled *The Media Are American*, the British media sociologist Jeremy Tunstall has shown how two widely held models of the Anglo-American domination of the international news media were both wrong. Some people imagine that the international news media gave way before the advance of American media; others suppose that British media succeeded in capturing a small share of an essentially American-dominated market. In fact, Tunstall showed, since before the First World War, the international news media have been very largely dominated by an English-language partnership between American and British firms, with the British always the junior partner. Something similar applies in a number of other 'software' industries, including shipping, banking, airlines, accountancy, commercial entertainment, advertising and even organized sport. In each case, while Japan, West Germany, France and other developed nations maintain a respectable measure of autonomy, buttressed by language barriers and in some instances by more or less overt protectionism, the United States is still dominant – far more dominant, in fact, than the diminished proportion of the American gross national product relative to the world GNP would indicate. Alongside the American giant, Britain too has a special position, stronger by far than the intrinsic size or contemporary performance of the British domestic economy would warrant.

That, certainly, is the way it is in the international insurance business. Thanks to their own energy and expertise, but thanks also to a network of contacts and acquired positions dating back in some instances to the earliest eras of the modern international trading system, the multinational insurance conglomerates which the Lloyd's brokers have turned into hold their own as prosperous satellites in a system that revolves around the sheer weight of the American insurance industry.

The First Eleven of big brokers has at its head a trinity of blue-bloods. Here they are, listed in terms of 1982 income from brokerage commission and broking fees only:

1.	Sedgwick Group	£176 million
2.	C. T. Bowring	£83 million
3.	Willis Faber & Dumas	£71 million
4.	Alexander Howden	£70 million (estimated)
5.	Reed Stenhouse	£59 million
6.	J. H. Minet	£56 million
7.	Stewart Wrightson	£55 million
8.	Hogg Robinson	£36 million
9.	Bain Dawes	£34 million
10.	C. E. Heath	£31 million
11.	Leslie & Godwin	£30 million (estimated)

(Note: all these figures exclude affiliates.)

In many cases, outside income from many diversified activities adds considerably to gross revenue. To take Hogg Robinson as an example, investment income and outside activities in underwriting (at Lloyd's and elsewhere), travel and leasing brought total turnover in 1982 to £53·4 million; in terms of profit, insurance broking provided £8·1 million out of pre-interest profits of £9·8 million.

Hogg Robinson is untypical in that it is one of only three of the major brokers where underwriting at Lloyd's makes a significant contribution to profit. Hogg Robinson's underwriting agencies – Janson Green (the family firm of the former Chairman of Lloyd's, Sir Peter Green, a major shareholder in Hogg's) and Gardner Mountain & Capel-Cure – earned nearly £3 million out of Hogg Robinson's total group profit of £9 million in 1981. Only two other brokers were heavily dependent on underwriting profit: Alexander Howden, with Ian Posgate as its underwriting star; and Minet, with the PCW agency, commemorating the underwriter Peter Cameron-Webb. Both were to be the focus of scandal in 1982.

These First Eleven are all public companies. Only one is unlisted on the London Stock Exchange: Bain Dawes, which is controlled by the giant Inchcape group of shipping and merchanting companies (more than £3 billion turnover), and is in many ways still very much the family business of the Earl of Inchcape. Four are controlled by North American insurance brokers: Bowring by Marsh & McLennan, Alexander Howden Group by Alexander & Alexander and Leslie & Godwin by Frank B. Hall. Stenhouse is controlled by the Canadian insurance group

Reed Stenhouse. The remaining six have their shareholdings more or less widely dispersed, between descendants of the founding families, London financial institutions and the British public generally.

As in all the best school stories, there is plenty of pressure to get into the First Eleven. A mixed group of young hopefuls and old faithfuls jostles to get into the Second Eleven. The batting order that follows is of no particular significance: but in the opinion of money experts, this is the team:

1. Thos R. Miller: the family business of the present Chairman of Lloyd's. It is now separate from Thos R. Miller & Sons, specialists in managing 'P & I Clubs', the mutual insurance associations that insure shipping fleets against third-party liability.
2. Fenchurch International Group: associated with the Guinness Mahon merchant bank.
3. Lowndes Lambert: owned by merchant bank Hill Samuel.
4. Holmwood & Crawfurd (whom we came across as the brokers for the owners of the *Bill Crosbie*): owned by Brown, Shipley, another London merchant bank, in turn associated with Brown Brothers Harriman in New York.
5. Wigham Poland: once controlled by the Anglo-French zillionaire Sir James Goldsmith, is now owned 57 per cent by the New York broker Fred S. James, itself now owned by Transamerica, and 35 per cent by the Thomson Organization, which owned the London *Times* and *Sunday Times* before selling them to Rupert Murdoch, and still owns diversified media interests in Britain, the United States and Canada. The Poland family still has a holding.
6. Clarkson, Puckle: the result of a recent merger between Peek Puckle and H. Clarkson. Clarkson originally belonged to Shipping & Industrial Holdings, then to Italian interests. Clarkson, Puckle is now controlled by the commodity brokers Gill & Duffus.
7. Frizzell: partly owned by the government-financed Industrial and Commercial Finance Corporation, partly by overseas insurance interests. It has a big British domestic and motor business.
8. Furness Holder: part of the Furness Withy shipping group.
9. Paul Bradford: created by a 1982 merger. Robert Bradford used to belong to Sime Darby, the plantation, trading and manufacturing group with headquarters in Kuala Lumpur, Malaysia. It now belongs to Mills & Allen, a London billboard advertising and money-broking house.

10. Seascope: started recently by David D'Ambrumenil, son of a chairman of Lloyd's, and now owned by the Henry Ansbacher merchant bank. It insures several big Greek and British fleets.
11. The Jardine group: controlled by the big Jardine Matheson conglomerate, based in Hong Kong. Jardine set about acquiring several middle-sized brokers, including Bache Insurance Services in the United States and Glanvill Enthoven in London. It is now said to be the fastest-growing insurance broker in the world.

These twenty-two Lloyd's brokers are varied enough in ownership, style and specialization. Yet they are linked together with a web of Lloyd's connections. Certainly it would be hard to imagine this network of insurance business having grown up without Lloyd's as its centre.

You can tell the brokers as they converge on the Room from their offices in the surrounding streets by the slipcases they carry under their arms, simple leather folders, buttoned over bulging stacks of slips, telexes and other insurance documents they will have to show to underwriters. They are as distinctive and traditional as the cotton bags in which, around the Law Courts, you see barristers carrying their wigs, or the bill brokers' top hats in the streets round the Bank of England. One in twenty of the slipcases that come into the Room are now carried by women.

The first stage of the process of acceptance for women at Lloyd's has come quickly and with little or no friction. A dozen years ago, no woman had ever been a member of Lloyd's, and no woman had ever set foot in the underwriting Room. Today there are more than 400 women broking risks there regularly. There are close to 4,000 women Names. Women have begun to climb most of the various career ladders in the Lloyd's community. There are women working on underwriting boxes, a handful of them as deputy underwriters (none as yet the active underwriter); women executives in broking companies, several in senior positions (none as yet on the main board of a major broker); women in positions of great responsibility in the Corporation of Lloyd's (none as yet elected to the Committee).

Characteristically, the decision to admit the first woman to work in the Room was taken without fuss, and apparently without much debate. It was a pragmatic decision rather than a conscious precedent on an issue of principle. The Honourable Mrs Liliana Archibald was already a director of a Lloyd's broker, the specialists Adam Brothers

Contingency, a tall, brusque woman who drives sports cars; her parents were Russian émigrés, and she was originally a professional historian of pre-revolutionary Russia. She has edited publications for the Royal Institute of International Affairs and is now adviser to Lloyd's on European problems. She came into Adam Brothers through her husband, but once there made a reputation for herself as an energetic and innovative specialist broker. Her field was the insurance of capital goods exports covered by the British government's Export Credit Guarantee Department. She had devised a number of contingency liability policies, without any thought of broking in the Room, nor had she applied to do so. But she did become an underwriting member of Lloyd's in 1972. Then, one bright morning, the Chairman, at that time Sir Henry Mance, summoned and told her she could feel free to broke risks in the Room if she wanted to. The first, as it happened, was to Sir Peter Green.

That was in 1972. More than two years previously the first women were admitted as underwriting members. In Britain and the United States, a substantial proportion of private wealth – according to some estimates, well over half – is owned by women. In the years after Hurricane Betsy and the Cromer report, Lloyd's was anxious to build up capacity. One obvious way to do this was by enlisting the largest pool of ineligible British money: that owned by women. The first two women admitted as underwriting Names were a self-made businesswoman, Margery Hurst, who founded the Brook Street Bureau, office staff consultants; and the wife of a prominent active underwriter, the late Mrs Margaret Alder. They both passed the Rota committee in 1969 in time to underwrite the 1970 account.

In 1973 Sylvia Horsey of the Corinthian motor syndicate became the first woman to work on an underwriting box. And as from 1 January 1974 brokers were allowed to send women into the market to broke risks as 'substitutes' even if they were not members. The first woman to do so was Mrs Maureen Swage of Willis Faber.

Lloyd's is just the kind of traditionalist, masculine preserve where you might expect women to run up against formidable overt resistance. That does not seem to have happened. 'It may well be that in the broking houses women have to be twice as good as men,' shrugs Liliana Archibald. 'But the doors are open. The feeling, and the fact of the matter, is that women are accepted at Lloyd's.' A young Sedgwick broker, Judith Bell, agreed that women were accepted, up to a point; but she was aware of underlying currents of resistance, if not hostility. She told me she more or less drifted into working at Lloyd's in the first place because her job in the public relations department of a newspaper was boring, and because she loved sailing and wanted to be able to sail on the Lloyd's yacht club's ocean racer, *Lutine*. She was grateful for the opportunities she had had at Lloyd's, but not naïvely so. She recalled an underwriter who had said he welcomed women on his box just because they didn't 'want a career structure'; and she suspected that some brokers, although not her own, were keen to hire women for lower echelons because you could get brighter, harder-working women than men for the same salary, but that they might not be keen on promoting women to top jobs. She conceded that some women had risen to middle-level executive jobs in broking firms, but wondered how much higher they would be able to rise. She said the atmosphere was intimidatingly masculine to begin with, 'like a boys' boarding school or an all-male club'. She had learned not to wear loose clothes in the market, for example; when she first started broking there, she wore a loose woollen cardigan, and found men would paperclip notes to it. Sylvia Horsey, the first woman on an underwriting box, says that men came round to stare at her as if they had never seen a woman before.

Most women at Lloyd's wear notably conservative clothes. Many of them wear suits and even ties, almost as if they were trying to look as much like men as possible; though at the same time it is not unusual for there to be more than a hint of sexual tension or at least sexual undertones in the relationship between a woman broker who is trying to persuade an underwriter and the man who has to make up his mind whether or not to do what a woman is asking him to do. Most of the women at Lloyd's are highly educated. Their manners are impeccable. They are on their best behaviour, and they pose no threat. Men always apologize if they swear in front of her, one woman broker told me. It remains to be seen whether the process of acceptance will move on to the next stage, where women are free to compete on equal terms with men for all jobs. But already that process is beginning. The Corporation of Lloyd's itself is leading the way. Its director of training is a woman, Andrea Bondi, and so is the head of the legal department, Irene Dick, who played one of the key roles in the long and delicate saga of the Fisher inquiry and the Lloyd's bill. It may surprise those who think of Lloyd's as a bastion of reaction. But the evidence suggests that – perhaps because Lloyd's has been so prosperous that it is free from defensive attitudes found elsewhere – the prospects for women there are as good as anywhere else in the British economy, and better than in most.

*

In the history of the Sedgwick group, the biggest insurance broker in Britain, and one of the biggest in the world, you can clearly see the individual Victorian entrepreneur succeeded by the Edwardian partnership, and finally evolving into the integrated international conglomerate. It is reminiscent of the genealogy at the beginning of the gospel according to St Matthew: 'And Ram begat Amminadab, and Amminadab begat Nahshon, and Nahshon begat Salmon . . .' The firm achieved its present form only in 1979, when Sedgwick Forbes merged with Bland Payne; each of those two firms in turn was the product of a series of mergers. As a result, Sedgwick can trace its history back, if not to our forefather Abraham, at least to the early days of marine insurance before the fire in the Royal Exchange in 1838.

It begins in 1825. In that year T. W. Forbes started transacting marine insurance in the old Lloyd's Room at the Royal Exchange, and five years later a certain Alexander Maclean quite independently started out in the same line of work. In 1890 Maclean's business was taken over by a firm of brokers called Bland Welch. In the same year a fellow called H. B. Sedgwick set up as a marine broker. The next development was for marine brokers to ally themselves with specialists in the growing field of non-marine insurance. In the middle of the century, two of the pioneers in non-marine broking had been Charles Price and Frank Collins. Now the non-marine Price firm teamed up with the long-established Forbes marine firm and just before the First World War marine Sedgwick joined forces with non-marine Collins. The last piece of the jigsaw was supplied in 1919, when Ernest William Payne founded E. W. Payne & Co., a broker that came to specialize in reinsurance. Sedgwick is now a complex international insurance conglomerate handling well over $4 billion in premium every year.

Many big British firms call themselves 'international' when in reality they have hardly managed to penetrate outside the game preserve of the old British Empire: the overseas operations, for such firms, tend to be in Melbourne, Auckland and Cape Town. Sedgwick is not like that. It is genuinely international, with a major group of subsidiary companies in North America (Lukis Stewart in Canada, American Insurance and Southern Marine & Aviation Underwriters in the United States) as well as broking subsidiaries in more than two dozen other countries, including Argentina, Chile and Brazil as well as the main Western European countries, Africa, the Middle East and the Far East. The group's interests, as a result of the merger, are widely spread, with strong representation in aviation, in the British domestic market and in reinsurance (through Sedgwick Payne), as well as in general marine business. But if you ask an insurance man anywhere in the world what Sedgwick are specially famous for, the odds are that he would mention oil rigs. The group has specialized in the complex business of putting together insurance programmes for underwater oil- and gas-drilling and pipeline equipment, a growth area where immense insured values are exposed to formidable perils. The most spectacular of Sedgwick Offshore Resources Ltd's achievements in this field, and the most widely reported, was the putting together of the insurance cover on the Statfjord 'B' oil-drilling platform. The problem was to cover the towing of the platform, said to be the largest object ever moved by man, from the yard where it was built in Norway to the offshore drilling field in the North Sea where it is now operating on behalf of a consortium of oil companies led by Mobil. Starting three years before in 1978, Sedgwick succeeded in placing the largest insurance cover ever placed on a single risk by July 1981, when the platform, over 1,000 feet high, was towed into position. The total cover, placed largely in London, including Lloyd's but also in many other markets around the world, was $1·625 million.

London began to emerge as the most important market for insuring oil-drilling rigs in the 1950s, and it was Lloyd's that took the lead. There were two trends at work. The oil industry was beginning to move offshore, at first in the marshes and bayous of Louisiana and eastern Texas, then in the open waters of the Gulf of Mexico. At the same time the big oil companies, which for many years had carried most of their own insurance risks, were beginning to move back to the market, at first largely for installations on land, such as refineries, pipelines and petrochemical plants. Between 1953 and 1960 a market of sorts developed in London. In 1960 six marine underwriters, most of them at Lloyd's – they included Sir Peter Green and Henry Chester – recognizing the potential of the offshore industry, got together and founded the unofficial Drilling Rig Committee. They wrote what became known as 'the memorandum', determining the basic guidelines of the coverage, including rating guidelines for different types of risk, such as contractors, drilling barges, oil company platforms and so on.

Between 1960 and 1965 the business continued to expand. The values covered also increased. In the early 1960s, the most a broker could place in the market on a drilling barge would be around $5 million, then the cost of a drilling barge of the type used in the Gulf. Then, in late 1965 and early 1966, came a freak sequence of disasters. A pioneer North Sea platform, *Sea Gem*, was lost in heavy storms. The *C. P. Baker* was destroyed by a gas blow-out in the Gulf. Another rig was lost on a tow from Japan, and a fourth lost in West Africa due to a volcanic accident. And Hurricane Betsy smashed fixed platforms in the Gulf to smithereens. Hurricane Betsy cost $100 million, and seven separate losses in the same period another $50 million. Many of the rigs were covered by package policies with oil companies, and widely spread through world insurance markets. But the impact on the London market came to many times the premium that had been earned. Estimates of the 'burn cost' – the rate of premium that would have needed to be charged to cover the losses – ran from 12.5 to 15 per cent. The London offshore market virtually collapsed. Underwriters were not refusing to pay on existing policies, but they did call a two-week moratorium on writing new business.

There were crisis talks between the Drilling Rig Committee, representing the underwriters, and the brokers representing the oil companies. The vast majority of the oil industry business in the London market was placed by three brokers: Sedgwick Collins, Bland Welch and Stewart Smith, now part of Stewart Wrightson. In the end the underwriters, as we have seen, agreed a new rate of 9.7 per cent, and it was left to the brokers to produce a 'master drilling rig line slip', placed by Sedgwick Collins and Bland Welch, and led jointly by the six underwriters on the Drilling Rig Committee.

The line slip is renewable each year. Every March since 1966, the two brokers (now merged into Sedgwick) have gone to the underwriters, and because the book of business is bigger, with a bigger spread and a better record, the brokers have been able to negotiate the rate down. By 1972 it was around 5 per cent. In time it was extended to cover fixed structures as well as drilling barges, and as the oil industry, especially in the North Sea, moved into deeper and deeper water, the values on individual platforms shot upwards. In the late 1960s, when the industry was developing Cook Inlet in Alaska, brokers had to scour the world for capacity to underwrite an Atlantic Richfield platform there called the *Dolly Vardon*, insured for $21.5 million. By the middle 1970s, completed platforms in British Petroleum's Forties Field in the North Sea were being insured for $150–200 million each.

Bland Welch's involvement with insuring offshore oil equipment dated back to the early days of the offshore industry. Bland Welch was controlled by a broker named Reggie Cheeseman, who took it over shortly after the Second World War. In 1953 Bland Welch took over Southern Marine & Aviation Underwriters Inc., a company that had been started by L. K. Giffin, a New Orleans broker who foresaw the insurance potential of the offshore industry, working closely with a

specialist surveying company, Charles D. Wood. Cheeseman persuaded Giffin to move his oil- and gas-drilling cover to Bland Welch,
and later, after Cheeseman's death, Bland Welch bought Southern
Marine.

Sedgwick Collins's involvement with oil goes back much further still.
Sedgwick executives are cagey about the extent to which the company
depends on its role as broker to the two British giants among the Seven
Sisters of the oil industry. But where Bland Welch's oil account came
from Southern Marine's drilling barge business, the growth of Sedgwick Collins has always been intimately linked with the Shell and BP
accounts. 'We grew along with them,' one Sedgwick veteran said
simply.

The Shell connection goes back into the mists of history, as modern
corporations measure their lives. There is a tradition in Sedgwick that
H. B. Sedgwick was Marcus Samuel's insurance broker even before
Samuel went into oil. The story is that, in the days when Mr Samuel
was importing seashells to decorate fancy boxes (that is how his oil
company got its name), Mr Sedgwick was lucky enough to have the
office next door, and that is how he got the Samuel account.

However that may be, the oldest reference to Sedgwick in Shell's files
is stamped on the cover of a memo which shows the meticulous record,
penned in copperplate handwriting, of 'Material Facts & Dates' in the
life of a tanker called the *Nerité* between 1905 and 1907. Turning over
its pages is like handling a fragment preserved from the world of Joseph
Conrad: a record of wanderings among the little ports of the Indonesian
archipelago, and an accounting for every penny and every Straits dollar
spent on repairs after each minor collision and temporary stranding.
But this was the second *Nerité*, launched on the Tyne in 1904 to replace
the first of the name, destroyed by fire in 1902. The first *Nerité* was
one of the original fleet of tankers, named after seashells, that were
commissioned for Marcus Samuel & Company in 1895 and subsequently transferred to the 'Shell' Transport Trading Company when
it was founded in 1897. (Shell tankers are normally still named after
seashells.) Since H. B. Sedgwick seems to have started out as a marine
broker in 1890, it is plausible that he had a business link with Marcus
Samuel before the latter went into oil in 1891–2, and very likely that
Sedgwick was Samuel's broker before the latter started Shell.

Even less is known about the origins of the relationship between
Sedgwick Collins and British Petroleum. But they were already brokers
to the Anglo-Iranian oil company's fleet, the forerunner of BP, before
1914. Continuity is all-important in British life. The son follows his

father's choice of tailor, hairdresser and gunmaker. A fleet is placed by the same broker from one generation to the next unless something goes strangely awry. Why change?

The connection of the firm of Bowring with oil goes back even further. Bowring later called themselves in their advertisements 'the Oldest Importers of Petroleum into Great Britain', and their New York office was busily shipping oil in barrels to Liverpool in 1867, less than eight years after the original oil strike at Titusville, Pennsylvania. Bowring was already an old-established business by then. It is a good specimen of those nineteenth-century family businesses that created the web of the British commercial empire, with the City of London at its centre. They were staffed by a seemingly inexhaustible brood of sons and nephews, cousins and sons-in-law. They were quirky but determined; they combined a strong respect for tradition with surprising flexibility. In each generation the mix and the emphasis shifted to whatever looked the most promising line. I was going to write that firms like Bowring were the soil in which the nineteenth-century Lloyd's grew. But soil is not the right metaphor. These firms all grew in salt water; their logic was defined only by the many ways you could make money out of the sea.

It was in 1811 that Benjamin Bowring, a watchmaker from Exeter in Devon, first voyaged to Britain's oldest colony: Newfoundland. Five years later he emigrated, and prospered by shipping cod and seal oil and skins back to England. In 1834 he returned home and set up an office in Liverpool. By the late 1840s the Bowrings were sending half a dozen ships and more than 200 men to the great seal hunts that stained miles of ice with blood. In the same years they were shipping salt cod to the Mediterranean to make *bacalao*, the same food that had once kept the Vikings alive on their interminable ocean voyages. By the 1850s the Bowrings owned a large fleet of fast trading schooners, then bigger, faster clippers, flying the Red Cross, and each named after a character in Shakespeare. In the 1860s they were running lines of packetboats from Liverpool to Rio de Janeiro, Bombay, Auckland and New York.

Next they got into the business of shipping oil, at first from the Pennsylvania oilfields to Britain and Europe, then from Baku on the Caspian Sea in the Russian Empire, and from the Dutch East Indies. At different times the Bowrings were agents or partners to the Mellons (in the Bear Creek Oil Company), the Rockefellers and Standard Oil, the Nobels in Russia, and Weetman Pearson, later Lord Cowdray, in the Mexican oilfields. They fought a famous fight on behalf of American interests in the vain attempt to prevent Marcus Samuel, the founder of Shell, shipping oil in tankers through the Suez Canal. Earlier, they had themselves been among the pioneers of shipping oil in tankers, and it was not until 1912 that Bowring finally sold their oil business to the Cowdray interests.

Bowring were badly hit by shipping losses in the First World War. They continued to be involved in shipping, though on a reduced scale; and they traded in teak, rubber, coffee and mother-of-pearl, as well as manufacturing fish-oil and fertilizers. Meanwhile the firm's involvement in insurance grew steadily. Individual Bowrings had written marine insurance in Liverpool early in the nineteenth century, but it was not until 1876 that the first of them became a member of Lloyd's. By the end of the century, as brokers, Bowring were expanding into the growing non-marine market. As early as 1897, they placed the re-insurance for the Fireman's Fund in San Francisco. In 1912 a young Bowring broker succeeded in insuring the *Titanic* in the overdue market after Lloyd's was closed and *after* the first news of the disaster.

The story, as it is told in a memorandum in the Bowring archives, is a classic instance of the imperatives of 'utmost good faith':

A cable was received in our office at 5.30 p.m. requesting us to place what was in those days a large line of reinsurance on the *Titanic* against total loss at 'best possible'. A young broker was dispatched to Lloyd's to see whether anything could be done. After searching the Room, the Captain's Room and elsewhere with no result, he met on the stairway of the old Lloyd's in the Royal Exchange Mr John Povah, a well-respected leader in the overdue market. On being offered the risk he remarked, 'The rate at the moment is 25 guineas per cent, but if you want me to write so large an amount as that, I must have 30 guineas.' Having an order at 'best possible' this offer was accepted and Mr Povah said, 'Bring the slip round to me tomorrow and I will put it down – I am in a hurry now.' By next morning there was no doubt about the total loss of the *Titanic*; there was likewise no doubt in anyone's mind that the verbal acceptance was binding.

In the years on either side of the First World War, the non-marine market was expanding rapidly, and Walter Hargreaves of Bowring was a leading figure there. His pet idea was the Lloyd's Policy Signing Office, an arrangement he thought would streamline the cumbersome procedures for signing and processing documentation. At first he could not get Lloyd's to accept this innovation so he and a few other brokers and underwriters simply ran a policy signing office of their own for several years, at their own expense, until Lloyd's was convinced and took it over.

In 1916 the pioneer American reinsurance broker Guy Carpenter brought the reinsurance of the Cotton Insurance Association to Bowring to place at Lloyd's, so Lloyd's became involved in insuring the Mississippi delta planters against the perils of drought and windstorm and burst levees. Bowring also placed reinsurance for Japanese insurance companies after the great Tokyo earthquake of 1923, and played a large part in setting up one of the first of the new 'protection and indemnity clubs' for shipowners, the West of England. In 1924 they got into the infant aviation market when they placed the entire fleet of Imperial Airways.

As early as 1901 Bowring started their first marine underwriting syndicate, and their first non-marine syndicate followed in 1921. Between the wars, as the British merchant marine declined from the dominance of the first decade of the century (when seven out of every ten ships afloat were British-owned), and British export industries lost out in world markets to German and American competition, insurance steadily pushed shipping and trading back into secondary roles at Bowring. The same trend continued after further heavy shipping losses in the Second World War and further difficulties for British manufacturing industry.

So conservative was the company's family-dominated management – until 1960 you could not become a director unless you were a member of the family! – that it never wanted to give up altogether any activity it had once been involved in. Long after the passing of the seal hunt, for example, Bowring maintained a small trade in sealskin. In the late 1970s, a trading subsidiary was still contributing £1 million a year (out of more than £40 million) to group profits, though from activities so diverse that their only logical connection was historical. A small shop at Gander airport, in Newfoundland, founded in 1959, grew into a chain of gift shops across Canada. In shipping, three bulk carriers, naturally with Shakespearean names – the MV *Capulet*, MV *Trinculo* and MV *Desdemona* – kept the red cross of Bowring afloat, but in 1978 they also lost half a million pounds between them. The new Bowring building next to the Tower of London – new, that is, in the long perspective of the firm's history, since it was opened in 1967 – is full of beautiful models of Bowring vessels in glass cases. The company's shipping business has long been little more than an expensive hobby, and has now been sold by Marsh & McLennan. Even more quixotically, Bowring financed an expedition to circumnavigate the globe from north to south, instead of from east to west, led by a former British army officer with the magniloquent name of Sir Ranulph Twistleton-Wykeham-Fiennes.

If Bowring have been loath to abandon any of their traditional activities, it is only fair to say that they have not been slow to get into new lines of business, including those involving advanced technology. They have been the leading brokers in London for the rapidly growing business of satellite insurance. The story began with a man called Jim Barrett, who read about the first communications satellite (Comsat) in 1962 and worked out for himself that anyone who was raising all that money to put up a satellite would need some insurance. He phoned up Marsh & McLennan in New York from a phone booth in Washington. As it happened, a non-marine broker from Bowring called Bob Rock happened to be in New York at the time, and Marsh asked him whether he was interested in placing some of the business in London. As Tony Bolton, who runs Bowring's aviation division, put it cheerfully, 'There are only two answers, and I'm glad to say Bob gave the right one!'

Satellite business is growing very rapidly at Lloyd's. 'In fifteen years it has gone from being like the 2.30 race at Kempton Park to being 25 per cent of our aviation division,' says Bolton. (Kempton Park is London's favourite race track.) At first it was a question of protecting Comsat's interest in Intelsat against the danger that the satellite would not go into synchronous orbit around the earth. That type of insurance continues, only there are now between forty and fifty communications satellites in orbit. Bolton believes that the premium that will be generated will soon be as great as that for the whole aviation market. A large airline, he points out, will spend something in the region of $10 million in insurance premium every year to cover its fleet. RCA spends that much annually on *each* of its five satellites.

Then came a breakthrough. Marsh and Bowring started offering insurance against interruption of business to clients who buy time on satellites. In each satellite there will be as many as twenty-four transponders, so the number of insurable interests at risk in each satellite is a multiple of that number. Brokers are now placing satellite insurance for two distinct types of client: major communications corporations who own satellites, like RCA; and anyone who is investing in time on satellite. That includes a company like Dow-Jones, who use the satellite to transmit stock exchange prices worldwide; banks; even Sotheby Parke Bernet, which is linking buyers into its art auctions from Europe and Japan via a transponder on an RCA satellite.

The losses are substantial, but so are the premiums. The first big satellite loss was the Orbital Test Satellite that malfunctioned in September 1977. That cost underwriters $29 million. That was nothing in comparison with the $77 million loss on an RCA Satcom F3 in

December 1979, and a Japanese geophysical satellite that went into elliptical orbit in error in February 1980 was a $25 million loss. But the values, and therefore the premium, in satellite insurance are big enough to give underwriters courage to face even losses like these. Bowring have just placed a European maritime exploration satellite for over $100 million, and a new European communications satellite is expected to bring in over $25 million in premium. About a quarter of that will find its way to Lloyd's, where the two leading underwriters for satellites are the Ariel aviation syndicate and Posgate.

By the end of the 1970s, Bowring thought of itself as 'a diversified multinational corporation'. It was active in over 150 countries, with 10,000 employees, a turnover of £1·3 billion and profit before tax of £41 million in 1978. Just over half of that profit came from insurance broking, and close to half of that from the United States. The shipping and trading business founded by Benjamin Bowring and his son Charles Tricks Bowring, ocean-going Forsytes, had evolved into an insurance and finance conglomerate in the modern fashion, though it stubbornly preserved its sentimental association with sail and spray. It was, however, more vulnerable than it looked, as we shall see.

Until the 1950s, Bowring, Matthew Wrightson and another small broker all had their offices in a building in Leadenhall Street which they shared with Willis Faber. By tradition none of the occupants ever competed for each other's business!

Henry Willis and Company, like Bowring, was founded in the early nineteenth century, and combined insurance broking with the business of a 'commission merchant', selling such diverse commodities as wheat, flour, barley and corn; bacon, cheese, tallow and turpentine; hides and hemp; horsehair and feathers; oak staves and isinglass; caviare and quicksilver on behalf of merchants in North and South America. The firm started out with five clerks in three rooms on the top floor of a house in Old Broad Street in the City, under the eagle eye of Henry Willis. This typical Victorian merchant wore white side-whiskers and a swallow-tail coat with shepherd's plaid trousers at all seasons, with a light beaver tall hat in summer, and a black one in winter. He is described as shrewd, with clear ideas and strong prejudices. 'He denounced drinking and smoking, urged the wearing of a stock tie, demanded that every one of his employees must speak audibly, and declared that "steel instead of quill pens, railways and telegraphs were the curse of the age".'

In 1877 – the year after the first Bowring came to Lloyd's – Willis sold his commission merchants business in order to concentrate on marine insurance. The Willis firm expanded rapidly; one partner explained that this was in part because they 'systematically cultivated the companies more than Lloyd's ... because I could get to them more quickly, because they wrote larger lines, and because they gave me reinsurance for our foreign companies'. Willis had an early connection with the Italia Company of Genoa, and later represented several important Japanese insurance companies in London. To balance their business, the Willis partners merged their firm with Faber Brothers, Lloyd's specialists, to form Willis Faber & Co. That was in 1898. The following year Willis Faber took a momentous step. They entered into an agreement with Johnson & Higgins in New York: Johnson & Higgins agreed to use Willis Faber as their brokers for all marine insurance placed in London; Willis Faber for their part agreed to refuse all American marine insurance from any other broker.

Between the wars Willis Faber, helped by this exclusive relationship with a leading American broker, benefited from the rapid increase in American non-marine business at Lloyd's. But it was in the marine market that Willis Faber was pre-eminent. 'We had all the big fleets,' reminisced John Prentice, who did not join the firm until after the Second World War. 'Cunard, Furness Withy, all the big American and Norwegian owners as well as the British fleets were with us. Most of the big French fleets came into London through us. We used to place a slip for 60 per cent of the Transat (the French Line) in London, half direct, half reinsurance. At the time when Willis Faber raised the cry of merging with Dumas & Wylie, the complaint was that it would mean a monopoly of the marine market.'

Dumas & Wylie was an even older enterprise than Henry Willis. The original Dumas was a grain-broker in the Huguenot colony at Altona, across the river from Hamburg. His father went bankrupt when the French government, during the Napoleonic wars, refused to honour its bonds (*assignats*); after the wars he came to London and started up as an independent broker. When he died in 1847, his son was only fourteen, so his widow, an Englishwoman, took her clerk, Wylie, into partnership. After Willis Faber merged with Dumas, it was estimated that they placed 30 per cent of the marine business at Lloyd's.

After the Second World War, Willis Faber & Dumas developed into an 'insurance conglomerate', on much the same lines as Bowring or the other major Lloyd's brokers. Like them, Willis Faber owned Lloyd's underwriting syndicates as well as agencies that specialized in underwriting on behalf of Japanese, German, French or Italian companies in the London market. Like them, Willis Faber has acquired a network of provincial brokers placing retail business from all over Britain, and set up broking companies around the world. Willis Faber has expanded in the same areas as its competitors – for example, in aviation, in reinsurance and in providing a total insurance service for big corporate clients. For a long time it remained at heart a marine broker; in its old offices in the heart of the shipping district, in Leadenhall Street, there was an unmistakable sense of the superiority of the marine brokers, so that it sometimes seemed that there were two separate companies, marine and non-marine.

Willis Faber's new head office maintains the splendour and, it has to be said, the pomposity of that old marine broking image. It is the old Port of London Authority building, opposite the Tower of London and across the street from Bowring, a monumental ziggurat in late imperial style, all twenty-foot ceilings and marble and bronze, and opulently carved female figures representing Commerce and Industry, the five continents and the seven seas.

That image is somewhat deceptive, however. The company changed in the middle 1960s, when chairman H. Elwyn Rhys was succeeded by Derek Ripley, who died on holiday almost immediately. The marine succession was broken. At that point the head of the aviation department, John Roscoe, took over as chairman. It says something about the company that, even today, he is regarded as having been a comparative outsider when he took over the chairmanship: he had only been with Willis Faber for eleven years at the time! So now the marine department remains strong, even though some of its traditional clients have fallen on relatively stony ground. Relatively, other departments have gained. The great strength of Willis Faber today is its worldwide reinsurance portfolio, built up historically through the company's links not only with Johnson & Higgins, but with companies like the Generali in Italy, the Allianz in Germany, the Tokyo in Japan.

In 1980, Johnson & Higgins ran a series of tongue-in-cheek ads with the theme: 'What's so new about transatlantic links?' The point was well taken. The relationship between Willis Faber and Johnson & Higgins goes back to 1898. But, more generally, Lloyd's has been heavily dependent on American business for almost a century, and all the big Lloyd's brokers have close ties with major brokers in the United States.

Over the first three-quarters of the twentieth century, that dependence steadily increased. Henry Kissinger has pointed out that in 1950 the American economy accounted for more than half of the Gross

National Product of the non-Communist world, but in every subsequent decade the American share has dropped by ten points, so that
it is now below 20 per cent of the world economy. This shrinking of
the American economy in relation to that of the rest of the world has
not come about because the American economy has been getting
smaller, but because of growth elsewhere. What is true of the economy
generally is also true of insurance. In 1950, according to Jack Bogardus,
chief executive of Alexander & Alexander, the number two American
broker, the United States supplied more than three-quarters of the
world premium income. Now the comparable figure is less than half.
First, people in Western Europe and Japan, and then more recently in
developing countries like Brazil, Korea and Mexico, began to insure the
property their new-found affluence brought them; at the same time
newly expanded enterprises in those countries, first in the more advanced nations, but before long in many other nations as well, began
to protect their property with the same range of comprehensive insurance programmes that once few but American corporations enjoyed.

At the end of the 1970s the big British insurance brokers found
themselves confronted with the prospect of corporate takeover from
the United States. John Regan, chairman of the biggest broker of them
all, Marsh & McLennan, is a diplomat. 'British brokers have been
wholesalers,' he told me in an interview. 'That means their business has
been dependent on talent. American brokers are retailers, and their
business has been dependent on organization.' Leaving out the flattery
– Regan does not need to be told that he has as much talent as any –
there is a fundamental truth in what he says.

The American insurance industry grew up as a retail operation. The
genius of the American economy has been not in building a better
mousetrap – there have always been good engineers in many countries
– but in beating a path to the world's door. What the American
economy has always been incomparably good at is arranging that once
something seems like a good idea, it should be within everyone's reach
at an attractive price as soon as possible. This may reflect the egali-
tarian tradition of American democracy. Certainly in Europe there is
a tendency to sell a new product to the few as a luxury, rather than to
the many as a new necessity they did not know they needed until
yesterday. Whatever the reason, that is the American way. It has
worked with cars and nylon stockings and TV games. And it has
worked with insurance.

The big American brokers, therefore, are big because they have built a highly organized, homogenized retail network. They have opened an office in Indianapolis, and then they have gone on and opened others in South Bend and Gary, Terre Haute and Evansville and Muncie and Fort Wayne, and then in every state of the union, until they have the nearest thing they can get to national coverage. But the vast majority of the business they have handled has been personal lines: 45 per cent of it is auto insurance, more than half is personal, and much of the rest is small business. That does not mean that American brokers do not specialize. They do. But it has been hard for them to break away from *volume*: from highly efficient, competitive processing of homogeneous business *en masse*.

The insurance industry in Britain, and especially at and around Lloyd's, developed in a completely different way. The kind of mass economic democracy that is characteristic of the United States – a chicken in every pot, and two cars in every garage and an insurance policy against every peril – came along much later in Britain and developed more slowly. The levels of car and home ownership that were reached in the United States in the 1920s were not reached in Britain until after the Second World War. There was no strong tradition of marketing and salesmanship. On the contrary, there was a certain disdain for mass marketing, and not least at Lloyd's.

The reason why British insurers did not compete in the more developed American insurance market was simply because they were kept out by protectionist laws. From the Progressive era in the early years of the century on, except in Illinois and Kentucky, state legislatures appointed insurance commissioners to enforce statutes that barred Lloyd's underwriters from taking any of the growing harvest of personal lines insurance. Instead, they were permitted to take only business that had already been turned down by a certain number of American insurers: the so-called surplus lines business.

So the Lloyd's underwriters, and the Lloyd's brokers, who had in any case developed as specialists in the exotic business of marine insurance, continued to evolve as wholesalers and specialists. They invented new, specialized types of insurance, such as personal accident and contingency. With their low overheads, long experience and substantial capital backing, they could sometimes bid for dangerous business, such as oil refineries, oil rigs and catastrophe insurance against, say, hurricanes, that prudent American underwriters did not want to accept. And they specialized in all types of reinsurance. Up until the Second World War, one American estimated to me, Lloyd's share of the world market in marine insurance and reinsurance was around 85 per cent, and that was on the whole, taking one year with another, highly profitable business. But Lloyd's did not do very much else.

After the Second World War, the competition, especially for re-insurance business, intensified sharply. The big German and Swiss companies, then American companies, then national companies in many other countries, all chipped away at Lloyd's market share. But the Lloyd's brokers had another advantage. Partly because of their point of vantage in the City of London, at the meeting point of a web of shipping, trading and banking connections, and partly because of the international links they had made in the specialist business of marine and reinsurance business, they were able to go international before the Americans saw any need to do so.

By the late 1970s, all this was changing. The domestic growth of the American market was slowing down, both absolutely and even more so as a share of the world market. Marsh & McLennan, Alexander & Alexander and Frank B. Hall had virtually completed national sales networks within the United States. They could look for no further growth from taking over new subsidiaries or from expanding into domestic markets where they had been unrepresented. At the same time American corporate business was going international. For all these reasons, the big American brokers went international too. They did it because, as publicly owned corporations, their stock listed on the exchanges, they needed continuing bottom-line growth. They did it because they wanted new worlds to conquer. And, decisively, they did it because their biggest and most profitable corporate clients were going international anyway. They followed them over.

By the mid 1970s, most of the large brokers in the United States had more or less completed worldwide networks of correspondents and associates. By 1973 Alexander & Alexander were having serious talks about a merger with Alexander Howden in London. In that same year, John Regan became chief executive of Marsh & McLennan and almost immediately started talks with Bowring. Both the Alexander & Alexander–Howden discussions and the Marsh–Bowring talks foundered for the same reason. In 1974 the 'secondary banking' boom in London collapsed, and the Bank of England had to step in and ante up several billions of pounds to stop several financial institutions that had expanded too fast from collapsing totally. Coupled with the miners' strike, the introduction of the three-day working week and the fall of the Heath government that same year, the banking crisis led to a sharp break on the Stock Exchange. Bowring shares fell from a high of over 170 to 18 pence. Edgar Bowring, the lawyer who became chairman because of a sudden death, knew relatively little about insurance, but he knew enough to spin out the negotiations while waiting for the price of his company's shares to recover, and Regan did not press the negotiations.

For the next three years – from 1975 to 1978 – Regan busied himself with acquisitions in Europe. 'We were so much larger than the firms we were talking to,' Regan told me, 'that we ran into the problem that they felt: "You will swamp us." So instead of acquiring control, we would buy a substantial minority interest.' On this basis Marsh bought into Faugère et Jutheau in France and Gradmann Holler in West Germany. 'To complete the circle,' Regan went on, 'we had to find someone in London. But in London it was more difficult. They were already multinational, and the amount of money involved was horrendous. The British company could say to us, "Aren't we the natural leader?" But we were half again as big as them.' In fact, depending on shifting stock prices and dollar–pound exchange rates, Marsh was twice as big as Bowring or more.

Regan is sensitive as well as shrewd. He could understand that, as he put it to me, 'you don't have to be English or to be a family business to want to hang on to your independence'. But Regan wanted Bowring. His whole strategy of making Marsh the first truly global insurance enterprise demanded a presence at Lloyd's. Bowring was the biggest Lloyd's broker, and it was with Bowring that Marsh had built up close ties over the years. With subtlety and tenacity, Regan set about manoeuvring Bowring into a position where they would have no option but to merge their insurance interests, at least, with Marsh on one set of terms or another.

Early in 1978, by chance, Regan was offered an alternative. He was not distracted. Générale Occidentale, Sir James Goldsmith's holding company, offered to sell him control of Wigham Poland, a respected but much smaller Lloyd's broker. It was too small for Regan's purpose. At almost exactly the same time, Frank B. Hall was negotiating to buy the middle-sized firm Leslie & Godwin. The two bids set off something close to a wave of paranoia at Lloyd's. People were afraid that one Lloyd's broker after another would be bought out by Americans. It was not, generally speaking, mere chauvinism. Most people at Lloyd's are consistently pro-American. Most brokers travel constantly in the United States, and it is not uncommon for them to have lived there for many years at one stage or another of their career. The business and political climate of the United States is congenial to them. They have no desire to kill the goose that lays so many golden eggs. Their hostility was not to Americans. It was to American *control* of the firms they worked for, and to the changes they feared that might bring.

On the Committee, this ill-defined and hardly rational dread took a more specific shape. Some members of the Committee were afraid that if a substantial number of Lloyd's brokers were to become subsidiaries of big, publicly owned American brokers, the Committee's ability to regulate the market might melt away altogether. As it was, the Committee's power depended to an alarming degree only on vague moral sanctions. It was one thing to summon a broker whose whole working life had been spent in the Lloyd's market, say, and who depended on that market for a substantial part of his income, and reproach him for some breach of market etiquette or the by-laws. It was not so easy to picture, say, Jack Regan of Marsh & McLennan standing before the Committee, in the guise of a humble penitent, to be told to go and sin no more.

In this dilemma, the Committee panicked and committed a clumsy error. In August 1977, the Committee happened to have set up a working party under a Bowring underwriter, Lambert Coles, to look into the whole question of the admission of brokers. The inquiry arose out of changes in British law relating to the registration of insurance brokers generally, and Lloyd's had simply to make sure that its own practice was in line with the new law. In the spring of 1978, when the Coles group was halfway through its work, the Committee saw its opportunity. As Ian Findlay told a committee under former prime minister Sir Harold Wilson that was looking into the regulation of the City of London, 'it so happened' that Coles had finished the part of his job that dealt with shareholding! Literally, one morning Coles was called upon to reveal his conclusions, and in the afternoon the decision was handed down. The Committee announced that the rule would be that insurance interests outside Lloyd's should not own more than 20 per cent of any Lloyd's broker. On 19 April 1978, Wigham Poland and Leslie & Godwin were so informed.

The Committee insisted publicly that the 20 per cent rule was not aimed at American brokers in particular. That need not be taken too seriously. Ian Findlay himself volunteered to me that it was the fear of American takeovers on the part of the other members of the Committee that led to the decision. 'I hated the 20 per cent rule,' he confessed to me, 'because all my life I've been a free enterprise man. I was prepared to take my chance and rely on the disciplinary process. But everyone was terrified of the Americans.'

The Americans, for their part, were furious. The 20 per cent rule went down very badly indeed in the United States. Leading figures in the American insurance industry permitted themselves tart comments. Newspapers were scathing. Lloyd's seemed to be behaving in a way that validated all the ancient stereotypes about the British: snooty, stuffy, protectionist and asleep.

One consequence of the 20 per cent decision was to bring to birth the New York Insurance Exchange and subsequently two further imitations of Lloyd's in Florida and Illinois. Newspaper coverage presented a simple morality tale of overweening arrogance in London, followed by condign retribution at the hands of the sturdy colonists of downtown Manhattan. 'It was just a year ago,' reported Rita Palmer in *The New York Times* in May 1979, 'that two American insurance brokers tried to win access to the hallowed trading room of Lloyd's by buying British brokerages. But Lloyd's, that venerable marketplace ... said no. The Americans were furious. They were fed up with having to split their commissions with the British brokers, particularly since they supply Lloyd's with half its $4 billion business. The brokers quickly became the driving force behind the New York Insurance Exchange, the new marketplace that plans to open its doors in October. "Lloyd's couldn't have done more for us than that," recalled Donald Kramer, the insurance consultant who is the architect of the New York Exchange.'

Such reports conveyed the impression that the New York Insurance Exchange was thought up in response to the exclusion of American brokers from Lloyd's. That did not give the complete picture. Ever since the capacity crisis at Lloyd's caused by Hurricane Betsy in the 1960s, insurance men in New York had been talking about starting an exchange modelled on Lloyd's to write reinsurance and big exotic risks. This idea was picked up in the early 1970s by a group of established New York insurers and brokers who in late 1976 formed an ad hoc committee to press for what was to be called a New York Reinsurance Exchange. Though there was broad support for the concept, the driving force behind it was Maurice 'Hank' Greenberg of American International, who for many years had been writing just the big, one-off risks that so often leave the United States for Lloyd's, and had the strongest business motive for keeping those risks in the United States.

In February 1978 – before Lloyd's passed the 20 per cent rule – the ad hoc committee was joined by the New York State superintendent of insurance, Albert B. Lewis. The bill approving the exchange was presented to the New York State legislature in May. So the Committee of Lloyd's ruling, admittedly a gaffe, accelerated the realization of plans that had been in existence for some time, and gave the new Exchange a splendid public relations send-off. 'This is the best time to take on Lloyd's,' said superintendent Lewis. And Senator John Dunne, chairman of the New York State senate's insurance committee, told me wrily that, after the Lloyd's decision, 'for a number of reasons, not all of them sound, the momentum grew'.

This is not the place to follow the history of the New York Exchange, or that of its rivals in Florida and Illinois. None of them has yet got up to full speed.

In the short term, the New York Insurance Exchange is not yet serious competition for Lloyd's, and perhaps will not be for many years. In the longer run, however, it and the other American exchanges must represent a serious challenge. The volume of insurance and reinsurance premium leaving the United States for Lloyd's and other international markets is immense. Inevitably, American underwriters will fight to keep more of it at home.

Still, for the time being the underwriters' enthusiasm for the Exchange seems to be greater than that of the brokers, though all the major American brokers support it in theory. It is said, no doubt with poetic licence, that in the Exchange's first year more than 90 per cent of the business there was written by Greenberg's syndicate. Brokers were less active. Some of them, at least, had a good reason. They had found a way into Lloyd's after all.

The prospect of Marsh & McLennan acquiring Wigham Poland did wake Bowring up, as John Regan had calculated, and for a good reason. Ever since the original Mr Marsh and Mr McLennan first came to London from Chicago before the First World War, Bowring had been their chief brokers at Lloyd's. Marsh was supplying around a third of Bowring's American business, itself roughly 40 per cent of Bowring's total broking volume. Moreover, the Marsh business represented an even higher proportion of Bowring's profit. In particular, Bowring had handled the lion's share of the highly profitable major reinsurance accounts from Marsh & McLennan's subsidiary Guy Carpenter.

There was another latent threat. At about this time Marsh & McLennan acquired an interest in a rival Lloyd's broker. It bought from Montagu Trust, itself 25 per cent owned by the Midland Bank, a substantial investment holding of around 20 per cent, in Bland Payne. 'From Day One,' says Bowring's managing director Gilbert Cooke, 'the Bowring board had this terrible dilemma. It wanted a resolution that would keep our relationship with Marsh & McLennan.' Dilemmas have two horns. What he meant was that the board wanted a solution that would *both* keep the Marsh & McLennan connection *and* leave Bowring its independence. That proved to be too much to hope for.

Regan was in a position to tie Bowring in one of those cruel nooses where, the harder you struggle, the tighter you draw it. In June 1978, Ivor Binney, head of the insurance broking side of Bowring and a member of the Committee of Lloyd's, flew to New York with Anthony Solomons of Singer & Friedlander to try to negotiate some arrangement with Marsh. Regan was obliging about the brokerage. As the talks went on, Marsh gave Bowring more and more business, until they were supplying half their American account, or 20 per cent of total volume. That was the kind of embrace it would be hard to disentangle from without accepting an offer of marriage.

For almost a year the two companies laboriously discussed what was called a 'Unilever arrangement' – that is, a profit-sharing agreement with no stock acquisition, modelled on the relationship between Unilever NV in the Netherlands and Unilever Ltd in Britain. Then, abruptly, in May 1979, Regan announced that profit-sharing would not work, ostensibly because it would breach the European Economic Community's regulatory rules. In retrospect, Bowring executives believe this was a pretext. 'There were those who said it was a Tar Baby situation,' Ivor Binney has said.

In the meantime, something very important had changed from Regan's point of view. At the end of June 1978, the Committee of Lloyd's had issued a release approving new proposals for Frank B. Hall's acquisition of Leslie & Godwin. Frank B. Hall bought the whole of Leslie & Godwin's capital. All Lloyd's brokerage would be handled by a subsidiary, and Frank B. Hall would hold only 25 per cent (not 20 per cent) of that subsidiary; the remaining 75 per cent was spun off to the Rothschild Investment Trust. The Committee of Lloyd's announced that these arrangements met the criteria laid down by the 'interim report' of the Coles working party; the main thing was that day-to-day control should be in the hands of people with long experience of the Lloyd's market.

Leaving aside the intriguing question of when 25 per cent is 'not more than 20 per cent', it is not unduly cynical to regard this as a climb-down. The Committee of Lloyd's had at least shown the wisdom of flexibility. It had been shaken by the bad press which the 20 per cent rule had received, in both the United States and London, and there was a general feeling that a mistake had been made. John Regan at Marsh & McLennan concluded that he might still have a chance after all.

From May 1979 until the end of the year, the Bowring board doggedly discussed various alternative relationships with Marsh. There was talk of a partnership, of a merger with a Bowring person as chairman of the combined company, even of Bowring selling its insurance broking interests only to Marsh. That was not attractive to the Bowring board; it would have given away the kernel and kept the husk. 'Because the talking had lasted for eighteen months,' Bowring's managing director, Gilbert Cooke, recalled, 'we got to a point where continuing it would inevitably be seen to be detrimental. So the Bowring board said that we didn't think there was a way we could get the businesses together formally. We preferred to remain in the sort of relationship that Willis Faber and Johnson & Higgins continue to have.'

'Finally,' John Regan takes up the story, 'Peter Bowring and his principal colleagues came to see me and said, "We'll have to make an announcement that we can't do it." I said, "That's not a good idea."' And at long last, having patiently exhausted all other alternatives, Regan made his move. He told the Bowring directors that he intended to make their shareholders a tender offer for their shares at 170 pence, a little more than 50 per cent above their price on the Stock Exchange.

The Bowring directors were deeply shocked. They felt they had been conned; that in the long, friendly talks Marsh had acquired an intimate knowledge of their business secrets that would now be used against them, and of one secret in particular: the extent of their dependence on profitable business from Marsh and Guy Carpenter. Peter Bowring, the chairman, wrote sorrowfully (and angrily) that the board would regard a tender offer as an 'unfriendly act'. Bowring filed suit in New York, asking for an injunction to restrain Marsh from making improper use of confidential information acquired during the talks.

There was never much doubt of the outcome, however. It has been suggested that Bowring lost their fight for independence because they were too 'gentlemanly', that if they had only been willing to bite and gouge they could have won. It is true that the Bowring family are not the kind of people to fight dirty. It is also true that they seem to have rejected advice from a top New York public relations man, Richard Cheney of Hill & Knowlton, on how they could have got in a few low blows. But that misses the point. The Bowrings could not bite and gouge, because while they wanted to retain their independence, they did not want to pay the price of independence if that meant contemplating the loss of all the easy and profitable business they were getting from Marsh. Perhaps it would be truer to say that they had already lost the substance of independence and were fighting only over its symbols.

They were also taken aback by the lack of support they received in London. The British Insurance Brokers Association welcomed the bid. The institutional shareholders were enthusiastic. The Committee of Lloyd's, as Regan had accurately calculated, did not oppose it. Marsh made a second tender offer, only five pence above the first, and that clinched it.

For a while there was some bitterness at Bowring, and the board was divided. By and large, the members of the Bowring family opposed the Marsh offer. There were two Bowrings, Peter and Edgar, and two Stoddarts (descended from a marriage between a Stoddart and a Bowring girl in the 1850s) on the sixteen-man board, besides other members of the family in top executive positions. Considering the family owned less than 10 per cent of the shares, that suggests how far Bowring had remained a family company in spirit. The non-insurance directors, for the most part, rightly anticipating that once Marsh gained control it would sell off their operations, were also against the bid. After it succeeded, four separate groups in management quit. Peter Stoddart and Clive Bowring, respectively chairman and chief executive of the important overseas broking subsidiary, left and set up a new brokerage under the umbrella of the Robert Fleming merchant bank. Michael Jenner, head of the marine broking division, left and went to work for the J. H. Blades brokerage in Houston. For a while, it was touch and go whether others would depart. Regan was taken aback, and said that if he had thought that Bowring employees didn't like him, he would have stopped his takeover bid. This need not have been mere sentimentality: the most valuable assets of a firm of brokers, they say, go down in the elevator with a briefcase under their arm at the end of the day. The defections did not reach critical mass, however. Bowring today is operating and, within the limits imposed by the current world recession, thriving as a subsidiary of Marsh & McLennan.

The anticipated American takeover bid for Lloyd's, however, did not take place. For two and a half years, from 1979 to 1981, Alexander & Alexander negotiated with Sedgwick about a merger. At the end of July 1981, the day after the royal wedding of Prince Charles and Lady Diana Spencer, the two brokers called their marriage off. Ostensibly the problem was the incompatibility of British and American tax laws. In particular, where a British stockholder can claim credit for tax paid by the corporation before he receives his dividend, American stockholders pay double tax. British investment bankers told Alexander & Alexander they therefore could not recommend the deal to the British shareholders. The larger problem was that the two firms were simply too close in size. Sedgwick's chairman, Neil Mills, made it plain that his company was not interested in being taken over, but only in a merger of equals. Unlike Bowring, Sedgwick was too strong to be taken over against the board's will. As the head of another major London broker told me, 'They gave tax as the official reason, but it was really who's going to be top dog.'

Alexander & Alexander, reluctant to be left on the shelf without a close tie at Lloyd's, went back to a childhood sweetheart. Now Marsh had Bowring. Fred S. James had bought Wigham Poland. Johnson & Higgins had the old amicable tie with Willis. Frank B. Hall had Leslie & Godwin. So Alexander & Alexander went back to the firm they had been talking merger with since the early 1970s, Alexander Howden. (In fact, Kenneth Grob and Ronald Comery had been approached by Alexander & Alexander before the two of them sold their brokerage to Alexander Howden in the 1960s.)

That relationship was to explode into a crisis that threatened the reputation of Lloyd's as a whole. But there, for the time being at any rate, the process of American acquisition of Lloyd's brokers rests, with a little fewer than seven Lloyd's brides for seven Yankee brothers.

Softly, softly, the Committee of Lloyd's backed off from the 20 per cent rule. In the spring of 1980 the Fisher report said: 'Once these new provisions have been introduced' – that is, the Fisher recommendations for tightening up discipline at Lloyd's – 'we do not believe that the Committee need seek to impose an absolute limit on shareholding in Lloyd's brokers by non-Lloyd's insurance interests.' Just before Christmas 1980 the Committee quietly backed down altogether, issuing a statement that it would be possible for those wishing to take over Lloyd's brokers to offer undertakings that they would accept the Committee's authority as an alternative. By that time, every major American broker had acquired, in one way or another, the access to Lloyd's that it wanted.

CHAPTER 6

THE STORM

Touching the Adventures & perills which we the assured hereafter named are contented to beare, & doe faithfully promise by these presents to take upon us in this present voyadge are of the Seas men of warr, fyer, enemyes, piratts, rovers, theeves, Jettezons, letters of marte & countermarte, arests, restreynts & deteynments of Kings and princes and all other persons, barratry of the Master & mariners, and of all other perills, losses and misfortunes whatsoever they be.

From the earliest surviving English marine insurance policy,
on the ship *Tiger*, 1613

For those who 'go down to the sea in ships', as the old English prayer has it, 'and occupy their business in great waters', the world is still almost as full of perils, losses and misfortunes as it was when Master Morris Abbot's ship *Tiger* set sail for Zante in the western Greek islands in search of currants and wine.

The perils that concern modern marine underwriters still include jettisons and fire; thieves on the dockside in Liverpool or Lagos; modern pirates operating out of Beirut and Hong Kong; and an epidemic of maritime fraud, sometimes on the part of masters and crew (which used to be called barratry), sometimes on the part of the owners themselves. In the late 1970s underwriters at Lloyd's made a lot of money in the war risks market, only to lose a lot when the Iran–Iraq war of 1980 trapped dozens of ships in the Shatt al Arab. And there have been several recent instances of the risks consequent on the high-handed behaviour of the modern counterparts of kings and princes, such as the sovereign governments of Angola and Somalia. In addition to these ancient perils, marine underwriters now have to contend with the new dangers of technology: supertankers, oil rigs and pipelines, liquid natural gas, satellites and computers.

None of this is necessarily bad news from an underwriter's point of view. When people are no longer afraid of the peril, the premium soon dries up. One of the first things he will have been taught when he went into the Room as a young man was that there is no such thing as a bad risk: only a bad rate. What worried underwriters was not so much that the highest peacetime casualty rate in history coincided with an unprecedented wave of marine fraud; it was the fact that all of this happened at a time when, because of competition and undercutting, rates were disastrously low. At the very time when Lloyd's as an institution was buffeted by a whole series of rows and scandals, Lloyd's as a market was confronting the underwriter's nightmare: exceptional claims at a time when he cannot increase his rate of premium.

In the late 1970s, in fact, the stately language of the old marine insurance policy seemed to have taken on a new and mocking metaphorical meaning. It was as if Lloyd's itself were a great ship, richly laden still but now vulnerable, steering blindly from one unforeseen danger to another, and wallowing lower and lower in the seas as the storm broke over it.

Nowadays few international passengers travel by sea. Even on the North Atlantic crossing, once a milk run, it takes some patience to find a passage. As a result most of us assume, unless we stop to think about it, that maritime trade is a declining or even an obsolescent business. It is not so. The total tonnage of merchant shipping has roughly tripled over the past twenty years. The tonnage of oil tankers came close to tripling in just ten years between 1968 and 1978.

It is quite true that, partly as a result of this rapid growth, there is at present chronic over-capacity. Silent navies of unwanted ships wait for the economic wind to change in Galveston Bay, in the Norwegian fjords and among the Greek islands. Freight rates have fallen to a fraction of their level of only a few years ago, and so have the rates of premium for marine insurance, though these are beginning to recover.

But if shipping is going through an economic trough that more than reflects the recession in the world economy as a whole, that does not mean that shipping is a dying industry. More than 90 per cent of all international trade is still shipborne, and the volume of trade has expanded spectacularly. It is bound to go on growing as the rich countries of the North export an ever higher proportion of their national output, and the developing countries import more and more of their food, their fuel and the capital goods that offer them their only hope of growing less poor.

Indeed, in a world where growing Third World populations depend increasingly on bulk shipments of oil and grain that can only go by sea, and airline economics are ravaged by the rise in fuel costs, it is aviation that begins to look obsolescent and shipping that could be the transportation industry of the future. Technological change has brought shipping up to date: radar, modern communications, computers, containers and the rapid growth in the size of tankers and bulk carriers. Cheap charter flights may fly holiday-makers from America to Europe, from Britain to Florida or from Germany to Bali and Bangkok in their hundreds of thousands. Yet shipping remains at least as important as aviation among the sinews of the world economy. Oil is one example. It was ships, not pipelines, that enabled the Persian Gulf's crude oil to reach the United States and Western Europe. The rise of Japan is another. However efficient her manufacturing industry, Japan could never have emerged as the world's second industrial power without ships: tankers from the Persian Gulf and ore carriers from Western Australia butting their way northwards across the South China Sea and general cargo ships streaming south and east with Japanese cars, television sets, steel and cameras for the American and European markets.

The rules of the game and the size of the pot have changed since Joseph Conrad's day. So too have the players. First, Scandinavians and Greeks challenged the supremacy of the Anglo-Saxon fleets. Then it was the turn of the overseas Chinese. The Onassis of today is Sir Y. K. Pao of Hong Kong, whose companies own more than 200 tankers. The Niarchos, until he died recently, was his rival C. Y. Tung. All of these owners have floated away 'offshore', where they are not troubled by regulation or taxes. Flags of convenience inadequately veil what was always a cowboy business, and falling freight rates have made it more cut-throat than ever.

It is a world game. A muttered conversation on the Baltic Exchange in London, and an Indian crew flies off to join a Greek-owned, Liberian-registered tramp that is shipping out of Antofagasta for Yokohama. Sikh, Thai and Chinese punters play it in seedy buildings in Hong Kong and Singapore. So do shady masters waiting for a ship to scuttle on the Akti Miaculi in the Piraeus, and tough Dutch tugboat skippers roaming the North Atlantic looking for a ship in distress to rescue, and uncommunicative lawyers in waterfront offices from Rotterdam to Panama. In one way or another, for insurance and reinsurance, but also for communications and intelligence, all these players depend on Lloyd's. Nine out of every ten contracts of insurance on hulls and cargoes in international sea trade (over and above the risks retained by shipowners' own mutual insurers) are placed at Lloyd's, and something between one-third and two-fifths of the value of all those hulls and cargoes is actually insured there. All their adventures, perils, losses and misfortunes will eventually wash up on the shore of the Room.

The gross tonnage of ships of all types lost in 1979 was the highest ever recorded in peacetime, according to the Intergovernmental Maritime Consultative Organization (IMCO), which is the United Nations shipping agency, with headquarters in London. The losses were especially severe in tankers. A total of 3·7 million tons of tankers was lost in the two years 1978 and 1979. And that was not just because the world's total tanker fleet was growing. On the contrary, this record rate of losses coincided with a record rate of tanker scrapping. Where over the four years from 1974 to 1977 tanker losses never rose above 0·22 per cent of the world's fleet in terms of tonnage, in 1978 the rate jumped to 0·4 per cent and in 1979 to 0·74 per cent. Altogether in 1979, according to Lloyd's records, 156 vessels with a known value of more than £500,000 (about $750,000) were written off as total losses for insurance purposes. That represented a total of over 2 million tons in a single year, and an aggregate money value of £326 million (around $489 million).

Most alarming was the sequence of serious casualties among the biggest, most expensive and potentially most dangerous class of ships afloat: the big tankers. (There is, as we shall see, one small group of even more dangerous ships: the liquid natural gas carriers.) As long ago as 1969, when the supertanker was still a relatively new concept, there was concern about the intrinsic safety of the type when three big ships, the *Kong Haakon*, the *Marpessa* and the *Matra*, blew up within a few weeks. But 1969 was nothing compared to 1979. In the fifteen months from January 1979 to March 1980, the London Salvage Association reported, there were thirty-five cases of fire or explosions on board tankers or combined oil-and-bulk carriers of over 100,000 tons deadweight (dwt), more than in the whole of the previous five years. For tankers alone, the rate was even more alarming: twenty-nine fires or explosions in fifteen months against only twenty in five years.

These were some of the worst. On the last day of 1978, the Greek *Andros Patria* (218,000 dwt) exploded and killed thirty crew members. Just over a week later the French-owned *Betelgeuse* blew up while unloading in Bantry Bay in the west of Ireland, killing fifty people.

In March 1979, the Portuguese-owned *Neiva*, an enormous ship of over 300,000 dwt, also caught fire while unloading, luckily without loss of life. In May five crewmen died when the *Atlas Titan*, of 213,000 dwt, exploded while cleaning her tanks near Lisbon. She was only five years old.

In July came the biggest casualty ever in terms of the sheer tonnage lost: the *Atlantic Empress*, 292,000 dwt, collided with the *Aegean Captain*, 210,000 dwt, off Tobago in the Caribbean. The *Atlantic Empress* was insured for $45 million and carried $40 million worth of naphthalene. The *Aegean Captain*, insured for $7·5 million, stayed afloat but lost $4 million of the oil she was carrying. Altogether over three million barrels of oil went up.

In November the *Benge Vanga*, 227,000 dwt, sank in the South Atlantic after an explosion in one of her holds with thirty crew on board. What was particularly unnerving, one leading marine broker at Lloyd's confessed to me, was that her owner was known to be exceptionally safety-conscious. The ship, only seven years old, was equipped with many of the latest safety devices.

In the same month the *Indepenta*, Romania's biggest tanker (150,000 dwt), collided with another ship and caught fire in the narrow Bosphorus channel close to the centre of Istanbul, arousing anguished concern in Turkey about the dangers of a major tanker route running in a narrow, twisting channel through the middle of a city with more than four million inhabitants.

Just before Christmas the very large *Energy Determination* (321,000 dwt) blew up and was paid as a constructive total loss. Only seven months later her sister ship *Energy Concentration*, also owned by the C. Y. Tung group, broke her back in Rotterdam's Europoort with more than 100,000 tons of crude on board. Crew fatigue was suspected as a contributory cause of that accident, which could have had catastrophic consequences if the oil had caught fire in the middle of the world's busiest port.

Perhaps the most shocking disaster of all came in March 1980. The Spanish *Maria Alejandra* (235,000 dwt) exploded and sank in under one minute off the coast of Mauritania. Neither poor management nor indifferent owners could be blamed for her loss. She was less than three years old and insured for more than $40 million. Thirty-six people went down with her: they included the owner, an enthusiast for ship safety, and his wife and daughter, whom he had taken along for the cruise.

By that stage something akin to panic was beginning to spread through the shipping world and to infect the Lloyd's market. Working parties set feverishly to work to find out what it was that caused big, modern tankers to go to the bottom, and to discover whether any precautions could prevent these disasters.

The London Salvage Association published a report that strongly recommended the installation of inert-gas safety systems to prevent tank and hold fires. Lloyd's underwriters were sufficiently impressed that they collectively took the comparatively unusual step of announcing a discriminatory rate of premium deliberately intended to encourage owners to install inert gas. Rates were raised by 0·1 per cent for VLCCs (very large crude carriers, or supertankers) *with* inert gas, but by 0·2 per cent for those without. The difference, on values of up to $50 million, was enough to make owners think twice.

Why was there such a spate of tanker losses?

The weather was exceptionally severe in many parts of the world in the winter of 1978-9. But that hardly explained the long series of casualties right through the summer, many of them in tropical zones. Some people blamed poor crews. 'It is hard to get good crews to go to sea nowadays,' said Peter Miller, a leading marine broker who is now the Chairman of Lloyd's, in an interview. But Miller admitted that some of the ships that went to the bottom, like the *Benge Vanga* and the *Maria Alejandra*, were modern ships with excellent crews. 'Partly it is lack of training,' said George Howard of the London Salvage Association when I talked to him. 'Partly it is lack of attention to duty. Unless people know how to use them, and do use them, the best safety devices are a waste of time. And partly, I'm afraid, it is commercial pressure.' Howard pointed out that the *Torrey Canyon* oil pollution disaster in 1967, which ruined half the beaches in the Cornwall peninsula in south-western England for a summer, was clearly caused by commercial pressure. The tanker's master, hurrying to catch a tide at Milford Haven in South Wales, cut inside instead of keeping safely outside the Scilly Isles, and ran aground.

Commercial pressures may have worked in an even more insidious way to cause this sudden sharp increase in the number of tanker accidents. It was because the economics of tanker operation were so unfavourable in 1978 and 1979 that so many tankers were scrapped. For most of 1978, tanker operating costs on average were less than the time-charter rate an owner could command for a one-year charter. Only small tankers of below about 60,000 dwt could earn a surplus over operating costs, and even that surplus could be wiped out by repair costs if they should become necessary. On the bigger ships, losses were running at anything from $450,000 a year for a modest 80,000 tonner, according to H. P. Drewry, the London shipping consultants, to an annual $1·2 million loss for a VLCC. The same conditions persisted for the first four months of 1979. Then charter rates began to recover. By the end of 1979, even big tankers were earning their keep.

The inescapable conclusion is that because of the recession in shipping, and after some years of low freight rates and charter rates, some shipowners were skimping on maintenance and repairs, so that the proportion of ships at sea that were not truly seaworthy was rising dangerously. Many experts warned what would happen. One of the most forthright warnings came from Roger Peterson, of the University of Tennessee, working in collaboration with the Netherlands Maritime Research Institute. He studied all tanker accidents between 1964 and 1977 intensively, and concluded that the most critical factor was 'the nature and attitude of the management who ultimately control the vessel and its operations'. Such fleets as Exxon, Japan Lines and P & O, Peterson pointed out, had excellent records, irrespective of the age and size of their fleets. In contrast, where 'ownership and control are hidden within a maze of interlocking companies', some owners were 'gambling on safety to make money'. Or, Peterson might have added, to save it.

The pattern of losses during 1978 and 1979 tends to support Peterson's allegation. The big increase was not, as you might have expected, in the older ships, but in the younger ones. And it was very heavily concentrated among ships sailing under flags of convenience, especially that of Liberia, and under the Greek flag. While some Greek shipowners are models of conscientious behaviour, others notoriously are not. 'The consistency of the trends between 1977 and 1979,' Drewry summed up, 'has the worrying implication that the overall standard of safety of tankers deteriorated during this period. One possible reason for this is that owners in general earned insufficient revenues in the poor freight markets, and some of them reacted by insufficient spending on necessary repairs and maintenance.' That could not explain all the losses. Many of the ships that went down were impeccably cared for. One even went down with the owner and his family on board. Still, the temptation to skimp undoubtedly explained the sudden leap in total losses.

Others hinted at even more sinister explanations. 'Cynics will doubtless argue,' wrote the London *Sunday Telegraph*, 'that a string of tanker losses may be a blessing in disguise, or more than just a coincidence, at a time when the tanker market is still depressed.' Scuttling, after all, is just another way of scrapping a ship, but with the rather important difference that, whereas when a ship is scrapped the owner is saved the expense of keeping it afloat and collects whatever he can get for the steel in the depressed scrap market, if the ship is scuttled, instead of the scrap value he collects the full insured value from the underwriters.

It might seem fantastic to suggest that any part of the increase in supertanker losses was due to deliberate scuttling. There is certainly no direct proof except in one instance. Yet, as we shall see, it is far from unknown for owners to throw their ships away, as the expressive phrase at Lloyd's has it, in times of depressed earnings. In those very same years there is good evidence that the owners of many small ships, faced with exactly the same economic dilemma, did resolve it by deliberately scuttling their ships. In at least one case the sinking of a supertanker, originally reported as due to an explosion, turned out to be a deliberate scuttling. There may have been others. 'There is a Boyle's law of scuttling,' says Donald O'May, a partner in the shipping law firm Ince & Co., 'to the effect that the volume of total losses is proportional to the downward pressure of the freight market. Ships and freight go down together.'

Whatever the reason, although by the spring of 1980 there were many alarmists who predicted that tanker losses would go on up for ever, that is not what happened. Whether by coincidence or not, it is a fact that, after charter rates began to recover in late 1979, the wave of tanker losses subsided. In fact, the rate of serious casualties as a proportion of all tankers at risk fell as abruptly as it had risen, from 3·24 per hundred ships in 1979 to 2·22 in 1980, which was actually a lower rate than in any year since 1974.

What effect did this epidemic of total losses in tankers have on the marine market at Lloyd's?

The layman might suppose that the effect would be disastrous. Much press comment took that for granted. After all, in effect marine underwriters are gambling that ships will not go down. So, if a lot of ships do suddenly sink, it seems reasonable to assume that underwriters will lose their shirts.

In practice, it is nothing like as simple as that. For one thing, though much of the market is represented on many important slips, some boxes will be cannier than others in choosing the slips they decide not to write. So even when the majority of boxes are losing money, some hold out against the trend. More important, underwriters plan their whole programme on the basis of the level of loss they can safely absorb, covering the big catastrophic losses by reinsurance. Above all, the effect of a given run of losses on the market (as opposed to the individual underwriter) will depend on two factors: on rates, and on the amount of competition. Or – to put the same idea in a different way – losses, competition and rates will all be factors in an equation that will produce a relatively slowly changing economic cycle.

It is not always so slow. In the late 1960s, the market went through a series of catastrophic losses that culminated in the unexplained explosions in the *Kong Haakon*, the *Marpessa* and the *Matra*. The market wanted to protect itself. It needed time to think, and to find out how dangerous these floating cathedrals full of fuel and inflammable gases really were. In three weeks, Sir Peter Green recalled, rates jumped from 3·75 per cent – already high – to 8·75 per cent. At times, in the market, underwriters wanted 12·5 per cent, a figure that was intended to deter brokers altogether but did not always succeed.

Ships, after all, must be insured. And brokers do not get their commission unless they can arrange insurances for them. As always, a time of catastrophic losses was a time of opportunity for those with the nerve to gamble. One of them was Ian Posgate. He recalls that, before the three big losses, the rate for the two dozen or so supertankers then in existence was around 0·3 per cent. The next time the Shell fleet came up for renewal – *Marpessa* and *Matra* were both Shell boats – the rate was up to 1·5 per cent. On another major fleet, that owned by Daniel K. Ludwig – the rate was 2·5 per cent. Such rates were low compared to the panic rates charged in the immediate aftermath of the three losses, but they were still very high. There were no more mystery supertanker explosions for several years. The world fleet rose from a couple of dozen VLCCs to several hundred. And Posgate and other underwriters bold enough to take the risk made a fortune.

While Lloyd's is an important part of the world marine insurance market, it is not the whole of it. Lloyd's marine underwriters compete with insurance companies in London in what is called 'the London market'. They also compete with insurers in the United States, Germany and other maritime countries, as well as with the captive companies owned by the big oil and shipping companies, many of them based in Bermuda, and with smaller, more marginal operators in the Middle East and Far East. After the big losses of the late 1960s, many of these competitors simply withdrew from the marine market. Few of them depended on marine underwriting for any major proportion of their income. So Lloyd's marine market was left with a much larger share of the business, and at higher rates of premium. That is how an insurance market works. When losses rise, insurers withdraw from the market. Those who have the nerve and the resources to stick it out, or who have no alternative, are in a position to ask and get a high price.

For a time they reap the reward of their quasi-monopoly position. Then, before long, they pitch their price too high. New competitors appear and old ones reappear. New money comes into the market. Rates fall once again.

That is just what happened in the marine market in the 1970s. For a while Lloyd's underwriters found themselves almost alone. They put their rates up and at first made a lot of money. Gradually the competition moved back, but by then inflation was gathering speed worldwide. More and more people were attracted by what insurance people call 'writing for premium' – that is, underwriting insurances not primarily because of the prospect of making money on the underwriting proposition itself, but because of the interest that could be earned on the premium before it was needed to pay claims. They could do this all the more safely because – again, thanks to the excess capacity in the world market – reinsurance was cheap and plentiful. Plenty of insurers in Bermuda and Hong Kong, Lloyd's underwriters complain, would ask what the rate was at Lloyd's and then offer to write it for ten cents less.

In both Britain and the United States interest rates reached record levels. More than ever it was tempting to write for premium, even at the risk of eventual underwriting losses, just in order to get hold of cash flow and invest it. When the big losses hit once again in 1978–9, the rate of premium in the Lloyd's marine market did not jump as it had done in 1969. 'Unfortunately,' Sir Peter Green told me wryly, 'the competition moved back into the market just as inflation really took off. So we lowered rates just when we should have been increasing them.'

The rate of premium in an insurance market reflects two separate sets of factors. First, it reflects the actuarial likelihood of losses. If tankers are sinking in disconcerting numbers (or satellites falling out of the sky, or houses being burgled), then – other things being equal – rates will rise to take account of a higher probability of loss. But other things are not always equal. Specifically, the amount of competition varies. Rates also reflect the balance between buyers and sellers. If there are more sellers in the market than buyers, which in insurance terms means if there is excess underwriting capacity in the market, then rates will tend to fall. The actual rates that can be obtained in the market will thus reflect the balance between actuarial and market pressures. Losses, competition and rates are all factors in an equation. As those functions vary, so will the market's economic cycle rise and fall.

When catastrophic losses hit the market in 1978–80, therefore, on actuarial grounds rates ought to have risen sharply. As it was, because of the competitive pressure of insurers looking for premium, they hovered for a while at a low level, then slowly began to edge up.

Lloyd's has always felt that heavy losses are to its advantage, because they frighten away the weaker brethren among the competition. Given enough losses, Lloyd's men seem to feel, they will once again enjoy their rightful place of unchallenged supremacy in the marine market. There is a certain arrogance in this attitude, and at the same time a certain realism. Richard Rutherford, who has retired from running the hulls side of the Lloyd's Underwriters Claims and Recoveries Office, told me a story that perfectly illustrates the market's traditionally ambivalent attitude to big claims. Rutherford's boss, a Mr Mitchell, used to tell him the story of an old underwriter who would ask him, every time he walked through the Room, how the claims were coming. No shortage of claims, Mitchell would admit. 'Good man!' the old underwriter would bark back at him. 'Keep those claims under control! But keep them coming!'

By 1980, the combination of high inflation and high technology made it hard to keep marine claims under any kind of control. In the summer of that year, Lloyd's announced with some pride that underwriters had just settled the heaviest claim in history. Privately they had reason to be grateful that it was not heavier.

In 1915 Godfrey L. Cabot of Boston took out the first American patent for transporting liquid gas by water. Not until the 1950s, however, did the technology become practical. The chairman of the Union Stockyards of Chicago, William Wood Prince, gave the impetus to development because of his belief that his company's gigantic cold-storage operations could be fuelled with Louisiana natural gas, liquefied at very cold temperatures and transported up the Mississippi on barges. Research and development continued through the 1950s in America, Britain, France and Norway. A renewed impulse came from the discovery of vast gas reserves at Hassi R'Mel, in Algeria, and by January 1959 the world's first ocean-going liquefied natural gas carrier, the *Methane Pioneer*, crossed the Atlantic from Lake Charles, Louisiana, to Canvey Island, in the Thames estuary. The *Methane Pioneer* was developed by a consortium ingeniously named Conch International Methane Ltd – in cooperation with the nationalized British gas industry. The first three letters stood for Conoco, who held 40 per cent of the stock, the last two for Union Stockyards of Chicago, with 20 per cent, and the entire bivalve for Shell, the owner of the remaining 40 per cent.

The shape of the international energy market changed in the next decade. In 1965 natural gas was discovered within fifty miles of the English coast in the North Sea, and at the same time the United States was becoming a major energy importer. In 1968, for the first time, the demand for natural gas in the United States exceeded domestic discoveries. In that same year El Paso Company, one of the major American gas production and pipeline operators, signed a contract with Sonatrach, the Algerian national oil and gas company, to buy 1 billion cubic feet of liquefied natural gas (LNG) a *day* and ship it to the United States. El Paso at the time had no experience whatever of shipping. With help from various companies with experience in the field, however, El Paso ordered and successfully operated, first, three ships built at the Chantiers de l'Atlantique in Dunkerque, in France, and then, because of American government subsidies available through the Federal Maritime Administration, three built in Mobile, Alabama. LNG from the Hassi R'Mel field was piped to the Mediterranean coast of Algeria at Arzew, where it was liquefied by a process that reduced its temperature to below the boiling point of methane, which is −260° Fahrenheit, and then shipped to two specially built regasification plants at Cove Point, Maryland, and Savannah, Georgia.

The aluminium gas tanks on the first six ships (like most but not all of the fifty or so other LNG ships in operation with other companies such as Shell and Exxon) were insulated with balsa wood. For the next three ships, *El Paso Columbia*, *El Paso Cove Point* and *El Paso Savannah*, to be built at the Ogden Corporation's Avondale yard in New Orleans, and each capable of holding 125,000 cubic metres of gas, a new form of insulation was tried. Avondale was to build the ships, the aluminium tanks were to be supplied by Kaiser Aluminium and the insulation was to be designed by Conch LNG, Inc., a subsidiary of Shell. They decided, in order to cut the man-hour costs of installing balsa-laminated panels around tanks ninety feet high, to insulate the tanks with polyurethane foam sprayed into position on site.

It did not work. Just why not was to be a matter of fierce dispute and the subject of much litigation. But when, after much testing and some delays, one of the three ships, the *El Paso Columbia*, finally went for her sea trials in May 1979, electronic sensors detected cold spots on the double hull. That meant that the insulation had failed, and back at the yard inspection revealed extensive cracks in the foam. The United States Coast Guard duly refused a certificate of seaworthiness. El Paso were now left with three ships that were useless for the trade they had been built for. Avondale faced the prospect of not being paid for three $100 million ships.

Both were insured. Avondale was covered by a construction policy, and El Paso was protected both against late delivery and against the abandonment of building. Avondale's brokers, Frank B. Hall, sent most of the business to Sedgwick to place in the London market. The slip was led at Lloyd's by Bill Maitland, from the box of the Chairman of Lloyd's, Janson Green. El Paso's brokers, Desert American Agency, also sent the business to Sedgwick, and again the slip was led by Maitland.

The insurance pattern was more complicated than that. Both El Paso and the Federal Maritime Administration had insurable interests under the construction contracts, and Kaiser was also named in them. Conch had insurances of its own, with Sedgwick again as the direct broker.

Other brokers and other underwriters were involved. (Some 15 per cent of the builder's risk was with the American Hull Insurance Syndicate, for example.) But it was clear that, with the biggest Lloyd's broker representing most of the parties in one way or another, and with the Chairman of Lloyd's box leading most of the slips, Lloyd's reputation was more than usually at stake.

The sums of money at risk were daunting. The total value of all policies was $625 million. Writs were flying about as each party's lawyers tried to safeguard their position. Kaiser was suing Avondale, Avondale was suing both Kaiser and Conch, and so on. In the context of public debate about potential conflicts of interest at Lloyd's, both brokers and underwriters were sensitive to even the appearance of conflicting interests. It was clear that the most satisfactory solution would be to get all parties round a table in London to talk things through. In the end, with a good deal of help from Frank B. Hall and Desert American, that was achieved. A long series of meetings began, some in Sedgwick House, some in Janson Green's office, and some at LUCRO, with Dick Rutherford of LUCRO and Bill Maitland representing underwriters, and Adrian Platt of Sedgwick Marine prominent on behalf of the assured, but with the top management of El Paso and Ogden and the head of the Federal Maritime Administration all taking a personal interest. One risk that all parties were conscious of was that the United States Congress might also take an interest if the Maritime Administration did not get its $200 million or so of loans back.

The immediate danger for underwriters was that all three ships could be declared a constructive total loss, in which case all the El Paso insurances would be activated, leaving underwriters liable for the full $625 million. The first repair estimates quoted a figure of $250 million for repairs; with inflation, that was dangerously close to the full value of the construction policy at $310 million. Naturally, underwriters vigorously contested the repair estimates. And there were weak points in the assureds' case, too, tactically speaking. They had to *prove* a constructive total loss. If they could get no settlement, then expensive litigation could drag on for years. It became clear that they were less interested in getting the ships repaired than in recovering a sum of money that would enable them to settle their own commitments to the federal government and their other sources of finance. There were moments of high drama, and more than one threatened walkout. But on 1 August 1980, after almost a year of negotiation, terms of settlement were announced. The total was the largest settlement ever paid by Lloyd's underwriters to date: $60 million in each of three annual tranches under the builder's risk policy, plus another three tranches of $10 million and a lump sum of $90 million to El Paso: a total of $300 million.

It had to be reckoned expensive advertising for Lloyd's, even though a major proportion of the settlement was covered by reinsurance. Still, it was excellent advertising. First, it advertised that Lloyd's was still able and willing to pay out spectacularly large sums. More subtly, it showed the smooth way the Lloyd's system can move in and unravel a potentially horrendous corporate quarrel and negotiate a solution with a minimum of friction.

Over the twenty years or so that LNG has been transported by sea in quantity, the specialized fleet of some fifty-six vessels built for the purpose (ten of which are now laid up) built up an excellent safety record. There have been no more than two or three minor spills on deck, and no injuries whatever to personnel. The ships have been built with more protection than oil tankers: double bottoms, double side-shells and in some cases double decks as well.

It is just as well, because if the liquefied methane ever were to spill, vaporize and then ignite, the consequences could be catastrophic. In 1944, admittedly in an early stage of LNG technology, an explosion caused by a leak in an LNG storage tank in Cleveland, Ohio, killed 128 people. Critics have pointed out that a 125,000 cubic metre LNG carrier contains more energy than was released in the atomic explosion at Hiroshima, and called the ships 'floating time-bombs'. The industry naturally reacts indignantly, citing its excellent safety record since the Cleveland accident, and insisting that the hazards are no worse than those involved in transporting gasoline or propane. An incident on 29 June 1979 – right in the middle of the unhappy trials of the *El Paso Columbia* – was a reminder that those hazards could nevertheless be considerable.

On that day the *El Paso Paul Kayser*, bound from Algeria to Cove Point, ran aground on the rocks at La Perla, in the Straits of Gibraltar, damaging her double bottom. Tense experts from El Paso, from the Dutch salvage company Wijsmuller and from the United States Salvage Association flew to the spot. Four big salvage tugs and another El Paso LNG stood by for a week as the damaged 'bomb' of 100,000 cubic metres of gas was refloated. The ship and its cargo were insured on the London and American markets for $160 million. If the salvage operation had not been brilliantly successful, more than money could have gone west. Experts do not like to speculate what the consequences would have been for the Rock of Gibraltar or the Spanish coast if any chance spark had ignited a cloud of combustible vapour anything up to ten miles long.

What the insurance market fears more than even the most cataclysmic imaginable single loss, though, is the unforeseeable aggregation of loss, and especially of 'liability' – that is, of damage caused to third parties. So not even the collision of two VLCCs like the *Atlantic Empress* and the *Aegean Captain* off Tobago, or the worst imaginable explosion of the *El Paso Paul Kayser*, was the worst of the catastrophic losses underwriters might have to face.

On 17 March 1978, right in the middle of the blackest month in the history of Lloyd's, Roger Lowes, of the Lloyd's casualty department at Colchester, sent out the following brief message to the International Tanker Owners Pollution Federation, known as ITOPF:

LLOYDS MESSAGES FROM LANDS END RADIO STATE:
FOLLOWING FROM LIBERIAN MOTOR TANKER AMOCO CADIZ CALL SIGN A8AN 109700 TONS GROSS, ON 500HZ AT 2326 GMT: SOS POSITION LAT. 48.36. 2 N., LONG. 04.45.9 W. (ABOUT 14 MILES NORTHEAST OF USHANT) AGROUND. NEED IMMEDIATE ASSISTANCE, IF POSSIBLE BY HELICOPTER. FULLY LOADED, POLLUTION.

After giving Lloyd's telex number – 987321 – and some details about the tugs standing by and the tanker's radio, Lowes added an even more pregnant line:

VESSEL IS LADEN WITH 230,000 TONS CRUDE OIL.

For more than a decade, a nightmare had haunted conservationists, bird lovers, fishermen, hotel owners and officials all along the narrow seas that link Rotterdam, the Thames estuary and Northern Europe's other oil ports with the ocean. With the grounding of the *Amoco Cadiz*, that nightmare had turned into a reeking, clogging, black reality.

At any moment, 100 million tons of oil are at sea, most of them threading half a dozen relatively narrow sea lanes between the Gulf, the United States, Western Europe and Japan. Western Europe alone imports more than 600 million tons of crude oil a year, or the equivalent of 3,000 supertankers the size of the *Amoco Cadiz*. Ever since the wreck of the much smaller *Torrey Canyon* on the opposite shore of the English Channel in March 1967, people had asked what would happen if one of the new big tankers were to spill its cargo on an inhabited shore. Now they were to get their answer.

Even if a third of the tanker's cargo evaporated or dissolved, a team of scientists from Texas A & M University calculated after the event, the rest of the oil would mingle with mud and water to deposit 500,000 tons of viscous mousse along the rocky coasts and sandy bays and estuaries of Brittany. More than 245 miles of the coast were affected. According to one French expert, almost one-third of all living creatures in and over the coast of Brittany were killed by the oil. They included 20,000 sea birds, among them rare guillemots, razorbills and gannets. For some reason the lobsters, crabs and shrimps, exported in great numbers·from that coast to the Paris restaurants, were not so badly harmed. But fish, especially the red mullet, were badly affected, and ulcerated fish, presumably infected by the heavy fractions of the oil that clung to the sea bed, continued to float to the surface for many months. The coves of north-west Brittany produce more than a tenth of France's total oyster crop in a normal year; in 1978 Breton oysters were virtually non-existent.

Brittany is also the second most popular tourist region in France after the Riviera. French visitors go there in July and August, and more than 1 million foreigners, mostly British and German, fill up the accommodations in June and September. The French especially, having watched the impact of the oil on television all spring, stayed away in massive numbers. Camping sites all along the north coast of Brittany were empty, and hotel bookings were down by more than 80 per cent. 'The 1978 season,' said an official report, 'is the worst the Finisterre hotel industry has ever known.' The economic implications of the disaster spilled over from fishing and tourism to secondary industries; boat repairers, truckers, food wholesalers and sand and gravel dredgers were all forced to lay off employees.

For several weeks some 6,000 naval and military personnel, plus an average of 2,000 volunteers, worked at cleaning up the foreshore, with a thousand vehicles and several flights of helicopters. (The most effective vehicles were the 'honeywagons' which farmers used to cart manure.) The impact on local community and local government budgets was devastating: $31·7 million for the department of Finisterre, $13·8 million for the Côtes du Nord. But in a highly centralized country like France the heaviest burden fell on the national government.

Worst of all, the *Amoco Cadiz* chose to drift on to the rocks at Portsall in the tense interval between the first and second round of voting in the French presidential election.

At the best of times the Bretons' attitude towards the national government in Paris can be compared with that of Texans towards Washington. Now they were quick to accuse the government of President Valéry Giscard d'Estaing of indifference or incompetence or both. French public opinion in general echoed the Bretons' anger that, because the main lane for tankers bound for northern Europe as a whole skirts their coast, they ran the risk of being devastatingly polluted by oil that was not even bound for French refineries. Some French newspapers whipped up Breton anger against the 'Americans' who were defiling the fair coasts of France (even though the tanker was on charter to, and the cargo belonged to, Shell, which is part-Dutch, part-British, with very substantial French minority shareholdings). No less promptly, American lawyers descended on the little ports and quayside bistros of Finisterre, expatiating beguilingly on the beauties of class actions and contingency suits.

The result was that damage claims totalling no less than $2·2 billion were filed in American courts. Both liability and the quantum of damages in all those suits remain to be determined. But it is certain that the wreck of the *Amoco Cadiz* will lead to some of the heaviest awards for damage ever made, and to one of the heaviest aggregations of claims for marine insurance – that is, unless an even larger oil spill takes place before it is resolved.

The French Republic is suing for the cost of the cleaning-up operation, including the pay of the thousands of soldiers, sailors and police involved. That claim alone comes to more than $300 million. The various departments, towns and communes affected are suing separately. So are the fishermen and the oystermen, individually and as classes. So are the hoteliers and the restaurateurs. And so too are the whole body of the citizens of the ancient province of Brittany in the name and person of a certain local doctor.

The reason why all these actions were brought in the courts of the United States is simple enough: the plaintiffs were advised that they stood to win more money there. This is not due to the greater generosity of Americans; it results from certain peculiarities of the international arrangements made by the oil companies and others for handling major oil spills, and also from certain differences between the legal systems of the United States and France.

After the *Torrey Canyon* disaster in 1967, the tanker owners set up a system for voluntary compensation for damages caused by oil pollution. It was called TOVALOP (Tanker Owners Voluntary Agreement concerning Liability for Oil Pollution). In 1971 the cargo owners followed suit. Their system was called CRISTAL (Contract Regarding an Interim Supplement to Tanker Liability for Oil Pollution). In many cases tanker owners and cargo owners are different wings of the same international oil company. What happened was that the private oil and shipping industries rushed TOVALOP and CRISTAL into the breach after the *Torrey Canyon* incident; both were intended to be interim expedients, to be replaced by international compensation arrangements between governments, then being negotiated under the auspices of the Intergovernmental Maritime Consultative Organization (IMCO). Those agreements were duly ratified: the Convention on Civil Liability (CLC) in 1975 and the Fund Convention in 1978. But by that time the maritime industry and its advisers knew that it would be a long time before all the world's dangerous seas were covered by signatory countries, and also that the sums allowed for compensation were being rendered inadequate by inflation. The effect of these industry and intergovernmental compensation funds by 1981 was like this: TOVALOP would put up the first $16·8 million and CRISTAL would top that up to $30 million if an oil spill damaged the territory of a nation not a party to the international conventions; if the damage was done to the territory of countries that were parties to the conventions, a total of up to $58 million might be available. At the time of the *Amoco Cadiz* spill, the total amount available under this system of limited liability would have been only $30 million: $16·8 million under CLC, and the balance topped up under CRISTAL (the Fund Convention not having come into force) to the then maximum of $30 million.

It was obvious to everyone, including the French government, which can afford lawyers every bit as sharp as any oil company's, that this sum would not go very far towards paying for the clean-up, let alone for all the potential contingent liabilities for damage to property, businesses and earnings. The lowest estimate for the cost of the damage to be heard even among the most committed partisans of the defendants is $50 million. A working party, funded by the United States government and chaired by Professor Thomas Grigalunas of the University of Rhode Island, estimated to the Organization for Economic Cooperation and Development (OECD) that the cost of the damage would be at least $175 million.

That was why the French brought suit in the United States. It was nevertheless a strange decision for the government, for France is a signatory to the CLC; and under the convention nations agree that suits may be brought only in the courts of the country where the accident occurred. The accident took place in French coastal waters. The United States is not a signatory power. To win an action in the United States courts, the plaintiffs would have to prove 'fault and privity' on the part of the defendants. Faced with the huge bill for the clean-up, the French government decided to try to do just that.

The registered owners were Amoco Shipping, a Liberian company. The management company was Amoco International in Bermuda. But most plaintiffs brushed them aside and went against the parent, Standard Oil of Indiana, whose head office is in Chicago. That is why suits were brought in federal court in Chicago and in Illinois state courts as well as in federal court in New York and later in Virginia. There were the usual side-issues, stratagems and counter-stratagems. At one point Amoco arrested a sister-ship of the tug that had tried to salvage the tanker, belonging to the Hamburg firm of Bugsier, because it was rash enough to stray into Norfolk, Virginia. But when the lawyers had finished playing their games, it was decided to consolidate all the actions in federal court in Chicago.

Like most big shipowners, Amoco insured 100 per cent of its whole fleet's liability for damage to third parties as a direct insurance with one of the 'P & I Clubs'. (P & I stands for protection and indemnity, and the 'clubs' are in effect mutual insurance companies, jointly owned by shipowners in proportion to the size of their fleets. They provide the first line of cover for third-party and certain other kinds of liability.) In this case, it was the London Association, whose money is put up by the shipowners who belong to it. It is managed by an old-established marine insurance specialist in the City of London called A. Bilbrough & Co. The London Association then reinsured with a pool made up of several P & I Clubs: it used to be called the London Pool, but the name was tactfully changed to the International Group Pool. But the London Association also reinsured a special excess of loss to cover catastrophic liability claims like a major oil spill. The broker was Peter Miller, of Thomas R. Miller, now Chairman of Lloyd's.

So at the end of this long chain of responsibility we come at last to Lloyd's. Not that Lloyd's is alone at the end of this chain. Miller has placed the reinsurance with great care. 'You can say the reinsurance was distributed on the world market,' says John Hawkes of Bilbrough's. 'It was extremely widely spread.' Some of the responsibility ended up with Lloyd's underwriters, some of it was taken by the rest of the London market and some of it went to the United States. There was even a small insurance company in Nepal that took a line.

Lloyd's was involved in another way, one that caused a certain embarrassment. The *Amoco Cadiz*'s distress signals were picked up by a Bugsier salvage tug, the *Pacific*, that happened to be on its way from the port of Brest, in western Brittany, to help an oil rig through the Straits of Dover at the other end of the English Channel. As he steered to the rescue, the tug's skipper, Captain Hartmut Weinert, routinely offered to carry out salvage under Lloyd's open-form salvage agreement. The worldwide acceptance of this form of agreement, proclaimed Wright & Fayle's standard *History of Lloyd's* 'without undue boasting',

is a tribute to British probity and to the administration of British law. The saving to world commerce by its adoption cannot be estimated. When a vessel is in distress much may depend on the promptitude with which assistance is rendered. In the absence of some standard agreement, acceptable to all parties, the subject matter of insurance might seriously depreciate, or even disappear ...

Quite so. That possibility was very present to the minds of Captain Bardari of the *Amoco Cadiz* and his British safety consultant, former Royal Navy officer Lesley Maynard, as they clung to the darkened bridge of the *Amoco Cadiz*, half-gassed and not daring to switch on a light for fear of igniting 223,000 tons of crude oil. Perhaps it was an argument over the Lloyd's open-form agreement that led him into that desperate predicament and contributed to the scale of the *Amoco Cadiz* disaster.

The basic principles of the open-form agreement are that it is a *salvage* agreement, not a contract with a tug company for help; that it is on the basis of 'no cure, no pay'; and that the amount payable for salvage is left to be determined by arbitration *in London*. Obviously, in dangerous circumstances at sea the open-form agreement, understood by all master mariners, has great advantages, since it can be agreed upon informally, without negotiation, and everyone knows what it means.

In the particular case of the *Amoco Cadiz*, however, the Lloyd's open form had an overwhelming disadvantage for Captain Bardari, so much so that he delayed accepting it for more than four crucial hours, apparently until he could get authority from his owners in Chicago. He thought he did not need salvage. He simply wanted a tug to keep his ship pointing in the right direction while he floated it off with its own powerful, intact engines. (It was the out-of-order steering gear that caused the tanker to drift off course on to the Portsall rocks.) A tow to the shelter of Lyme Bay on the English coast opposite, which is what he wanted, would cost a few thousand dollars; once he accepted salvage, the arbitration award might cost the owners millions.

If Bardari had accepted the agreement, it might or might not have saved his ship. It would certainly have meant that his owners accepted arbitration in London by a British Queen's Counsel. They would also have been represented there by one or more barristers practising in the specialist law of Admiralty, and they in turn would not be permitted to act unless instructed by one of fewer than a dozen London law firms that do 'Admiralty' – marine – work. There are serious criticisms to be made of a system that compels so many of the world's maritime disputes to be brought to London to be decided by a tiny cartel of Admiralty lawyers. But the saga of the *Amoco Cadiz* illustrates a more general, more subtle point. The international shipping and marine insurance industries are still dominated by an Anglo-American community that is to a significant degree centred on the City of London and on Lloyd's.

The British merchant marine may have shrunk. (It is still the world's third largest, after Liberia and Japan.) The American fleet may have virtually all gone offshore under flags of convenience. Other nations have increased their share of world seaborne trade at the expense of the United States and Britain, though the Anglo-American share remains very significant. Banks from Western Europe, Japan and the Middle East are breaking into what was once an Anglo-American near-monopoly of the financing of international sea trade. Major fleets are now owned by Greek, Scandinavian, Chinese and Japanese interests, among others. Yet London remains the economic and cultural centre of the business. International shipowners visit London regularly, maintain offices there, use London lawyers and insurers and experts of all kinds. The main organizations dealing with tanker insurance and pollution compensation, to take one example among many –

IMCO, ITOPF, CRISTAL and the rest – have their offices either in the City of London or in the British colony of Bermuda. If the world of aviation speaks English with an American accent, the world of shipping still speaks the Queen's English – or a hundred broken approximations to it! This international world uses Lloyd's in the specific ways I have described. More vaguely, yet in a way that has pervasive importance, it gravitates around Lloyd's. That fact has undeniably been a great advantage and a source of profit to Lloyd's over the past thirty years. In the late 1970s, it was also a cause of perils and misfortunes.

This world of ships and shipping, with the Lloyd's marine market and the Lloyd's intelligence network at the very heart of it, has a sedately Victorian reputation. It brings to mind sober, businesslike men of unassailable caution and probity, Scots or Scandinavians as like as not, going through time-honoured rituals in offices furnished in mahogany and identified by engraved brass plaques. Many of the old-established shipping lines are indeed impeccably correct, and so are many of the ancillary professions that support them. Yet few industries offer such opportunities to scoundrels, and there has never been any real shortage of scoundrels to take advantage of them.

It is, first of all, an industry that works to a remarkable degree on trust. It is commonplace for ships and cargoes worth millions of dollars to be entrusted to almost total strangers after minimal checks. It is a world that works necessarily at long range. It would be hard to police at the best of times; now that so many ships are registered under flags of convenience (the Republic of Panama once toyed with a scheme for registering ships at a moment's notice over the telephone!) and ownership is often concealed under a web of offshore companies, policing it is well-nigh impossible. In most cases, there is no single jurisdiction where the authorities have a clear incentive to take on the time-consuming and expensive work of tracking down an international shipping fraud. And the basic system by which most international trade is financed, c.i.f. (cost, insurance and freight) contract, is almost absurdly easy to defraud.

There are two main systems in use for international trading. Under one, the f.o.b. (free on board) system, a shipper is responsible only for delivering the goods he is selling to a port nominated by the buyer, and for loading them on to a suitable ship. Once they are loaded, title passes to the buyer, who is then responsible for freight and insurance. In c.i.f. contracts, on the other hand, the seller is responsible for insurance and freight during the voyage. So that the seller can be paid without having to wait for the goods to reach the buyer, however, there has grown up the system of financing named after the 'bill of exchange', traditionally a 'ninety-day bill on London'. The effect is that, in the words of one eminent legal authority, there are two quite distinct elements to a typical c.i.f. transaction. One concerns the physical transfer of goods, and the provision of documents covering their description, sale and insurance. Then, quite separately, there is the transfer of the documents in exchange for value. As the code of the International Chamber of Commerce, the bible of most banks in international trade, succinctly puts it: 'All parties concerned deal in documents and not in goods.' That means that a bank is quite willing to hand over very large sums of money against production of documents. Those documents – essentially a bill of lading, evidence of transferable insurance cover and a commercial invoice describing the goods – can be comparatively easily forged. Banks, moreover, tend to check that the documents are in order, not that they correspond to any external reality. Many frauds depend on documents that show goods as having been loaded on a ship that was far too small to carry them, or was in dry dock at the time. A good example happened in the spring of 1981. The Iranians, at war with Iraq, were desperate for arms. An official in the Iranian defence ministry had a contact, a Lebanese businessman living in Paris, who agreed to supply and ship a large quantity of American arms and ammunition, including 20,000 rocket launchers and shells. The businessman's company, Universal Oil Trade, with offices in Paris but a Panama registration, produced bills of lading issued in Rio de Janeiro to show that the arms had been loaded on to a ship called *Sydkust*. On presentation of these shipping documents, the Iranian Bank Melli paid over no less than $56 million. The ship turned out to be one of only 200 tons, and could not possibly have loaded the cargo listed. The building where the bills of lading were issued turned out to be still under construction. The ship was swiftly sold and resold. And the Lebanese businessman disappeared, after transferring at least $30 million of the missing millions into an account in a bank in Geneva.

It was not altogether surprising, in these circumstances, that the late 1970s, a time of worldwide financial stringency and political turmoil, saw a veritable epidemic of marine fraud. 'During the second half of the 1970s,' according to one expert, 'the minimum amount netted by fraudsters, both the organized rings and the entrepreneurs, topped $650 million ... with the toll still rising. And that takes in only reported crimes.' Many big multinationals, rather than have to admit to having been taken for a ride, prefer to hide their embarrassment and never report their losses. In the first half of 1980, this same authority estimates that marine fraud cleared at least $200 million more. Another expert, Eric Ellen, director of the International Maritime Bureau and former chief constable of the Port of London Authority Police, calculates that in 1979 there were on average three frauds of $1 million or more each reported every month, and that even that, because of failure to report, 'can only represent the tip of the iceberg'.

This epidemic of fraud may have been in part an indirect consequence of the oil price rise in 1973, when oil-producing countries found their revenues tripled or more overnight. Several of them, notably Saudi Arabia, Iran and Nigeria, embarked on ambitious investment programmes, involving massive purchases of capital equipment from abroad, and hurried to import consumer goods of all kinds. Their ports were unable to handle this rush of business. At Khorramshahr, the chief port of Iran, ships had to wait 160 days and more before entering harbour. More than a million tons of goods were waiting in the holds of over 200 ships, and even when goods were unloaded they might wait for months and even years before being driven away. It was the same at Jeddah, in Saudi Arabia. Worst of all were conditions at Apapa, the port of Lagos in Nigeria. The English writer Patrick Marnham has described conditions there in 1976:

As far as the eye could see there were lines of ships at anchor, four hundred or five hundred of them, waiting for berths in a port that was already blocked, with more ships arriving by the hour to join the serpentine line. Each of the ships was loaded with cement. It was one of the most extraordinary moments in the development of Africa, this great fleet of ships, carrying the means to construct half a dozen modern cities, inching their way solemnly towards the quay – while the closer they approached it, the more unusable their cargo became. For after a number of months cement becomes unreliable, and the structures it supports are liable to sudden collapse.

Struggling to partake in this profitable calamity were all the cement suppliers of the Northern world, equipped with the leakiest vessels and the most watertight contracts they could obtain. Any boat would do, as long as it could survive the single voyage to Apapa, where in waiting fees it would earn a daily fortune. Some suppliers did not even bother to load up the cement; they just undertook to deliver it and then sent an empty boat to wait outside the port.

The Nigerian government is said to have ordered 18 million tons of cement for its defence ministry. Because the port at Apapa could not cope, the government was obliged to pay out what are called demurrage charges to compensate shipowners for wasted time. Unscrupulous shipowners quickly learned how to fiddle demurrage payments by 'dashing' – bribing – port officials. (Bribery and theft took place on a spectacular scale in European and American ports. But it is fair to say that West Africa holds the record in this respect. Dash is an established custom. If a bribed crane driver, for example, deliberately bounces a container on its corner so that he and his mates can see what is worth stealing in it, veteran expatriates shrug philosophically and murmur, 'Wa-wa!, – which means West Africa wins again!')

Other rackets soon sprang up in the waiting ships. Fires broke out, followed by inflated insurance claims. Rather than wait in line, masters sold their cargo, already paid for by the Nigerians, at other ports. Pirates even raided some of the ships and took them over. At one point Lloyd's underwriters threatened to impose special additional premiums for ships bound for Nigeria.

The effect of the Apapa cement queue was more than local. It attracted criminals the world over and alerted them to the possibilities of marine fraud. There was a definite geographical pattern to the epidemic of fraud, which spread first from West Africa to other parts of the continent, then to the Middle East, especially Lebanon, and finally to the Far East.

It has to be said that the vectors of this epidemic of marine fraud were in a disproportionately high percentage Greeks. An analysis of ninety-three cases involving $1 million or more reported to the International Chamber of Commerce up to 1979 showed that forty-six involved ships were under the Greek flag, twenty-four under that of Panama (many of them also no doubt owned by Greeks) and sixteen under that of Cyprus. The remaining seven ships were of six other nationalities. It is also true, of course, that a high proportion of all the world's shipping is in Greek hands – but not so high as the proportion of marine fraud. As the Union of Greek Shipowners is quick to point out, Greeks are also prominent among the victims of fraud. There are in any case plenty of ingenious rogues of all nationalities at the game. But it has to be said that Piraeus is the world capital of marine crime, the home of many petty defrauders of the sea and of some of the master criminals who have organized its grandest coups.

There are four main kinds of marine fraud. Insurers in the marine market at Lloyd's, who insure both hulls and cargoes and often both, end up paying for all of them: documentary frauds, where the defrauder gets paid on the basis of faked documents; charter frauds, where he pays just enough money to get control of a ship and load it with valuable cargo, and then decamps with them both and sells them;

scuttling, sometimes called the rustbucket fraud, whereby the whole profit comes from the insurers; and infinite varieties of cargo theft. All these scams are as old as the sea, and all of them multiplied dramatically in the late 1970s. The most successful known exponent of documentary fraud, mixed with a few refined charter swindles, is a young Greek of genius (he is only in his mid-thirties) called Costas Kameteros. His career is supporting evidence for the theory of the West African connection. In 1976, joining the throng of his enterprising countrymen, he contracted to deliver 100,000 tons of cement to the Maduako Transport Company in Nigeria. The first 70,000 were duly delivered and paid for. Then Kameteros produced faked documents to show that another 25,400 tons had been loaded on to three ships, against which papers the London branch of an African bank paid out $1·7 million. Kameteros then added an elegant touch. He sent off messages saying that most of the (imaginary) Maduako cargo had been loaded from the three ships on to one, the *Cindy*, at Rostock, in East Germany. (The *Cindy* was in fact in Poland at the time.) Then he sold the imaginary cement to another Nigerian firm, Ekimpex. With the money from them, he then really did buy a load of cement, and sent it to Nigeria ... in the *Cindy*! Both Maduako and Ekimpex were firmly convinced it was theirs ...

The next year, 1977, he made several million dollars from another Nigerian firm by selling it condensed milk, supposed to be on board a ship whose name Kameteros changed in rapid succession five times. The cargo was sold in the end in Beirut – a good example of the way quick-witted criminals moved from one target of opportunity, Nigeria, to another, Lebanon. Kameteros then pulled off a whole string of daring coups. In one of them he was alleged to have collected no less than $30 million from shippers for goods that were never delivered. The bait was an offer of cheap freight on a proposed shipping line from Europe to Africa. But Kameteros's masterpiece was the voyage of the *Aristoteles*. In the summer of 1978 she loaded a general cargo worth over $7 million for various consignees in West Africa. She got as far as Dakar. Then she disappeared. Several months later she turned up in the Piraeus with most of the cargo, including a large quantity of powdered milk, still on board. The creditors managed to arrest her. But then she was sold at auction, for less than her scrap value, to a Cypriot company with links to an entity Kameteros had used before: the Arab International Bank and Trust Company of Florida, registered, in spite of its name, in, of all places, the tiny island of Montserrat in the Leeward Islands. The *Aristoteles*'s new owners first tried to tow her to Cyprus. They were stopped by a court order. Then the *Aristoteles* quietly slipped her moorings and sailed for Tripoli in the Lebanon. Minimally disguised as the *Tote*, with the first four and the last three letters of her name crudely painted out, she unloaded her cargo, no doubt for famine prices, to one of the factions in the chaotic Lebanese civil war. Then she disappeared again.

But that was not the end of the story. The ingenuity of Costas Kameteros was not exhausted. The story is best told in the words of Barbara Conway, of the London *Daily Telegraph*, as she unravelled it in her book *The Piracy Business*:

In early 1979 a Greek called Papadopoulos [a name roughly as common in Greek as Smith is in English] rented a small shed at the side of a farmhouse in Assendelft in Holland, installed a telex and set up as a shipping office. The shed was rented in the name of Omega Marine of Cyprus, a non-existent company.

In March 1979 Omega registered a ship, the *Gloria L*, in Panama ... whose description matches in every way that of the vanished *Aristoteles*. [The *Gloria L*] loaded a general cargo, including steel bars, cement, joists and a large consignment of batteries, in European ports, destined for Abu Dhabi. She started the voyage for the Gulf on 14 July, and was logged en route at Suez on 12 August. Nothing more was heard of the *Gloria* for over a month. Then, in late September, she appeared off the Lebanese coast at Aquamarine and discharged her cargo to the local faction, the Christian PNL party.

This was only one of a whole series of incidents in the late 1970s when ships were diverted to the Lebanon. The Manchester *Guardian* reported no fewer than four such incidents in the single month of October 1979. World attention was focused on this strange business by the international row over one of those four incidents, the case of the *Betty*, a.k.a. *Black Eagle*, *Ares* and *Star Five*. Owned by the Greek Pero Shipping Company of Nicosia, Cyprus, the *Betty* was chartered by a firm in Genoa, and loaded 3,500 tons of steel in Chioggia, Italy, and 500 cubic metres of wood in Rijeka, Yugoslavia, bound for Jeddah in Saudi Arabia. On 18 August she called at the remote port of Pylos, home of Homer's legendary King Nestor, on the west coast of Greece, ostensibly for stores. While she was there, she changed her name and her crew. Again, her cargo found its way to the improvised port at the beach resort of Aquamarina, near Jounieh, north of Beirut, where it was sold for $1·7 million. Saudi merchants learned that goods they were waiting for were being sold in the Lebanese street markets. They were furious and put pressure on the Saudi government, which promptly banned from its ports all ships that had previously visited the Lebanon. The Greek authorities arrested two lawyers, one of them a well-connected figure who served as director of the port of Piraeus under the Greek military dictatorship, and a shipowner.

A similar case, that of the *Alexandros K*, is worth noting because its protagonist, Captain Dimitrios Georgoulis, cropped up later in an even more famous episode. *Alexandros K* loaded up with 3,000 tons of steel bars in Bulgaria in December 1978. The cargo had been pre-sold. But when the ship put into Piraeus in March 1979, the cargo, now shown on the *Alexandros K*'s documents to have been loaded at Ravenna in Italy, was sold to a Spanish company, which swiftly resold it to an Egyptian. The Egyptian flew to Piraeus to check his cargo. It was the last he was to see of it. That same night, in a thick fog, the *Alexandros K* slipped her anchor and stole out into the Aegean. Six weeks later, a ship called the *Leila* discharged 3,000 tons of steel bars at Zouk in the Lebanon. It was the *Alexandros K*.

What was happening was that a number of astute and well-connected Greek businessmen saw in the Lebanese civil war an opportunity for extraordinarily profitable fraud. Because of the war, the port of Beirut was closed to the Christians, and all factions, Christian and Muslim, were reduced to landing urgently needed supplies at improvised ports, some of them little more than beaches. Sometimes the goods were sold direct from their containers on the shore, sometimes spirited away by armed men belonging to the private militias that proliferated in the savagely divided country. The Lebanese desperately needed supplies of almost everything. They would ask no questions about where it came from. And they would pay high prices. The Greeks masterminding the operation could make several profits. They could be paid for the cargoes by the original buyers. They could claim insurance on both vessel and cargo. If they could make the ship disappear, and that was not always possible, they could sell that too. And finally they could make the Lebanese pay through the nose at the end of the line.

The Saudi government was not the only one to be infuriated by such barefaced frauds. It was in 1976 that the Angolan government import agency, Importang, bought 1,000 tons of palm oil from a forty-four-year-old Lisbon businessman with Angolan connections called Manuel José Pires. Pires and his partner, Mario Rogowski of Madrid, guaranteed delivery and asked the Angolans to open a letter of credit in their favour at the Union Bank of Switzerland in Zurich for $560,000. Soon afterwards, a bill of lading in proper form and the other necessary documents were produced, showing that the oil had been loaded on to a freighter, suitably called the *Cool Girl*, for delivery to Angola. The

Union Bank duly paid over the money.

Two months later – still not having received the palm oil, which was not surprising, given that at the time when she was supposed to be loading her cargo, the *Cool Girl* was in fact in dry dock in Rotterdam – Importang contacted Pires and Rogowski and ordered 1,500 tons of beef. This time the bills of lading were made out showing the cargo as loaded on the *Maco Viking*, owned by the same helpful Copenhagen businessman who had procured the *Cool Girl*. This time the ship was undergoing major repairs at a shipyard in Norway. Nobody bothered even to go through the motions of buying any beef. And this time the Union Bank of Switzerland, on the production of documents, handed over $1·6 million.

In the meantime the Angolans had placed an even bigger order with Pires, for 13,420 tons of 'dehulled groundnuts suitable for the extraction of oil', c.i.f. Luanda and Lobito. The order was worth $6,844,200. Pires asked for the money to be sent to the Union Bank, and Importang specified the documents he would have to produce in order to be paid. They included, as well as the usual bill of lading, insurance policy and invoices, certificates of origin, weight, quantity, quality and packing. This time Pires – Rogowski and the Danish businessman had by this time dropped out of the story – contacted Doraldo Perreira Lima, owner of Lima Navigation, a shipping company operating out of Hamburg but registered in Bermuda. Lima owned no ships, but chartered two, both Greek-owned, the *Pistis* and the *Saronicos Gulf*. In Greek, *Pistis* means 'good faith', which is ironic, because at the time when the Lima documents stated that both ships were loading with groundnuts at the port of Beira, on the east coast of southern Africa, one of them was already at Luanda, on the Atlantic coast, and the other was in dry dock in Greece. Nevertheless, having been presented with documents certifying that the *Pistis* had been loaded with 57,401 bags of groundnuts, and the *Saronicos Gulf* with 116,885 bags, for a total weight of 13,420 tons, the officials of the Union Bank of Switzerland considered that they were obliged to pay out the full $6,844,200.

To cut a very long story short – a story of freighters wandering aimlessly from one small African port to another, of sealed envelopes to be opened only when the vessel was at sea, of altered documents and convoluted chicanery – the two ships finally landed in Angola with cargoes, and shortweight cargoes at that, not of groundnuts but of groundnut cake, which is what is left when the oil that the Angolans so badly wanted has been extracted from the nuts.

The Angolans had been sold a suitcase full of rocks. Understandably they were furious. Eventually they got their money back. They sued not Pires and his fellow-conspirators, but the Swiss Bank and the ship-owners, and including their legal costs they won a total of over $9·5 million. But they were so angry that they arrested not only the *Pistis* and the *Saronicos Gulf*, but two other perfectly innocent Greek-owned freighters unfortunate enough to be in the port of Luanda at the time. More than four years later, all four ships were still under arrest there. Pires and his friends are still free to enjoy the more than $9 million they deftly removed from a country that was trying to make up with imports for the shortfall of its own food production.

Angola is a poor country, but Somalia is even poorer. According to the World Bank, it is the eighth poorest country in the world, with an average income per inhabitant of between $130 and $140. In 1974, hit by a drought, the Somali government decided to buy 10,000 tons of sugar, and entrusted the purchasing to a Somali with Kenyan nation-ality in Mombasa, Kenya. This man was put in touch with a Chinese-owned trading company in Singapore, which in turn opened negotia-tions with a Chinese businessman in Bangkok known as 'Mr Chern'. Chern agreed to supply the Somalis with the sugar, and asked for a letter of credit to be sent by them to the Moscow Narodny Bank's branch in Singapore. He duly handed over documents indicating that 10,000 tons of sugar had been loaded before 24 June 1974 on a ship called the *Delwind*, bound from Bangkok to Berbera. On receipt of these documents, the Russian bank paid over the money it had been credited with by the Somalis, $5·9 million, to a company fronting for Mr Chern. It had been created only two weeks earlier, and had a paid-up capital of just two US dollars.

The *Delwind*, of course, was nowhere near Bangkok or Singapore at the time. In May she made her way across the Pacific from Van-couver to Osaka, in Japan, where she went into dry dock, was sold to an Italian owner and changed her name. As for the sugar, the Somalis were surprised to receive a telegram purporting to come from a Captain Michalopoulos, master of the Greek freighter *Lord Byron*, announcing that 687 tons of sugar had been transferred from the *Delwind* to his vessel in the Nicobar Islands, in the middle of the Indian Ocean. The *Delwind* at the time was nowhere near the islands. Nothing was ever heard of the rest of the sugar. And poor Michalopoulos sailed in-nocently into Berbera to face the wrath of the Somali Revolutionary Council. In spite of the combined efforts of representatives of the Dutch owners, the Greek agents and British lawyers representing the P & I Club involved, and several embassies, the Somalis could not be prevented from throwing Captain Michalopoulos into prison. Released after nine months, he died in hospital of heart failure. The *Lord Byron* was held in Berbera for more than five years.

In terms of international maritime law, the Somali Revolutionary Council's actions had been as high-handed as those of any Barbary pirate. But see it from their side. In dire need to feed their people, they had handed over – admittedly with absurdly inadequate precautions – a sum equal to more than 1 per cent of the country's gross national product, only to see it disappear into thin air, or rather into the bank account of a wealthy Chinese crook in Bangkok. The *Lord Byron* and its crew were the only cards they held. Who can blame them for using them to try to get back either their money or their sugar? The go-between in Mombasa is said to have made $1·5 million. 'Mr Chern' is said to have died. But it is also said that reports of his death are premature, and that he has been seen around Bangkok, several million dollars to the good.

Barratry in marine law is the offence of 'fraud or gross and criminal negligence on the part of the master or mariners of a ship, to the prejudice of the owners and without their consent'. That, too, can be a danger for modern underwriters, just as it was one of the perils the owner of the *Tiger* wanted to be insured against in 1613; and not always in the most obvious ways. That was what underwriters learned from the case of the *Michael*, properly known as *Piermay Shipping Co. SA and Brandt's Ltd* versus *Chester*, heard over forty days in 1977 and 1978 in the Commercial Court in London.

The story went back almost ten years before that. In December 1968 a ship called *Gold Sky* sank in the Mediterranean thirty miles off Gibraltar. The Greek owners sued Lloyd's underwriters, who refused to pay the claim because they suspected that the *Gold Sky* had been scuttled. The law is that, since barratry is a crime, a court will not find that it has been committed unless it has been proved beyond all reasonable doubt. In a civil action, however, a court is entitled to find that barratry has been committed on the balance of probabilities, and this is what Mr Justice Mocatta did in the *Gold Sky* case. In particular, the judge clearly did not believe the evidence of the *Gold Sky*'s third engineer, a man with a criminal record called Stylianos E. Komiseris. Komiseris testified that the ship sank because of a crack in the hull. The judge clearly believed that she had beeen scuttled, and found that the owners had failed to establish that she had been lost 'by the perils of the sea', even though the evidence was not sufficient to establish beyond reasonable doubt that she had been scuttled.

The solicitors who acted for Lloyd's underwriters in the *Gold Sky* case were the well-known firm of Ince & Co., and the Ince partner in charge of the case was Michael Baker-Harber. For several days he sat a few feet away from Komiseris while the latter gave evidence. That was in the spring of 1972. In January 1973 another Greek-owned freighter, the *Michael*, was on a voyage from Baton Rouge, Louisiana, to Puerto Cabello, Venezuela, with a cargo of soda ash when she developed engine trouble in heavy seas. The engines stopped. The master sent an SOS and two salvage tugs hurried to the rescue. At the very moment when the first tug to arrive was attempting to pass a towing cable (subsequently cast off by the *Michael*'s crew for no good reason), the engine room began to flood. The officer of the watch in charge of the *Michael* during this double calamity was none other than Komiseris, who had flown out to join the ship in Mobile, Alabama, immediately before her last voyage. The crew, aware that the water was shark-infested, quickly abandoned ship and were taken by one of the tugs, the *Cardon*, to Curaçao. The *Michael* sank and became a claim for a total loss on underwriters at Lloyd's, where the slip was led by the Chester box.

By chance Michael Baker-Harber of Ince had business in Curaçao, and certain similarities between the *Michael* and *Gold Sky* losses aroused his curiosity. So he was there when the crew came down the gangplank of the *Cardon*. What happened next was described thus by Mr Justice Kerr in the subsequent trial: Baker-Harber 'immediately recognized Komiseris, and Komiseris immediately recognized him. Komiseris apparently said something like, "Oh, not you! It is not possible!" Both appear to have roared with laughter; in one of a number of photographs taken by Mr Baker-Harber, Komiseris does not seem at all put out by the encounter.'

So here was a man with a criminal record, suspected in court by a judge of scuttling one ship, and now caught close to red-handed scuttling another; it was common ground between the parties in court that the *Michael* had been deliberately scuttled by Komiseris. The only question was whether the owner, Nestor Pierrakos, shared responsibility or not. Mr Justice Kerr found that he did not. 'Since Komiseris sank the *Michael* deliberately without any consent or foreknowledge on the part of the owners,' the official record shows, 'the claim for barratry succeeded' and the underwriters had to pay up. It is worth pointing out as a footnote that, since the *Michael*, Nestor Pierrakos has been unlucky enough to lose two more of his ships: the *Prosperity* in 1974 and the *Pallas Athene* in 1978.

The *Michael* case was a blow to underwriters. Many privately took the view that, if they had to pay up in a case like the *Michael*, they would have little chance of standing off any other claim. Henry Chester, however, was characteristically philosophical. 'In a year,' he told me, 'we will be on ten losses we don't like the look of. Of those, seven will be paid straightaway. Two more will be paid eventually. One won't be paid, because the chap will know we've got him to rights.' But the onus of proof is on the underwriter. He has got to prove to the owner that he will win if the case comes to court. Sir Peter Green takes a similar view. 'We often suspect fraud,' he told me. 'The difficulty is to prove it. You can try to call the chap's bluff. But if you can't, then you'll have to pay up, even if the crew came ashore in their best suits.'

Sometimes they do just that. Sometimes, indeed, they get the cook to cut them sandwiches before they take to the boats. But if you are an underwriter, you still have to prove that a ship was scuttled, or pay.

In the late 1970s, though, there was one part of the world where scuttling was getting so brazen that marine underwriters from Lloyd's and other markets took the unprecedented step of getting together and paying for an investigation of suspicious claims.

In 1977–9 more than forty ships sank in dubious circumstances in the South China Sea. The pattern of claims led to rumours that a single syndicate, with its headquarters in Taiwan but with branch offices in Hong Kong, Singapore and Bangkok, was coordinating an epidemic of scuttling and fraudulent cargo insurance claims.

Two casualties in 1978 brought insurers' indignation to a head. One was the *Delta Sigma Pi*, owned by a Hong Kong company called Tyler Navigation. Tyler had lost two ships previously in suspicious circumstances, the *Andy* in 1976 *en route* for Lagos, Nigeria, and the *Atalanta*. The *Delta Sigma Pi* sank in shallow water near Bangkok, apparently trying to make it out to sea before going under. The crew tried to set the ship on fire, no doubt in order to conceal the fact that she was empty, though a large cargo of rice and fish bound for West Africa (again that connection!) was insured on her. She had only a small quantity of bunker oil on board for the long voyage. And all of this was observed from an Interpol helicopter overhead.

The second case, that of the *Starter*, was equally embarrassing. She was in ballast, in spite of insurances claiming cargo on board. The crew abandoned her not far from Hong Kong, and the master reported her sunk in heavy seas. But the seas were not too heavy for mainland Chinese fishermen, who spotted her, plugged her leaks and towed her to their commune. The owner's ill luck with other ships was described by one cynical expert as 'bordering on the supernatural'.

As a result of these scandals, and of suspect insurance claims totalling at least $100 million, $45 million of them still outstanding, the marine insurance industry in the Far East decided to suspend its normal internecine competition. Lloyd's Underwriters Association and the Institute of London Underwriters (representing the London companies) joined the marine insurance associations of Hong Kong, Japan, Taiwan, Singapore, Indonesia and Malaysia. Together they set up the Far Eastern Regional Investigation Team, appropriately acronymed FERIT, in April 1979.

The FERIT investigation was carried out by only four men, and it ended after only four months – neither enough hands nor enough time to get to the bottom of such a tightly woven network of ingenious rackets. Underwriters were unwilling to spend more than £50,000 ($75,000) on it, not much in proportion to the amount they had lost and were losing because of the frauds. All told, FERIT did not delve as deeply into all the ramifications of the scuttling business as it might have done. And in the true Lloyd's spirit its report was kept confidential, ostensibly to avoid prejudicing subsequent criminal prosecutions, but perhaps also to throw the mask of charity and oblivion over the extent to which – as the shipping journal *Seatrade* put it – 'insurers have paid out on claims they knew to be fraudulent in order not to prejudice future business, the reinsurers thereby having to follow on although on occasions they have delayed payment long enough for investigators to be able to put a case together'.

Still, with all its imperfections, the FERIT investigation assembled some suggestive information. It looked at more than sixty sinkings, and chose forty-eight of those for a closer look. Of those forty-eight, twenty-eight within the past two years were judged to have been lost in 'suspicious' circumstances; and of those, sixteen were in all probability scuttled. The same was true of at least another eleven earlier sinkings. So at least twenty-seven ships, in the team's estimation, and perhaps many more, have been scuttled; and in many cases cargo frauds will have milked underwriters of far larger sums than the insured values of the predominantly small, old ships that were sunk.

FERIT rejected the rumours that a single syndicate was responsible for all the losses, but it acknowledged that a number of identifiable groups – perhaps five of them – were each responsible for more than one loss, and that these groups seemed to have cooperated with one another to some extent. The majority of these groups, operating out of Taiwan, Hong Kong and Singapore, were run by overseas ethnic Chinese, though at least one Indian businessman, in Hong Kong, was also involved. A Chinese businessman, known as 'Mr A' and also sometimes referred to as the 'Boss', was said to have been connected with no fewer than eleven ships that sank in suspicious circumstances. He and others involved in the scuttling and insurance rackets were also said to have been implicated in the cruel traffic in 'boat people' trying to escape from Vietnam.

The essence of the racket was simple. The scuttlers got hold of smallish, ancient ships. (The typical rustbucket involved would be at least fifteen years old, probably built and inspected in Japan, of less than 3,000 gross rated tons, and, in no less than 84 per cent of the cases examined, registered in Panama.) They insured them for high but not incredible figures, say anything from $500,000 to $1 million. They faked bills of lading saying that valuable cargoes (in one case Japanese stereo equipment, in another a most improbably large proportion of the world's clove harvest) were on board. Sometimes the cargo was real, but was unloaded before the ship was sunk. Sometimes it was never there at all. Then the ship was sunk, and the insurance claimed. Simplicity itself, given nerve and connections, and the overseas Chinese are not short of either. A high proportion of all these doomed ships, indeed, turned out to belong to fly-by-night companies registered in a single office building across from the Western market in one of the less elegant neighbourhoods of Hong Kong, the Kai Tak Commercial Building.

Scuttling, then, was in high fashion in the Orient in the late 1970s, and it was very much on underwriters' minds. But nothing in their experience, or in the *modus operandi* of the scuttlers they had so far come across, Greek or Chinese, prepared them for what was to come in the New Year of 1980, which must be rated as the most ambitious marine crime since Sir Francis Drake stole the Spanish treasure fleet. For the first time, in a plot whose sheer international scope illustrated the dangerous new world Lloyd's had to cope with, a gang of modern pirates hijacked a supertanker, stole her cargo and scuttled her. Once again, Lloyd's was painfully involved.

On 17 January 1980 the marine radio station at Portishead, near Bristol, that citizen's band of the sea, picked up and relayed to the Lloyd's intelligence services at Colchester a terse and seamanlike message from the master of the 210,550 dwt tanker *Salem*. He was no longer on board his command, which was then settling slowly into one of the deepest trenches in the North Atlantic, 150 miles or so south-west of Dakar, at the tip of West Africa. He was reporting over the radio of the British Petroleum tanker *British Trident*, which had fished him and his crew out of their boats a couple of hours before:

At 1509 G M T Jan 17: Vessel due fire and explosions abandoned 0530 G M T Jan 16 and sunk 1136 Jan 17 in lat 12 38N, long 18 34W. All crew collected safe by *British Trident* at 1235 Jan 17. Proceeding Dakar for disembarkation E T A 2300 today – Master s tank *Salem*.

That message concealed much more than it gave away. It passed over, for a start, a moment of supreme farce. We have met the master of the *Salem* before: Dimitrios Georgoulis, master of the *Alexandros K*, the freighter that slipped away from Piraeus in May 1979 and turned up as the *Leila* in the Lebanon. 'Captain' Georgoulis maintains that he knows nothing of that adventure, and that he left the ship at Piraeus. But then he also maintains that he has a Liberian master's certificate, when it is in truth that of a Pakistani third engineer. Georgoulis was asked by the Greek police not to leave the country until he had finished helping them with their inquiries into the *Alexandros K* affair. Instead, on 10 October, using a United States passport in the name of Jimmy Georgoulis, he flew to Malta to take charge of a crew of Greek officers and Tunisian sailors waiting to take over a tanker called the *Paula*. Around 1 November the crew flew to Dar-es-Salaam, in Tanzania, to pick up another ship. Only on 30 November at Dubai, in the Persian Gulf, did Georgoulis and his crew go on board the *Salem*. He declined the usual offer of her previous owners, Hong-Kong-based, British-owned Pimmerton Shipping, to lend him one of their officers to break him in to his new command. Instead, the chief engineer was surrepti-tiously offered $5,000 for a short-term contract, which he refused. It is said that one of the first things Georgoulis said after coming on board was to ask whether the *Salem* had charts for South Africa.

Georgoulis took his ship up the Gulf to Mina' al Ahmadi, in Kuwait, and there loaded a cargo of 193,000 tons of Kuwaiti light crude. On 27 December he unloaded 178,000 tons of that cargo at the Shell oil terminal off Durban, South Africa. That night Georgoulis telephoned two men in Zug, between Zurich and Lucerne, Switzerland, from the Royal Hotel in Durban. One of the men was a Greek, Nikolaos Mitakis. The other, Anton Reidel, is a Dutchman who has connections with a Swiss company called Beets Trading A G in Zug and with South Africa. The next day the *Salem* set off again, ostensibly for Gibraltar and Europe. Two and a half weeks later, Georgoulis was on the point of crowning four months of work and waiting by putting the finishing touches to a perfectly executed operation and sliding the *corpus delicti* into 2,000 fathoms of water when the officious *British Trident* had to spoil it all by bustling up over the northern horizon.

From that moment on, it was always going to be hard to keep the true story quiet. The crew were in the lifeboats with their suitcases packed, and the lifeboats had been abundantly provisioned, with plenty of cigarettes. There had been time for that; but not to rescue the *Salem*'s log! No SOS message was sent until the crew were already in the boats; interestingly enough, the radio officer, Vassilios Evangelides, had failed to use his radio until a very late stage in the sinking of another ship he was on, the *Brilliant*. Even more curiously, the *Brilliant* belonged to Gregorios Makrygiorgos, the owner of the *Alexandros K*, involved in a notorious case of piracy in 1979. Although Georgoulis's version, duly relayed to Lloyd's by Portishead, was that there had been explosions thirty hours earlier, it emerged later that the *Salem* went down in sight of the *British Trident* and her crew, who saw no explosions but only orange smoke from emergency signal rockets, artistically ignited. There was, moreover, a small oil slick from the sinking tanker, but nothing like what there would have been if she had been full of 193,000 tons of crude, almost as much as the cargo of the *Amoco Cadiz*.

Where had the oil gone? It was only a matter of days before one of the Tunisian crewmen, on his way home through Paris, spilled the beans. The *Salem* had unloaded its cargo in South Africa.

The oil boycott of South Africa is a striking result of the new alliance between the Arab and black African nations. The Organization of Petroleum Exporting Countries (OPEC), largely though not entirely made up of Arab countries, boycotts South Africa in return for the black African countries boycotting Israel. South Africa, with a major manufacturing economy and virtually no domestic oil supplies, is perpetually thirsty for oil, and the state oil refining and distributing company, Sasol, is always ready to buy crude at well above the world market price and ask no questions. Not only that: strict censorship makes it hard for anyone else to ask too many questions about where South Africa is getting her oil.

So South Africa provided one component of a tempting deal: a willing buyer. To satisfy the South Africans it would be necessary to put together three other elements: the ship, the cargo and the crew.

The story of how the *Salem* came to be the ship begins with the meeting, somewhere in the world, probably by chance, of Anton Reidel, the Dutch businessman with a Swiss company and South African connections and incidentally a previous conviction for smuggling American cigarettes into Italy, and a young Lebanese–American businessman, living in Houston, Texas, called Frederick Ed Soudan. He had gone to the United States in 1972 at the age of twenty-nine, and for the next six years made a modest living as an insurance salesman. His home was in Missouri City, Texas, an unpretentious suburb of Houston. In 1978 he branched out into commodity broking and began to travel widely, apparently trying to do deals in cement, steel and oil. But as one of his partners said, 'We were never able to complete a deal.' It was this obscure businessman who suddenly set out to buy a super-tanker. Beginning in September 1979, he began approaching ship-brokers in New York and London looking for a tanker to buy and a shell company registered in a flag-of-convenience country to own it. He found what he wanted. Northern Ships Agency, of 1 World Trade Center, New York, owned a shell company called Oxford Shipping, registered in Monrovia, Liberia, and Soudan made arrangements to buy it. In the meantime, through a London broker, Elder Smith Golds-brough Mort Ltd, he had found a ship.

She was built by Kockums in Malmö, Sweden, in 1969; a 210,550 ton single-screw steam-turbine tanker. At the time she was an ultra-modern ship. She was built for a Stockholm shipping line, Salenrederierna, who called her *Sea Sovereign* and operated her until 1977, when they pulled out of tankers and sold her to Pimmerton Shipping, whose president is an Englishman, Michael Steele, who is also a director of Wallem Shipping in Hong Kong. For two years, renamed the *South Sun*, she was chartered back to Salenrederierna and operated profitably. But now she was getting old, and she was due for a refit, costing $1·25 million, so Pimmerton decided to sell. Pimmerton wanted $11·5 million for the *South Sun*, plus $750,000 for the 5,000 tons of fuel in her bunkers. 'There was no argy-bargying,' Michael Steele remembered. Soudan produced a letter of credit from the London branch of Manufacturers Hanover Trust, and the sale went through.

Soudan later claimed that the purchase money came from his father's estate. His father had died in Beirut, he said, 'leaving me an awful lot of money'. In fact, Manufacturers Hanover Trust were simply acting as the London correspondents for a Johannesburg bank, Merca Bank, and it was paying the money on behalf of a South African company called Haven International.

Back in August, Soudan had gone to South Africa at the suggestion of Anton Reidel and with introductions from Reidel to two South African businessmen, Jim Shorrock and Jack Austin. These two registered Haven International on 19 October after they first met Soudan. According to Soudan, he discussed deals in several other commodities, including coal, and was asked if he could arrange any oil deliveries. The $12·3 million advanced by Haven to pay for the tanker was completely unsecured except for the contract Haven had with Sasol. Indeed, it may have been an advance against the purchase price of the oil.

It was on 27 November that the memorandum of agreement was signed between Pimmerton and Oxford Shipping, represented by an associate of Soudan's, Dr Wahib Attar. But one section of the document was countersigned by Anton Reidel. The contract of sale transferring Oxford Shipping from the New York shipbrokers to Soudan was dated the same day, 27 November, although it was not actually signed until later. And, indeed, the deal was to go badly wrong.

The very day after the oil was delivered in South Africa, 28 December, Fred Soudan called Andrew Triandafilou, one of the partners in Northern Ships, and asked him how he wanted to be paid. He was asked to call back. When, after suspicious delays, his lawyer contacted Triandafilou's lawyer, he was told it was too late, and furthermore that Soudan himself had already been told in Europe by Anton Reidel that he, Reidel, was going to buy Oxford Shipping and so become the owner of the *Salem*. A furious dispute resulted, and Soudan filed for an injunction in New York. In order to do so, he had to file a copy of his original agreement with Northern Ships, and that agreement contained two immensely interesting clauses which were now on the public record.

Clause 3 reads: 'Purchaser agreed to pay the purchase price of $300,000 to Northern Ships Agency, Inc., or its nominee on or about 27 December 1979 upon arrival of the vessel SOUTH SUN off Durban, South Africa (closing date) or any other discharge port.'

Clause 14, however, states: 'This Agreement is exclusively contingent upon and subject to the lifting of a cargo of crude oil by the vessel SOUTH SUN and the arrival of the vessel at Durban, South Africa and commencement of discharging. In the event that the said contingency does not occur, Purchaser shall then pay to the Sellers the amount of TWENTY-FIVE THOUSAND DOLLARS ($25,000) . . .'

In other words, when Soudan bought Oxford Shipping, and Oxford Shipping bought *South Sun*, he knew, and in all probability his friend and mentor Anton Reidel knew, that it was intended to use the tanker to deliver a load of crude oil to Durban on 27 December. And that is exactly what happened.

Where did the oil come from? From Kuwait. Who owned it? By the time it was unloaded off Durban, it belonged to Shell International Trading of London, an operating subsidiary of the Royal Dutch-Shell Group, the world's second-biggest oil company. Shell bought the oil on the 'spot' market on 14 December, while the tanker was still *en route* from the Persian Gulf to Durban, from an Italian firm called Pontoil of Genoa. Shell paid $56 million, to be completed on 23 January 1980 after the oil had been delivered to France.

That is all simple enough, though eyebrows have been raised at the fact that Shell bought a cargo on a ship with totally unknown owners, and also that the price was a fraction above the spot rate at the time. What takes a little more explaining is how the Pontoil cargo found its way on to the *Salem* in the first place.

Back in October, a man calling himself Bert Stein rented a small office at 43 Schaffhauser Strasse in Zurich from Heinrich Frey, who owned the building, and put up a shingle for a Liberian-registered shipping company called Shipomex. 'Bert Stein' was almost certainly not his real name. The passport he used was one of a series of stolen West German passport blanks. Shown a picture of the man they had known as 'Stein', a number of people in Zurich identified a West German businessman called Thomas Jurgen Locks, aged thirty-three. Locks says he knows nothing about the affair. But it appears that it was Shipomex, in the person of the mysterious Stein, that arranged to charter the *Salem* from Oxford Shipping to lift the Pontoil cargo, and to arrange the crew.

The man who called himself Stein arrived in October in the office of Captain Nikolaos Mitakis in a building in the Piraeus. Out of one room in that building Mitakis runs the Mitzinafir Navigation Company and the Euroafrican Corporation with the aid of one secretary. According to Lloyd's intelligence services, he also owns a shipping company in Cyprus. He has owned two vessels and had the misfortune to lose them both. Mitakis undertook to recruit a crew for Stein's tanker, and he also found the cargo.

Pontoil in Genoa asked their brokers, Nolarma, to find them a tanker for a load of 193,000 tons of Kuwaiti light to be picked up at Mina' al Ahmadi. Nolarma contacted the well-known London shipbrokers Galbraith Wrightson, who have a long-standing relationship with the equally reputable firm of Genpe Shipping in the Piraeus. Mitakis told the senior partner of Genpe that he represented Shipomex and that he had a tanker looking for a cargo. Pontoil quickly agreed to charter the *Salem*.

It was Mitakis who recruited the crew, it seems. He has stated that the name of the Captain, Georgoulis, was suggested to him by 'Stein'. That may or may not be true. The chief engineer was Antonios Kalo-miropoulos, aged thirty-four. There were peculiarities about Mitakis's team. For one thing, though the master, Georgoulis, had no valid master's certificate, the first officer, Andreas Annivas, did; not only that, he was a shipowner in his own right. Georgoulis, again, had been the skipper of a small dry cargo. He is not known to have had any experience of driving a supertanker. There are reports that he did do some training on a VLCC called *Albahaa B*, and that at one time it was intended to use her, rather than the first choice, the *Paula*, for the South African venture. The *Albahaa B* was saved, but not for long. On 3 April 1980 she exploded and sank off the East African coast with the loss of six lives, among them the master's nephew. She was linked with another tragedy, too. She was owned by the Fadi Shipping Group of Saudi Arabia, whose president, Aladin Hasan Bari, disappeared in his private jet with five people, including his English secretary, on a flight from Athens to Saudi Arabia.

Now all four corners of the deal – the ship, the cargo, the crew and the buyer – were in place.

It remains only to count the profits and losses; that, and to unravel what may have been one plot, or several plots that became intertwined.

The South Africans gained 1·3 million barrels of oil, or enough to keep their economy going for a week or so. There are some indications that the original plan may have envisaged Haven International buying not one but six cargoes of oil from Soudan. If so, then the cost of the tanker would have been spread over six times as much oil.

Sasol, the South African state oil company, paid $43·5 million through the Volkskas Bank of Johannesburg into the account of Beets Trading – the company Anton Reidel was associated with – with the Crédit Suisse's branch at Zug. The price sounds low, considering that Shell paid $56 million two weeks earlier for the same cargo. But if the purchase price included the advance paid through Haven International to buy the tanker, $12·5 million, then the South Africans paid about the same price for their oil, except that they only received 178,000 tons out of the 193,000 on board.

Both the Tunisian crewmen and the Greek officers are said to have been handsomely paid off. The principals and organizers profited even more. The lion's share of the profits went to an entrepreneur, or syndicate of entrepreneurs, who stayed in the background throughout the venture. That would seem to be the implication of the movement of funds from the Crédit Suisse account in Zug. The same day the money arrived, 28 December, $3 million was shifted to an account with Paribas (the biggest French private bank) at its branch in Geneva. Of that, some $300,000 went to the principals of Haven International as commission, and around $100,000 to another South African who helped to arrange the financing. Another $8 million was paid into a number of nominee accounts in various countries. It is reasonable to guess that this represented the appropriately generous wages for the men who carried the scheme out. That left at least $20 million, on the assumption that the South Africans paid themselves back the $12·5 million they had advanced before paying out; or well over $30 million if it is assumed that the full price was $56 million and the advance was deducted from that. This balance was paid into an account at the Union Bank of Switzerland in Geneva in the name of a Greek national. One investigator claims that, shortly afterwards, five hired Mercedes cars drew up outside the bank. The five chauffeurs accompanied their master into the bank. Each carried two briefcases. The millions from the *Salem* were withdrawn in cash, stuffed into the briefcases, loaded into the Mercedes and driven over the border into Italy. Whether that happened or not, the millions in the UBS must be the reward of the man, or men, who conceived of this audacious enterprise.

So much for the winners. Who were the losers?

Captain Georgoulis and Chief Engineer Kalamiropoulos at least had to sweat for their reward. They were exhaustively questioned, first by the Senegalese, then by the Greek authorities. Then they were extradited to Monrovia, Liberia, and were due to go on trial in June 1980 on charges carrying a maximum of ten years' imprisonment. Before they could be tried, however, Master Sergeant Samuel Doe had overthrown the government of President Tolbert of Liberia. He showed no mercy to members of the old régime, some of whom were publicly shot on the beach near the capital. But he personally visited the jail where the two Greeks were held and freed them.

Fred Soudan is back in Houston, though he has moved into a bigger house in one of the smartest sections of town. He is being sued by Shell, and warrants have been issued by the British authorities against him, Georgoulis, Reidel and Locks on fraud charges. Unless he is irresistibly drawn to visit England, Soudan can probably afford to ignore that warrant, and so can the others. Soudan has not tried to claim the insurance on his ship; he has tried to sell the insurance rights, no doubt at a substantial discount on their face value of $24 million.

Shell paid out $56 million for a cargo that never arrived. No doubt in some embarrassment, Sasol has paid a proportion of that. Shell has been helpful to the South Africans over oil supplies in the past, not least by helping to break the sanctions that barred international oil companies from sending oil to South Africa's ally, Rhodesia (now Zimbabwe). Sasol paid $30.5 million. The balance is in dispute between Shell and Lloyd's underwriters.

The cargo was insured on a slip initialled by sixty-nine Lloyd's syndicates and twenty-nine companies. Lloyd's is resisting the claim. In April 1982, a London court found for Shell, holding that the *Salem*'s cargo was lost as a result of a peril, namely scuttling, against which Shell were insured. Underwriters appealed, and the case goes to Britain's highest court, the House of Lords, on the question whether Shell were insured under the standard ships' goods contract, or on a wider form of policy that covered all risks, including that of being scuttled.

Lloyd's therefore stood originally to lose as much as $80 million as a result of the *Salem* affair. Because the *British Trident* steamed over the horizon in the nick of time, no claim for the loss of the hull has been made, and rather more than half of the value of the cargo has been made good by the South Africans. In the end, even if underwriters do lose in the House of Lords, the *Salem* will be no more than one big claim among many.

There is another, more delicate question: whether underwriters will have done their reputation any harm by fighting this claim. On the one hand, $25 million is a lot of money, even when spread among almost a hundred syndicates and companies. No one can blame underwriters for feeling it is their duty to protect their Names from losses of that magnitude if they are advised by their lawyers that they do not have to pay. On the other hand, the decision to dispute the claim was hardly in the tradition of Cuthbert Heath's famous telegram after the San Francisco earthquake: 'Pay all our policy-holders in full irrespective of the terms of their policies.'

More disturbing even than the vast financial losses at stake were the sheer scope and audacity of the conspiracy. The men who stole the *Salem* were capable of thinking on a global scale. They coordinated every element to a precise timetable, yet they were capable of adapting their master plan flexibly to the means available. The action swooped from Houston to the Persian Gulf, from Durban to Switzerland, with the tumblers all clicking meticulously into place. They did not hesitate to take on one of the toughest and most ruthless governments in the world: for it is clear that the organizers turned the tables on the South Africans. They allowed the South Africans to set up a plan for them to supply them with their precious oil; then they planned to add a refinement, by scuttling the ship, and so carrying out a classic manoeuvre, but on a scale a hundred times bigger than that of the routine cargo and rustbucket frauds of the Levant. A detail illustrates the efficiency of their intelligence, the ingenuity of their planning, their determination to leave nothing to chance. Why was the *South Sun* rechristened *Salem*? The choice may not have been accidental. The oil terminal at Durban is operated by Shell, on behalf of a consortium of oil companies. What if someone asked questions about an unknown tanker unloading there? Before arriving off Durban, the tanker's name was changed to *Lema*, an easy change with a bosun's chair and a pot of paint. But not a random change. For Es and Is are almost interchangeable in Greek and sound the same in English. And within a day's sailing of Durban on 27 December there was a real Shell tanker called *Lima, en route* from the Persian Gulf to Holland. Was that sheer coincidence? Or had someone noticed her whereabouts, worked out her inevitable route and cunningly calculated that if the *South Sun* were renamed *Salem*, that could easily be changed to a name that would disarm any casual inquiry when a strange tanker turned up at Durban?

Enemies, pirates, rovers, thieves, jettisons – all those perils of the sea are still with us. The fate of the *Salem* was a reminder that the good ship Lloyd's also ventures through waters that are infested with sharks.

CHAPTER 7

FIRE ON BOARD

Ships and cargoes are sometimes condemned, not so much from real necessity, as because it is in the interests of the parties to abandon, and throw the loss upon the underwriters . . . The too common practice of selling an entire package of goods because a few pieces in it have been injured is entirely illegal.

Letters of instructions to Lloyd's Agents, 1811

On 20 January 1975 two Lloyd's brokers met for lunch at the Savoy Hotel in London. The lunch was pleasant enough. The consequences, for both men and for the society of Lloyd's as a whole, were comprehensively unpleasant. For in a sense that lunch was the starting-point of what came to be known as the *Savonita* affair, an exceptionally bitter, if intrinsically trivial, market row that led to sharply unfriendly scrutiny of Lloyd's in the press and in Parliament. As a result, it played a crucial part in setting up the Fisher inquiry, and thus in the whole process of reform at Lloyd's.

One of the two brokers who met for lunch at the Savoy that day was a short, dark, dynamic man in his early thirties named Malcolm Pearson, chairman and moving spirit of his own firm of Lloyd's brokers, Pearson Webb Springbett. The firm had been founded in September 1964. In April of the following year, Pearson married Francesca Frua de Angeli, daughter of Umberta Nasi, a granddaughter of Senator Giovanni Agnelli, founder of the Fiat automobile and engineering empire and of one of the greatest family fortunes in Europe.

The other man at lunch was an Ulsterman called Robert Arnold, then a senior reinsurance executive with Willis Faber & Dumas, the biggest firm of brokers in the marine market at Lloyd's. Willis Faber alone account for more than one-quarter of all the premium in the Lloyd's marine market; it is a sign of the relative decline of Lloyd's in relation to world markets, and of the success with which the big British brokers have themselves managed to expand beyond the horizons of Lloyd's, that the business Willis Faber bring to Lloyd's is now also only one-quarter of Willis Faber's total brokerage business.

After some non-committal fencing, the two men soon got down to the subject at hand: the competition between their firms for the brokerage to be earned from reinsuring the Fiat group's captive insurance business. At that time the Fiat group's very substantial insurance account was divided between two companies, both affiliates of IFI, the Agnelli family holding company which controls the group. Non-marine business was handled by the Società Assicuratrice Industriale (SAI); marine business was handled by the Società Italiana Assicurazioni Trasporti (SIAT). SIAT was formed in 1968 and was an amalgamation of SAI's cargo insurance interests and the hull-insurance connections of Ugo Fassio. It had originally been owned by various Italian shipowners, but a few years earlier a controlling interest had been bought by the Fiat group, through SAI. Italian shipping interests still owned some 35 per cent of the shares and 4 per cent were owned by Willis Faber. John Prentice, a senior executive and later deputy chairman of Willis Faber, sat on the board.

SIAT's cargo insurance was the responsibility of a man called Gigante. The far more important hull insurance was looked after by Giorgio Mitolo, general manager of SIAT; his superior as managing director was Luigi Atzori. For many years, both the hull and cargo insurance written by SIAT had been reinsured at Lloyd's through Willis Faber. In 1970, however, after the Fiat takeover, Willis Faber lost a piece of SIAT's reinsurance business to Pearson Webb Springbett. In that year Fiat brought in new, specially built ships owned by a Norwegian firm, Ugland, to keep pace with the growing demand for their zippy little sports cars in the United States. Because each ship could carry more than 2,000 cars, worth more than $6 million, SIAT, at the prompting of Fiat management, arranged a top-up 'surplus' reinsurance over and above the normal reinsurance arranged through Willis Faber. It was this surplus cargo cover that was placed through PWS. ('Surplus' simply means surplus to the original underlying reinsurance treaty, whose limits were inadequate for the large values involved. So on a shipment of cars the first layer would be taken by SIAT and its 'treaty' reinsurers; the rest would go to PWS's surplus reinsurers.) PWS placed one-third of this cover with underwriters at Lloyd's, and the balance with various companies in the London market. The arrangement specified that if there was any loss, SIAT would pay Fiat the first $1 million or so, and the underwriters who had signed the PWS slip, No. 74/54126, would be responsible for reinsuring SIAT to the extent of the difference between SIAT's retention and the full potential value of the cargo: in the worst case, for some $5 million.

The proportion of SIAT's reinsurance placed by Willis Faber was only a small proportion of the SIAT business they handled. But at one time there had been a danger of Willis Faber losing all of it: at one point a directive had been issued by the Fiat group that PWS were to be treated as a member of the group, with the implication that all SIAT's reinsurance would by placed by PWS. Giorgio Mitolo did not believe that PWS could handle the SIAT hull account, and he was also less than pleased when one of the PWS directors, John Webb, was made a director of SIAT. John Prentice was not pleased either. The loss of the comparatively small facultative cargo cover that did go to PWS in the event was something that Prentice could contemplate with equanimity, but the loss of the entire SIAT hull account was something else, for it would have meant the severance of old and valued business connections, not least with his friend Giorgio Mitolo. There was some discussion at Willis Faber of what ought to be done. Bob Arnold suggested that the simplest thing might be to buy PWS. With Prentice's knowledge, he invited Pearson to lunch and floated the gentlest preliminary fly over his nose.

Good-naturedly, over the veal, Arnold needled Pearson about his success in winning the facultative business. Pearson admitted that Webb had been installed at SIAT partly through the influence of his wife's stepfather, Giorgio Ajmone Marsan. But, Pearson retorted, John Prentice was on close terms with Mitolo. And then Pearson confided in Arnold his suspicions about Mitolo and specifically that special arrangements were being made to keep the SIAT business. Arnold was shocked. This was a serious charge, and he insisted that he must report it to his colleagues. Pearson protested that he had spoken in confidence, and asked for an undertaking, which Arnold gave, that his allegations would not go back to the Italians.

Through no fault of Arnold's, however, it did. When he got back to the office, meaning to report Pearson's allegations and at the same time to insist on his own undertaking that the Italians would not be told, he found that Prentice was in Tokyo. When Prentice got the message, by telephone, he was not told that Pearson had spoken in confidence. He immediately interpreted Pearson's criticism of Mitolo as an attempt to attack Willis Faber's position as the reinsurance broker of the SIAT hull account. Mitolo was told about Pearson's accusation, and insisted on coming to London, with his superior Atzori, to have things out.

The meeting, again at the Savoy, was thunderous. Pearson found himself alone, confronted by John Prentice, Bob Arnold, another colleague from Willis Faber and the two Italians. He found the atmosphere so different from that of his friendly lunch with Arnold that he could only conclude that his suspicions were well founded. The powder trail was well and truly laid. Each side now suspected the other of behaving dishonourably. Pearson believed that something was wrong in Italy, and only three days after the meeting at the Savoy his suspicions were further strengthened.

He was in an acquaintance's office in the Fiat office in Turin when the man abruptly scribbled something on a scratch pad, tore it off and shoved it across to him. These were the twenty-four words he wrote in Italian. Pearson had already been given a sibylline warning by a contact inside SIAT that things were not as they should be. Now that warning seemed to be confirmed.

> *301 vetture*
> rimaste a SAVONA
> *perchè molto daneggiate*
> che fine hanno fatto?
> a chi sono state vendute?
> rottamete? NO
> sono state messe all' ASTA?

Which means:

> *The 301 cars*
> left behind at SAVONA
> *because very damaged*
> how did they end up?
> who were they sold to?
> written off? NO
> were they put up for sale at AUCTION?

By coincidence the first personal involvement Malcolm Pearson had with the 301 cars that were to be so important in his life occurred on the morning of the day he met Bob Arnold for lunch at the Savoy. From the Lloyd's intelligence services sheets pinned up in the Room, PWS learned that a fire had broken out on board the *Savonita* only eight hours after she sailed from Savona, near Genoa, for Wilmington, Delaware, and New York City on 26 November. There were 2,697 cars on board, all Fiats except for 300 Alfa Romeos. The claim was treated as routine, with SIAT asking PWS for payment and underwriters asking PWS for details, until 20 January. That day, before leaving for the Savoy, Malcolm Pearson drafted a telex to be sent to Giorgio Mitolo asking SIAT to settle some unpaid premium. As an afterthought, at the prompting of his marine department, he also asked for a copy of the survey report on the *Savonita* loss.

The whole story turns on what exactly happened when the *Savonita* got back to port and the 301 cars were taken off.

It seems there was a certain amount of discussion as to what ought to be done. Representatives of SIAT, Fiat, Ugland and later of Fiat-Roosevelt, the American importers, took part. The shipowners wanted to sail again with a full or almost full cargo, and the SIAT and Fiat representatives disagreed. In any event, 301 cars were discharged. The *Savonita* sailed for Wilmington, where the rest of the cars were cleaned of the traces of smoke and of the sea-water and carbon dioxide used to put out the fire. The 301 cars in Savona were sold to one Antonio Dotoli, Fiat's main dealer in Naples. Dotoli paid Lire 81 million (about $81,000) for them, or about 15 per cent of their sale value when new. He later sold them at a discount of 22 per cent. Since the cars were built to American specifications, many of them were sold to American military personnel at the NATO headquarters in Naples.

On 5 December 1974 SIAT reported to PWS that the *Savonita* 'discharged 301 cars from decks nos 7, 8, 9, 10B, which are now lying on quay at Savona, and appear to be very seriously damaged by fire and/or water'. To be precise, they were in a fifteen-storey silo near the quay, and most of them had been so little damaged that they had been driven to the silo under their own power. On 14 January 1975 SIAT supplied more detail. 'All these cars,' they wrote to PWS, 'appeared immediately very seriously damaged, and were indeed discharged also because their prosecution [sic] to the USA would not have been practical and economical.' Out of the 301 cars, SIAT said, '44 have been completely destroyed, 176 from deck 7 and 8 appear to be very seriously damaged by the direct consequences of the fire, 125 from deck 9 and 10 appear again to be seriously damaged mainly by water and/or other extinguishing means'. It was no doubt a slip, but the 176 cars from decks 7 and 8 and the 125 from decks 9 and 10 add up to 301. Forty-four 'completely destroyed' cars seem to have disappeared into thin air.

'Following our surveyors' recommendations,' SIAT's letter went on, and in view of the damage, the cost of repairs and the port charges, 'we are endeavouring to sell all the cars on "as is, where is" basis.' The letter added that SIAT's representatives were 'in touch with prospective buyers', and that they expected to conclude a sale for a price in the region of Lire 80–85 million. The letter was perhaps too cautious. For the investigator Robert Bishop, of the international firm of loss adjusters Graham Miller, subsequently reported to underwriters and to Giovanni Agnelli, the head of the Fiat group, that 'undoubtedly the cars were sold to Dotoli on 10 January', four days before the letter was written.

Fiat-Roosevelt in New York, PWS were informed, had already claimed the full insured value of the 301 cars, and PWS were politely requested to collect their share of the reinsurance, which came to $711,643·13.

The hint passed to him in Turin on 6 March put Malcolm Pearson in a whole maze of dilemmas. As a broker, he owed a duty to his client, SIAT, but now he was in possession of an allegation of an attempted fraud in relation to the SIAT claim. He knew, of course, of the personal hostility of the management of SIAT, as manifested at the Savoy meeting. But so far the suggestion was that the fraud was in Fiat, not in SIAT. Given Pearson's relationships within the whole group, it was not possible for him to see his relationship as being exclusively with one company in it, rather than with another.

Secondly, as a Lloyd's broker (though he was not himself a member of Lloyd's) he felt himself bound by the ideal of 'utmost good faith'. He was most unwilling to damage the name of his company by pushing a claim that might turn out to be fraudulent, and knew the danger that if he did so, he might himself become a party to any fraud.

Lastly, he was most uncomfortably aware of the complexities of his own relationship with the powerful clan who control the Fiat empire. Fiat alone is one of the four biggest corporations in Europe, producing ships' engines, diesel trains, aircraft and earth-moving equipment as well as cars. The descendants of Senator Agnelli who hold shares in IFI, the family holding company, also control banks, a great newspaper (La Stampa in Turin) and Juventus, one of the perennial champion soccer clubs in Europe. All the enterprises together have a turnover in excess of $20 billion.

Pearson's father worked as a broker for Bowring and did well enough to buy a shooting lodge on the Moor of Rannoch in the Scottish Highlands. Shortly after Malcolm left Eton, and while he was hesitating whether or not to go into Lloyd's, he was offered a job as tutor to the children of Susanna Rattazzi Agnelli, Member of the European Parliament, one of the ten shareholders in IFI and the favourite sister of Gianni Agnelli, head of the family. He took it and went to work for the family in Italy. In April 1965 he married Francesca, the daughter of Umberta Nasi, another of the IFI shareholders; Umberta subsequently married Giorgio Ajmone Marsan.

The Agnelli family presents a more or less united front to the world. But, as in most dynasties, concealed resentments smoulder under the surface. Some members of the family are said to chafe at the dominant position of the brothers Gianni and Umberto Agnelli. If Pearson had friendly contacts throughout the family, that did not necessarily mean he could count on being automatically backed up as a member of the family. This slightly ambivalent position was not, however, affected by the break-up of his marriage in 1970, for he remained on good terms with his former parents-in-law.

Pearson makes no bones about the fact that the success of Pearson Webb Springbett owed a lot to his Agnelli connection. But, naturally and reasonably, he also points out that he would not have kept the Fiat business he got if he had not pursued it with competence and energy.

There was yet another dimension to the relationships with his former wife's family, however. Not only had they put money into his business. They had put money into an aspect of it which was later to run into trouble. Indeed, there was more to the Agnelli clan's involvement with PWS than the mere fact that a young member of the family had married Malcolm Pearson and invested some of the money she received from family trust funds in it. Pearson's company, PWS, became a part of the great Agnelli financial machine; a small part, no doubt, but one that played its part in the family's financial and tax strategies.

When in 1965 the capital of PWS was increased and it began to get off the ground, Susanna Rattazzi Agnelli and Giorgio Marsan each took 10 per cent of the shares. Pearson and his wife had 30 per cent, and the two brokers Pearson had brought with him from Bowring, John Webb and David Springbett, had 17.5 per cent each. The remaining 15 per cent went to a man called Ralph Delbourgo, who was both a shareholder in PWS and the underwriter for a new insurance company called the Bastion, incorporated in September 1965.

Many years later a case came to the Court of Appeal in London which arose out of a reinsurance treaty negotiated by PWS together with Delbourgo, whose company, Delbourgo Ltd, had an underwriting contract with the Eagle Star insurance company, plaintiffs in the case. In judgement Lord Denning referred to Delbourgo as 'one of those smart young men who get a lot of business in a short time but leave a lot of trouble behind'.

The Fiat group controlled a holding company in Luxemburg originally called Profina SA; in 1972 its name was changed to PWS (Holdings)

SA. When the Bastion was set up in 1965, Profina took up 180,000 £1 shares, and SAI, the Fiat insurance arm, took up another 250,000, while the rest belonged to Malcolm and Francesca Pearson and to Webb and Springbett. The underwriter was Delbourgo. The Agnelli dynasty, through SAI and Profina, was reposing considerable confidence in its new kinsman and his friends.

In 1971, Pearson, Webb and Springbett as individuals sold the Bastion for a price which took account of a deficit of more than £300,000 on profit and loss account. Then, under different ownership and management, it collapsed altogether. In late 1966, in any case, the Agnellis insisted that SAI pull out of the Bastion. At first Delbourgo, through a company called the Coronet, joined with the Pearsons, Springbett and Webb in buying out the SAI holding. Then, in November 1967, the Pearsons bought out Delbourgo. (Mrs Pearson had recently inherited a substantial sum as a result of the maturation of trusts established on her behalf.) After Malcolm Pearson had severed any connection with the company, it fell under the influence of a man called John Follows, who enters this story in quite a different context. It is one of the incidental pleasures of the fringes of Lloyd's that the same characters come round again and again, like Falstaff's army. In April 1974, in any case, the Bastion crumbled and went into liquidation. Sixty-four brokers and ten insurance companies, under pressure from the Department of Trade and Industry, established a support fund of more than £2 million.

In February 1974, in the meantime, an agreement was made between the two Fiat group insurance companies, SAI and SIAT, and a company called PWS Agency AG Zug in Switzerland. As part of the deal, Pearson's partner, John Webb, moved to Italy permanently to become reinsurance director for both SAI and SIAT. The lion's share of the brokerage on reinsurance business given to PWS by SAI and SIAT was to be paid not to London or to Luxemburg, but to PWS Zug.

PWS Zug was a properly organized trading company, subject to the tough requirement of Swiss audit law. As a Luxemburg holding company, PWS Luxemburg was not allowed to trade under local law. So PWS Zug received the brokerage from Italy and passed on only the profit (which amounted to a large proportion of the brokerage) to Luxemburg, having paid tax in Switzerland. Of course Swiss company tax is lower than the equivalent tax in Britain or Italy, and the Swiss franc is a stronger currency than the Italian lira.

Pearson was even more perplexed when, on 21 March 1975, he got confirmation from what he regarded as a reliable source inside Fiat that the 301 cars from the *Savonita* had indeed gone to Dotoli. By that stage, half of them had been sold, some to Italian, some to American buyers, for about Lire 2·8 million ($2,800) each, but purchasers were given an official invoice for only Lire 500,000. By 17 April, Pearson's friends had actually bought a car, chassis number 0091033. It seemed to be in brand-new condition. They paid for it with two cheques: one was made out to the Dotoli firm for Lire 560,000 ($560), which represented the 'official' price, to be reported for tax purposes, of Lire 500,000, plus Italian value-added tax at 12 per cent; the other for Lire 2 million (just over $3,000 at the then prevailing rate of $1 : Lire 650) was made out to a man of straw. Whatever else might or might not be said of the transaction, it was clear that the disposal of the cars from the *Savonita*, like so much else in Italy, was being done in such a way as to deprive the Italian government of tax revenue. Before the end of May Pearson had a complete list of the chassis numbers of the cars unloaded from the *Savonita*. He was not surprised to find that 0091033 was among them.

One of the strongest points against Malcolm Pearson's view of the case throughout was the fact that reinsurance normally follows the terms of the original insurance. (This point of law has been confirmed by Mr Justice Leggatt in the case of *Insurance Company of Africa* v. *SCOR*, in which, incidentally, Bob Bishop, the investigator in the *Savonita* case, was criticized by the judge.) The reinsurers, according to this principle, do not separately investigate the circumstances of claims settled by the direct insurers, unless they could prove fraud on the part of the direct insurers. The contract between SIAT and Lloyd's underwriters under which the *Savonita* claim was brought was of this kind: on the slip signed by Roy Hill as the leading underwriter at Lloyd's, it was specified that reinsurance was 'to follow all settlements and agreements of the ceding company'. On 8 April Giorgio Mitolo came to London to make this point to a meeting of the leading underwriters and Gordon Edwards, manager of the Lloyd's Underwriters Claims and Recoveries Office, in PWS's offices.

Neither Edwards nor the underwriters were prepared to accept Mitolo's argument without question, however. Edwards insisted that where fraud was suspected underwriters did have the right to ask questions about a reinsurance claim. Two days later PWS informed Mitolo by telex that underwriters were not prepared to pay, for two reasons: they were not happy with the survey report, and they felt that 'not all the cars could have been a total loss'. (Of course SIAT were

claiming that they were a *constructive* total loss – not that they had
been physically annihilated, merely that the cost of repairing them
would exceed their insured value.) Pearson's suspicions were now
shared, to the extent that they were not prepared to pay up without
further investigation, by the leading underwriters both at Lloyd's (Roy
Hill) and in the London companies market (the Ocean) as well as
by Edwards of LUCRO. Edwards and Hill decided to send in a
surveyor, and not an ordinary surveyor at that.

Bob Bishop is a heavyweight Yorkshireman who started life as a
soccer pro before becoming a policeman. He worked for the City of
London Fraud Squad before going to work for the loss adjusters
Graham Miller as a surveyor who was in effect a detective. Within the
next couple of years he was to play a part in many Lloyd's rows,
including Sasse and the scuttling of the *Salem*. He was originally retained by underwriters, but Malcolm Pearson, who believed the key to
the *Savonita* mystery might lie inside Fiat, took Bishop with him to see
Gianni Agnelli, and Bishop found himself retained by Agnelli as well
as by the London underwriters.

The investigation was to take months, and Bishop did not find it easy
going. He speaks no Italian, and had to interrogate reluctant witnesses,
some of them downright hostile, through interpreters. Nevertheless,
he persevered. He saw Mitolo and other SIAT personnel in Genoa, as
well as the surveyor, Pietro Ferrigno. He got hold of photos which
suggested that damage had been limited to a comparatively small
number of cars. He interviewed rival bidders who admitted that their
bids had all been typed on the same typewriter. In Naples, the dealer
Dotoli threw Bishop out of his office, though not before he had seen
large numbers of cars from the *Savonita*, apparently in good condition.
And in Turin he talked to a number of Fiat executives, including two,
Raimondo Meak and Franco Scarpa, who knew Dotoli well since the
days when they worked in Naples. Bishop secured admissions from
both of them that they had been involved in helping Dotoli buy the cars.

Bishop produced two interim reports to Agnelli as well as his report
to underwriters. Eminent counsel who later studied the reports said
that 'a good deal of Bishop's information has been obtained in a form
that would not be admissible in a criminal court – for example, a certain
amount of it is hearsay'. That was perhaps inevitable, given the circumstances in which Bishop had to work. However, the same authority
concluded that Bishop had indeed 'disclosed positive indications of
fraud' and that a prosecutor would 'very probably' be able to prove it.

This legal opinion was to play a considerable part in influencing

Malcolm Pearson's actions as the story unfolded. It was written for him by John Mathew QC, the senior prosecuting counsel for the Crown, whom he consulted as a private client. Mathew distilled from Bishop's reports a number of reasons for believing that fraud had taken place.

There was, first of all, the fact that when the ship turned back to Savona, the owners were ready to set out again with a full load of cars. It had been the Fiat representatives who insisted on unloading the slightly damaged cars. Then there was the matter of the survey reports. Mitolo at first refused to produce any reports to P W S; later it was said on his behalf that he regarded the mere request for them as a slur. But altogether four survey reports were eventually produced: one, by Dr Mattarelli, a surveyor associated with the local Lloyd's agent in Genoa, was done on behalf of the P & I Club, covering the shipowners; another, by Gian Carlo Serrati, was dated 14 March 1975; and two separate reports from Captain Ferrigno, S I A T's surveyor, bore the same date, 29 January, though they did not agree in all respects, and in fact the second, more detailed one was produced only in June.

The mint-fresh car bought from Dotoli by Pearson's friends was described in one survey as damaged by 'water and smoke: cause of damage 70 per cent water, 30 per cent smoke', and in the other, ostensibly written by Ferrigno on the same day, as 'severely damaged by fire or heat'. The photographs Bishop got from the files of Mitolo's assistant, Enzo Rosina, showed large numbers of apparently un-damaged cars, and Rosina agreed, according to Bishop, that some of them were in 'very good condition'. Bishop later tracked down the lawyer and surveyor who acted for Ugland, the *Savonita*'s Norwegian owners, both of whom had also inspected the cars when they were unloaded, and they both agreed that only about fifty seemed damaged.

Finally, Bishop's conversations inside Fiat convinced him, rightly or wrongly, that the sale to Dotoli had been set up from inside Fiat, and that some pressure had been brought on S I A T staff to make sure that the Dotoli bid was accepted.

Bishop slogged away at his inquiries all through 1975; his second report was not ready until February 1976. If Malcolm Pearson hoped that Bishop would find a 'smoking gun', however, or that Agnelli would be convinced by the reports, those hopes were to be dis-appointed. Roy Hill, too, the leading underwriter, was getting nervous. Partly to reassure him, Pearson now for the first time brought the *Savonita* affair to the attention of the Chairman of Lloyd's, Sir Have-lock Hudson. The Chairman seemed surprised that they had come to him. To him, it seemed a simple matter: if the claim was a bad one, they should resist it. Hill suggested there might be pressure from Agnelli, Pearson that there might be pressure from Willis Faber. Sir Havelock dismissed both these fears. Characteristically, he employed a metaphor from cricket. Bat straight, he said, and they would have nothing to worry about. Cricket, unfortunately, has never caught on in Italy, and developments there were disturbing from Malcolm Pearson's point of view.

On 7 January 1976 he flew to Turin and met the Fiat high command, including Gianni Agnelli himself, armed with a report from his legal department. The meeting lasted only half an hour, and was a bitter blow to Pearson's hopes. In itself, said the Agnelli lawyers, the Bishop report contained no evidence of either irregularity or irresponsibility on the part of Fiat. (In passing, the lawyers did ask, as if with raised eyebrows, how it came about that, though the cars, as salvage, belonged to SIAT, the invoices to Dotoli had been made out in the name of Fiat!) Unwisely, perhaps, Pearson went on the offensive, and asserted that Fiat personnel had improperly influenced SIAT. If Agnelli was annoyed by this charge, he did not show it. He would not go beyond his lawyers' advice; if they were wrong, was the most he would say, so much the worse for them.

Less than three weeks later, on 26 January, the stakes were raised. A fire broke out on the *Savonita*'s sister ship, the *Torinita*. The circumstances were similar. The blaze was put out with sea-water and carbon dioxide, and the *Torinita* put in to Freeport, Texas, where David Springbett of PWS, who happened to be in the United States, was able to inspect her. Springbett reported that about forty cars were burnt out. Cars even as little as ten feet away from those that had been completely burnt out were in 'surprisingly' good condition, Springbett found. However, he thought that all cars on the upper seven decks were badly sooted, and a major cleaning operation would be needed. The cars were taken on to Los Angeles and sold there on an 'as is, where is' basis. This time, reinsurers appointed a recognized car damage surveyor, and a solution acceptable to all parties was reached.

Each side could cite the *Torinita* fire in support of its own point of view. Pearson's critics later argued that it showed that the *Savonita* had been correctly handled. Pearson maintains to this day that it showed nothing of the kind. What is beyond dispute is that it made it even more urgent from SIAT's (and Fiat's) point of view to collect the reinsurance on both claims. On 26 March the Italians made what was to be almost their last attempt to work through PWS to get underwriters to pay. Giovanni Nasi, chairman of both SAI and SIAT, and Benedetto

Salaroli, general manager of S A I, flew to London and met underwriters at Lloyd's. Salaroli conceded that Dotoli had made some money out of the deal, but not much. Gordon Edwards, Roy Hill and the leading company underwriter offered to pay 10 per cent of the claim and refused to discuss its quality.

Deadlock had been reached. But a new round of the game was about to begin.

Pearson did not know it yet, but top management at Fiat had decided to finish with him and his suspicions. He still had friends in Turin, but for the moment they were overruled. Whatever the reason, the decision was taken to remove the responsibility for collecting the reinsurance from P W S. In this the Italians could hardly be blamed. Pearson, after all, was lobbying underwriters with all his might to persuade them not to pay. But what made the decision even more painful for Pearson was that the Italians now gave the job to Giorgio Mitolo's good friend John Prentice, of Willis Faber.

Prentice was approached by Pasquale Chiomenti, a Roman lawyer with excellent connections and offices in the exquisite ancient Roman Teatro di Marcello, one of the few buildings in Rome known to have been begun by Julius Caesar. Besides advising numerous other major European corporations, Avvocato Chiomenti acts as Fiat's top legal troubleshooter. Prentice had two long conversations with Chiomenti, and eventually agreed to recover the claim on two conditions: he must be convinced that it was not fraudulent; and he must be free to arbitrate or litigate the issue. The Italians at first said he could go to arbitration, but not to law. Later, when underwriters persisted in refusing to settle, Prentice persuaded his Italian clients to let him go to law.

His two conditions met, Prentice threw himself into the task of collecting the *Savonita* claim with an energy that suggested it was something more than a piece of routine business for him. Prentice's amiable, even debonair manner does not conceal a pair of remarkably steely blue eyes. The needle between him and Malcolm Pearson might have its origin in business competition, but there were personal elements in Prentice's determination to teach Pearson a lesson too. The episode of the Savoy lunch rankled on both sides. Prentice felt that Pearson had made unforgivable imputations against his friend Mitolo. Pearson thought Prentice had behaved unforgivably in passing on his suspicions, vented in confidence. Each man, in a word, felt the other fellow did not know how to behave like a gentleman, and proposed to teach him a lesson. It was a very English quarrel – but then Lloyd's is a very English place.

Prentice was advised by a veteran Willis Faber lawyer, Richard Millett, who has vast experience as a commercial solicitor and a shrewd and combative nature. Millett treated the accusations of fraud with great scepticism. It was when he professed himself satisfied that there was no evidence of fraud that Prentice too was convinced.

The day after Willis Faber were appointed to collect the claim, the other member of Prentice's team for this project, Desmond Baker, a senior Willis Faber broker and director, arrived at PWS's offices to read the file. In the first two hours he formed the opinion that PWS were making no serious effort to collect the claim, a judgement that cannot be challenged. By 21 April Baker was in Genoa, and on 26 April he signed his four-page report. It was clear and forthright. 'SIAT handled the claim properly,' Baker judged, 'and SIAT's reinsurers have no grounds for refusing settlement ... while the completely negative and passive role played by PWS may well have encouraged the re-insurers to resist the claim' – Pearson had certainly been negative, but passive he had not been! – 'nevertheless they must acknowledge their liability and settle the claim without delay, because any doubts they have as to the validity of the claim and the handling of the claim by SIAT are quite unfounded.'

Baker did his best to sweep Bishop's case away. What were Bishop's main points? he asked. That the cars ought not to have been treated as a constructive total loss (CTL)? But under the Marine Insurance Act of 1906 the definition of a CTL is expressed in these words: 'where the cost of repairing the damage and forwarding the goods to their destination would exceed their value on arrival'. Three surveyors – Ferrigno, Serrati and Mattarelli – said Baker, agreed that forty-five cars were damaged 100 per cent, and that the remaining cars were damaged by fire, water and smoke in varying degrees. The most economical solution, they therefore agreed, would be to sell the 301 damaged cars as a single lot, on an 'as is, where is' basis, leaving the buyer to pay the cost of cleaning and transport, and also the cost of the fourteen cars which the surveyors judged fit only for scrap. On that basis, Baker calculated, Dotoli's total costs would come to twice the actual cost price of Lire 81 million. Indeed, given the depressed state of the Italian car market, Baker suggested, Dotoli would be running a 'very high commercial risk'. That, perhaps, was overstating the case. Dotoli, after all, had hardly shown reluctance to run this particular risk. More than a year earlier, in March 1975 (if Malcolm Pearson's information was accurate), when he had already sold more than half the 301 cars for around Lire 2·5 million each, Dotoli would, on Baker's own calculation of his costs, have more than doubled his money. Baker made a more technical point of some force: according to British marine law, when a consignee rejects a shipment or part of a shipment short of its destination (as Fiat-Roosevelt did at Savona), the only way to deal with the claim is on a 'salvage loss' basis, which was what SIAT did. On that basis, however, the underwriters should have received the benefit of any salvage, which they did not.

Baker had an explanation, too, of the strange dating of the survey reports. Immediately after the fire, he was told in Genoa, SIAT commissioned Ferrigno to produce not one report, but three: a general report, a report for the specific purpose of General Average (the ancient term used in marine insurance for calculating the share of a loss due to damage caused intentionally by efforts to save hull or cargo; in this instance, the damage caused not by the fire, but by the sea-water and carbon dioxide used to put it out) and a third limited to the cause of the fire. 'Is it surprising,' Baker asked Prentice, 'that all three were dated 29 January 1975?' He did not explain why SIAT had been so slow in producing these reports for underwriters. Nor did this explanation really account for the contradictions Bishop had noticed between Ferrigno's two reports.

Baker is an experienced claims man with the highest reputation in the market for straightforwardness. His report was impressive, especially to anyone unaware of the detailed doubts Bishop had unearthed. A sceptic might have noted that it was based on talking only to Mitolo, Rosina and their lawyer – in other words, only to those who had every interest in finding answers to the difficulties Bishop had raised. But John Prentice was not a sceptic where the honesty of his friend Mitolo was the issue. If he ever felt serious doubts about the *Savonita* claim, Desmond Baker's report demolished them.

Only two days later Prentice met Roy Hill and the leading company underwriter. He showed them Baker's memorandum and left it with Hill. He also presented Hill with a memorandum of his own which asked underwriters – 'when you are persuaded that it is reasonable to do so' – either to pay the claim in full or to go to arbitration.

Prentice's own memorandum attacked Bishop's memorandum as 'innuendo and supposition' and worse. He assured Hill that the top management of Fiat and SAI, including Gianni Agnelli himself, remained utterly confident of Mitolo's ability and integrity, and so did he. He had heard, he added, that Hill and Pearson had been to see the Chairman of Lloyd's and had told him they were afraid that pressure would be brought on underwriters to settle. Prentice assured Hill he had no intention of bringing 'any unduly heavy pressure' to bear himself.

What constitutes 'unduly heavy pressure' in pursuit of a legitimate business objective, of course, is a matter of opinion. What seems mere forceful advocacy in a just cause to the advocate may feel painfully like bullying at the receiving end. And advocacy from a senior executive of a firm of brokers with more than a quarter of the marine premium in the market can feel uncomfortably forceful for a small independent underwriter like Roy Hill.

Matters came to a head at a meeting on 1 June at which Prentice became incensed with Hill and Gordon Edwards. Accounts of what passed differ. Even one sympathetic to Prentice records that it was 'a very stormy meeting' and that the Willis Faber case was presented with 'robustness'. It is possible that the very forcefulness of these tactics backfired and made the underwriters more stubborn than if they had been more gently handled. At any rate, they held out for more than another eighteen months. They were still refusing to offer more than 10 per cent when, on 13 July 1976, there was a surprising development in Italy. On that day the Agnelli holding company, IFI, issued a press release announcing that it had just sold its 52 per cent controlling interest in SAI to the Ursini group. With SAI, of course, went the controlling interest in SIAT.

Now the connection that had created the *Savonita* story in the first place was broken. IFI and Fiat had washed their hands of the business. Malcolm Pearson, to his chagrin, found himself replaced by Willis Faber. The pace of events slowed down. But the story did not stop and the claim had not ceased to exist; nor had Willis Faber's determination to collect it evaporated. So far from fading away, the *Savonita* affair was about to emerge from the obscurity of a market row into an incident that could no longer be swept under the carpet, which is where the instinct of all good Lloyd's men tells them rows ought to be kept.

By the autumn of 1977 Roy Hill was expressing a willingness to compromise. He was talking about paying something halfway between the 10 per cent he had offered all along and 100 per cent of the claim. For one thing, Hill and the other underwriters were now in possession of advice from Brian Waltham, a partner in the leading shipping solicitors Ince & Co., to the effect that there were no grounds for refusing to settle. And no underwriter, least of all an independent, could hold out against Willis Faber without some second thoughts. It was not just that Willis Faber were big and for many of the underwriters on the *Savonita* slip were the biggest source of business. It was quality as well as quantity. 'It was all prime beef,' one veteran broker told me. It included fleets like Cunard. If an underwriter took nothing else, he was bound to prosper. Twenty years ago, it was not unknown for an underwriter to stand up when a Willis Faber broker came to his box. And Willis Faber's walnut-panelled image was also based on their being straight and never hiding anything from underwriters that they ought to know. 'The real truth of the matter,' one broker said, 'is that Willis's power in the market is such that they were bound to win.'

Malcolm Pearson knew this. He made desperate efforts to stave off a defeat that could not be long delayed. In so doing, he made a move that was interpreted as eating crow to get his business back. As he saw it, it was more a desperate effort to make sure that, though the heavens fell, justice would be done. Justice, for Malcolm Pearson, now meant that Willis Faber in general, and John Prentice in particular, must be taught that might was not right.

Pearson had already threatened a libel action against them, based on Baker's remark that PWS had played a 'completely passive and negative role'. In his determination to deny Willis Faber the glory of victory, he now did a surprising and ill-judged thing. Roy Hill felt that if he had to compromise, he preferred to do so through PWS. Through his contacts in Turin, Pearson passed on to SIAT his willingness to do this. He flew to Milan and met Giorgio Mitolo for lunch at the airport restaurant there. Pearson said he was willing to act for SIAT again, but only on conditions. He was not retracting his doubts about the quality of the claim. He would give no undertaking as to the percentage he could recover. And he insisted that Willis Faber be removed from the account. That, no doubt, was the real reason why he tried to get back into the action; that, and his sense that it was his duty to get the money for his client if anyone could. On 24 January 1978, three years and four days after his lunch with Bob Arnold, he met Mitolo in London at the Savoy. By this time Mitolo had succeeded in getting some money from the shipowner's insurance under General Average. Now all he wanted was a little over $600,000, and he said he had given Willis Faber until the middle of February to get it. Pearson never did get to represent Mitolo. And he realized that Willis Faber's final assault would be going over the top before very long.

Pearson's last-ditch attempt to get back on to the account had infuriated John Prentice. If Pearson did collect the claim after all, when Prentice so far had failed to do so, then Prentice would be a laughing-stock in the market. Pearson's move stiffened Prentice's already formidable determination to win. It also handed him a most effective argument. Pearson had maintained all along that he refused to collect the claim because he suspected fraud. Well, what had changed? Now he was willing to collect it after all. Did it mean that he no longer believed there had been fraud, or merely that he no longer felt so squeamish about it?

On the last day of January Roy Hill telephoned Pearson to say that the pressure was coming on hard. On 21 February he offered 60 per cent. But the very next day he telephoned Pearson again to say that the slip had collapsed behind him 'like a pack of cards'. Willis Faber had deployed a classic tactic of the claims broker: if the lead underwriter resists a claim and the broker believes it should be paid, it is standard operating procedure to go down the slip getting other underwriters to signify that they would be willing to settle. When you have achieved enough success with this operation, you go back to the leader and make him feel he is isolated. For weeks and months Willis Faber's men had been sapping and mining in this way. Once the trenches had been softened up, the assault was almost a formality. On 24 February Willis Faber formally collected 96 per cent of the *Savonita* claim, of which, the underwriters noted with a last touch of stubbornness, 'a certain percentage was *ex gratia*'.

For three years now, Malcolm Pearson had acted with superb disregard for his own self-interest. He had stuck to his contention that the *Savonita* claim was fraudulent, that it would therefore be dishonourable for him to collect it and that if the Lloyd's system obliged him to grit his teeth and do so anyway, then there must be something wrong with the Lloyd's system. Plenty of members of the Lloyd's community called this behaviour obsessive, or unprofessional, or arrogant. It can perhaps be said that it was also courageous. Pearson had incurred the bitter enmity of Willis Faber. He had appealed to the Agnellis, and they had rejected him. He had taken his worries to the Chairman of Lloyd's, and found no active sympathy there. His troubles were not over; the worst was still to come. Yet only a couple of weeks after what seemed his utter defeat in the market, support appeared from an unexpected quarter. On 7 March Pearson was telephoned by an old acquaintance, the Conservative Member of Parliament Jonathan Aitken. The phone call did Pearson little good, as it happened. What it did do was to start a train of events that ensured that the *Savonita* row could no longer be kept mum in the traditional Lloyd's manner.

Aitken was thirty-six years old at the time, independently wealthy and politically independent. Before he went into Parliament he was a reporter on the *Sunday Telegraph*. He was once the central figure in a trial under the Official Secrets Act after he published a secret report on British involvement in the Biafran war in Nigeria; he was acquitted. He is now the chairman of a small investment bank backed by Saudi investors, among others. He is a kinsman of that highly independent figure Max Aitken, the self-made Canadian millionaire who as Lord Beaverbrook became the close friend of Sir Winston Churchill, a member of his wartime cabinet, and one of the most powerful press lords in Britain. Later there were mutterings in the market that Pearson and Aitken were members of an 'old Etonian clique'. In fact, though they were friends as boys at Eton, they had completely lost touch for a dozen years. Aitken happened to hear of John Mathew's opinion about the *Savonita* case from another lawyer at a dinner party. He called Pearson out of sympathy. The next day Pearson wrote to the new Chairman at Lloyd's, Ian Findlay, reporting that Aitken proposed to raise the *Savonita* affair in the House of Commons.

Aitken's original intention was to do no more than ask a question in Parliament. This is the lightest and least formidable way in which an individual Member can draw Parliament's attention to something he considers in need of remedy. Then he went to see Ian Findlay. His misgivings increased. The Chairman met him in a defensive posture, flanked by half a dozen members of the Committee. His answers did not impress Aitken. He maintained that his powers as Chairman were enormous. Then, in the middle of the meeting, he called Ronald Taylor, chairman of Willis Faber, on the intercom, and asked him to see Aitken. Taylor's answers, pitilessly relayed to the meeting by the intercom, led Aitken to wonder whether the Chairman's powers were as great as Findlay claimed. In due course, however, Taylor did see Aitken. He in turn was well supported by Prentice, Baker and Millett. The acrimonious meeting confirmed Aitken in his feeling that all was not well.

Aitken maintains that if at any time Lloyd's had offered to hold what he regarded as a genuine inquiry into the *Savonita*, he would have been satisfied. As it was, he decided to draw a far heavier weapon than the parliamentary question and raise the whole story in what is known as an 'adjournment debate'. (Just before Parliament recesses at the end of a session, a whole day is given over to about eight adjournment debates. Half a dozen of these are balloted for by Members, and two are chosen by the Speaker. Aitken went to see the Speaker and got his approval for an adjournment debate on the *Savonita* and Lloyd's.)

Aitken was surprised by the weight of the indirect pressure mobilized against him by Lloyd's in the effort to make him drop it. There were about seventy-five members of Lloyd's in that Parliament, all but a handful of them Conservatives. They included the Conservative Chief Whip, Humphrey Atkins, who intimated pretty broadly that this was not the kind of behaviour that would help Aitken in his career. Aitken was annoyed enough to go ahead.

Jonathan Aitken is a committed believer in free enterprise, so he began his speech with 'a warm tribute to the London insurance market' and its contribution to Britain's international balance of payments. 'I hope it will be clear that any criticism of individual situations should not be taken as an implied suggestion in favour of more government regulation, government intervention, nationalization or state control. Those would be the Four Horsemen of the Apocalypse for the London insurance market.' But the price of the market's success, Aitken argued, was eternal vigilance. He called for improvements in the self-policing mechanism, especially at Lloyd's. He then proceeded to give his version of the *Savonita* story, as he had heard it from Malcolm Pearson, in terms highly critical of the Chairman and Committee of Lloyd's. He cited Mathew's legal opinion. 'What did the Chairman and Lloyd's actually do?' he asked. 'The sad answer is that they did nothing.' And Aitken quoted the words of Edmund Burke: 'The only thing necessary for the triumph of evil is for good men to do nothing.' He ended by making a discreet but unmistakable allusion to the pressures that Lloyd's had deployed to get him to drop his debate. 'There have been moments,' he said, 'when I have felt like that over-advised soldier who is described in Macaulay's Lays of Ancient Rome as the person to whom

> Those behind cried "Forward"
> And those before cried "Back".'

Lloyd's was stoutly defended in the ensuing debate by another wealthy Old Etonian Conservative, Timothy Renton (so much for the suspicions at Lloyd's of an Old Etonian clique ranged against them), and, more surprisingly, by the Labour junior minister responsible for insurance, Stanley Clinton Davis.

The adjournment debate was fully reported in the press. At the same time it was reported that the City of London Fraud Squad was investigating the *Savonita* affair. Findlay was privately furious with Pearson, whom he suspected of both tipping off Aitken and bringing in the police. Nothing could have been more irritating at a time when Lloyd's and its new Chairman were getting more and worse publicity in the media than ever before. Findlay decided that the *Savonita* could no longer be left to breed lawsuits, rumours and newspaper investigations. On 8 April the Committee yielded to his persuasion and set up a board of inquiry to hold a full-dress in-house investigation. By 5 May a board of five members had been appointed, four of them members of the Committee of Lloyd's, chaired by a professional arbitrator, Clifford Clark. In six months it had twenty formal sessions, interviewed fifty witnesses and consulted more than 2,000 documents.

The result was a harsh attack on Malcolm Pearson. The board's report described him as 'young, able and ambitious', not, in context, quite such complimentary adjectives as they might sound! The report found that he had 'embarked on a course of conduct in furtherance of his own personal interests and without regard for his responsibility to his client, namely SIAT'. Pearson saw his responsibility, the board said, as being towards Fiat rather than to SIAT. 'On his own admission,' the report stated, Pearson 'saw the claim as a means of unseating senior management in SIAT, particularly Mitolo.' The report went further. It found that Pearson's judgement became 'irrational' and led him to a course of action 'which cannot be supported on any view'.

The nub of the board's argument was this: when a broker becomes aware of circumstances that make him suspect fraud, what should he do? First, said the board, he must report his suspicions both to underwriters and to his client. Then he should *either* press the claim (even though he suspects it of being fraudulent) *or* withdraw from acting for his client. Pearson, the board said, did neither. 'The Board deeply regrets,' the report said, 'that a client should be effectively deserted by his Lloyd's broker without explanation.'

Both in his own mind and in his defence of his conduct when he was interviewed by the board, Pearson had set great store by the legal opinion he had obtained from John Mathew. Mathew had confirmed Pearson in his belief that he was right to refuse to press the claim when he believed it to be fraudulent. Pearson was under no *legal* obligation to report his suspicions, Mathew had found, though he was under both business and personal obligations to see that the information he had was available to all interested parties. He could best discharge those duties, Mathew had advised, by informing the Chairman of Lloyd's (which Pearson had already done) and the chairman of the Institute of London Underwriters on behalf of the companies involved (which he was subsequently to do). 'If Pearson takes this course,' Mathew had concluded with all the authority of his position, 'there can be no possible criticism of him.'

The board now referred only briefly to this weighty opinion. 'It is noteworthy,' its report commented, 'that the opinion is primarily concerned with the question of Pearson's legal and personal responsibility as chairman of PWS rather than with PWS's responsibility as brokers.' That was not, perhaps, the most even-handed way of putting it. It is a fair criticism of Mathew's opinion that it did not consider the question of Pearson's responsibility to his client in any detail. This was not mere omission, however, but followed from the whole tenor of Mathew's argument. Mathew had explicitly stated that he shared Pearson's belief that 'there is a strong probability that this is a fraudulent claim', and therefore that 'Mr Pearson undoubtedly took the right course in refusing to press the claim against underwriters'. Indeed, Mathew had pointed out in the roundest terms that if he had been a party to causing underwriters to pay a claim which he believed to be dishonest, then he would have been in danger himself. 'In our opinion,' Mathew had formally cautioned, 'Mr Pearson must have nothing whatsoever to do with the collecting of this claim, whatever may be the commercial consequences to his company, because by doing so he lays himself and his company open to charges of fraud.'

Now, great as is the authority of someone in Mr Mathew's position, he was advising on this instance as Malcolm Pearson's counsel, and Lloyd's board of inquiry was not bound to agree with him. What is surprising is that there was not one word about his argument in the board's report, though his was surely advice that anyone would have hesitated to ignore. The only further allusion to Mathew was as follows: 'With regard to the aspect of fraud upon reinsuring underwriters, the opinion states: "It is of course a different matter if underwriters, having been made aware of all the information available, for their own commercial reasons nevertheless wish to pay, because it cannot be a fraud upon them unless they are dishonestly misled."' Thus the board of inquiry extracted from Mathew's opinion a brief qualifying passage that might be taken to justify the underwriters' eventual decision to pay the claim, while it omitted Mathew's lengthy arguments for believing that the claim might well be fraudulent and his unqualified conclusion that Pearson was justified in his efforts to bring this possibility to the attention of interested parties.

The board brushed aside the powerful legal warrant Mathew gave for the course Pearson took. It took no account of the genuine difficulty in which Pearson had been placed by events. It looked no further than the fact that SIAT was Pearson's client, and pronounced that it was to SIAT alone that he owed his duty as a broker. It stated – surely erroneously – that Pearson saw his responsibility as being to Fiat rather than to 'his client'. But what was SIAT? Pearson's difficulty arose precisely from the fact that, rightly or wrongly, he suspected fraud on the part of some, but not all, of the management *both* of SIAT *and* of Fiat. It was nonsense to imply, as the board of inquiry did, that the SIAT management had no inkling of Pearson's suspicions. Mitolo knew. That was why the whole story had arisen. Moreover, Pearson had met and discussed his suspicions with the Agnelli brothers and with Giovanni Nasi, then the chairmen and chief executives of IFI, Fiat, SAI and SIAT. It was scarcely Pearson's fault if the management of all four companies decided that Pearson's suspicions were unfounded.

The report also dealt in an unsatisfactory way with the important question of Pearson's dealings with the Chairman of Lloyd's. 'Up to 21 December 1977,' it stated, 'there is no evidence of any request to the Chairman of Lloyd's for assistance.' The unwary reader might well take that to mean that Pearson had not approached or informed the Chair at all before that date. The report's formula, however, is only true if heavy emphasis is placed on the words 'for assistance'. The truth is that Pearson, with Roy Hill, did see Sir Havelock Hudson, then the Chairman, as far back as December 1975, two years earlier than the board's choice of words suggests, and conveyed his suspicions to Hudson on that occasion. Moreover, as the report actually notes, on 4 August 1976 Pearson sent a copy of Mathew's opinion to the Chairman.

In striking contrast, the Lloyd's board of inquiry dealt lightly with Willis Faber. 'WFD did not seek to use the weight of their account in order to persuade reinsuring underwriters to settle this claim,' it concluded. It made only two criticisms. 'At one meeting,' it acknowledged, 'the behaviour of the WFD personnel concerned was robust beyond the normally acceptable standards of broking conduct.' And the board also said that it regretted 'the manner and haste' with which Pearson's remarks made in confidence to Arnold at the ill-fated Savoy lunch had been relayed to Prentice and then to Mitolo.

It was perhaps unintentional. But the contrast in style and language between the report's castigation of Pearson and these gentle slaps to the collective wrist of Willis Faber was so sharp that many readers doubted the impartiality of the inquiry, or at least the board's grasp of that wise precept that justice must not only be done, it must be seen to be done. The report stuck to the simple view that Pearson's responsibility was merely to collect the claim at the direction of the SIAT management in the person of Mitolo. It assumed, without thorough investigation, that Willis Faber were right, and Pearson was wrong, about the substantive question of whether there had been fraud. The result was that the report appeared to be unfair to Pearson, not only in the conclusions it reached, but also in the way it reached them.

The result was a public relations disaster for the board, and for the Committee and Chairman of Lloyd's, when the report duly appeared on 8 December 1978. (A revealing detail: it was not shown to Pearson before publication!) The reception, however, was made ten times worse by the method Lloyd's chose for making the document public. Newspapers were allowed to have copies of the report only if they agreed to sign a document beforehand acknowledging that 'having regard to the privileged nature of the report, neither the board of inquiry nor the Committee of Lloyd's will accept responsibility for the accuracy or otherwise of the report'. In addition, newspapers were required to indemnify the board and the Committee in advance for any legal costs arising from publication.

The Committee had adopted this bizarre stratagem on legal advice from a leading expert on libel and slander, Peter Carter-Ruck. However sound in law, the advice was disastrous from a public relations point of view. In principle, there is something ridiculous about a body that claims the privilege of self-regulation and is so nervous about making public its exercise of that privilege. In practice, it caused a crisis in Lloyd's public relations. The press was not just horrified, but contemptuous. Lloyd's should have taken the risk of publishing its own report, said the august *Financial Times*, and not have tried to pass the risk on to others. 'The report is a shoddy document that smacks heavily of kangaroo justice,' said the *Economist*. 'The way in which Lloyd's of London has mishandled the *Savonita* affair,' said the *Sunday Telegraph*, 'has dealt its reputation the worst blow in living memory. Not to put too fine a point on it, Lloyd's has succeeded in making itself appear both incompetent and somewhat cowardly.'

The attention of the board of inquiry focused almost exclusively, not on whether Malcolm Pearson was right or wrong about the substance of what happened in Italy in the first place, but on whether he had behaved correctly or incorrectly afterwards. It was with some difficulty, indeed, that Pearson and his solicitor, Sir Percy Rugg, prevented the Chairman of Lloyd's, Ian Findlay, from so confining the scope of the inquiry as to exclude altogether any matters 'extraneous to Lloyd's', which would have ruled out any inquiry into what happened in Italy at all. Pearson believes passionately that he has good reason to suspect fraud in the original *Savonita* claim. John Prentice and Richard Millett and their colleagues at Willis Faber are equally confident that after a thorough investigation no evidence of fraud was discovered. They are equally insistent that even if there had been fraud, it would have made no difference unless Pearson was able to prove fraud by the senior management of SIAT; short of that, they maintain, his duty was to press the claim with underwriters, because in all other circumstances reinsurance must follow the fortunes of the direct insurer.

By the summer of 1981 the Italian authorities were investigating the disposal of the cars from the *Savonita* in order to discover whether fraud was committed. Official notices were served on twelve men, warning them that they were under investigation. Four were arrested and charged with fraud: Raimondo Meak, former commercial director of Fiat for the Mediterranean area; Antonio Dotoli, the Fiat dealer in Naples; Pietro Ferrigno, the surveyor on whose repoits Mitolo and Baker placed such reliance; and Enzo Rosina, a director of SIAT and, at the time of the *Savonita* fire, Giorgio Mitolo's deputy for cargo insurance. The Italian proceedings have not been resolved. Until they are, nobody can be certain whose version of the *Savonita* story is correct.

It is of course a matter of some importance to those directly involved. But, in a larger context, the *Savonita* row was important because it opened up – fairly or unfairly – a great breach in Lloyd's reputation for behaving according to the standard of 'utmost good faith'. It was one of the events that led to the setting up of the Fisher inquiry and so to the long contest over the passing of the first Act of Parliament to change the constitution of Lloyd's in 111 years.

CHAPTER 8

MAN OVERBOARD!

IBM doesn't know how to make computers, they don't know how to program at all, but what they really know is how to sell. The genius of IBM is marketing.

Dr Herbert Grosch, a computer expert,
quoted in Rex Malik, *And Tomorrow the World? Inside IBM*

On 19 June 1979 Federal Leasing, Inc., of McLean, Virginia, a middle-sized firm specializing in leasing computers to various agencies of the federal government, filed suit in the United States district court in Baltimore against Lloyd's and fifty-seven underwriters. The 168-page claim asked for $10 million allegedly due in claims under insurances written at Lloyd's and by London companies on computer leases. In addition, the suit claimed $50 million in 'consequential damages' and $500 million in punitive damages for alleged disruption of federal business because of the non-payment of claims by Lloyd's underwriters.

The story broke slowly, but with explosive effect. Before the end of the month *Computer Weekly* in London was reporting that Lloyd's was being sued for $630 million (it is not clear how the magazine arrived at that figure), while the London *Financial Times* reported that 'computer leasing insurance business has presented Lloyd's with one of the most serious problems that its market has ever experienced'. A couple of weeks later the same paper headlined that 'Lloyd's of London faces its biggest losses'.

There is an ancient piece of folk wisdom in Fleet Street, where every possible story has been told a thousand times, that divides the infinitely various experiences of the human condition into only two ideal types. One kind of story is accompanied by a diagram and a legend saying: 'Arrow Points to Defective Part'. A far better kind of story is accompanied by a photograph showing both the subject's ears, with the words: 'We Name the Guilty Man!'

Any attempt to explain the malfunction of the rather elaborate machinery of computer leasing insurance would require both diagrams and copy of forbidding complexity. So from a journalistic point of view it was a relief when the *Washington Post* discovered a man who, on his own admission, was guilty of something, and presented him with some admiration as the anti-hero of the computer leasing affair. There is another sound journalistic rule: that a story should accord with the readers' most cherished prejudices. The youth of America, said Oscar Wilde, is their oldest tradition, and part of that myth is the stereotype of the 'brash young American hustler' running rings round the 'venerable' but tired financial brains of Europe. This piece of folklore has survived undamaged while successive generations of young American hustlers have retreated westward across the ocean, their pockets turned inside out by the supposedly naïve bankers of London and Paris, Geneva and Zurich. Still, it continues to give innocent pleasure, as in the front-page story by John F. Berry in the *Washington Post* on 3 July.

'The conference had just gotten underway at the Chemical Bank headquarters in New York City on 16 March 1975,' Berry's story began, 'when one of the bankers spotted a small object drop to the floor from under the table.' The object was a bug; an electronic eavesdropping device ordered by a '29-year-old jet-setting high school drop-out from Dallas' called Charles S. (Chris) Christopher, described by Berry, deferentially, as a 'brash young hustler'. The bug at Chemical Bank was 'just one episode in a fast-paced, cut-throat game of international finance that now threatens the venerable Lloyd's of London with the biggest loss in its 291-year history'.

'It is a story,' Berry went on breathlessly, 'of how a young American salesman with virtually no technical knowledge was able to sell one of the world's most famous insurance combines on an insurance scheme that made him, and many of his imitators, overnight millionaires. In effect, Christopher convinced Lloyd's to pay off computer leasing firms if their business was canceled by new technology in the industry.'

The preconceptions of this account are the stuff of myth-making. Brash young David is set against venerable Goliath; though among those who did well out of Lloyd's in this matter were such underdogs as the Chase Manhattan Bank and the leasing subsidiary of the Bank of America. Again, the same lack of technical knowledge that is accounted a virtue in Charles Christopher is held to be the cause of Lloyd's misfortunes. Nevertheless, it was this version of events that was reimported back into Britain. The London *Daily Express*, for example, took a whole month to pick up the *Washington Post* story, but then adopted Charles Christopher's version of events with uncritical gusto.

'DISASTER AT LLOYD'S' said the big black headline, over a picture of a smiling Christopher in the act of shooting the contents of a well-shaken champagne bottle into a swimming pool. 'One rich American has good reason to celebrate.' The story quoted Charles Christopher, adding insult to injury, as saying, 'Lloyd's have only themselves to blame.' He warned them, he added magnanimously, 'but they became greedy ... Lloyd's were suckers. It was as if they built a wooden house in the middle of the desert and then insured it for twice what it was worth and made an arsonist the beneficiary of the policy.'

The press coverage of the computer leasing affair is an intriguing example of the way a number of statements, true in themselves as far as they go, can be woven together to leave an impression in the public mind that bears very little relation to what actually happened.

It is quite true that computer leasing turned out to be a disaster for underwriters. It is too soon to say what the total losses will come to. The $560 million asked for by Federal Leasing was, of course, a figure pulled out of the air by Federal's lawyers, over and above the $10 million in actual claims. It owed something to the fact that you cannot increase the quantum of damages once an action has begun in American courts, so that from the start lawyers habitually ask for the largest figure they can put in without absurdity. By coincidence, however, the aggregate of all claims on computer leasing insurance, for all assureds, in all countries, and in all the years of account for which the business was written, may come to a figure not far short of the Federal claim. The latest loss forecast by Lloyd's own lawyers in New York and in London is $444 million. That would be a larger amount than any single claim paid at Lloyd's to date; some 50 per cent bigger, for example, than the $300 million paid out on the El Paso LNG ships. But the computer leasing losses were spread out over thousands of different policies; a fair comparison would be with other whole books of business, say, supertankers or oil rigs, or product liability, including asbestosis, rather than with an individual claim. By those standards, the losses sustained by underwriters on computer leasing were heavy, even disastrously heavy. They were not unprecedented.

Much of the coverage, again, interpreted the computer leasing fiasco in terms of naïve gentlemen at Lloyd's being taken for a ride by slickers from the United States. That may be a valid interpretation of what happened; though naïveté is not one of the most obvious characteristics of Lloyd's underwriters as a group. But very few of the losses were directly due to Charles Christopher, who dropped out of the story before most of the business that turned sour was written. If there were slickers, they were not high-school drop-outs or brash young hustlers from Texas; they were in some of the biggest banks in the United States, and they were marketing strategists in the IBM corporate headquarters at Armonk, New York.

Lastly, it has become part of the legend that the trouble arose because people at Lloyd's were ignorant about the technology of computers. A British computer leasing expert, Parry Mitchell, has argued this case passionately, and he has been persuasive. 'I don't think they ever understood the technology they were dealing with.' True. But few insurance men anywhere ever feel they need to understand the technology of the aircraft or the factories they insure. Lloyd's losses in the computer leasing affair had precious little to do with being ignorant of technology, everything to do with being naïve about the ferociously aggressive marketing strategies with which IBM holds on to its monopoly.

Charles Christopher does indeed play an important part in the computer leasing story, even if it was not his policies that led to the big losses. He was the first person to succeed in getting computer leases insured at Lloyd's against the risk and the financial consequences of cancellation. He was not, however, the first person to try. Late in 1971 a Lloyd's broker came to Adam Brothers Contingency and asked if, as specialist brokers, they could help. A leasing company in the United States was in the business of getting bank finance for buying equipment and leasing it to the federal government. The United States government is not permitted to enter into a binding commitment for more than twelve months, because Congress will not give budgetary authority for any longer period. The government therefore insists on a mandatory right to terminate any leasing arrangements each year. The leasing company was asking, through its brokers, whether there was any possibility of getting insurance cover on the lease to protect the bank in the remote event that the government exercised its right and cancelled a lease. The inquiry concerned a specific risk; a lease covering a mainframe computer leased to the federal government. Adam Brothers consulted leading underwriters and reported back to the leasing company's brokers that the answer to their inquiry was: 'Probably not.'

Two years later, however, in late 1973, Adam Brothers were approached again by a major firm of Lloyd's brokers, acting on behalf of a firm of brokers in Texas. This time the assured was Charles Christopher's company, Surety Leasing, Inc. The equipment was not a mainframe computer, but 'peripherals' – extra storage, disc drives, tape drives, printers and other equipment that the user can add on to his computer. And this time the answer from underwriters, relayed by Adam Brothers along the chain of brokers, was: 'Why not?'

'Chris' Christopher had dropped out of high school and started out in life as an encyclopaedia salesman, a breed famous for their ingenuity and tenacity above all other predators in the sales field. He then switched to selling insurance for W. Clement Stone, the Chicago insurance man with an almost revivalist approach to the benefits of salesmanship, who contributed $3 million – more than any other single donor – to the Nixon presidential campaign in 1972. In 1969 Christopher went into leasing, and in 1971 he started Surety Leasing in Dallas. It was a boom time for leasing generally, and also for the installation of mainframe computers and, increasingly, for the peripherals that Christopher made his speciality. 'We leased all sorts of equipment,' Christopher told the *Washington Post*, and he claimed that his earnings climbed from $75,000 to $300,000 in just three years.

Contingency insurance is the bespoke tailoring of the insurance world. It covers assureds when there is no standard form of policy in existence. It does not cover physical property or a person, but the possibility of losses arising out of fortuitous events in the future. Adam Brothers Contingency is a small firm of Lloyd's brokers which has been specializing in placing contingency insurance since 1936. (The firm dates back to the 1870s, but it was not until the 1960s that its directors decided to handle only contingency business.) Until computer leasing, it was perhaps best known for the fact that one of its directors, Liliana Archibald, was the first woman to broke a risk in the Room at Lloyd's; for that, and for placing insurances protecting businessmen against the financial consequences of the cancellation of major events like the Olympic Games or the World Cup soccer championships.

That was the backbone of contingency insurance since the 1930s: insuring promoters, distributors of souvenirs and the like against the risk of cancellation of events, big and small. (It included insuring theatrical managements, impresarios and film producers against loss due to the non-appearance of artists.) Over the years the scope of the business grew steadily, so that now Adam Brothers place some sixty different classes of contingency insurance at Lloyd's, and almost all underwriters write this kind of business from time to time. The main leads are the Janson Green, Merrett and PCW boxes in the marine market, and in the non-marine market Ralph Rokeby-Johnson of the Sturge syndicate and E. F. Williams.

As well as covering the organizers against loss due to physical

damage, strikes, non-appearance of performers and bad weather ruin-
ing – to quote Adam Brothers' promotional literature – 'exhibitions,
fairs, conferences, conventions, meetings, carnivals, pageants, film
productions ... television film series, theatrical productions, concerts,
lectures, sporting events, air shows, tours, cruises, flights, jamborees
and social functions of all kinds', Adam Brothers have placed insurances covering the risk of cancellation of such major events as the
World Cup soccer championships in 1970, 1974, 1978 and 1982, the
1984 summer and winter Olympics, the wedding of Prince Charles and
Lady Diana Spencer in 1981, and the Pope's visit to Britain in 1982.

Almost all contingency insurance originates with an assured who has
a special problem. He approaches his broker, who eventually (in some
cases after passing the business along a whole chain of other brokers)
gives it to a Lloyd's broker. And almost always the Lloyd's broker takes
it to Adam Brothers, as the specialists. It is their job to assess the client's
real need, and to devise the language of a policy that meets the case.

It may be a one-off situation: a single assured wanting cover for a
single event. In that case, it is placed in the market on a single slip. Or
it may be a class of risk that is likely to be repeated over and over again:
an exhibition, for example, involves much the same risks as any other
exhibition, and one conference is much like another. In that case Adam
Brothers will arrange a cover facility, or what is known as a line slip,
to save having to take every single piece of business of the same kind
round the market. Or the assured may be coming to Adam Brothers
to cover one particular risk associated with a specific major event, like
the Olympics, where experience teaches there will be many more. In
that case, too, Adam Brothers will set up a line slip, and any client with
an insurable interest in that particular event can get the same cover.

The first significant placing of this kind for a major event was the
Festival of Britain exhibition on the South Bank in London in 1951. The
next was the coronation of Queen Elizabeth II in 1953. Since then the
values insured have risen dramatically. The 1981 royal wedding
brought placings to a total insured value of between £11 million and
£12 million, mostly on behalf of souvenir manufacturers; the 1982
soccer World Cup, more than £40 million ($60 million), much of it for
tour operators.

Adam Brothers had been steadily extending the range of their contingency insurances even before computer leasing came along. Or
perhaps it would be truer to say that the range of contingencies that
clients want to insure against in an unpredictable world has been
steadily widening.

One important growth area has been permanent or temporary total disability cover for highly paid individuals, such as surgeons, racing drivers or professional golfers. An extension of that is the policy insuring parties to a lawsuit against an increase in their legal costs in the event of the death or serious illness of the judge hearing their case. Then there is a whole shelf-load of Dickensian-sounding policies available in sundry obscure legal contingencies: for example, 'recovery of sanity', covering trustees against costs that might arise if a person in the care of a mental institution were to recover testamentary powers; or 'issue risk', covering trustees or other interested parties against the chance of the life beneficiary under a trust unexpectedly having an heir.

A far more popular branch of contingency insurance recently has been cover for exporters and contractors, mainly British and American, in the Third World, both against 'political' risks and also against technical problems such as contractual penalties for delay or performance failure. A particularly flourishing branch is what Adam Brothers call 'contract frustration risks'. This is in demand from manufacturers, construction firms or design engineers signing contract for the design, supply and commissioning of plants. These contractors can cover themselves against termination of the contract due to *force majeure* preventing them completing the contract on time.

In practice, a substantial proportion of this business is what people at Lloyd's call 'political' insurance. Many of the contracts involve exporting plant or services to countries in the Middle East, Africa or Latin America that either actually are, or are regarded by timorous and prejudiced Anglo-Saxon businessmen as being, politically unstable. Middle Eastern business in particular has led to a big increase in bank guarantee insurance. For many years now, Middle East governments have been buying huge quantities of plant and equipment from Western manufacturers. Dozens of whole refineries, harbours or petrochemical plants have been bought in deals costing many hundreds of millions or even billions of dollars each. Instead of asking firms bidding for these contracts to put up a surety bond for their ability to carry them out, therefore, Middle Eastern governments, in a buyer's market, have demanded bank guarantees cashable 'on first demand'. That means the company bidding for the business must give a guarantee that their bank, for example in London, will allow the Middle Eastern government to claim a given amount at will, irrespective of its performance of the contract.

As long ago as the mid-1960s, a big British engineering firm, faced with a demand from a Middle Eastern government for bank guarantees of this kind, approached Adam Brothers through its own brokers, asking for insurance against the customer cashing the guarantees without any fault on the contractor's part. Adam Brothers successfully broked this risk to the Peter Green box, and a trickle of similar business followed. After Colonel Gaddafi of Libya called in the bank guarantees of several Italian contractors (none of them insured at Lloyd's), nearly bankrupting some of them, many American and British firms took the risk of losing their guarantees more seriously, and the trickle became a useful flow of business.

Standard Lloyd's policies follow various forms of words. An underwriter may use one of these, or he may use what are called 'J' forms, which are in effect blank policies except for the standard exclusions for war and fraud. The J(a) form is even blanker, since it does not even have a war exclusion clause. There are basically two rules any Lloyd's policy must conform to. Any business written must be subject to a war exclusion for war on land. This dates back to 1936, when – with war in Abyssinia, Spain and China, and the threat of war in Europe – underwriters signed the War Risk Exclusion Agreement. Later this was refined. You can now insure the abandonment, because of war, of any event scheduled within twelve months. With regard to political risks, one exclusion is war between any of the five major powers – that is, the United States, the Soviet Union, the United Kingdom, France or China. 'If we have war between any of those,' Lloyd's men say, 'there won't be much left to cover anyway.' The other exclusion is war between the country of the buyer of any goods and the country of the seller.

None of these various exclusions has any bearing on computer leasing insurance. But there is another exclusion that might appear to forbid it. The Committee of Lloyd's does not allow underwriters to write financial guarantee insurance. This rule, too, dates from 1936, but the restriction had its origin in the concern following the Harrison fraud in the 1920s and other scandals between the wars. The provision might seem to rule out insurances like those on bank guarantees or computer leasing. In fact it does not. The language of the Committee's definition of what constitutes an unacceptable financial guarantee insurance is contorted, but still decipherable:

The test to be applied ... in deciding whether an insurance is a violation of the financial guarantee agreement is whether the happening of any one or more of the following events, viz.
 (a) the financial default or insolvency of any party;

(b) the financial failure of any venture;
(c) the shortage of receipts, sales or profits of any venture; or
(d) lack of support;
will cause a loss to become payable under the insurance, or brings into operation a peril or contingency insured against which will cause a loss under the policy, *unless it is a condition of the insurance that any loss recoverable must be a direct result of a specified contingency, which is not precluded.*

The last clause is the operative one. If an insurance makes it a condition that any loss recoverable must be the direct result of a specified contingency, then it escapes the ban on financial guarantee insurance.

So when Charles Christopher, through his American broker and their Lloyd's broker, was put in touch with Peter Nottage at Adam Brothers, there was no bar to Nottage doing his best to place it in the market. Nottage was eminently qualified to do this: he has been specializing in placing contingency insurance since 1946. He put it to the underwriter for the E. F. Williams syndicate as the leader. This time, there was enough background information coming from Christopher via his brokers. The business was placed long before Nottage had encountered Christopher. Later, Christopher commuted to London. But the initial business was placed without his persuasive skills being brought to bear. On its merits, as they saw them, underwriters accepted the risk as one more innovative and potentially lucrative contingency insurance.

To understand Charles Christopher's proposition, it is helpful to grasp, in the barest outline, why and how a leasing industry had grown up in computers in the first place. And that in turn means understanding at least the skeleton of the history of IBM's monopoly and its long, defiant and so far successful trench warfare against the United States Department of Justice as it tried for fifty years, with little success, to make IBM conform to the anti-trust laws.

IBM was being prosecuted for illegal monopolistic practices long before it had anything to do with computers, indeed before computers existed. The company grew out of a merger between three firms making business machines, one of them founded by Dr Herman Hollerith, of the United States Census Bureau, to manufacture his invention, an electric tabulating machine that depended on cards punched with a pattern of holes to sort and count electrically. In the 1920s and 1930s IBM (it changed its name to International Business Machines in 1924) *rented* punchcard machines and *sold* the cards to go with them. In 1932 the Justice Department first brought anti-trust charges, alleging that IBM and also Remington Rand were breaking the Clayton Act of 1914 by tying in sales of cards to the rates of rental for their machines; if a customer tried to buy cheaper cards elsewhere, the Justice Department said, IBM made them pay a higher rental for their machine, and this was clearly prohibited by the statute. IBM took the case to the Supreme Court and lost. But in practice it won, for it was left free to draw up specifications for the punchcards that could be met only by cards made on machines it controlled. IBM was also left free to rent its machines and to refuse to sell them.

In 1952 the Justice Department brought suit again, this time under the fundamental Sherman Anti-Trust Act of 1890, which banned contracts and combinations in restraint of trade. This second suit was settled in 1956 when the government and the company signed what is known as a consent decree. No admissions were made. The government dropped its prosecution, and IBM agreed to drop certain practices. One of those practices was IBM's refusal to sell its machines. Under the terms of the consent decree, IBM was required to offer equipment for sale at a discounted price according to its age.

The 1952 Justice Department action, leading to the 1956 consent decree, was aimed not at electronic computers, but at IBM's 90 per cent grip on the market for conventional electro-mechanical tabulating machines. Even as late as 1956, at the time of the consent decree, fewer than 100 IBM computers had been installed. Then the market for computers expanded rapidly. IBM was one of nine American manufacturers poised to become major suppliers to that market. The story of how IBM acquired a dominance in computers almost as great as its earlier dominance in tabulating machines is a story not of technological brilliance, but of acumen and ruthlessness in marketing.

One threat after another was beaten off, usually in circumstances that left bitterness and lawsuits behind. The first threat came from Control Data, a small Minnesota-based computer manufacturer started by William Norris, a breakaway from IBM's major rival, Sperry Rand. In the early 1960s Control Data made serious inroads into the market for the biggest 'number crunching' computers, used largely for scientific research. IBM was afraid that big scientific institutions, in the words of its chief scientist, 'set the tone for industrial users'. In other words, IBM was afraid that Control Data, whose 6600 machine was fifteen times more powerful than anything IBM had to put up against it, would first capture the top end of the market for big scientific computers, then move down into the heart of the market. IBM responded with a campaign of price-cutting, but also with what are called 'fighting ships': computers that were not really ready to be delivered, that in some cases, indeed, existed only on paper, but could be used to prevent sales of the competition's products.

In 1962 a second phase of the campaign began. IBM took the decision to build a product line, the one that eventually reached the market as Series 360. Again, the new machines were hardly a triumph for computer design or production engineering. IBM's chief executive, Thomas J. Watson Jr, admitted later that, as a result of a deliberate management decision, Series 360 was offered for sale two years before it was really ready. It was, however, a marketing coup of Napoleonic daring. What IBM has always been best at is selling: what its salesmen call 'shifting iron'.

In the case of Series 360 it added a refinement. It had agreed to offer machines for sale at an age discount. In late 1963, it suddenly announced that there would be no age discount after 1 January 1964. Users rushed to buy while the company would still allow them credit for the rental they had already paid against the purchase price. Then, without warning, and before it was ready, in April 1964 IBM announced the new Series 360, making all its previous machines obsolete. The cash collected from all those customers who had rushed to buy their machines before the deadline helped to pay for the new products that would make the old ones obsolete!

One reason why IBM likes renting machines better than selling them is that it is immensely profitable. It normally sets the purchase price of its machines at fifty-four months' rental. But by putting the rental so high in terms of the purchase price, IBM made possible the growth of an independent leasing business, once the Justice Department had insisted that it make some machines available to purchasers. IBM was interested in high monthly *rentals*. Now a new industry could grow up of independent *leasing* companies, offering IBM machines over a fixed-term contract. Because they could finance the cost over a longer, fixed-lease period, say for five to seven years, the leasing companies could offer IBM machines at a lower rental than IBM was charging.

There were two bursts of leasing. The first was created by Saul Steinberg, whose company was called Leasco. Steinberg saw that a gap had opened up because of IBM's high rentals, and he exploited it, leasing IBM 360 mainframe computers for far lower monthly figures than IBM's own rentals. His success brought imitators into the market. At any stage IBM could have wiped the leasing companies out, and eventually that is what it did. In the meantime, Steinberg made a lot of money and bought other businesses with high-priced Leasco stock.

The new leasing industry was not limited to the computers them-selves, or to what were coming to be called 'central processing units' (CPUs). In the 1960s the size of the market for peripherals had grown steadily, until by 1968 it was calculated that it accounted for two-thirds of the whole market for electronic data processing equipment. By 1971, IBM's top management was seriously worried by competition from manufacturers of what are called 'plug compatible peripherals' – that is, peripherals that could be fitted on to IBM machines. In April that year the IBM management review committee set up a 'blue ribbon task force' to look at the problem. The solution was called the 'fixed term plan': peripherals would be offered on one- or two-year leases with price reductions; the lost income would be siphoned back by higher charges for servicing. One of the peripheral manufacturers, Telex Inc., was seriously hurt by this riposte. Like Control Data's management before them, the Telex management thought IBM was out to get them. They sued, and were eventually given the highest damages ever awarded by a United States court, though the amount was later reduced on appeal. IBM also began to move into fixed-term leasing for main-frame computers. It had decided to beat the leasing companies at their own game.

This, then, was the business that Charles Christopher was in when he was introduced to Peter Nottage at Lloyd's. The computer industry was dominated by IBM, and IBM had shown that it was willing to defend its monopoly position tenaciously by litigation, by price-cutting and by aggressive, even unscrupulous marketing. At the same time, the emphasis was drifting away from CPUs to peripherals. Partly because of the Justice Department's insistence that IBM must sell its machines, partly because of IBM's own policy of setting its rental rates so high, a competitive independent leasing business had grown up, both in mainframes and in peripherals. And now IBM had threatened that industry with destruction by going into the fixed-term leasing business itself. The independent leasing companies could not hope to compete – unless they could find a way of increasing the 'residuals' – that is, the value that could be assigned to machines or peripherals at the end of the lease, so that the amount that needed to be covered by monthly payments, and therefore the monthly payments themselves, could be drastically reduced. It was this that Lloyd's enabled them to do.

Charles Christopher's firm, Surety Leasing, did not handle IBM equipment. He would get finance from a bank to buy peripherals from other manufacturers and lease them to a user. (Or, if the manufacturer had already contracted with a user, he would take over the contract.) The bank would get the rental stream from the user to pay off its debt (after Surety's expenses had been paid). Once the debt was paid off, then the rental stream would be shared between Surety and the manufacturer in an agreed proportion; typically, the manufacturer would get the smaller proportion. The lease might be of varying lengths with breaks; for example, five years with a break after three, or seven years with a break after five. If the user did cancel the lease at the break for whatever reason, then the equipment would revert to the manufacturer, or to Christopher if he had bought the lease, and it was up to them to remarket the equipment as best they could.

Christopher's bright idea was to see that if he could persuade underwriters at Lloyd's to insure him against the risk of cancellation of the lease, he would thus eliminate one major anxiety for the banks, who would therefore be willing to lend him more money. Bank officers were eager to accept what looked to them like a guarantee that removed one of the few risks attendant on some highly profitable business.

Indeed, Christopher's problem was that the business was too attractive to the banks: they wanted in on it themselves. He had no sooner begun to approach banks with his bright idea than he found some of them trying to cut him out by going straight to Lloyd's for a policy of their own. Christopher told the *Washington Post* that he approached Chemical Bank in New York for a leasing deal armed with his new Lloyd's policy. 'Six weeks later,' he complained, 'Chemical had its own representative in London trying to get the same policy.' Soon after, Christopher went on, he was lent $25 million by the Bank of America to buy peripherals from Storage Technology in Denver. The very next morning, according to Christopher, Bank of America had second thoughts. Why not get Lloyd's cover for its own leasing arm, Decimus? 'The very next week,' in Christopher's version, 'ten Bank of America representatives were in London.'

Christopher's account may be coloured by resentment. But it is certainly true that, within a very short time after he had first used his Lloyd's facility to get financing for computer peripherals leasing from a bank, American banks were getting Lloyd's policies for their own leasing subsidiaries.

Until April 1974, banks had been forbidden by American law to compete with independent leasing companies. Up until then, subsidiaries of bank holding companies could offer only full pay-out leases – that is, leases whereby the lessor recovers his full investment within the term of the lease. On that basis, the banks could not compete. That prohibition was contained in the Federal Reserve's banking regulation 'Y'. But in April 1974 Regulation 'Y' was liberalized as a result of strong representations from the banks. Now their leasing subsidiaries *would* be allowed to finance non-full pay-out leases, on certain conditions, among them: (1) the 'residual value' assigned to the equipment being leased must not exceed 20 per cent; (2) they were allowed to take a third-party guarantee for a maximum of 60 per cent of the acquisition cost of the equipment. Here is how it works: the cost of the equipment plus the cost of the financing totals $x,000. The rental, plus the residual value (no more than 20 per cent), plus the third-party guarantee (not more than 60 per cent), plus any tax benefits, must come to exactly $x,000.

The upshot of this change was that the banks could now compete in the leasing business, and compete they did. The very next inquiry Peter Nottage received, after the initial approach from Christopher, was from a subsidiary of a major American bank holding company, covering the cancellation of leases and the financial consequences. Very quickly independent leasing companies and bank subsidiaries made further approaches. Among those that were insured at Lloyd's were Itel, the world's biggest leasing company, Lease Financing Corporation, Federal Leasing, and leasing subsidiaries of Bank of America, Chase Manhattan, Citicorp and other major banks. 'The word had got around,' said Nottage.

Charles Christopher does not appear to have accepted that, once Adam Brothers had developed a new kind of contingency policy, there was no reason why other assureds should not be covered. He remained intensely suspicious of the banks in general, and of Chemical Bank in particular. His suspicion was to lead to a tragicomedy. But first there had been second thoughts about the cover at Lloyd's.

It was in early 1974 that the rush of computer leasing business was written. In October 1974 Adam Brothers had a meeting with the leader, Cecil Street-Porter, and other underwriters. Nottage: 'Here is the business you've got. Here is a waiting-list of new business you can write if you want to.' The underwriters' reaction was that it was time to call a halt. Every new kind of insurance business must be evaluated over a certain amount of time. It takes time and experience to see that the wording of the policy is right, and to see that the rates accurately reflect the risk. So the underwriters decided not to accept any more computer leasing business for a time, and Adam Brothers so notified the brokers who continued to approach them, asking for cover for more and more clients. But new business continued to be written for existing clients.

In March 1975 Christopher's brokers invited Peter Nottage and Geoff Fox of Adam Brothers to visit Texas for a briefing on the Surety Leasing operation. After spending a few days in Texas, they were due to go to New York for meetings with Chemical Bank and another leasing company, Commonwealth Leasing of Fort Lauderdale. They asked Christopher's secretary if she would make reservations for them at a particular New York hotel. Instead she made reservations at the Plaza. Nottage and Fox flew to New York and went to the meeting at Chemical Bank.

No one thought anything of it when one of the bankers picked up an inch-square black plastic box off the carpet under the table and tossed it into an ashtray.

That night, back at the hotel, Nottage was on the phone to a broker in California when the FBI arrived. 'We've just arrested two people in the next-door room!' was their opening.

One of the two men was Richard Geyer, a private detective from Palm Beach, Florida, owner of the Geyer Detective Agency and Tracer Corporation, which sells electronic surveillance equipment. The other was Charles Christopher's personal Learjet pilot. The two men had electronic bugging equipment with them, which, they said, they were going to try out for a client. The FBI accused them of planning to eavesdrop Nottage in the next-door room at the Plaza. Just over a year later Charles Christopher and Geyer pleaded guilty to several charges.

What had happened was that, suspicious of Nottage and Fox, furious with Chemical Bank and curious to learn what he could of a competitor's business, Christopher had hired Geyer to bug the conference room at the bank, Nottage's hotel room and Commonwealth Leasing's private plane. In February 1976, under pressure from Surety's biggest creditor, the Bank of America, Christopher resigned as chairman, president and chief executive officer, though he continued to be a consultant and stockholder. Bank of America bought his portfolio of leasing contracts.

There was a curious sequel. Two former officers of Surety, Richard Reid Wadsworth Jr and Irvin E. Barlow, started a cluster of computer leasing firms known as Intercap. They had access to a Lloyd's policy through a Dallas insurance brokerage house called Nationwide General. Nationwide belonged to Charles Christopher. Using the Lloyd's policy, Intercap leased $77 million in computer equipment to the Southwestern Bell Telephone Company in St Louis. In testimony in a federal criminal case in Dallas, Ray Allen Acker, a retired vice-president of the telephone company, testified that he had received about $2 million in bribes from the two Intercap executives.

The business written for Charles Christopher mainly covered peripherals. It is a matter of record that on all the insurance written at Lloyd's on leases covering peripherals, on a total of several thousand separate transactions on behalf of both Christopher and his competitors, underwriting losses were no more than marginal. The big losses came on the big computers, on deals mainly made with some of the biggest banks and leasing companies in the United States, most of them after Charles Christopher's fall from grace in the spring of 1975; on the deals, in short, that were most vulnerable to a decision by IBM to bring out a new generation of big computers.

From October 1974 until the spring of 1976, underwriters stuck to their cautious policy. They continued to write new business for existing clients, but they took on no new clients. By the spring of 1976, Adam Brothers had a waiting-list of no fewer than 130 leasing companies who wanted to get in on the act. One of them even threatened to sue if he was not allowed a Lloyd's policy. So, at the prompting of Adam Brothers, underwriters agreed to look at new clients, though they did so with ostentatious care. They reviewed their claims record on the business to date, and found that it was not bad. They polished up the wording of the policy, and produced a new proposal form. In the end, these tactics discouraged or eliminated most of the 130 potential clients: of these, only thirty applied and only fifteen were accepted. The biggest of them was Itel, and it was for Itel that almost half the total covered by Lloyd's policies was eventually written.

In 1976–7 the flood tide of computer leasing business came into Lloyd's. There was something about this of the giddy euphoria which attends those perennial financial follies that have visited the world since the 'tulipomania' in seventeenth-century Holland, when speculators paid thousands of guilders for a single bulb. For a moment, people in the computer leasing business seemed to think that the laws of financial gravity had been suspended, so that what went up need never come down. Leasing companies, insured or not, started writing leasing contracts for $5 million or so apiece on the big IBM 370/158 and 370/168 computers on the assumption that the residual value left at the end of the lease would be as high as 40 per cent on their value when new.

No one knew better than Itel how risky that was. Itel was started in 1967 by a former McKinsey consultant. Its first line of business was leasing IBM 360 computers. For a while, that was very profitable. Then IBM brought out the 370s. Itel was kicked sideways, and so were many,

many of its competitors. Its stock fell from $37 to $6 and the company had to write off $300 million in obsolete computers as IBM slashed the price of its 360 series. Itel survived, diversified, prospered. It leased containers, ships, railroad rolling stock, even Boeing 747s. It eventually owned more than $1 billion in assets of all kinds. It became a byword for success California-style: for high expense accounts, pretty secretaries and obsessively aggressive, optimistic salesmanship. Itel, like its competitors, knew precisely what IBM could do to its leasing portfolio, much of it comprising machines made by National Semiconductor to compete with the IBM 370s. Only, this time, there was a difference. What was the worst that could happen? A wave of cancellations? They had insured the risk of cancellations, and with Lloyd's of London at that.

Altogether, counting the business written both on the original 1974 policy and on the tighter 1976 wording, underwriters at Lloyd's accepted some 14,000 separate computer leasing risks placed by brokers on behalf of some seventeen assureds. With the exception of two French leasing companies, all of them were American. Some of them were subsidiaries of major banks like Chase Manhattan, Citicorp, Chemical and the Bank of America (Decimus), and the rest were leasing companies like Itel, Commonwealth and Federal. The total amount insured was about $1 billion.

In the spring of 1977, when underwriters had been writing under the new policy for just a year, there came a clear warning of what might be expected. It took the form of a press release dated 25 March 1977 from IBM's data processing division at White Plains, New York, announcing that IBM was about to bring out a new top-of-the-line computer, the 3033, with 'an improved level of price-performance to large system users'. This was a number-crunching machine designed with big users in mind, such as government agencies, major research laboratories and oil companies. This was competition for IBM's 370/168 models, and the release said it would provide between 1·6 and 1·8 times better performance for a comparable monthly rental.

The leasing companies and the banks went right on financing leases of 370s. But the writing was on the wall. As IBM's chief scientist had explained fifteen years earlier at the time of the fight with Control Data, the big scientific computers set the fashion. The institutions, in both public and private sector, that buy them want the maximum in processing capacity, and are prepared to pay for it. But the big profits are made further down the market, with the workhorse computers used by the big corporations in the *Fortune* 500 for routine accounting, stock control and payroll functions. That was where IBM's biggest and most profitable market lay, and that was where most of the machines that Lloyd's insured had gone. Most of them were 370/148s and, especially, 370/158s.

So the news of a new model that would compete with the 370/168s did not ruffle the waters at Lloyd's. Underwriters went on writing computer leasing business undeterred. They were living in a fool's paradise, however. The introduction of the 3033 ought to have been an unmistakable alarm signal. For it was plain enough that this was the first of the '3000' series, a new generation of computers the market had been expecting for years. It would only be a matter of time before IBM marched down into the 148 and 158 market with new models.

In a press release dated 6 October 1977, IBM announced the arrival of two new computers, the 3031, replacing the 370/148, and the 3032, replacing the 370/158. The 3031, IBM claimed, was 2 to 2·5 times faster than the 148, and the 3032 2·5 to 3 times faster. The new models would be available in the spring of 1978, and they would cost no more than half the price of the models they replaced, whether it was expressed as a rental, a four-year lease or a cash sale price.

This time the reaction at Lloyd's was very different. The same day that the *Financial Times* carried a story reporting the IBM announcement, Street-Porter of E. F. Williams got on to Peter Nottage and said, in effect, 'That's it, you can pull the plug out right away!' He asked Nottage to contact the brokers who had instructed him and find out from their clients what they thought the effect of the new product line would be on existing portfolios of leases. The consensus of opinion was that it would be serious, but not disastrous. The underwriters, who had put a temporary ban on writing any new computer leasing business as soon as they heard the news of the new models, swiftly made it permanent as far as mainframe computer leasing was concerned. Peripherals, being compatible with successive generations of mainframe technology, were far less seriously affected, and in fact to the end the loss record was not bad. In 1978 the aura of computer leasing generally was so bad that underwriters stopped writing them too.

In the nature of things it was some time before the full extent of the losses was known. What Lloyd's underwriters had insured, after all, was the cancellation of leases; what they were indemnifying was the shortfall in rental income due to such cancellation. The IBM announcement might make it inevitable that large numbers of leases would be cancelled. But until the cancellations actually happened, no one could be sure how many, and even then the extent of the shortfall would not be clear at first.

Over 1978, however, the cancellations and the consequent claims on underwriters began to come in like waves. In August and September, representatives of Itel, the biggest single insured in terms of the potential claims, came to London and admitted that customers were returning their National Semiconductor machines in droves because they wanted to switch to the new IBM products, and that they would therefore be making massive claims.

A working party of six underwriters was set up, chaired at first by Cecil Street-Porter, then – after Street-Porter's retirement and a brief period with his colleague J. C. Ryman in the chair – by Murray Lawrence, the top Bowring underwriter and later a deputy-chairman of Lloyd's. The immediate problem was to close Lloyd's 1976 account. The working party asked the loss adjusters, Toplis & Harding, for a report and a forecast. By mid-February 1979 the 1976 account was closed, and Toplis & Harding had come up with a preliminary estimate for total losses on computer leasing insurances as a whole: $225 million.

That was bad enough, but the situation was confused, and it was clear that the losses could come to far more than that. One difficulty was that each insurance covered a lease running up to seven years. Another was that in many cases any money paid as losses by Lloyd's would go not to the assured, but to the banks who had put up the finance. The whole situation was complicated by the machines themselves. The leasing companies in some cases were obliged to repurchase them at the values assigned in the leases; but residual values had fallen, in some cases by as much as $500,000 for a single machine, since the introduction of the new IBM model line. In short, the whole computer leasing industry was in a shambles, and everyone looked to Lloyd's to bail them out.

Lloyd's needed someone to sort things out in the United States. It was not easy to find someone suitable. It needed to be a big, sophisticated financial institution, preferably a bank, with experience of leasing, and with staff to spare to do a big investigation and report in a hurry, yet who were not inhibited by any conflict of interest. Most of the obvious candidates either had leasing subsidiaries of their own that had been covered by Lloyd's policies, or had financed lessors who were insured at Lloyd's. In the end Lloyd's hit on the First National Bank of Boston. They were asked to produce a data base and a more detailed loss report. By 5 December FNBB had produced a global loss forecast for the whole class of computer leasing business, covering all assureds in all countries in all years of account, of $340 million. Part of the deterioration since the Toplis & Harding report under a year earlier was due to the steep fall in the residual value of 370 series computers, a decline accelerated by the efforts of the leasing companies caught in the squeeze to get rid of their own machines at almost any cost.

In such a tangle, litigation was inevitable, and by the second half of 1979 the situation was crisscrossed with lawsuits and rumours of lawsuits. Federal sued Lloyd's underwriters, and underwriters sued Federal in return. One of Federal's bankers, the Bank of Lincolnwood in Illinois, sued both Federal and Lloyd's. Itel did not sue underwriters, but instead sued its brokers, Marsh & McLennan and America Insurance of New Orleans, a subsidiary of Bland Payne (and now of Sedgwick). Even the unfortunate Bank of Boston found itself being sued for its pains.

Lloyd's strategy was to try to negotiate out-of-court settlements with as many of the assured as possible. But it was a slow process. One final settlement was reached with Commonwealth (the Florida leasing company that had provoked Charles Christopher's electronic curiosity) in August 1980. Lloyd's appeared close to an agreement with Itel, whose mainframe computer leases represented almost half of the total losses. But in January 1981 Itel filed a petition for bankruptcy under Chapter 11 of the Federal Bankruptcy Act, so Lloyd's settlement was conditional on the agreement of a Federal judge in San Francisco. In June 1982, Itel reached a final agreement with Lloyd's. Lloyd's paid a further $6 million, making a total of $120 million paid by Lloyd's. At the time of writing, the litigation with Federal Leasing has not been finally determined.

The latest forecast of total losses stands at $444 million, and, in the opinion of those in a position to judge, it is not likely to go much higher than that.

It has been an embarrassing as well as an expensive experience for Lloyd's. It was not good, for one thing, to be in the posture of challenging so many claims, fighting so many lawsuits, in the United States. After all, Lloyd's reputation there owed much to the legendary willingness to pay that had its origin in Cuthbert Heath's inspired act of enlightened self-interest.

That was not the worst of it. What was even more discomfiting was that Lloyd's collectively was made to look foolish, naïve and, in particular, guilty of an out-of-date ignorance of technology.

That was, rather predictably, the burden of much of the American press coverage. In London, too, critics charged that Lloyd's had failed to understand the technology of computers. On 20 July 1979, for example, just over a month after the Federal Leasing suit, the chairman of a British company called United Leasing, Parry Mitchell, who had previously operated the computer leasing subsidiary of a major British bank, wrote a scornful letter to this effect to the *Financial Times*. Lloyd's losses, Mitchell charged, were the consequence of 'myopic thinking'. Computer leasing, he wrote, was a classic risk business, and the major factor 'is machine obsolescence in an industry where technological change has become famous'. The key to success in computer leasing, Mitchell went on, was to make any investments that assumed residual values – that is, any but full pay-out leases – as early as possible in the technological life of the equipment. His own company, he said, designated an eighteen-month investment 'window' after the first deliveries of a new IBM product. After that, he implied, it was just too risky.

Another computer expert, the chairman of a major British software business, agrees. 'It was absolutely certain,' Philip Hughes of Logica told me, 'that IBM would bring out a new range, and about when they did. If there was any surprise at all, it was that they did stick to the same architecture as their previous series, and not go to their Future Series.'

Lloyd's, in other words, in the opinion of many people in the computer business, were suckered into thinking they were insuring against random cancellations of leases, when what underwriters were doing in effect was insuring against the coming of a new generation of technology; that is, betting *against* a certainty.

Does the charge lie against them? Murray Lawrence is categorical. 'It is not true that we don't know about advanced technology. What killed us was that IBM, for the first time in their history, cut their prices.'

Peter Nottage takes a similar line, though with an interesting difference. 'Leasing companies thought the IBM 370 was going to be there for many years more,' he told me. And he recalled that at the time when Watson announced the cancellation of IBM's projected Future Series in 1975, he had predicted that in the future IBM's model changes would be evolutionary, not revolutionary. 'And that was true, so far as it went,' Nottage commented wryly. At least the 3000 series was compatible with the 370. 'What IBM did that *was* unprecedented was to introduce a better price/performance ratio: the 3000 series came in either with higher performance at a comparable price to the 370, or with similar performance at a lower price.'

The remark reveals, on the one hand, how closely Nottage followed IBM's new product policy, and thus disposes of the idea that the gentlemen at Lloyd's were utterly innocent of the risks of new technology: and, on the other hand, suggests a certain naïveté about the commercial methods by which IBM, not once and forever, but again and again over fifty years, had moved to enforce their market domination, methods that include price cutting when and if necessary.

It is hard to escape the conclusion that both the broker, Peter Nottage, and the underwriters were taken for a ride. The people who were providing them with the business knew very well what they were doing, and that it was only a matter of time before IBM would cut their prices and crush the leasing industry as they had eliminated so many competitors before. In effect, therefore, Lloyd's underwriters found themselves betting not against the progress of technology, but against a commercial strategy.

For Peter Nottage, the whole experience of computer leasing had been a profound trauma. 'I've been handling contingency business since 1946,' he said. 'You could count on the fingers of one hand the number of cases of attempted fraud I've run into.' He was not suggesting that there had been conscious fraud in the story of computer leasing insurance. He meant that he had grown up in a world where brokers, underwriters and clients saw themselves as partners in an enterprise that ought to benefit each and all; and that he now realized that even the most respected of American corporations, the most admired of leasing whiz-kids, took it for granted that the world was a very different kind of place, where the devil took the hindmost; and that even the great white shining IBM was not moved only by the crystalline logic of technology, and was not above seizing an opportunity to destroy competition from leasing companies whose right to invade its serene monopoly IBM's management had perhaps never fully accepted.

In the computer leasing affair, Lloyd's learned that the moral universe of American corporate business is some way from the ideal of 'utmost good faith' that is supposed to govern the Lloyd's market. Whether that is entirely a matter for criticism of Lloyd's and its values, of course, is a different matter.

Computer leasing, at any rate, has been 'no end of a lesson'. It remains to be seen whether it will do underwriters 'no end of good'.

CHAPTER 9

A MUTINY IN FIRST CLASS

What connection can there have been between many people in the innumerable histories of this world, who, from opposite sides of great gulfs, have, nevertheless, been very curiously brought together.

Charles Dickens, *Bleak House*

The village of Swinbrook in the Cotswolds is about as different from the fire-trap tenements of the South Bronx as one human habitation can be from another. Broad tracts of that part of New York City look like Dresden the morning after the great fire-raid. Hollywood made a film about the police precinct there that used to be known as Fort Apache, in celebration of the custom, among the local seekers after *machismo*, of competing to see how close to the front door of the station house they can deposit the cadaver of their latest victim. The grim jest is that now it is known as the Little House on the Prairie, because it stands almost alone amid the surrounding wastes.

Swinbrook is a snug hamlet of immemorial trees and mellow stone cottages, clustered round the twelfth-century church and the Swan Inn on the trout-filled River Windrush, whose inhabitants compete, if at all, only to breed dogs and grow sweet-peas and marrows in their trim gardens. The seventh earl Fortescue, who lives in an ancient but comfortable farmhouse in Swinbrook, might seem unassailably cocooned against the changes and chances of this fleeting world. He is the descendant, according to *Burke's Peerage*, of a soldier 'of extraordinary strength and courage ... said to have borne a huge strong shield' (*fort escu*, in old French) 'before William, Duke of Normandy, at the battle of Hastings'. Yet Lord Fortescue, in the summer of 1979, had to face the disagreeable probability that a substantial proportion of the fortune he had inherited from twenty generations of Devonshire squires, lawyers and soldiers was at risk, along with the frail fabric of crumbling apartment houses in the South Bronx and other slum property in the less salubrious corners of North America.

Nigel, fourteenth baron Napier and Ettrick, is a witty and unassuming former stockbroker who lives in a place that is, if anything, even harder to associate with the South Bronx. Apartment 2, St James's Palace, London SW1, is a home he enjoys, as the phrase goes, by grace and favour of Her Majesty the Queen and by virtue of the fact that he is private secretary to Princess Margaret. Lord Napier, too, found himself in the disagreeable position of facing a demand for more than £250,000 ($375,000), with less than a month to pay, as a result of the same chain of circumstances that connected Lord Fortescue with the South Bronx. Their misfortune, in both cases, was that they were underwriting members of non-marine Syndicate No. 762 at Lloyd's, whose active underwriter was F. H. Sasse.

In 1975 'Tim' Sasse, as everyone calls him, was a wealthy and popular underwriter. At fifty-one he seemed to be on his way at Lloyd's. He was writing risks on behalf of several syndicates managed by his Sasse–Turnbull agency. Besides Lords Napier and Fortescue, the 110 Names on his main syndicate, 762, included a number of other well-known and well-connected people: Major the Honourable Sir Francis Legh, who is an equerry, or personal assistant, to the Queen Mother; Murray Gordon, chairman of the Combined English Stores group; Sir Sigmund Sternberg, a somewhat mysterious tycoon with interests in East–West trade who is a close friend of former prime minister Sir Harold Wilson; Humphrey Swire, a director of Sotheby's, the fine-art auction house, whose family has vast interests in Hong Kong; Nigel Leigh-Pemberton, an opera singer, whose brother is Governor of the Bank of England; and many more.

Sasse was conned by a parcel of rogues, who used his syndicate to push an enormous volume of dubious American and Canadian property insurance through the Lloyd's market. The Lloyd's label gave them the respectability they needed both to get hold of a flood of business in the first place, and then to reinsure it with the Instituto de Resseguros do Brasil (IRB), the Brazilian state-owned reinsurance company, one of the dozen biggest in the world. But Sasse also lost his Names a lot of money because of plain bad risks, including computer leases. The upshot was that his Names found themselves owing more than $40 million between them, which was a good deal more than they could pay.

They did not take this with a stiff upper lip. As Earl Fortescue put it in the House of Lords: 'I do not in any way deny that I agreed that my liability should be unlimited against normal underwriting risks. However, I never agreed, nor do I now feel like agreeing, that I should accept unlimited liability if the underwriter or his agents act fraudulently or outside Lloyd's rules, or if in particular the loss is due to negligence or breach of duty on the part of the Lloyd's Committee ...' As a result, sixty-three of the Names refused to pay that part of their losses that arose from business written in breach of Lloyd's rules. Instead, they sued.

The Sasse affair was that rarest of marine perils, a mutiny among the first-class passengers. It shook Lloyd's to the keel. More acutely even than the *Savonita* row, the Sasse affair seemed to pose the question whether Lloyd's could truly live up to the ideal of its motto: 'In Utmost Good Faith'. This was not just a matter for head-shaking by sentimental old-timers. More than half of Lloyd's premium income comes from the United States. Though there was never, at any stage of the Sasse affair, any doubt that even those Lloyd's policies obtained in the most dubious ways would be honoured, still, the Sasse story was even worse publicity for Lloyd's than computer leasing or the *Savonita*.

It drew attention to practices, notably 'binding authorities', that at least seemed to involve underwriters in conflicts of interest of a startling kind. It made it possible to argue that the Fundamental Rules of the 1871 Lloyd's Act had been systematically broken for many years, with the Committee's full knowledge. At the same time the affair cast serious doubt on the Committee's ability and even on its willingness to act effectively to police the market.

In a very real sense it threatened Lloyd's very existence. It struck at the Names' willingness to put up their money. If ever the outside Names as a group were to lose confidence either in the competence of underwriters in general, or in the efficacy of the Committee, that could bring the whole system down like a house of cards. On the other hand, if the idea were ever to spread that Names could always hope to evade their responsibility for paying losses by reaching for their lawyers, that would undermine the credit of the Lloyd's policy. In the event, the Sasse saga did not bring Lloyd's to the brink of either of these ultimate dangers. But it brought home to thoughtful watchers what could happen if Lloyd's did not put its house in order.

The piece of business that led to all this sorrow was called the 'Den-Har binder'. One of the 'fundamental rules' of Lloyd's – Rule II – says that all business done by Lloyd's underwriters and brokers must be done in the Room. But because Lloyd's is so dependent on business from abroad, and especially from the United States, it has long been willing, if not to bend this rule, at least to make special arrangements to facilitate bringing in overseas business. Over the years one of the most important devices that has grown up to find a way round Rule

II is the 'binding authority', or 'binder'. This means, in effect, that an underwriter at Lloyd's gives authority to a 'producer' – in other words, a broker – to write insurances in his name. As they say at Lloyd's, he 'hands him his pen'. To protect himself, the underwriter naturally specifies limits. He says how much business the producer can commit him to under the binder. He sets an upper limit on the amount of premium that can come in under it and therefore, he hopes, on the amount of claims that will be made on it. He gives authority only for a particular kind of business and in a particular area; in the United States, that typically means in a particular state. And the business must pass through a Lloyd's broker.

Tim Sasse's recollection is that the Den-Har binder was first broked to him in one of the members' men's rooms at Lloyd's. This was early in 1975. A broker friend of his called John Newman slid into the stall next to his and asked him how he would like to write $250,000 worth of business. 'Bring it to me in my office,' said Sasse, 'and if I like it, I'll write it.' A few days later, Newman, who was a director of a firm of Lloyd's brokers called Brentnall Beard, brought the binder to Sasse's box, where it was accepted, not by Sasse personally, but by his partner, Thomas Turnbull.

This was a general binding authority for fire and other property risks granted by Syndicate 762, through Brentnall Beard, to a Florida firm called Transworld Underwriters. One of the officers of Transworld was an Englishman, then living in Coral Gables, Florida, called Dennis Harrison. The binder was to be effective from 1 April 1975. Later that year a firm called Peter King, Inc., was added to the binder; this company had been started by another émigré Englishman in America, Peter King, who by coincidence had once been Turnbull's neighbour in Bedfordshire. Later still, a new name was added to the binder, and that was the one that stuck: Den-Har Underwriters, from the first syllables of Dennis Harrison's first and last names. The Den-Har binder was effective from 1 November 1975. Even earlier, a third English insurance man who had emigrated to the United States became involved: Ted Smith, whom first, IntraGlobal, was given reinsurance facilities by IRB, the Brazilian state reinsurance company, in July 1975.

The three expatriate Englishmen, Smith, King and Harrison, had all worked at Lloyd's in one capacity or another before moving to the United States. Now they were in a position to ship business back there, using the Lloyd's anchor badge to get business that would never have been given to them otherwise, and at the same time they were able to reinsure it with one of the world's biggest reinsurers. It was the opportunity of a lifetime, and they took it with both hands. We shall see what sort of business they found, and what they did with it. But first let us take a closer look at the two central figures in the Lloyd's end of the story, as they stand side by side in the members' men's room.

Tim Sasse, then fifty-one years old, is taller than John Newman by almost a head, a dozen years older, and – at least on the surface – far more confident socially. Fond of horse-racing, devoted to his wife Sarah but at the same time with an eye for a pretty girl, he looked the epitome of the chap who is making the right friends, making the right kind of money and making a success of Lloyd's as a gentleman's club. Underneath, he was a good deal less secure than he looked; but there was no special reason why an outsider like John Newman with a two-by-four chip on his own shoulder would notice that.

Sasse's father died when he was a baby, and he was brought up by his mother, an Australian, in France. She could just afford to send him to 'a good public school'. That matters to him. He mentions it frequently, as if he were torn between wanting you to know that he had been to an expensive school and concern that you might make the mistake of jumping to the conclusion that therefore his family were very well off. He went straight from school into the Ghurkas, one of the regiments raised in India with British officers and other ranks recruited from the ferocious little tribesmen from the Himalayan foothills who like to cut off their enemies' heads with their curving *kukri* knives. He had what his generation called 'a good war'; he won the Military Cross in Italy. His best friend in the regiment was a Lloyd's man; but after Sasse came out of the army in 1947, he was planning to go to Australia to look for a job when he met a man playing cricket who talked him into trying Lloyd's. He had 'just enough money' to become a working Name.

His wife Sarah came from a wealthier background. Her father was an underwriter who earned a large income even during the Depression of the 1930s, and lived in style outside London with a butler and half a dozen other servants. Gradually Sasse began to get on. He became the active underwriter of a well-known syndicate. (It had once belonged to H. F. Tiarks, whose daughter, Henrietta, Marchioness of Tavistock, is married to the heir to the Duke of Bedford.) But he didn't really begin to feel that he had made it until the episode of the Rheingold syndicate.

Rheingold was a horse, jointly owned by a syndicate of half a dozen people, most of them connected with Lloyd's. It was a smart crowd, the sort of people whose boxes at the races were always full of pretty women and vintage champagne, not to mention some high-rolling friends from New York. One of the co-owners was Tim Sasse. Another was Nancy Weller-Poley, wife of John Weller-Poley; the horse was in training at their stud at Boxted Hall in Suffolk.

Weller-Poley, like Sasse, had won the Military Cross during the war. Unlike Sasse, he came from an old landed family. His father had been High Sheriff of Suffolk, and the son was the archetypal squire at Boxted, near Sudbury: a justice of the peace and chairman of the local Conservative Association; a keen hunting man, handsome and social; a heavy swell, in Lloyd's terms, though some of his business associates were less distinguished. The fact that about this time he sold a large quantity of the family silver suggests that his financial position, while affluent, may have been under pressure.

Another member of the Rheingold syndicate, equally smart, though in a very different, international jet-set style, was Charles Anthony Barbaro St George, chairman of Lloyd's brokers Oakeley Vaughan and also head of his own Oakeley Vaughan underwriting agency. In 1981 Oakeley Vaughan was to be the subject of an inquiry by the Committee of Lloyd's. Both Charles St George and his lawyer brother Edward have many connections in the Bahamas as well as in New York.

It was certainly doing Sasse no harm, either in social or in business terms – except perhaps with very stuffy people – to be seen at the races with this smart, fast set. Then Rheingold won the Prix de l'Arc de Triomphe in 1973, the biggest and richest race in France, and the syndicate sold him for £1 million. Now Sasse felt he had really arrived in a world that fascinated him. He had made the first big dollop of easy money in his life. Life seemed easy, and so did underwriting.

Tim Sasse's style as an underwriter made him more vulnerable to the type of error which occurred. He had a box in the Room, but he didn't use it much, preferring to operate from his office. He neither led slips himself, nor did he often follow on slips led by others. He was not writing large risks, but giving binding authorities to retail producers. He liked to write 100 per cent of the slip himself, because that way there were no other underwriters in a position to tell him what to do. He was, as the Lloyd's Establishment saw him, 'a bit of a loner'. He thought the Establishment was stuffy and that only jealousy prevented people from acknowledging how profitable his way of doing business was. He was, in short, in a mood where he felt confident he could handle anyone and anything – certainly including John Newman and his business propositions.

If Tim Sasse is very conscious of being a public school boy, John Newman is equally conscious of being a grammar school boy. 'I am concerned with the question whether a grammar school boy with no friends in high places can get a fair hearing at Lloyd's,' he said to me once with sharp bitterness. The distinction is a piece of English social history with more than casual relevance to Lloyd's. The 'public schools' in Britain are expensive private boarding schools on which American prep schools have modelled themselves to a great extent. There are about two hundred of them altogether, of which the most famous are Eton, Winchester, Harrow, Westminster and Rugby. The grammar schools, originally charity day schools, many of great antiquity, were taken over by the state after the Education Act of 1944, and most of them were turned into the top ability stream of the free state system of secondary schools: tests at the age of eleven would send the brightest children to the grammar school. A public school boy, therefore, was one whose parents paid a great deal of money to send him to a prestigious boarding school; a grammar school boy was a bright boy from a family that either couldn't or wouldn't pay school fees. The Labour government in the 1970s abolished the grammar schools because the process of selection was considered too elitist for socialists; all state school pupils now go to the same 'comprehensive' secondary schools.

What was happening at Lloyd's in the 1950s and 1960s was that for the first time a substantial number of young men who did not come from the assured and generally moneyed public school background were refusing to be content with jobs as clerks or book-keepers and beginning to compete to be underwriters in their own right, or to be directors of firms of brokers. Many grammar school boys went on to great success at Lloyd's without experiencing hostility or discrimination. They include some members of the present Committee. But in the years when John Newman was making his way at Lloyd's, class prejudice could be open and ugly. Newman feels that a boy from his background simply had to take more risks, to be farther out, even at times to be something of a clown, in order to be noticed and to get the business that might go automatically to a less able but better-connected competitor. There is no way of proving or disproving that assessment objectively. What matters is that Newman and others like him felt it, and reacted accordingly. They felt that no one would give them a fair break. And after a time some of the ablest and most ambitious of them began to derive a contemptuous satisfaction from finding that they could take for themselves what others expected to have handed to them on a plate.

Newman went straight from a North London grammar school into Price Forbes and started at the bottom as an 'initialling boy', taking slips round the Room to be corrected for minor omissions. The two other young men who joined the firm at the same time were respectively the sons of a wealthy cotton-mill owner in Lancashire, with plenty of property to insure, and the son of Price Forbes's auditor. In the 1950s, Lloyd's was like that. If you had neither social nor business connections to bring to a firm, you might well feel that you had to run a little harder than the rest, and perhaps cut a corner or two as well. Newman did not stay long with Price Forbes, but went the rounds from one firm of insurance brokers to another, learning all he could about the business. On the first day of 1967 he joined the board of the interesting firm of Follows, Weller-Poley, Lloyd's brokers.

Follows, Weller-Poley was controlled (through an associated company called Liverpool and County Discount) by an even more interesting enterprise called the Vehicle & General Insurance Company – the 'V & G'. In the 1960s, this was about the hottest property in the entire British insurance industry. Run by three aggressive young businessmen, the V & G's success was based on the somewhat nebulous concept of 'the proven motorist', who was to be attracted to insure with the V & G by high no-claim discounts. The V & G was a rate cutter, and it refused to have anything to do with such cosy insurance practices, common in Britain, as 'knock-for-knock' claims settlement. There was another gimmick. In theory the 'proven motorist' would make so many fewer claims that the company needed far lower reserves than its competitors. If there was ever any intention of applying this idea strictly, it fell by the wayside.

Premium expanded, often by 50 per cent and more a year, and the V & G also grew by acquisitions, not all of companies that had pursued 'the proven motorist' so single-mindedly. Before long the company was insuring more than one in ten of all the drivers in Britain. Obviously its accident record approached closer and closer to the average, and its reserves became more and more inadequate. Management, commented the subsequent official report, was 'running blind'; it was 'conducting its affairs with the panache and imprudence of a gambler, and with a risk of future insolvency if the gamble did not succeed'. It couldn't, and it didn't. In 1971 the V & G collapsed in one of the worst insurance smashes in British insurance history.

In the meantime, John Follows and John Weller-Poley, strangely ill assorted though they might seem – the brilliant, aggressive young hustler and the sociable East Anglian squire – had been on to a first-

rate thing. Their firm got all the non-motor business dredged up by
V & G's high-powered sales force. It also broked all the V & G's
reinsurance. In addition, Follows brought in a good deal of business
from Israel, and Weller-Poley brought in more from his vast circle of
social acquaintances.

John Newman was soon bringing in a lot of business of his own,
mostly from the United States and Canada. But not long after his
arrival, the firm began to be divided by fierce internal rivalries. In the
end, Newman succeeded in lining up a majority, organizing a board-
room coup and getting rid of Follows. This was early in 1968.

Follows was, perhaps justifiably, furious. He was shortly to be
avenged in bizarre circumstances. About a year earlier, Charles Raw,
a business writer on the London *Sunday Times* (later to become the
most formidable financial investigative journalist in London), had
written two shrewd comments hinting that the V & G's reserves must
be inadequate. In April 1968, Raw suddenly received through the mail
the top half of a letter on Vehicle & General letterhead.

The letter was addressed to a leading Lloyd's underwriter (and he,
too, comes into the Sasse saga) named Basil Edmunds, of the
d'Ambrumenil syndicate. 'Dear Basil,' it said, 'You will no doubt
remember that it was agreed that claims paid from 1963 for five years
would be protected to the extent that the difference between the gross
premiums paid by ourselves and the net payments by yourselves over
this period would be in effect "stop lossed" by ourselves ...' What the
letter meant was that the V & G was in effect relieving its reinsurers
of their obligations to repay all claims in the first layer of reinsurance,
the all-important one, covering claims from £2,500–£10,000 for each
loss. That meant the company was effectively not reinsured, and
therefore that its liabilities were far higher than they appeared to be.
In effect, it meant that it was insolvent. Raw's resulting article did not
bring the V & G to an immediate end, but the company soon began
to ship water and finally foundered three years later.

The Vehicle & General's associated company that controlled J. H.
Weller-Poley (as the company was called after the angry departure of
John Follows) disappeared with the collapse of the V & G. But J. H.
Weller-Poley lived on. It passed through a number of hands (including
those of the Cardiff financier Julian Hodge, sometimes known as the
'Wizard of the Valleys') before being bought by a firm of brokers called
Brentnall Beard.

Brentnall Beard had been started in Shrewsbury, a small country
town near the Welsh border, before the Second World War by its

chairman, Fred Beard, and had developed outside London. The moving spirit now, however, was an ambitious Londoner named Stanley Elsbury. Relations between Elsbury and Newman were not good. Newman complained about the office he had been given; in return, according to Newman, Elsbury said something about 'cows that don't give milk'. It was that remark, Newman reflected long afterwards, which led to the Sasse affair. For he now determined to drown Elsbury in milk. As a first step, he started forming small insurance companies in the United States and Canada.

I have told the story of John Newman, John Follows and John Weller-Poley at some length for a number of reasons. One is that it is not generally known that there was any connection at all between the Vehicle & General crash, the most spectacular insurance scandal of the 1960s in Britain, and the Sasse affair, the most spectacular scandal of the 1970s. The second is that the cast of characters reappears in other contexts in Lloyd's recent history. The link between John Newman and Tim Sasse, the broker and the underwriter on the Den-Har binder, was that amiable enigma John Weller-Poley, who died of a brain tumour in 1980. Weller-Poley introduced his business colleague Newman to his racing friend Sasse, and Newman took to dropping by once a week or so at Sasse's office, a pleasantly unbusinesslike place with racing prints and a few nudes on the walls, where Tim Sasse could be relied on to rustle up a sandwich and a glass of wine at lunchtime. On one of these companionable occasions Sasse confessed to Newman that he had a problem. He had a loss on his 1974 account. Most of it – some £160,000 – was due to a 'tonner' he had written for Christopher Moran. A tonner is a kind of insurance policy – now, but not then, illegal at Lloyd's – which is pure gambling. It started as a form of excess-of-loss re-insurance for marine underwriters. If they were afraid of the freak aggregation of loss that could arise if, for example, the *Queen Mary* were to ram the *Normandie*, they would cover themselves by taking out an insurance against two ships of more than 50,000 tons each being involved in a casualty in a given year. But tonners evolved into a form of gambling; for example, you could take out an insurance against the possibility that more than five tankers of over 100,000 tons would be involved in casualties in a given year. Since it is virtually certain that they will be, the premium will run well over 100 per cent, perhaps as high as 1,000 per cent.

Christopher Moran was another of the young men in a hurry at Lloyd's. From 'a very middle-class background' – his own description – he left a London grammar school at seventeen and went to work for a big aviation broker. Ten years after leaving school, his broking company went public with profits of more than £1 million a year. He complained that the then Chairman of Lloyd's did not like him parking his Rolls-Royce outside the main entrance. In 1980 Moran lost a libel action he brought against the London *Daily Telegraph* for reporting certain transactions involving reinsurance in which he had been involved. In 1982 he was acquitted of separate fraud charges relating to large aviation reinsurances at the Old Bailey. As we shall see, he was later expelled from Lloyd's. Moran, advised by the redoubtable Lord Goodman, is appealing against his expulsion and is also seeking to acquire an underwriting agency.

Largely as a result of the tonner Moran had broked to him, Tim Sasse was looking at a loss for his Names on the 1974 account. It was not a big loss. But most underwriters try to avoid giving their Names a loss at all if they can help it.

John Newman found Sasse a way out. He showed him a way, using a Canadian company, of carrying forward his 1974 loss into 1975 (a year Sasse then expected to be profitable!) by means of an accounting device. Newman maintains stoutly today that what he did was not illegal. On the contrary, he is proud that he was able to help his friend Sasse, and sorrowful that Sasse does not now appear to appreciate his help.

Sasse had written a binder to a Canadian company, Deslauriers Wilkins & Associates, Inc. (DWI). Newman got the board of Brentnall Beard to set up a Canadian insurance company and transfer the whole portfolio of premium and claims under the DWI binder to it.

What Newman had noticed was that a lot of the business attributed to 1975 actually belonged to 1974. He explains how this could happen. If business explodes over the New Year, a lot of the business that is reported in the bordereaux, or records, for January and February will be business that rightly belongs in December, but was delayed in the processing. In this way, Newman found a way for around Canadian $500,000 in premium, which would otherwise have been attributed to 1975, to be attributed to 1974 instead. That was enough to wipe out the Sasse syndicate's embarrassing 1974 loss. In this way Newman had not only helped a friend and, he hoped, earned his gratitude, but also earned a healthy chunk of brokerage commission for Brentnall Beard.

Sasse had an additional reason to feel grateful to Newman. After Rheingold won the Prix de l'Arc de Triomphe, Sasse bought a 25 per cent stake in a firm of brokers called Popple, Lock. He needed capital for this venture, and Newman talked about helping him to raise it by buying some of the Names on his syndicate from him.

Whatever the exact weighting of gratitude and complicity in his mental processes, Tim Sasse felt, as John Newman stood beside him in the Lloyd's men's room, that Newman had a hold on him, and that he could not refuse the Den-Har binder.

Dennis Harrison's firm, Transworld Underwriters, which was given the original binding authority broked by John Newman to Tim Sasse, ran into a little financial bother in the course of 1975. So, that autumn, another of the enterprises Harrison was running in the intervals between living the good life in Coral Gables, Florida, was added to the binder. With effect from 1 November 1975, the Den-Har Corporation was empowered to accept fire and other non-marine risks up to a limit of $500,000 per risk and per loss anywhere in the United States on behalf of the unknowing members of the Sasse syndicate.

Dennis Harrison had moved from London to Florida in 1974, where at first most of his business came from Norstrom–Larpenteur, a big American insurance broker. Before long he had renewed his acquaintance with Ted Smith, who had worked at the Meacock box at Lloyd's, and was now established in Texas. In mid-1975 Smith had flown to London and been introduced to John Howell, at the I R B's London office, who gave his company, IntraGlobal, a reinsurance facility. All Harrison and Smith needed now was a flood of business to flow into the channel they had dug. Sometime in late 1975 or early 1976, they made contact with the very man to provide that business. His name was John Valentine Goepfert.

Jack Goepfert, then forty-eight, slim, balding and endowed with great charm, was in a spot of bother, not for the first or the last time in his career. The latest field of his operations had a coincidentally appropriate name – the Argonaut Insurance Company, named after the band of Greek heroes who set out to find the Golden Fleece, a commodity Goepfert and his friends, too, had pursued for many years. In November 1975 the Argonaut took out a full-page ad in the *Wall Street Journal* to assure the world that Goepfert had no connection with it, and on 13 February 1976 the company filed suit against him in federal court in New York.

Over the years Goepfert has been involved in a whole string of insurance frauds. He was sued by the Resources Insurance Company after it collapsed in the middle 1970s, and he was mentioned in press comment after the failure of the Heritage Insurance Company in

Illinois a couple of years later. In 1980 he was indicted on a federal criminal charge for swindles connected with fraudulent construction bonds and financial guarantees. His firm, Casualty and Indemnity, with an office in downtown Philadelphia but set up under the laws of Belize, in Central America, used worthless securities as collateral for loans. These were issued, *inter alia*, by a company called the Phoenix Trust Ltd, itself subject to the laws of an even more obscure jurisdiction, that of the island of Tortola, in the British Virgin Islands, described in the federal indictment as 'an old stamping ground for insurance fraud'.

Goepfert lived on a 200-acre estate in Wall Township, and kept an office in Manaquan, both in New Jersey. He and his associates were adept at operating out of a suitcase if they needed to, however, and acquaintances say that at one time Goepfert transacted much of his business from a telephone brought to his table at a New York financial-district restaurant called Stan's Other Place, near the Brooklyn Bridge. These old haunts no longer see him, since he is serving a ten-year federal prison sentence.

Goepfert is a master who has woven infinite variations round a simple theme. Somehow, he acquired a book of low-quality insurance business worth at least $10 million and perhaps as much as $30 million in annual premium. This book of premium from owners wanting to insure slum housing and cheap commercial property, mostly in New York, New Jersey, Pennsylvania, Illinois, Michigan and Florida, was Goepfert's stock in trade, so to speak. His method of operating was to find a rundown insurance company that was hungry for premium, make his book of dubious business available to it and then move in and milk the flow of premium by means of a truly dazzling repertoire of scams. To the basic devices of 'churning' commission by passing premium through an absurdly long chain of insurers controlled by himself and his friends, Goepfert began in the late 1970s to add the refinements made possible by reinsurance.

In most American states, property owners are obliged by law to insure their buildings. High-risk, low-quality property – whether it is tenements in the South Bronx, over-the-road trucking companies in the West, tract housing in the hurricane belt of Florida, or bars in marginal urban neighbourhoods in the Middle West – is no fun for insurers. Such property is often overvalued. It attracts more than its share of fraudulent claims. And because fire and other hazards are more common in marginal areas, even legitimate claims can come to many times the price of the premium.

To ensure that even this low-grade property is nevertheless covered, it is shared out among all domestic insurance companies in most states under an arrangement known as 'Fair Plan'. All insurers agree to take a proportionate share, and the rates of premium are correspondingly high. In theory, they are set at such a level that the companies are supposed to break even. In practice, they are usually in the red, because once a neighbourhood or a batch of commercial property starts to go downhill, it can sink with alarming speed.

Unscrupulous operators can make money out of 'Fair Plan' property in countless ways. The crudest is to insure the buildings as close as possible to replacement value, which could be ten or even twenty times the market value, pay someone to put a match to them and claim the insurance. It is done all the time. But sophisticates like Jack Goepfert and his friends know better ways of skinning a cat than that.

Dumb crooks, in short, cheat on the claims. Smart crooks operate on the supply side. Instead of – or as well as – making fraudulent claims, they use a dozen devices to divert premium before it ever reaches the underwriters. Given the inevitably high rate of claims on poor-risk property, that means that the rate of claims as a proportion of the premium actually reaching the underwriters is ruinously high. A plaintive inquiry from a French underwriter who had been burned in one of these time-honoured scams to a friend in New York makes the point. ''ow come,' this outraged Gaul asked, 'when the worst underwriting risk I 'ave ever seen is 140 per cent per annum, that I 'ave lost 340 per cent of premium on this?' The answer, his New York friend pointed out, was that claims were probably no more than 100 per cent of the premium paid by the insured, but that perhaps as much as three-quarters of the premium got lost on the way to Paris.

There are many, many tricks for skimming premium. One of the simplest is the 'Chinese papers' trick. Each copy in a set of insurance documents has a different figure written into the box for the premium. The highest figure, naturally, is the premium actually paid by the insured; the lowest, by far, is the premium finally paid over to the underwriter.

The basic point is that Fair Plan property offers an opportunity of getting hold of a large cash flow. The insured, faced with high premiums from Fair Plan itself, is tempted to jump at any cut-rate premium on offer. Underwriters, thinking of the investment income they stand to make on a big cash flow with interest rates at their present high levels, are tempted to grab the cash flow and not ask too many questions about where it comes from. (Of course an underwriter will not knowingly accept a mass of poor-quality business at low rates of premium. The trick is to conceal the quality of the business from the ultimate underwriter.) Brokers, too, even if they are not going to skim any of it illegally, are apt to salivate over the commission to be earned on big flows of premium.

One of the mysteries about John Valentine Goepfert is the true nature of his relationship with another legendary figure in the New York insurance world, Raymond E. Karlinsky. Goepfert worked for an agency called B & R Excess, controlled by Karlinsky. In 1970 the New York State insurance department revoked Karlinsky's licence as an excess and surplus lines broker because B & R Excess was putting business into a Florida insurer, State Fire and Casualty, of which Karlinsky had been owner and board chairman until 1967, although he knew State Fire to be in 'a hazardous financial condition'. State Fire went bankrupt in 1969. In 1970 Karlinsky was indicted by a federal grand jury in Miami, but all charges were dismissed.

Karlinsky is also involved in the far more remarkable story of Promotora de Occidente SA, or POSA, a Panamanian reinsurance company that is at the centre of a major international scandal. POSA was the brainchild of Pedro Reyner, former son-in-law of Mexican President Emilio Portes-Gil, a dapper Latin diplomat and a United Nations adviser. Reyner's idea was that Third World countries were being milked by American and European insurers, and his plan was to create a Third World reinsurance company. He travelled round the world in pursuit of his dream, accompanied by Karlinsky, who drew up an elaborate set of reinsurance arrangements. Many of these involved two intermediaries that produced the business – one of them, MIR in London, owned by a New York concern controlled by Karlinsky and associates. When the POSA scandal broke, many of the best-known insurance companies in America, not to mention the Posgate box at Lloyd's, woke up to find that their reinsurance premiums had gone to more than eighty reinsurers, many of them in the Third World, and began to fear that they would never be able to collect claims under the coverage. Now POSA is in liquidation and, in the United States, under investigation by federal and state authorities. Its affairs are the subject of lawsuits by more than forty companies. Pedro Reyner and Raymond Karlinsky exchange accusations: Karlinsky insists that POSA was always controlled by Reyner; Reyner insists that it was used by Karlinsky to pass unprofitable business to associated reinsurers without their knowledge.

Karlinsky is a man of some style. One of the ironies of the Sasse story,

given the past connection between Karlinsky and Goepfert, is that Tim
Sasse met Karlinsky at the races in England and was much impressed
by his geniality. 'When I'm in my little box at the Derby, drinking
champagne with a few of my friends,' Sasse reminisced modestly to me,
'Ray Karlinsky is in the big smart box with Charlie St George and all
the pretty models and the smart people, and he still comes over to me
and says, "Hi, Tim!"'

Karlinsky insists that he fell out with Jack Goepfert years ago and
has not so much as seen him since 1975. At least since the Argonaut
affair in that year, however, Goepfert has been in the business of
putting his book of low-quality business into the account of one insurer
after another. He can rarely have seen a more tempting opportunity
than the proposition put to him by Dennis Harrison. In the binding
authority from Sasse, they had something like a blank cheque. True,
Newman had broked it to Sasse on the understanding that the premium
income would not exceed $400,000 and that the risks would be mainly
in Florida, and there was a limit of $500,000 on any one risk. That was
not going to stand in Goepfert's way. The binding authority was in the
name of Lloyd's of London, a name of magic that might persuade any
suspicious insurers to overlook the low rate of premium. And Lloyd's
of London would not be in any hurry to refuse claims or to repudiate
the binding contract, for fear of adverse publicity in the United States.

Jack Goepfert personally had to keep a low profile because of the
Argonaut affair. But two close friends and business associates, Alan
Assael and Richard Mamarella, were out front for him on the operation. There are awed tales of Mamarella in New Jersey stamping the
Lloyd's anchor on to policies as hard as he could go. It was at the
beginning of March 1976 that Goepfert began to give Harrison what
he called his 'special book of business'. It was special, all right. By the
summer, a good share of all the rubbishy insurance business in the
eastern half of the United States had been bound to the account of the
unsuspecting Names on Syndicate 762. Lloyd's has undertaken many
innovative insurances before, but this was the first time one of its
syndicates became insurer to organized crime.

Even if they had played it straight and confined themselves to
pocketing their share of the brokerage on this tide of premium, Goepfert and Harrison, Assael and Mamarella, would have done very well
out of it. But of course they didn't. For a start, they fraudulently billed
the policy-holders for property inspections that were never carried out.
They skimmed some of the premium due from Goepfert's Connecticut
company, U.S. Excess (whose offices in reality were in New Jersey), to

the Sasse syndicate by fraudulently claiming that policies had been modified by co-insurance clauses, under which premium should be returned to the policy-holders. In fact, no premium was returned, and the Sasse syndicate was done out of more than $200,000 in premium. The biggest skim of all was even simpler. The policies were supposed to be processed by Den-Har in Florida, but in fact Mamarella processed them, mostly in New Jersey, through U.S. Excess. More than $1 million of premium due from policy-holders to Den-Har, as agents for the Sasse syndicate, was diverted from U.S. Excess to a whole string of companies and partnerships controlled by Goepfert and Assael, including such solid-sounding entities as Northeast Facilities, Atlantic Reinsurance and Garden State Reinsurance, not to mention John V. Goepfert Associates, before finding its way to Goepfert, Assael, Harrison and others. At least $300,000 ended up in bank accounts in the names of Goepfert and Harrison in one of the classic offshore tax havens, Curaçao, in the Netherlands Antilles. Altogether, according to the United States Attorney at their subsequent trial, Goepfert diverted about $1·7 million, and Harrison about $900,000.

One of the most striking aspects of this complicated story swirling around Tim Sasse is how quickly the damage was done and how long it took Lloyd's to realize what had happened, let alone do anything about it.

In part, no doubt, this was because Lloyd's machinery for dealing with such an extraordinarily bold raid was inadequate. But it is impossible to escape the conclusion that the situation was made worse by the instinct of those in authority at Lloyd's to sweep unpleasantness under the rug at almost any cost. There were plausible reasons at every stage for this reluctance to get to the bottom of the problem and root it out: the desire to protect the policy-holders, the reputation of Lloyd's, Tim Sasse and his Names. But the consequences of the combination of secretiveness and an unwillingness to face facts were disastrous.

Goepfert and his friends did not begin to stuff their 'special book of business' into the Sasse syndicate's portfolio, through the Den-Har binder, until March 1976. The main mass of dubious business did not begin to flow before May. By the end of May, the broker John Newman said later that he knew that something strange and dangerous was going on. And the board of his brokerage firm, Brentnall Beard, knew. Tim Sasse, the underwriter, knew. LeBoeuf, Lamb, Leiby & Macrae, Lloyd's general counsel in New York, knew. And, informally at least, the Committee knew. Yet it was not until 31 July 1976 that Sasse gave

written notice of termination of the Den-Har contract, and even then
he said he would accept business already quoted up to the end of
August. And it was not until 29 December 1977 – twenty months to
the day after the extent of the mess was known in London – that the
Sasse syndicate was suspended from doing business at Lloyd's.

As early as March 1976, LeBoeuf sent a telex to Lloyd's passing on
what were then no more than rumours that Goepfert and another man
with a track record for insurance fraud were involved. By the end of
April John Newman had reported something of the situation, in particular the large volume of premium income, to the board of Brentnall
Beard and to the Committee. At about the same time, Tim Sasse got
the first inkling that things were getting out of hand. His colleague John
Scott got a call from an insurance friend in the United States. This man
had discovered that there were sub-agents offering to be able to plan
risks at Lloyds – presumably he had come across one of Goepfert's
many fronts – and wanted to offer the same facility himself!

Complaints began to pour in to LeBoeuf and also to Lord, Bissell &
Brook in Chicago, Lloyd's 'attorney in fact' under the special system
in Illinois. Both law firms were so well known in the insurance world
that when unfamiliar competition cropped up with a Lloyd's policy at
the end of the line, the wires were going to buzz. It was not many weeks
before insurers both in the New York area and in the Mid-West were
aware that there was a new tiger out there in the jungle, a man-eater,
with the Lloyd's anchor badge on his collar. They made their disquiet
extremely plain.

Later in the summer, complaints from insurers were followed by
complaints from policy-holders. Some were unhappy about their documentation. Others wanted to know why claims had not been paid.
These complaints, too, were passed on to Lloyd's by LeBoeuf. This,
more than anything, ought to have lit up a little red light in somebody's
head at Lloyd's. For if there is one thing that sends a chill down the
spine of the stoutest at Lloyd's, it is the faintest suggestion that anyone
at all in the United States might harbour the smallest doubts about
whether Lloyd's of London would pay up on its policies to the last
penny. The United States market is simply too important.

Yet, if the Committee had been made aware informally as early as
the spring, by Newman as well as by LeBoeuf, that there were serious
doubts connected with the Den-Har binder, it was – almost un-
believably – not until December 1976 that the Committee first took
official notice of what had happened.

When John Newman had first mentioned what was to become the

Den-Har binder to Tim Sasse, he gave Sasse the impression that the premium income would be around $250,000. When he signed the binder, Sasse thought it would be at most $400,000. By the end of March 1976, Newman already knew it was more than that. What he did not know was that by July the true premium figure was four times higher than the number he had been given. This was because of the IRB reinsurance. On a new slip, written on 5 May but backdated to 1 March, 'Lloyd's underwriters' had been added to the reinsurance. That meant Sasse, since he had written 100 per cent of the Den-Har slip. Unknown to Sasse, on this new reinsurance slip, the IRB was reinsuring up to $100,000 on each loss and in return was to get 75 per cent of the premium.

This was all wrong, of course. The proper chain would have taken the premium for the direct insurance from the policy-holder to Dennis Harrison in Florida to Brentnall Beard in London to Sasse; and then the premium for the reinsurance would go back from Sasse to Brentnall Beard to Smith through a firm called Austen & Balcon to the IRB. What Harrison and Smith were doing was what is known at Lloyd's as 'net accounting' – in other words, subtracting reinsurance premium before it reached the accounts of the underwriting syndicate, so as to enable a bigger volume of business to be written without breaching Lloyd's premium income limits. The premium was going from the policy-holders, theoretically to Den-Har, but in reality to Goepfert's and Assael's various firms. Some of it was then going on through Harrison to Brentnall Beard and Sasse. Some was going from Harrison to Smith and so to the IRB. And some of it was being skimmed off through U.S. Excess, Garden State Reinsurance and the rest.

John Newman, in London, knew nothing about this. As soon as he learned about the IRB reinsurance, sometime in the spring of 1975, he told Tim Sasse. Total premium income, he said, was not $250,000, nor yet $400,000. It was about $3·8 million. Sasse was aghast. Newman told him not to worry too much. After all, the IRB was taking three-quarters of the premium. In June 1975, Newman passed to Harrison orally Sasse's order to cancel the binding authority, and this cancellation was confirmed by telex from Brentnall Beard to Harrison on 23 July. Sasse's cancellation became effective on 31 July, subject to the concession that business already quoted could be bound if the orders were received before 31 August.

John Newman was now making frequent trips to the United States, working with the lawyers at LeBoeuf Lamb and with the accountants Kroll Edelman to try to sort the situation out. He was also reporting to the sleuths at Lloyd's. The two deputy chairmen were then Alec Higgins and Peter Foden-Pattinson, but in the autumn of 1976 Foden-Pattinson had a heart attack, and another member of the Committee, Leslie Dew, took over as acting deputy chairman; Newman reported through the advisory service at Lloyd's to Dew. Leslie Dew, to his bitter disappointment, learned in November that he was not going to be the next Chairman of Lloyd's, and early in 1977 he accepted an appointment as underwriter to the Gulf Oil captive insurance company in Bermuda; he now divides his time between Bermuda and a splendid apartment on Fifth Avenue in New York. On 1 March 1977 he was succeeded as deputy chairman by Bruce Gray. Before he left, Dew told Newman there were three things to be done. As the first priority, Lloyd's reputation must be protected 'at all costs'. Then Newman must do what could be done to 'salvage' the Sasse syndicate. And then the accounting had to be sorted out.

This was easier said than done. The accounts were in chaos. The Lloyd's advisory service reported to the Committee later that it was not until July 1977 that any 'meaningful' figures were available. Even then it is hard to see that they could have been very realistic, since no attempt had been made at that point to unravel the Goepfert conspiracy. When Leslie Dew contemplated the situation in late 1976, no documentation and none of the premium received had been sent to the Lloyd's Policy Signing Office in the usual way. Indeed, the Den-Har binder had not even been signed. It was obvious that, a great mass of poor-quality risks having been bound, a great tide of claims was about to follow. 'We had to batten down the hatches and wait for the storm to break,' one of Lloyd's lawyers reminisced years later. So in January 1977, on Dew's instructions, the LPSO signed and processed the Den-Har binder with a 1976 date (meaning it would count against the 1976 account). The brokers at Brentnall Beard were instructed to hand over the documentation and such premium as had arrived. It came to just over $1 million gross of commission, $711,000 net. Finally, Dew ordered Sasse to treat the contracts made under the Den-Har binder (cancelled by Sasse in July) as binding on the Names.

Dew's anxiety to regularize the position was entirely understandable. So was his concern to make it absolutely impossible for anyone so much as to whisper that Lloyd's were welshing on policies that carried Lloyd's name. Yet, with hindsight, one can see that the consequence of the dispositions he made was disastrous. In effect, Lloyd's had countermanded Sasse's instructions to cancel contracts that were in breach of Lloyd's own rules in several respects.

Lloyd's had failed to enforce those rules. Even if binding authorities as such were not in breach of the Fundamental Rules (and Rule II does specifically forbid underwriting outside the Room), everyday practices and precautions had been trampled on wholesale. The Den-Har binder had not been processed or even signed. Again, under Lloyd's rules, no binding authority could be given to anyone to underwrite on behalf of members of a Lloyd's syndicate in the United States or Canada unless approved by a tribunal set up by the Lloyd's Non-marine Underwriters Association, or 'tribunalized'. None of the people who had produced the Den-Har business had been tribunalized, nor had Dennis Harrison. And the whole operation was in breach of American and federal law in numerous ways. Dennis Harrison, to take only the most glaring example, was not authorized to underwrite insurance in the state of Florida.

By ordering the LPSO to sign the Den-Har business in spite of all the flagrant irregularities, Dew was storing up trouble for the future. The responsibility indeed lies with the Committee, whose decisions he was presumably carrying out. But in effect he was transferring responsibility for losses due to Lloyd's failure to enforce its own rules to the Sasse Names. Or so the Names' lawyers would argue, successfully, three years later. And all this was done in secret. The intention might be to save the Names. But they were not consulted about their own salvation, or not fully, and not yet.

For a time, the Committee of Lloyd's appears to have hoped that salvation would come from Brazil and the IRB. If so, then the problem became merely temporary. It would be necessary to bridge the Names over a difficult time; then the IRB would pay up on the reinsurance and the worst of the losses would disappear. For a few months, it looked as if the IRB might go along with that scenario. In November John Howell, the underwriter who had given Ted Smith the rein-surance facility at the IRB in London, resigned. At about the same time, the IRB made an initial payment of $500,000 to the Sasse syndicate, pending investigations. But then its attitude hardened. After all, it too had been a victim of the conspiracy in the United States. On Christmas Eve 1977 the investigator Robert Bishop flew out to Rio to begin work on the IRB's behalf. Soon afterwards, the IRB made it plain it would not pay up before a full investigation had taken place.

Back in London, once again, the approach of the year-end audit was concentrating minds wonderfully. A new Sasse syndicate, 828, was due to take over from 762 on 1 January. It was becoming urgent to decide whether it should be allowed to continue accepting risks. And it was becoming clear that the premium put through the LPSO the previous winter was only a small proportion of the total and that a huge volume of Den-Har business had still not been processed. In late December the Committee bit the bullet and decided to suspend the Sasse syndicate.

An experienced underwriter, Basil Edmunds, was called in to investigate the tangled paperwork. The Committee decided that the priorities should be: (1) the prompt payment of claims; (2) the protection of the Names; and (3) the protection of the good name of Lloyd's. That was admirable so far as it went. But it scarcely recognized the extent to which the first two objects, in particular, might be in conflict. No one could decide that it was more important to pay claims on Jack Goepfert's 'special book of business' than to protect the Names until he had thoroughly investigated what had actually happened on the ground in the United States. It is hard to avoid the suspicion that the Committee was so frightened of bad publicity if it refused to pay claims in the United States that it preferred to make Sasse pay, even though it already knew, from LeBoeuf Lamb, that there were grounds for believing that the claims were dubious.

The Committee again gave orders for the unprocessed business to be put through the LPSO with a 1977 signing date, so that it could be seen what effect it would have on the Names' audit at the end of the year, and on their premium income limits. Basil Edmunds established that there was $7·6 million in unprocessed premium and $8·4 million in unprocessed claims; losses were estimated at $7·7 million. A comprehensive mess. But Edmunds was still optimistic about the chances of recovering from the IRB on the reinsurance. If a full recovery could be made, he calculated, the outstanding claims would dwindle to $1·3 million, an altogether more manageable figure.

For the time being, then, the problem seemed to be how to tide the Names over so that none of them would have to realize assets and pay up large sums only to discover, when the IRB coughed up, that they need not have done so. The position was complicated by the fact that many of the Names' realizable assets were in sterling, then standing at a low exchange rate, while the claims were in US dollars. For the time being, however, the Names' 'deficiencies' – they would not become losses until the three-year accounting period was over – would have to be calculated 'gross' – that is, without offsetting them with any recoveries to be expected from the IRB.

On 15 March 1978, the Committee met to hear the auditor's report. For the 1975 account, the one that was now to close under the three-year system, the final loss would come to £6,600 for each Name. That was bad enough. But the 1976 deficiency was nothing less than catastrophic: £40,750 per Name, of which it was estimated that £30,000 would ultimately be recovered from the IRB. That was to prove wildly optimistic. And for 1977 there was a further deficiency of £8,800. The Committee arranged for a banking facility for a total of $6·5 million to help the Names over the interval before the IRB paid them back. Each of them was to have a letter of credit in US dollars so that they would not have to draw down on their sterling assets to cover their dollar deficiency.

Tim Sasse could not be allowed to underwrite any more, and someone would have to take charge of steering his Names through a very difficult period. The Committee's solution to this problem was revealing: a commercial answer to an essentially non-commercial problem, and a classic Establishment reaction – 'Get hold of a good chap, we knew his father' – and, it has to be said, an appeal to that good chap's good nature to undertake difficult, potentially expensive and dangerous duties for no reward except an implicit promise of gratitude from the Committee of Lloyd's.

Stephen Merrett is the son of one of the most famous and best-liked underwriters in the recent history of Lloyd's. The story of how Roy Merrett negotiated with the Indonesian government to release forty Dutch ships, insured at Lloyd's, in 1957–8, is a classic Lloyd's success story. In his early forties now, married to a financial journalist, Stephen Merrett looks younger. He is a blond, square-jawed man with a pleasant but unmistakably determined, if not stubborn, manner.

Late in April, 1978, Merrett was asked to go and see the Chairman of Lloyd's, Ian Findlay. To his surprise, Findlay asked him if he would be prepared to help Tim Sasse. Merrett was not keen, and asked pointedly whether this was a request that could not be refused. Findlay said mildly that someone had to help, and that there were not many substantial underwriters who were independent of brokers and who had the necessary expertise. What the Chairman really wanted, it turned out, was for Merrett's syndicate, Merrett Dixey, to buy Sasse Turnbull.

Stephen Merrett agreed reluctantly to take on the assignment, and he saw Sasse. Tim Sasse was delighted. He saw this as his great opportunity to continue underwriting, perhaps with a few new Names to give him additional capital, and all would be well. Merrett disabused him of any such dreams and offered him £20,000, with the proviso that if it turned out, after investigation, that the business was worth more than that, he would pay more. Sasse tried for several weeks to get a better deal elsewhere, and then accepted.

Merrett now threw himself into the negotiations with the IRB. He went to Rio and talked to the company, and he went to New York to try to sort out the Den-Har documentation there. But he could see a difficulty that had not, apparently, occurred to the Committee. The Committee seemed to think it was just a matter of negotiating amiably with the IRB, who would pay most of the Names' losses in the end. Merrett could see that there would be no recovery without at least the threat of litigation, and perhaps not even then. Sasse had already issued a writ after the IRB had made it plain they would not pay unless there was a full investigation. But Merrett could also see that he was in a dilemma: the more digging he did, and the more he found out about the murky side of the Den-Har binder, the weaker that would make his claim for recovery against the IRB.

Then, in August 1978, as he dug deeper into the affairs of Syndicate 762, Merrett discovered something that changed everything. He found out about the Canadian fire binders, broked to Sasse by John Newman of Brentnall Beard and collectively known as the 'DWI binders' after one of the firms involved, Deslauriers, Wilkins & Associates. But Newman had arranged for Sasse to give binding authorities to several of the companies he had set up back in the days when he was intent on drowning Stanley Elsbury in milk. One of them had a name, Follwell Inc., that commemorated the firm of Follows, Weller-Poley. Merrett also discovered what he considered manipulation of the accounts relating to these Canadian binders. Specifically, he found evidence both that money had been taken into the 1974 account from the 1975 account. As we have seen, John Newman maintains that the money rightfully belonged in the 1974 account. These two discoveries – of the losses on the Canadian binders, and of the apparent manipulation of their accounts – changed everything.

First, it hardened the attitudes both of Stephen Merrett and of the Committee of Lloyd's. There was now no longer any question of Merrett buying the Sasse Turnbull agency, since it was plainly to all intents and purposes insolvent. Instead, Merrett agreed to act on an unpaid basis. (He did eventually get an indemnity against legal costs from the Committee of Lloyd's, though there was to be disagreement about that too before it was finally arranged, and in any case the indemnity scarcely compensated him for the sheer time consumed by Sasse's affairs, let alone the unpleasantness of the litigation.) As for the Committee's attitude to Tim Sasse after the discovery of the DWI losses, it can be compared to that of Lady Bracknell to Mr Worthing in Oscar Wilde's comedy *The Importance of Being Earnest*: 'To lose one parent, Mr Worthing,' she says, 'may be regarded as a misfortune; to lose both looks like carelessness.'

Secondly, the discoveries led to recrimination between Tim Sasse and John Newman. And of course they changed the situation of Syndicate 762's Names. Almost immediately it became apparent that the DWI losses would increase each Name's loss on the 1976 account by at least £30,000–£35,000.

Finally, DWI put an end to the illusion that the Sasse affair would blow over once the Brazilians could be persuaded to pay up.

Merrett discovered the DWI losses only because Brentnall Beard, which had up until then been meeting claims on the Canadian fire business out of premium without putting either claims or premium through the Lloyd's Policy Signing Office, ran out of money. The losses could be concealed no longer. It was estimated that the losses came to a total of some Canadian $12·4 million. Much time and temper were consumed over the last four months of 1978 over the question whether Stephen Merrett should sign the DWI business, discovered in 1978, into the accounts of the 1977 year for Syndicate 762, which had ceased underwriting at the end of 1977. In spite of heavy pressure from the Committee, Merrett refused, on the grounds that it would not be fair to the Names. Eventually, on legal advice, a compromise was reached and a 'dummy' syndicate set up to deal with the losses.

By January 1979, even the Canadian binders did not seem to be specially significant against the welter of other bad news. The Syndicate's troubles were not limited to the Den-Har DWI binders; there had been a lot of plain unsuccessful underwriting that had nothing to do with John Newman or Brentnall Beard. Tim Sasse had lost heavily, for example, like other underwriters, on computer leasing. But even without DWI and computer leasing, the figures were appalling. Many Names would fail the audit at 31 December 1978 and on 16 February 1979 Stephen Merrett told the deputy chairman that the syndicate's total loss for the two years 1976 and 1977 would come to between £15 million and £20 million. It was another six months before the full implications of the disaster were brought home to the members of Syndicate 762.

Not only are the rich different from us, as Scott Fitzgerald said to Hemingway. They are different from each other. That is true even in England, where they all go to the same two or three schools and all dress up in the same uniform and troop off to the races together several times a year. The 110 members of Syndicate 762 would make a superb subject for a dissertation by some student of the sociology of wealth. They were a cross-section of that moneyed class in England that somehow manages to survive and to ensure that, in spite of sixty years of economic stagnation and high taxation, there will always be enough money for the boys to go to Eton and for the girls to hunt, for long drinks under the big cedar on the lawn, and old wine and old silver on polished mahogany at night.

The English upper class has always made room for new money, and there was new money as well as old in the Sasse syndicate. There was the Marquis Sauvage de Brantes, descended from an old lady who was a friend of Proust, of whom someone said that she was 'a whole Council of Trent on her own'. And there was Fred Smith from Sleaford in Lincolnshire, who made his brass in the wholesale fish business. There was the twelfth earl of Kintore, who lives in an ancestral hall in the Scottish Highlands and tells people, as his little joke, that when he needs a little more money he just takes another family portrait down off the wall and sends it down to London to be sold. There was a British Airways captain. There were self-made property men like George Szpiro and Joe Benjamin. There was an eminent doctor, Dr Jamison, who lives in Guernsey, and an eminent lawyer, David Karmel, QC. There were a couple of Australians, a Canadian and four members of the Rhulen family from upstate New York. There was also an exotic: Anthony Bentley-Buckle, who was the biggest trader in Mahé, in the Seychelles Islands, until a Marxist government took over in 1980 and he fled to South Africa. It was to his house that Archbishop Makarios of Cyprus was exiled by the British government in the 1950s.

'What is gentility,' asked the seventeenth-century antiquarian John Selden, 'save ancient riches?' The backbone of the syndicate, like the backbone of Lloyd's, was provided by what are called in England 'county families'. That means families who, whatever the original source of their wealth, have now become so established in one place that they seem almost as firmly implanted there as the hills and the woods. Sir Francis Legh, for example, is one of the 'Leghs of Legh', singled out by Benjamin Disraeli more than a hundred years ago as the archetype of the old English gentry family. The addresses, even more than the names, identify them: The Estate Office, Atherston-on-Stour, near Stratford-upon-Avon; Owlpen Manor, Gloucestershire; Manor Farm House, Ryme Intrinseca, Dorset.

To all of these comfortable addresses, as to Lord Fortescue in

Swinbrook and to Lord Napier and Ettrick in St James's Palace, the postman throughout 1979 delivered a stream of increasingly disagreeable letters. Among them were the ominous envelopes that went to Paddy Davies at his home in Slinfold, Sussex. Davies is a deceptive-looking man in several respects. He is, for one thing, a Brazilian citizen and did his military service in the Brazilian army, which is surprising, since you would take him for the epitome of the English gentleman. He seems easy-going, and that too is deceptive. From rather nondescript offices in a street in Mayfair full of expensive restaurants and gambling clubs for Arab oil sheikhs, he runs a group of international trading companies with a strong Latin American connection. He is not, as Lloyd's was to discover, a man to take for granted.

Davies began asking his member's agent, Clarkson's, awkward questions about Sasse and his underwriting as far back as the days of the Rheingold syndicate. Then one day he was warned that he would have to pay some £5,000. And from then on the sums he was told he was going to lose kept getting bigger and bigger. By March 1979 he decided that things were getting beyond a joke. Through friends, he made inquiries. 'Who is the best litigation solicitor in London?' he asked a top barrister. (A solicitor, in the British legal system, manages litigation as well as carrying out all sorts of routine legal business, such as drafting wills and conveyancing property; he may ask a barrister, or 'counsel', for an opinion on the prospects of success on a particular point, and he will brief counsel to act as advocates in court when an action comes to trial. Counsel also helps solicitors – for example, with drawing up pleadings.) The answer to Davies's question was unhesitating. 'The man you want is Leon Boshoff. He is a litigation partner at a law firm called Clifford-Turner. And he is six foot four of South African granite.'

The two men got on well from the start. At the very first meeting Boshoff told Davies that he might bring a successful action against several parties, but he also warned him that the cost of taking on Lloyd's would be beyond any one litigant. Get a group of Names together, spend a little money, investigate the whole story thoroughly, he said. Davies took his advice, got hold of a list of the Sasse Names and started calling them cold. Gradually a little group of Names came together as Boshoff's clients. They called themselves the 'Davies group'.

For several months, Paddy Davies was sure that in the end Lloyd's would help them out. There were a lot of meetings, and the news got steadily worse all summer. Stephen Merrett discovered another great pile of losses, this time on amusement and leisure insurances in the United States. That was almost the last straw. As late as 8 August Merrett told Names at a meeting in the library at Lloyd's that it was unlikely there would be any further call for funds before the end of the year. Then, on 13 August, another letter went out from Merrett Dixey asking for more money.

It was not Stephen Merrett's fault. The Committee of Lloyd's was now in a tight spot and was putting heavy pressure on Merrett to get the Sasse Names past the audit. Much more than the future of the Sasse Names was at stake, as the Committee saw it. Every year each underwriting member of Lloyd's has to pass the audit or be put in default. When all its members have passed the audit, each syndicate then completes a 'certificate of underwriting account'. And only when each syndicate has passed the audit does Lloyd's as a whole receive a certificate from the Department of Trade. This is one of the major requirements the government makes of Lloyd's under statute. To fail to comply was unthinkable. Even any serious delay would be embarrassing.

Late in July the Committee was informed that it would not be possible for the auditors to give the Sasse syndicate unqualified audit certificates. Any qualification might mean that Lloyd's as a whole would not get a certificate from the Department of Trade. And that would register in every one of the statements that Lloyd's must lodge with regulatory authorities all over the world, not least in the United States. LeBoeuf Lamb advised that any qualification in the Lloyd's audit, because of difficulties with the completion of the Sasse syndicate accounts, would be a public relations disaster of the first magnitude.

The only way out was to arrange a reinsurance in the Lloyd's market, limiting the Sasse 1976 losses to the figure estimated by Merrett Dixey. That at least would reassure anyone with any doubts that the losses could not go beyond an admittedly catastrophically high figure. The reinsurance was successfully placed in the market. Even so, the submission of the audit certificate to the Department of Trade was slightly delayed. The Committee insisted that the Names must pass their audit by the last day of August, whatever happened.

So Paddy Davies found that he was being asked for £258,000, with just three weeks to pay. And that was in August, when the Stock Exchange is closed and lawyers and accountants are likely to be on holiday. Leon Boshoff was away, so it was with his assistant, Terry O'Neill, that Davies sat down to draft a careful letter to the Chairman of Lloyd's. Davies still believed that Lloyd's would be understanding and would find ways to fund the Names' losses so that they could pay them gradually. So the letter began by reaffirming that the dozen or so members of the Davies group fully accepted unlimited liability for their entire obligations 'when these have been properly determined'. Still, they were playing out a strong lead. It was not the kind of letter Chairmen of Lloyd's are accustomed to receive from lawyers. 'It has now become crystal clear,' O'Neill wrote, 'that the affairs of the Sasse Syndicate No. 762 were in a near-chaotic state as a result of questionable conduct.' And he proceeded to list the things that were troubling his clients. Apart from the breach of Lloyd's own rules by the syndicate's overwriting of its premium income limits and by the reinsurance arrangements, there were half a dozen matters, including the amusement and leisure insurances, the way the Canadian losses had been treated in the accounts and, first of all, 'the payment of claims in the United States in order to preserve "the good name of Lloyd's" when circumstances perhaps indicated the need for further detailed investigation'.

It was a shrewd thrust. But still Davies believed he could persuade Lloyd's to come to the Names' help. The next day, 23 August, he went to see Ian Findlay. He wanted some sort of a moratorium: time to find out what had really happened, so that the Names would not have to pay any losses that were not properly due.

Ian Findlay was sympathetic, but utterly unresponsive. The Names' problems were the result of bad underwriting, he said, and there was nothing to be done for them.

'Bad luck, old boy,' he said. 'Wrong syndicate, bad luck!'

Paddy Davies came out of the meeting and said to O'Neill with feeling: 'I've never been so depressed in my whole life.' He walked to the phone in the Chairman's Waiter's office, just down the hall, called Leon Boshoff and said: 'The gloves are off now. We need counsel's advice, and we need it now.'

Paddy Davies was not the only one of the Sasse Names who had been talking to his lawyer. Murray Gordon, chairman of Combined English Stores, and Joe Benjamin, chairman and chief executive of a property company called Thames Investments & Securities, were also experienced businessmen. As it happened, they shared a lawyer, Martin Mendelsohn of Adlers & Aberstones, a burly extrovert with a passion for cricket, who among other things is a recognized authority on the law of franchising. Mendelsohn was talking to both Gordon and Benjamin about Lloyd's before the end of March 1979, and not long afterwards wrote Benjamin two long letters, setting out possible grounds for action against Lloyd's if the Names were not given some help to meet the Sasse losses. Mendelsohn took the point that Lloyd's might be beyond their rights in pushing the Den-Har binder losses through the Policy Signing Office, and more generally that the Names were being called on to pay losses due to business being written that Lloyd's had no power to authorize, because it was in breach of its own Fundamental Rules.

Lloyd's was breaking two of its own rules, as Mendelsohn saw it. First of all, all binding authorities seemed to be in breach of Fundamental Rule II, which prohibits underwriting business at Lloyd's outside the underwriting Rooms. Secondly, Rule V forbids the opening of an insurance account in the name of anyone who is not a member. Mendelsohn was particularly confident about Rule II. If a court ruled against his clients on that, he reckoned, it would be saying in effect that Lloyd's had no reason to exist. 'If it can be done anywhere,' as he put it to me, 'who needs Lloyd's?'

On 24 August, the day after meeting Ian Findlay, Terry O'Neill wrote him a sharp letter, saying that if he and the Committee failed to intervene, the Names might have 'no option but to resort to open defiance or to the law'. The Names were getting desperate, and they were getting annoyed. By the deadline of 31 August (which was, however, soon postponed), there were twenty-nine members of the 'Davies group'.

Terry O'Neill did not need to get his own counsel's opinion. Martin Mendelsohn had already arranged that. On 28 August the two lawyers and Joe Benjamin, Murray Gordon and Paddy Davies met in the Temple, at the chambers of Terence Cullen, QC, for what British lawyers call a 'con'. (This is not a confidence trick, but a conference!) Cullen was being asked for his opinion, informally at first, on the law bearing on whether the Names were truly liable for the full total of the Sasse syndicate's losses. Cullen came up with what one of the lawyers called afterwards 'wonderful stuff'.

Cullen advised on two points. Were the American and Canadian binders legal? And what was the liability of the agents for breach of contract, and of Lloyd's for failing to exercise its duty of care towards its members? Cullen pointed out that binders were not allowed under the Lloyd's Acts and Fundamental Rules; that underwriting agents had been given no authority by the Names to allow the underwriter to delegate his power; and in any case, the people to whom power had been delegated, such as Harrison, were not properly 'tribunalized'. Therefore, Cullen argued, the Names were not bound. Under the second heading, he made an even more ominous point: Lloyd's already possessed information in 1976 that might have alerted the Committee to irregularities, yet neither Lloyd's nor the agents did anything to warn the Names. Losses arising in 1977 ought to be recoverable from either Lloyd's or the agents.

The day after next, O'Neill telephoned Stephen Merrett and asked to see him right away. Merrett told him to come round. O'Neill's and Paddy Davies's visit to Merrett was a turning-point in the history of Lloyd's.

O'Neill outlined to Merrett what Cullen had stated as the law. Merrett was cordial, but flabbergasted, and at once he demanded to see the Chairman. An emergency meeting of the Committee was assembled within minutes. The young lawyer – O'Neill was not yet a partner in his firm – the underwriter and the Name were ushered into the presence of the Chairman, Ian Findlay, flanked by the two deputy chairmen, Sir Peter Green and Charles Gibb. They listened politely to what O'Neill had to say, asked some questions and decided to consult their own lawyers, Waltons & Morse. By the end of that afternoon, although the atmosphere remained civilized, hostilities had begun.

Now Ian Findlay was faced with an open rebellion. A group of Names were making a sweeping challenge to the legal status of much that had been routinely done at Lloyd's for many years. What was horrifying about this, from the Committee's point of view, was not so much the possibility that Lloyd's had been breaking the law all these years. It is safe to assume that they took it for granted that anything that had been done at Lloyd's for as long as they could remember *must* be legal. These were not men much given to abstract intellectual speculation. The problem for them was rather immediate and practical. A complicated legal wrangle with some obviously determined people advised by good lawyers would waste time. It would delay the audit yet more. 'They were in a cleft stick,' one of their lawyers said long afterwards. 'The whole market was in jeopardy.' It had been worry about the audit that led the Committee to press the Names for money before the end of August, and that was what drove the Names to fight. Now the fear of a further delay drove the Committee and its advisers to overplay their hand again.

Things began to move fast.

Armed with the Cullen opinion, Boshoff and Mendelsohn were in a position to bring legal action against Lloyd's, and in fact Boshoff was soon writing to his Names, warning them that he was getting ready to sue Lloyd's and Sasse, and that it might be necessary to sue some of the members' agents, because they controlled some of the Names' money, and Merrett Dixey as well, for technical reasons.

The Names' lawyers had to consider their strategic and their tactical interests, however. The first objective must be to put an end to escalating demands for money, at least until the question of whether the Names were liable for losses on the binders was decided, which meant keeping open lines of negotiation with Lloyd's. That was why Waltons & Morse beat them to the draw.

On 4 September they got an opinion from another leading counsel, Peter Webster, QC, which flatly contradicted Cullen's interpretation of the law. Rule II might say that business must be transacted at Lloyd's, said Webster, but the business that counted was the signing of the binder, not the signing of the policies written under its authority. If that had not been done at Lloyd's either, that was only a technical breach of the rules, and in any case the liability of Names would not be affected.

The layman may be permitted to register passing astonishment that two of Her Majesty's counsel, learned in the law, should differ so utterly as to what the law was. At any rate, armed with this version of the law, Ian Hattrick of Waltons & Morse made his move. The audit had to be completed: that was paramount. He was afraid that Boshoff would leave the matter until the end of the month and then apply to the court for an *ex parte* injunction, which would delay the audit. He had no desire to litigate, but he did need to draw Boshoff's fire. So he sued the Names, demanding that they produce a 'certificate of underwriting account' by 30 September.

The writs were not actually served until Saturday, 15 September. Paddy Davies, waking up groggy at his place in Sussex after taking a couple of sleeping pills, was surprised by the process server at the front door of his house at 8.45 a.m. and wandered back through the house calling out his own name to give himself time to think. Charitably, in the circumstances, he gave the man a cup of coffee.

On 13 September Boshoff had served *his* writ. It asked the court for an injunction restraining Lloyd's from enforcing claims against the Names or from realizing their Lloyd's assets; for declarations that the Names were not liable for losses arising from the American and Canadian binders, and that Sasse and the members' agents had exceeded their authority in giving the binders; for an indemnity; and for damages. The Names were ready for a fight. Twenty-seven of them, or almost a quarter of the syndicate, agreed to be plaintiffs. Morale was higher now that something seemed to be happening again.

One man spoke for this League of Gentlemen. Brigadier Peter Acland was seventy-seven in 1979. He lives in a Devon manor-house, the archetype of the country gentleman who has done the state some service in peace and war. In 1939 he was a colonial civil servant in the Sudan. When the war came, he raised a company of native irregulars and took them to serve under the legendary Orde Wingate in Abyssinia. After the war he commanded the Royal Devon Yeomanry. (Traditionally, yeomanry regiments are territorial cavalry, their officers recruited from the hard-riding foxhunting gentry of the shire.) One of the Brigadier's sons is the top civil servant in the Foreign Office, another is the British general who went with Lord Soames to organize the handover of what had been the Rhodesian army to the Mugabe government when Zimbabwe became independent in 1980.

Every four or five months, Brigadier Acland had been getting a telephone call or a letter from his agents, Clarkson's, saying that the loss would be worse and worse. Finally he was faced with a loss of £250,000, 'which I couldn't have done'. He makes it plain that he entirely accepts that he was responsible for commitments entered into in good faith. 'What we were not prepared to pay for was Lloyd's failure to enforce its own rules,' he says very firmly. He felt, too, that the professionals at Lloyd's – he called them the 'pundits' – no longer treated people like him as true members but as outsiders, as just so many punters. He resigned at the end of 1978. In September 1979, Leon Boshoff telephoned the old gentleman to explain that it might be necessary to sue Lloyd's, and that as his name came first in alphabetical order, the action would be known as *Acland and Others* versus *Lloyd's*. Was he game?

'Count me in,' said the Brigadier. 'I haven't been to war for forty years.'

Each side was now suing the other.

Among others, the Names (for purely technical reasons) were suing Merrett Dixey. Stephen Merrett had not been consulted about the decision to sue the Names and strongly disapproved of it. He was deeply unhappy to find himself rewarded for his willingness to help the Committee out by finding himself sitting in the middle of no man's land with writs flying past him like bullets. On 17 September he resigned, though in the event he was persuaded to stay on for a while until things were sorted out.

The next day, 18 September, the two summonses were heard before Sir John Donaldson of the Commercial Court in chambers. After some argument Lloyd's counsel were induced to admit that their writ was 'a red herring'. It was, in truth, little more than a tactical manoeuvre to get the Names to defend a writ from Lloyd's, if possible, instead of bringing an action of their own. It subsequently turned out that the 'certificate of underwriting account' was one that had never been asked of an individual member before, and that in any case, even if the Names had been willing to submit to the audit, the auditors could not have produced the certificate before the deadline.

The judge expressed his concern at the damage the whole row and the resulting bad press were doing to Lloyd's. He took the comparatively unusual step of descending from the bench, metaphorically speaking, into the arena, in an attempt to knock the two sides' heads together and get an agreement. For this purpose he took the even more unusual step of adjourning his court to meet two days later at Lloyd's. His lordship lunched with the Committee.

The result was that the Committee lifted the 30 September deadline and agreed to arrange a second loan to enable the Names to pass the audit. This took the immediate pressure off both sides. As for the central issue, whether the Names were liable to pay the losses arising under the Den-Har and Canadian binders, both parties agreed to submit their case to judicial arbitration.

Parties to a dispute in English law can elect to go to arbitration as an alternative to litigation. The arbitrator in a judicial arbitration is a High Court judge, in this case from the commercial court. The parties are represented by counsel, and the proceedings are informal. The arbitrator's decision is binding on all parties who have accepted the arbitration, though of course not on anyone else. The great advantage for Lloyd's was that the proceedings are confidential.

Leon Boshoff recognized from the start that this was a disadvantage for his clients. He believed that there would be great reluctance for the Committee of Lloyd's to go into the witness box and describe the procedure for policing the market, and how these had been applied in the Sasse affair. For the time being, however, he accepted the arbitration as part of the package that would remove the financial axe from his clients' heads. He could hardly communicate individually with all his clients: there were now more than forty members of the 'Davies group'. So he took to sending out circular reports to the whole group; he called them his 'comics'. By 25 September, he was able to report to the Names that the first objective had been achieved. The loan arrangements meant that there would be no further demands for money made on them until the central legal issues had been determined.

That was easier said than done. For three months the lawyers wrangled in vain over the arbitration agreement. The complexity of the negotiations was becoming mind-boggling. More and more parties were getting involved, and they all had their lawyers. Many also had 'errors and omissions' insurers, and they had their lawyers too. At one meeting at Clifford-Turner's offices, twenty-six lawyers argued all afternoon and all evening without succeeding in hammering out an agreement.

Progress was made in one important respect. In the summer of 1979 another underwriting agent, Ashby & Co., ran into trouble not dissimilar from what had happened to Sasse. Once again a binding authority was written in London that brought in a flood of business, in this case from New Zealand and the Far East, that soon swamped premium income limits. (The business came from POSA: Lloyd's was feeling the long arm of Raymond Karlinsky.) Eventually the syndicates were suspended. Even before that, the Committee had to consider who would 'run off' their business if the worst came to the worst. In the past, it had always relied on another syndicate to step in and help out. Stephen Merrett's experience suggested that it might be harder to rely on the goodwill of syndicates in the future. So, even before the Ashby case came to a head, plans were drawn up for a new underwriting company, backed by the Corporation of Lloyd's, to step in and tidy up the affairs of any syndicate that ran into trouble. It was called Additional Underwriting Agencies Ltd (AUA), and the Committee's first instinct was that it should take on Sasse as well. In the end, a separate company called AUA 2 Ltd was set up to do the job, with the Names as well as the agents and Lloyd's represented on the board, and a well-known accountant as chairman.

On the central issue, however, as golden October declined into sombre November, no progress was being made, and the Names were losing ground. By the end of November, the timetable for the arbitration had slipped so badly that the Committee's second loan would have fallen due for repayment before the Names knew how much they were obliged to pay. That first position Boshoff and Mendelsohn had fought for, a 'freeze' on financial demands until the legal issues had been determined, was thawing badly.

Boshoff decided it was time to stop messing about with arbitration. He would litigate. Privately, that was what he had been longing to do all along. But how could he get all the other parties and their lawyers to agree with him? He cut through the tangle with a characteristically forceful stroke. The original September action was still extant. Lord Justice Donaldson had convened yet another meeting in the unavailing effort to get the parties to agree the terms of arbitration. So Boshoff simply issued a summons in the High Court before Mr Justice Mustill asking him to give directions how the original action was to be heard. The parties were summoned to appear and defend the action. If they turned up, then they would have to drop the arbitration and litigate.

They turned up.

That was on 20 December. The judge laid down what turned out to be an unrealistically strict timetable. The trial would start on 14 April, and Boshoff must get in his pleadings by 7 January, only two and a half weeks away, with Christmas and the New Year intervening.

It was a herculean job. In any lawsuit, one very important stage is discovery, when each side has a right to see the other side's documents, except for privileged communications, like those with their lawyers. This normally takes place after pleadings have been exchanged. Sometimes lawyers drag their feet for months before giving the other side discovery. In this case, Waltons & Morse behaved ultra-correctly. The very next day, on 21 December, Clifford-Turner got discovery of thousands of pages of documents relating to the affairs of Syndicate 762 and Lloyd's efforts to police its affairs. This was informal discovery. The formal numbering and listing of documents took many months more.

It was, however, enough to give the Names' lawyers an idea of the strength of their case. Even the informal discovery, for example, gave Boshoff and his colleagues access to a good deal of the correspondence and telexes between Lloyd's and LeBoeuf Lamb in New York. From that traffic it was plain that as early as March–April 1976 Lloyd's knew a great deal about the Den-Har binder, including the names and track records of Goepfert, Harrison and the others involved, and the questionable character of the business. Then again, the informal discovery showed how the deputy chairmen, Dew and Higgins, had ordered Brentnall Beard and the LPSO to process the Den-Har business, and told Sasse to pay the claims on behalf of his Names, even though he had already cancelled the binder.

The mass of documents was so great in this case, and the pressure of time so heavy, that the plaintiffs' points of claim were a collective achievement. The first draft was done by a barrister, Murray Pickering, as an almost terse statement of the legal case. Boshoff's instinct was that the pleading should be meaty, full of fact that conveyed a graphic impression of Lloyd's failing to protect the Names while a notorious mess got worse and worse. The case fell into two halves: the 'authority issues', as they came to be called, and the 'breach-of-duty issues'. What it amounted to was that the Names were saying, first, that they had not given legal authority to their agents or to Tim Sasse to grant binding authorities in their name; and, second, that Lloyd's had failed in its duty to protect them by enforcing its various rules and regulations. The points of claim on the authority were served on 7 January, and by 25 January 1979, after various legal manoeuvres, the complete points of claim had been served.

Early in February, Waltons & Morse had served Lloyd's defence. Much of the substance of the defence was summed up in a single paragraph, paragraph 14:

(i) It is not admitted that the Plaintiffs had no knowledge of the granting of the Binding Authorities ...
(ii) It is denied that the Agents [i.e. the Members' Agents] or the Sub-Agent [i.e. Sasse] lacked authority to grant such binding authorities. Such authority was granted:
    (a) either by the express terms of the Agency Agreements: and/or
    (b) by virtue of the trade custom at Lloyd's in the non-marine market.

Lloyd's were on strong ground when they argued that the Names either had known about the binding authorities from 1978 on at least, or could have known about them. But on the whole their case was not particularly impressive. It might well be true that anyone who worked in the Lloyd's market knew perfectly well that binding authorities were a common practice. It might also be that one would expect Names, committed to unlimited liability, to have found out about such a routine type of commitment. The fact was that the great majority of the outside Names had no idea that binding authorities were used. Only two of the Names who were plaintiffs, according to their pleadings, had even heard the expression 'binding authority'. And Lloyd's might well be on even weaker ground when it came to the breach-of-duty issues.

If it came to a trial, the plaintiffs would have great fun drawing in as gory detail as possible a picture of Lloyd's covering up while they knew perfectly well that an appalling mess had been created. And not just covering up. The plaintiffs would make the most of those actions on the part of Lloyd's, such as the insistence that the Den-Har losses must be paid, that portrayed the institution making the Names pay for its mistakes. Of course, from the point of view of the Committee of Lloyd's, that was a monstrously unfair way of looking at it. The priorities had been honourably set, and the first priority was that every assured who had a valid claim on a Lloyd's policy must be paid. That was right, because the honour of Lloyd's demanded that it must keep its collective word and maintain the credit of the Lloyd's policy. It was also essential, politically speaking, that Lloyd's maintain a reputation in the United States like Caesar's wife: above suspicion. What was it that the young lawyer had said in his letter – 'the payments of claims in the USA in order to preserve "the good name of Lloyd's" '? Well, the inverted commas were a trifle offensive. But that was why the Committee had acted as it did, when you came right down to it. The intention had been honourable. But the more they thought about it, the more the worry grew: if it did come to a trial, *how would it look*?

The date for the trial was firmly set now: 22 January 1981. The lawyers settled down to the routine of formal discovery, and to a long wrangle about whether all members of the Sasse syndicate should be added to the action as plaintiffs. Clifford-Turner briefed Robert Alexander, QC, perhaps the top lawyer currently practising at the commercial bar in England. Alexander was consistently optimistic, and promised to write a comprehensive opinion in the summer of 1980, spelling out why he thought the Names would win if it came to a trial.

Lloyd's, too, were taking advice, but the prognosis they were getting was not so favourable. They had been advised from the time when the writs were issued by one leading counsel, Nicholas Phillips, QC. When the arbitration collapsed and it looked as though there would be litigation, they had brought in an extremely able lawyer in the same chambers, Sidney Kentridge, a South African who practises both in London and in Johannesburg and who was later to expose official hypocrisy with his deadly questioning at the inquest on Steve Biko. In the spring, they brought in a third heavyweight: Robert McCrindle, QC. McCrindle is already a legend at the English bar, although he is still in his early fifties. He has been described as 'intellectually quite brilliant', 'the best commercial barrister in England'. A few years earlier, McCrindle had quit the English bar and gone to work for the biggest New York law firm, Shearman & Sterling, at its Paris office. McCrindle was also a household name at Lloyd's, having done a good deal of work there at one time or another.

Privately, Ian Hattrick of Waltons & Morse had been thinking of possible solutions short of trying the case from the start. It had not been his wish to litigate, even though he had found himself obliged to sue first for tactical reasons. The costs of a trial were intimidating. It would last some six months, and the cost, for all litigants, would probably come to something in the region of £3 million ($4·5 million). The publicity was not something he looked forward to with any pleasure either. As early as January, Martin Mendelsohn had outlined some proposals for a settlement and Hattrick had asked him to put them on paper. But Hattrick was not going to rush to settle until he had seen the other side's pleadings and listened to his star array of counsel.

The opinions of these heavyweights are still confidential, but it is not hard to guess their essence. It was that Lloyd's were in danger of losing.

They were in danger of losing because it was going to come out in open court that they had known a lot more about the Sasse affair much earlier than they had told the Names; because in November 1976 they had made the wrong decision, to put the Den-Har business through the Lloyd's Policy Signing Office, and as a result the Names had been burdened with the Den-Har losses. Whatever the customs at Lloyd's might be, in law it was not absolutely clear that the Names had given authority to Sasse to delegate his underwriting power, least of all to Harrison. (Robert Alexander had made some play with the fact that Lloyd's appealed to customs, without seeming to be very clear what the customs were.) Even more clearly, Lloyd's had laid down rules for the protection of its members, and had failed to enforce them. Whatever proportion of the 1976 losses could be attributed to that failure, and that must include the Den-Har losses, might therefore be held not to be the Names' responsibility. As for 1977, Lloyd's position was even worse. Knowing what had happened, the proper course would have been to go to the agents and the Names, and warn them in good time to get off the Sasse syndicate. That the Committee had failed to do, and therefore Lloyd's might be called on to pay the whole of the Names' loss for the second year.

If that, or something like that, was the advice that Lloyd's were getting from some of the most eminent lawyers available, it must have come as a profound shock to members of the Committee. For it was one of the most deeply rooted traditions of the market that the Committee's function was merely 'to keep the coffee house'. Ian Findlay had blurted out the traditional view in his meeting with Paddy Davies in August 1978, and on 7 November 1980 he spelled it out at the general meeting of members. His tone was unconsciously patronizing, ironically so in the light of the way the story was to end:

Our experience of the problem of Syndicate 762 has revealed a number of misconceptions ... it is no part of the Committee's function to intervene in matters of day-to-day underwriting judgement and it is not in members' interests that the Committee should do so. Indeed, were such a control to be imposed over the underwriter by the Committee or any other body, Lloyd's would ... cease to keep its place among the leaders of the world's insurance markets. To those who work at Lloyd's all this is a truism. But these facts need emphasizing to those many Names who have joined in recent years and who may not as yet fully appreciate how Lloyd's functions.

Naïve as they might be in Findlay's eyes, the Names in the 'Davies group' and the 'Gordon group' were neither supposing nor asking that the Committee should intervene in 'matters of day-to-day underwriting judgement'. They did not regard the Den-Har binder as an everyday affair. If it was, there would perhaps be few outside Names willing to venture their all at Lloyd's. They were simply asking that, if they were to comply with their obligations, the Committee ought to obey its own rules. And now the Committee was being told that a court would probably agree with them.

It was part of Hattrick's job to lead the Committee to a more realistic assessment of the legal situation. That took time. It is hard to believe, but it was not until 1980 that the Committee really came to terms with the fact that there was indeed more than 'bad underwriting' to the Sasse losses. The Committee was not stubborn, though. These were pragmatic men, with a strong sense of their duty to do the fair as well as the sensible thing. By June 1980 there were such insistent rumours in the market and suggestions in the press – some of them no doubt the result of inspired leaks – that negotiations for a settlement were under way that Sir Peter Green took the trouble to deny them at a general meeting. By July, Lloyd's had reached agreement in principle. Now it was the agents who were parties to the suit, and the underwriters (and insurance companies) who had written their errors and omissions insurance, who were dragging their feet. In the end, it took a threat that Lloyd's and the Names would make a separate peace, leaving the agents on their own as defendants in a suit that Lloyd's would already have settled, to bring them to surrender.

The final negotiations were done over the telephone, between Sir Peter Green and Ian Hattrick at a conference phone in the Chairman's room at Lloyd's, and Leon Boshoff in a hotel room in Miami. The Committee accepted the proposals at a meeting on 23 July 1980. The next day, Sir Peter Green faced a meeting of Names and members' agents as if in the Forest of Compiègne.

It was clear to him beyond reasonable doubt, he said, that 'certain grave irregularities took place in 1976 in the handling and accounting of one contract'. It had been a little more than that, perhaps, but let it pass. 'In the light of this situation and other matters emerging as a result of information gathered by lawyers on discovery, the Committee of Lloyd's is prepared to accept that a negotiated settlement between the parties concerned would be in the best interests of all involved.' That, too, was putting the best face on things. The information that had emerged on discovery, after all, was information that had been in the possession of Lloyd's all along. Sir Peter Green made it sound as though the discovery had been a joint process of enlightenment. But that, too, was forgivable in a Committee that was putting a brave face on a rather bitter humiliation.

The final settlement was complicated as usual by the number of parties involved, but in essence it was simple. The Names put up £6·25 million of the 1976 loss, and the Corporation of Lloyd's made up the remaining £9 million of the total of just over £15 million. And the Corporation agreed to pay the whole of the loss of almost £7 million for 1977. In return for this, the Names gratefully dropped their actions.

There was much celebration, tempered by the reflection that, even in victory, the Names had lost £80,000 apiece. Fred Smith, from Lincolnshire, called Paddy Davies up and said that his wife, Mabel, a practising doctor, had something to say to him. Davies listened to the telephone and heard only one loud smacking kiss. Dr Smith was too shy to express her feelings in words, Fred explained.

Of the protagonists, John Newman is perhaps the bitterest, though he keeps his feelings veiled under a melancholy charm. He has left Brentnall Beard, and time seems to lie heavy on his hands.

Tim Sasse is surviving. He has had two heart attacks. His wife, of whom he is very fond, has left him. He can no longer practise his profession, and he has lost most of his money. He is still a gambler. He spends a lot of his time placing bets over the phone. Strangely enough, he is making a little money at it.

The impact of the story that will always, perhaps a little unfairly, carry his name is incalculable. Most of the Sasse Names, after all, are still members of Lloyd's. There are no signs of any lasting damage done to the willingness of people to accept unlimited liability, though every sign that they will be more alert and more inquisitive about the under-writing that is done in their name.

Yet few people would deny that Lloyd's will never be quite the same. Leon Boshoff, as usual, put it forcefully but accurately in a draft settlement he dashed off in the flurry of the early days of the lawsuit. It was 'probably common ground', he wrote to Lloyd's and their lawyers, among others, that 'the Sasse débâcle has finally proved that the modern complexities of Lloyd's operations cannot adequately be controlled by the outdated regulations and controlling mechanisms now in existence. Lloyd's is organized as a club but operates worldwide in a complex industry.'

No doubt the Chairman and Committee of Lloyd's were not particularly enchanted to be told that by a South African solicitor. But it was true, and in their own way they knew it. That was why they had invited Sir Henry Fisher and his coadjutors to advise them on what now became the next urgent item of business: what to put in the place of those outdated regulations and mechanisms.

CHAPTER 10

CALM SEA AND PROSPEROUS VOYAGE?

I forgot to mention that there is also a body called the 'Council', which consists of men who are firmly convinced that they are businesslike. There is no doubt that some of them are Good Business Men. [A Good Business Man] is one whose mind has not been warped and narrowed by merely intellectual interests, and who at the same time has not those odious pushing qualities that are unhappily required for making a figure in business anywhere else.

F. M. Cornford,
Microcosmographia Academica

It was on 27 September 1978 that the Committee of Lloyd's took the first step in what was to be the lengthy process of reforming the Society's constitution. The reform proposed was more radical than anything at Lloyd's since 1871. That was the measure of the buffeting the ship had taken. Was it also to guarantee for the future, in the words of the title of Mendelssohn's idyllic overture, 'calm sea and prosperous voyage' for both passengers and crew?

On 4 January 1979 Sir Henry Fisher accepted the Chairman of Lloyd's invitation to chair a proposed 'working party' to look into how the government of Lloyd's should be reformed. Within the week he was at work. In February the names of his colleagues were announced. The group's composition was carefully balanced: one broker, one underwriting agent, one marine and one non-marine underwriter, and two outsiders. (Did underwriters outnumber brokers to refute talk of 'broker power'?) They included one present and one past member of the Committee of Lloyd's; two who were members of Lloyd's but not of the Committee; and two who were not associated with Lloyd's at all. The deputy chairman of the working party was Thomas Langton, who had been on the Committee of Lloyd's from 1968 until 1971 and again from 1973 until 1976. The current Committee member was Bruce Gray, a non-marine underwriter. The other underwriter was Gordon Hutton; the sole broker was Norman Frizzell. One of the two outsiders was Robin Broadley, managing director of the august merchant bank

Baring Brothers; the other was a distinguished former journalist, David Watt, then director of the Royal Institute of International Affairs, but previously the authoritative political editor of the *Financial Times* of London.

Even before these names were made public, Fisher himself had launched himself into an energetic process of information gathering. Soon he was firing out salvoes of questions. A young lawyer, Irene Dick, who was secretary of the working party, had the job of coordinating the process of chasing up the answers to Sir Henry's questions from the various market associations (the Lloyd's Underwriters Association for the marine market, the Lloyd's Underwriters Non-marine Association, the Lloyd's Insurance Brokers Committee and so on), as well as from the Lloyd's bureaucracy and various law firms. The focus of Sir Henry's questions was the apparent lack of specific constitutional regulations governing important parts of the Lloyd's system. By virtue of what legal authority did the Committee seek to regulate the market? What powers did it have to enforce its regulatory efforts? What could it do if its authority were flouted and its powers failed?

The formal terms of reference for the inquiry were simplicity itself:

To inquire into self-regulation at Lloyd's and for the purpose of such inquiry to review:
   (i)   the constitution of Lloyd's (as provided for in Lloyd's Acts and Bye-laws);
   (ii) the powers of the Committee and the exercise thereof; and
   (iii) such other matters, which, in the opinion of the working party, are relevant to the inquiry.
Arising from the review, to make recommendations.

There is an important point to be noticed about these terms of reference and therefore about the whole Fisher exercise. It was from the start an inquiry into *self-regulation at Lloyd's* – not an inquiry into how best Lloyd's ought ideally to be regulated. The members of the working party were not asked to join an open-ended inquiry, free to consider all possible solutions. All plans involving any regulation of Lloyd's from the outside – by Parliament, for example, or by some public authority set up under the authority of Parliament – were virtually foreclosed from the outset.

Right at the beginning of the Fisher report, when it duly appeared, all alternatives to self-regulation were summarily, almost perfunctorily, dismissed.

There are those who question the whole concept of self-regulation and would prefer to see a system of control by government (or by statutory bodies set up by government) along the lines followed in some other countries. **We have no doubt that Lloyd's will be best served by a properly conducted system of self-regulation.** Indeed, we do not see how it could function in anything like its present form under any other system of regulation.

The report leaves the impression that the alternatives are on the one hand self-regulation, and on the other 'a system of control by government'. Put like that, the alternative to self-regulation sounds authoritarian, even perhaps Marxist. The fact is, of course, that not just 'some other countries', but all countries, including Britain, regulate the insurance industry. In the United States, an elaborate corpus of federal and state insurance laws are enforced by state insurance commissioners with large staffs. In West Germany, Canada and Australia, indeed in every economically developed country, including specifically those nations to which the City of London looks with admiration on the grounds that they are thought to be more hospitable to the spirit of free enterprise than Britain, insurance is regulated both by statute and by statutorily established regulatory authorities. In Britain, too, the insurance industry is not allowed to regulate itself, with one conspicuous exception. The insurance companies are closely supervised by the insurance branch of the Insurance and Companies Division of the Department of Trade in accordance with the Insurance Companies Acts. Only Lloyd's regulates itself.

It is quite true that the working of the Lloyd's system would make it hard to introduce the kind of regulation that insurance companies elsewhere are accustomed to, because regulation implies record-keeping on a scale that might be impracticable in an underwriting box in the Room at Lloyd's. This argument is not decisively conclusive, however, for two reasons. First, underwriting agencies do already keep rather comprehensive records for their own purposes and for the purposes of the Lloyd's audit. Second, the coming of micro-electronic technology, which is already entering the Room at Lloyd's, makes it far more practicable to keep the sort of records that would satisfy any public regulatory authority.

It is equally true that many insurance people in countries that do have regulatory authorities, including the United States, think that the system is wasteful and burdensome, and envy Lloyd's its privilege of self-regulation. That is hardly surprising. The contrast is not only between burdensome state regulation and self-regulation. It is between two possible systems of regulation, either of which may be more or less burdensome. In one system – that adopted in virtually every other country and in Britain, except for Lloyd's – the statutory duty of checking possible abuses is entrusted to a public authority. At Lloyd's, it is subcontracted out to the Committee. That way of policing the market has advantages and disadvantages. The most serious of the latter is that there may be a conflict of interest between the police function and the commercial interests of Lloyd's as a whole. How early, and how firmly, for example, should the Committee act to cut off dubious but highly profitable business?

The issues involved are not simple. Open-ended inquiry might well have led the Fisher party to the conclusion that Lloyd's ought indeed to regulate itself. But it was not in fact an open-ended inquiry. Strategically, indeed, it must be seen as an operation designed to forestall the danger of Parliament imposing outside regulation on Lloyd's. That was regarded by the Committee and no doubt by the great majority of the members of Lloyd's, both working and non-working, as a fate worse than death.

This general fear of government regulation, perceived as tantamount to state socialism, gave both the Fisher working party and the Committee great political strength. It meant that the membership of Lloyd's would accept even quite radical change, and change to their own financial detriment, if that were seen as necessary to head off the far worse alternative of outside interference. The Fisher exercise was to be many things to many people, and it led to positive results. But it must be understood as essentially defensive, a response to mounting criticism of Lloyd's in the media and in Parliament.

The working party held its first meeting on 20 February 1980 and sent out circulars to all Names and to the market, inviting any 'interested persons' to submit written evidence on any topic relevant to its terms of reference by 30 March. It held seventy-nine meetings altogether in one of the Committee's dining rooms at Lloyd's over a period of about seventeen months. It heard seventy-two witnesses, and studied 437 written submissions of evidence. On 23 May 1980, its 198-page report was lodged with the Committee, and this time (unlike the Cromer report, never published at all, or the *Savonita* report) it was freely handed out to the press.

It was a foregone conclusion that the Fisher working party would accept the principle of self-regulation. The question was how radical would be the constitutional changes it would prescribe as necessary for self-regulation to be effective. The report argued that, if self-regulation were to work, substantial changes would be needed. The fundamental flaw it identified in the existing constitution of Lloyd's was that 'sovereignty' lay not with the Committee but with the General Meeting of all members. That was all very well in Victorian times when there were only a few hundred members and a high proportion of them were to be found daily in the Room, or at least in the City of London. But now, because of the growth in the sheer number of members, most of them outside Names, not to mention the number of overseas Names, the General Meeting has become a hopelessly unsuitable instrument whether for legislation, adjudication or discipline. The Fisher working party was impressed by the sharp decline in the proportion of members who actually attended general meetings: from around 300 out of some 6,000 members in 1970–72, or over 5 per cent, to only 513 out of over 17,000 members, or under 3 per cent, in 1979.

In many ways and on many questions, in fact, the problem was that the Committee was expected to act, but did not have the authority to do so. The General Meeting, on the other hand, had the theoretical authority, but could not in practice be expected to exercise it. Fisher's remedy for this fundamental constitutional problem was ingenious. (To what extent 'Fisher' was the personal work of Sir Henry, and to what extent a product of collective drafting, is a matter on which some coyness is displayed. It is a reasonable guess that the main lines of the report were laid down by the former judge, with one important exception which will be noted. The proposed remedy was this: the legislative and disciplinary powers vested under the Lloyd's Acts in the General Meeting should be transferred to a new body called the Council of Lloyd's. This would have twenty-five members, sixteen elected by the 'working' members, six (later changed to eight) chosen by postal ballot by the 'non-working' members, and three, later four, lay members nominated by the Council with the approval of the Governor of the Bank of England, making twenty-eight in all.

The radical departure from tradition in this proposal was that it drew a distinction, familiar in practice but new in constitutional theory, between 'working' and 'non-working' members. The report argued that this was a fair exchange: the outside Names would lose their theoretical right to exercise sovereignty at the General Meeting; in return they would be compensated with a limited right they would be far more likely to be able to use.

Under the new Council, there would be a separation of functions. Discipline would be delegated to a standing disciplinary committee, with power to impose penalties including fines, suspension and expulsion in case of breaches of bye-laws and regulations. The executive function would be entrusted to an executive committee made up of the sixteen members of the Council elected by the working members.

The report spelled out in great detail how the new system would work. It prescribed how members should be elected and on what conditions, and how they could be suspended or excluded. It provided for the supervision of underwriters, brokers and members' agents, it proposed disciplinary procedures and penalties, and a system of appeals. It armed the Council with power to investigate the affairs of any syndicate, broker or agent, and toughened up the audit system. And it suggested dropping the controversial '20 per cent rule' that had threatened to prevent American brokers acquiring Lloyd's brokers as subsidiaries.

Much of this was commonsensical reform, needed to clear up the quaint imprecision and the sometimes Gilbert and Sullivan procedures of the existing system as it had evolved since Victorian times. But the Fisher report did propose one truly bold and intensely controversial departure. It recommended that brokers should be made to 'divest' themselves of the underwriting syndicates they owned. Most of the bigger underwriting agencies ('managing agencies'), it pointed out, were either broker-controlled or part-owned by a Lloyd's broker. To be exact, 45·39 per cent of underwriting capacity was managed by broker-controlled agencies, and another 5·87 per cent was 'broker-involved'. The eight biggest broker-controlled underwriting agents, with 59 per cent of the premium income of Lloyd's between them, were controlled by the eight biggest Lloyd's brokers.

'In our deliberations and conclusions,' Fisher said, 'we have never lost sight of the fact that Lloyd's is a market for the transaction of insurance business between Lloyd's Brokers, acting for Assureds, and Underwriters accepting risks on behalf of Syndicates of Names.' The interests of brokers and underwriters, therefore, at least in theory, are fundamentally in conflict. Yet many underwriting agencies were in fact owned by brokers. Could that anomaly be allowed to stand?

The Cromer report in 1970 had been clear enough about the anomaly. 'A substantial body of opinion at Lloyd's,' Cromer said, 'believes that broker control is undesirable and should be discouraged, if not brought to an end. There is a conflict of interest which cannot be ignored.' But the Cromer report backed off from recommending mandatory action to make brokers give up their underwriting agencies. 'We should hope,' it said weakly, 'that brokers might take the view that, in the light of experience and of possible future developments, they ought to reduce their involvement in underwriting.' Not surprisingly, brokers (who had, after all, the financial interests of their shareholders to consider, since almost all were now publicly owned companies whose shares were quoted on the Stock Exchange) were not going to give away profitable underwriting subsidiaries in response to so feebly expressed a pious hope. All that happened was that the Chairman of Lloyd's at the time discussed the idea with some representatives of brokers and underwriting agencies. Nothing was done.

The Fisher working party was determined not to be brushed aside so lightly. It conceded diplomatically that evidence of actual abuse of ownership of underwriting agencies by brokers was 'conflicting', but it insisted that the potential for abuse was there. A broker, for example, might put pressure on the active underwriter of a controlled syndicate to write risks against his better judgement, or to write it at lower rates than another underwriter might do, or to settle claims that he ought not to settle. Or a broker might give business to his own syndicate, even though better terms were available elsewhere. Or again,

it is said that some brokers owning syndicates are prone to 'load' syndicate expenses on to the Names, e.g. to allot to the underwriting agency a disproportionately large share of the group's expenses, which are then charged out as expenses to the Names ... that some brokers are prone to exert undue pressure on their owned managing agencies to accept new Names on syndicates which do not have sufficient premium income to justify an increase in capacity.

Most underwriters, the report said, still mustered the fortitude to resist undue pressure from their broker-owners. But not all did, and the ranks of the robust resisters might be expected to decline. The Fisher working party was decisive:

Faced with the position as it is today, we are agreed that logic points towards a complete divorce between Lloyd's Brokers and Managing Agents.

Unfortunately, it was also divided:

The question is whether the undoubted difficulties, both of principle and practice, of a compulsory divestment by Lloyd's brokers of shares in Managing Agencies should be allowed to override this logic. We have discussed this problem at length, and the majority of us have reached the conclusion that divestment should be enforced and the formation of such links prohibited for the future.

The majority, but not all. There was one dissenter. One of the three non-Lloyd's members of the working party was 'of the opinion that compulsory divestment of assets is too draconian a solution'. This man thought that measures short of compulsory divestment, both by reducing the risk of interference by brokers in the managing agencies they controlled, and by improving investigatory procedures, would do the trick. Who was it? Broadley, the banker? Watt, the journalist? Or Fisher, the judge? There is good reason to believe it was Fisher; if so, we are left with the remarkable fact that the most notable recommendation of Fisher the report was against the better judgement of Fisher the man. In any event, having registered this conscientious objection, the report went ahead and recommended that

the Council should have power to provide that from a stated date approximately five years ahead ... no Lloyd's broker who owns an interest in a Managing Agency will be permitted to show a brokerage account at Lloyd's and no Managing Agency in which a Lloyd's Broker owns an interest will be allowed to remain on the Register.

Other, less contentious, recommendations were that no managing agency should own shares in a Lloyd's broker, and there should be no shareholding links between managing agency companies and non-Lloyd's insurance interests. So Fisher came out against broker control of underwriting agencies, but stopped short of recommending that divestment should be immediate and mandatory. Instead, it gave the Council power to require divestment 'from a stated date approximately five years ahead'.

The Fisher report was sent to the Chairman on 23 May 1980. By now Lloyd's had a new Chairman. Sir Peter Green had taken over from Ian Findlay on 1 January, less than five months previously. One of the four or five most successful marine underwriters in the market and the son of a famous marine underwriter, Green was personally affected by the divestment issue. His family underwriting agency company, Janson Green, had been sold to the brokers Hogg Robinson, and Green is a major Hogg Robinson shareholder as well as director. He is a stocky, powerfully built man with an approachable but determined manner; he gives the impression more of force than of subtlety. The personal touches he imported into the Chairman's elegant office suggested a rather broad sense of humour. The rump of a stuffed raccoon stared down, if that is the right word, from the wall above his big mahogany desk, and on a side table the backsides of soft toy pink piglets lined the flank of a soft toy white sow. Such tastes could easily lead the fastidious to underestimate Green. He was to show both generalship and leadership in the campaign that was now beginning.

The first thing Green did was to persuade the Committee to lock itself away for a weekend somewhere, where it could be completely undisturbed to thrash out what its response to Fisher was going to be. For various practical reasons, the place chosen was the London Hilton

Hotel. With only three or four advisers, the Committee met at the hotel at six o'clock on a Friday evening and worked through with a minimum of interruptions until lunchtime on the Sunday. There was plenty of earnest discussion, but no serious division except on the question of what was now coming to be called 'the divestment issue'. At least one weighty member of the Committee, Robert Kiln, had deep misgivings on that subject. The Chairman himself had some private reservations. 'I have always felt divestment was probably the right course,' he told me after the battle was almost over. 'But I wanted it decided within Lloyd's rather than decided for us by someone else.' At the press conference held to present the Fisher report, he made it clear that compulsory divestment would be a damned nuisance and perhaps a cause of financial loss to himself and others. He also made it clear that he wholeheartedly accepted the recommendation and meant to do his best to carry it out.

The Committee decided at the Hilton that it accepted the Fisher report in general, especially the new Council and the new disciplinary procedures. On divestment, it accepted the broad conclusion that something had to be done about brokers owning managing agencies. It also accepted the recommendation that the bill to be put before Parliament must contain powers for compulsory divestment if all else failed. But at this stage there was no unanimity that there would have to be a complete separation of ownership between brokers and managing agents. Some Committee members believed that complete separation of management would be enough. Secondly, the Committee at this time was assuming that divestment was something that would happen *after* the passage of a Lloyd's Act. (The Fisher report contained in an appendix a draft bill giving the Council power to require divestment, but not requiring divestment under the terms of the bill itself.)

Reform on the scale Fisher was proposing would certainly require an Act of Parliament. For various reasons the decision was taken to ask Parliament to pass what is known as a private bill. (This is not the same as a private member's bill, which is no different from a public bill except that the latter is brought in by the government, whereas the former, as the name suggests, is proposed by an individual Member of Parliament.) A private bill – it becomes an Act of Parliament once it has passed both the House of Commons and the House of Lords and then receives the royal assent from the sovereign – is one that affects the rights, interests and duties of a limited group of Her Majesty's subjects. In the nineteenth century, private bills were much used to grant rights of way to railway companies. Since the Second World War, the private bill has enjoyed a revival because of the rapid expansion of Britain's labyrinth of laws and regulations dealing with planning permission for real-estate projects. In order to get Parliament to hear a private Lloyd's bill, Lloyd's would first have to get the assent of three-quarters of the membership, which would have to be done at what was known (after a nineteenth-century member of the House of Lords) as a 'Wharncliffe meeting'. If the meeting rejected the Committee's case and there was no Lloyd's bill, or at least no private bill on the lines the Committee wanted, the danger of outside regulation would be greater than ever. Then truly the ship would be drifting towards a lee shore, like the *Amoco Cadiz*, with steering gear that did not respond to the signals from the bridge.

So Green and his colleagues on the Committee were faced with a dilemma that had to be handled with some finesse. Fisher had recommended constitutional reform, which would have to be ratified by Parliament, but Fisher had also recommended divestment. The Committee could not get constitutional reform unless it won overwhelming support from the members, but it was far from certain that a majority would support divestment. It was not just that the Committee hesitated to go against the wishes of the broker barons, though in truth the barons were well represented on the Committee (at least eleven of the sixteen members were connected with brokers, as was the Chairman himself). It was also that the brokers' cooperation, even in such mundane matters as circulating the arguments for it to 'their' Names and busing them in to the meeting, would make passing the bill so much easier. If the big brokers actively campaigned against divestment, then in all likelihood the bill would be lost. And, after all, divestment meant that the brokers would be stripped of extremely valuable assets.

Sir Peter Green admits that he did not see through the whole tangled game from its opening like a chess master, but his tactical instinct was sound. He and the Committee in the first place put to the members the essence of the Fisher case for constitutional reform. The issue of divestment, for the time being, was in the background – not hidden, but simply subordinated to the question of the new Council. That was both right and clever.

On 25 June Green sent the Fisher report to every member of Lloyd's with a personal letter. The Committee, the letter said, 'welcomes the three fundamental recommendations: the concept of a Council as set out by the Fisher report; the transfer of authority to the Council' – Green noticeably did not add the words 'from the members'! – 'and the need for an Act of Parliament'.

On the subject of divestment, all the letter had to say was this:

The proposals in respect of Underwriting Agents, and the ownership of Managing Agents, present a number of practical problems. Nevertheless the Committee accepts the force of the arguments in the report and is confident that these changes can be implemented in the time scale envisaged.

Neither the Chairman nor the Committee, of course, was foolish enough to imagine that they could run the issue of divestment past 20,000 members (many of them lawyers!) without anyone noticing what was at stake. No doubt some hoped that compulsory divestment would not be necessary. Perhaps some even hoped that safeguards short of full divestment would meet the argument that a fundamental conflict of interest existed between brokers and underwriters, and at the same time provide practical safeguards against abuses in the marketplace. Parliament did not agree. In the end, after a process – as some wit put it – 'as long as *The Borgias* and as expensive as *Brideshead Revisited*', Parliament insisted that divestment must be mandatory, and made it a condition of the passage of the bill.

Ian Findlay was not in all respects fortunate in his time as Chairman of Lloyd's. It covered a year the market would prefer to forget: the *annus terribilis* 1978, the year of the *Savonita* and Sasse, the *Amoco Cadiz* and computer leasing. But in another way Findlay was lucky. For where it fell to Sir Peter Green to preside over the rebuilding of Lloyd's constitutional structure, it was Ian Findlay who took the decision to build Lloyd's a new home.

The Room was already crowded by the early 1970s, and Lloyd's membership was increasing by leaps and bounds: not only total membership, but the number of syndicates needing boxes. A members' writing room was knocked into the gallery to make more space, but it was clear that such shifts would not be enough for much longer. When Findlay became deputy chairman at the beginning of 1977, Sir Havelock Hudson asked him to take over as the chairman of a working party that had been trying for some years to decide how to find new space.

'We would have spent a vast amount of money,' Findlay told me, perhaps as much as £30 million ($45 million), '*not* to have a new building.' So Findlay went to Hudson and said, 'Am I crazy?' And Hudson said, 'No, I think you're right.' Findlay talked privately to some of the people he respected most at Lloyd's. 'Look,' he said to them, 'this is the most important thing we'll do in our lives, let's get it right!' One of his friends said to him, he remembers, 'All our predecessors have thought too small.' They had certainly underestimated the physical growth of Lloyd's. In 1928 the new building was supposed to last forever. It lasted until the late 1940s. So Lloyd's built again. And little more than a dozen years after the market moved, the new building was too small.

If Ian Findlay was lucky enough to have to take the crucial decisions about a new building, Courtenay Blackmore has been lucky enough to be involved in commissioning two major buildings on behalf of Lloyd's in his time. Blackmore, a friendly man who communicates intense vitality and enthusiasm in spite of walking with a stick, was an executive buying and selling petrochemicals with ICI (Britain's biggest chemical company) before going to Lloyd's as head of administration. When Lloyd's decided to build a new office complex at Chatham, on the Medway river thirty miles south-east of London, it was Blackmore who took the initiative in breaking with tradition.

The Chatham building, on a spectacular waterfront site, holds the Lloyd's Policy Signing Office and the membership department with their computers and about half of the Lloyd's staff. But now Blackmore and Findlay were talking about something of a different order of magnitude: perhaps the most important building that would go up in the City of London in the 1980s, and a building whose character would affect the whole atmosphere of Lloyd's for a generation or more.

The decision was taken to go to the Royal Institute of British Architects (RIBA) for advice. A competition is a good way of choosing a design. But all too often the winning architect has little understanding of what the client really needs. Lloyd's wanted an architect to design them a building, but first they wanted one to help them work out what sort of a building they wanted.

Over lunch with Ian Findlay the president of the RIBA, Gordon Graham, suggested a different approach. Instead of a competition, he said, why not put up the money to hire several good firms to produce alternative studies? There and then Findlay accepted the idea. In the end the list was whittled down to six. There was Arup Associates, famous for their engineering, who had designed the Lloyd's building at Chatham; a French firm, Serete; Foster Associates, headed by the Yale-trained Norman Foster, who had just won a great many prizes for his Sainsbury Centre for the Visual Arts in Norwich, England, and went on to design the spectacular headquarters for the Hong Kong & Shanghai Bank; Piano & Rogers, an Anglo-Italian firm; the Webb Zerafa Menkes Housden Partnership from Canada; and from the

United States, I. M. Pei. Blackmore wrote to each of them asking them to produce not a design, but a study which they were to present at a briefing. For this they would be paid £10,000 ($15,000) each. (Pei had previously decided with his partners to do no further foreign commissions, but he made an exception for Lloyd's. Every morning as a boy in Hong Kong, he told Courtenay Blackmore, he and his uncle would pass the offices of Jardine Matheson, greatest of the British trading houses in the Far East, and his uncle would say, 'They are the agents of Lloyd's of London.')

In the spring of 1978 each of the chosen six came and made a presentation to Findlay, Blackmore and a small subcommittee of the Committee of Lloyd's. 'The one assumption we made,' Courtenay Blackmore told me, 'was that the Western world will survive, and that the City of London will survive and will still be playing an important part in world trade into the twenty-first century.'

The two finalists were Arup, which had just finished a highly satisfactory commission for Lloyds, and Piano & Rogers. Arup's design was a delicate arched chamber that cleverly echoed the shape and rhythms of the Leadenhall market on the next-door site, a soaring Victorian wrought-iron structure reminiscent of the Milan *galleria*. But it was Piano & Rogers, the one firm that did not offer a specific design, that got the job.

Richard Rogers was in the United States when he learned that he had won the Lloyd's commission, and some of his friends think he would have taken an academic job there and emigrated if he had not got it. Renzo Piano was already spending more and more of his time in his native Italy. Richard Rogers, too, in spite of his name, is in many ways more Italian than English: he was born in Florence, his grandfather was an Englishman who married an Italian girl and settled there; his father also married an Italian. But the family kept their British passport and came back to Britain just before the war broke out in 1939. Richard went to boarding school in England and trained at the Architectural Association school in London, then did graduate work under Paul Rudolph at Yale. He and Norman Foster came back to England and practised architecture together. In the 1960s, after that partnership split up, Rogers plunged into avant-garde modernism with an emphasis on marrying architecture with technology. Then, in 1970, he joined Renzo Piano, and together they won a competition out of a field of 680 entries to build the Pompidou Centre in Paris.

That building is one of the most dramatic and controversial modern monuments in Europe. It is a multimedia centre, with libraries for books and videos, lecture halls, exhibition galleries and theatres, to commemorate Charles de Gaulle's successor as President of the French Republic, Georges Pompidou, who had a passion for modern art. Rogers' design is uncompromising. In glass and metal, it looms over a maze of narrow streets and twisting alleys between the site of the old Les Halles markets and the seventeenth-century palaces of the Marais. It is a bold slab with all its innards – moving staircases and heat and air-conditioning ducts – painted primary colours and stuck to the outside of the building. Richard Rogers, avant-garde experimentalist, flamboyant showman, self-consciously un-English, might be the last architect you would expect Lloyd's to hire. But they did hire him.

Rogers and his two partners, Marco Goldschmied and John Young, and a couple of dozen of employees, work in a converted workshop in Holland Park, in Kensington. It is in a backstreet between a tough council housing estate and a trendy neighbourhood inhabited by successful journalists and advertising men. The design studio bustles with casually dressed young designers and draughtspersons. The old office of the workshop has been converted into a kitchen. Smells of aromatic, deeply un-English coffee waft from it. Rogers uses a motorbike to cover the seven or eight miles from this West London outpost of cosmopolitanism to Lime Street. Culturally, you might think, the distance is far greater.

'They didn't ask for a design,' Rogers told me. 'They asked for a strategy.' And what he gave them was a crisply argued document called *A Design Strategy for Lloyd's.* The brief as he understood it was to

provide for the expansion of Lloyd's business by an approach which can:

1. Cater for the need of the market for a period of at least fifty years whilst retaining a single Room . . .

. . .

3. Create a building of quality which not only contributes to the environment of the City but also maintains Lloyd's prominence as the centre of world insurance.

4. Make optimum use of the land available allowing for a high degree of flexibility and choice of alternative strategies during design, construction and occupation . . .

5. Maintain full continuity of trading . . .

With a shrewd sense of what practical businessmen would be looking at, Rogers analysed how to optimize use of an awkward-shaped site, how to conserve energy and heat, and the various options for phasing a building programme and maximizing rental income. At the same time he boldly enunciated his aesthetic and social ideas about the City and its 'intricate mesh of narrow streets', and deftly slid the stiletto into any idea that traditional architects might have the edge on him in practical matters. He pointed out the poor 'net to gross ratios' of the traditional City palaces, and dismissed the tower blocks rising round the Lloyd's site as unjustifiable for 'visual or even practical reasons'. In a section called 'The Building as Public Performance', Rogers bravely put forward some of the main lines of his own philosophy, even though some of its strands might well be dangerous to his chances of winning the contest:

The days of the fortress and the glass box are over. Both are inflexible straitjackets for their users, suppressing self-expression and technologically indefensible for different reasons. We propose a free and open-ended framework where the ever changing performance is the dynamic expression of the architecture of the building ... A place where ever changing activities overlap in flexible well-serviced spaces, the café, the restaurant, the pub, the tailor, the bank, the meeting rooms, the underwriting Room, the food market, the sports room, the corner shop, the offices, each playing its role, growing or shrinking depending on demand.

Lloyd's wanted to avoid the problems they had encountered because they had not allowed for growth, Rogers saw. But they did not know how fast growth would be in a world in recession. The only thing they could be sure of, they said, was that there would be change they had not thought of. *Therefore*, said Rogers, structuring to me the argument he had made to himself, the building must be suitable for a number of different uses. *Therefore* it must be one that can be used as a standard office building. *Or* as an underwriting Room three times as big as the present one. *So* the division between offices and underwriting space must be fluid. *Then* you must be able to put in all the support systems in such a way that you can change them.

Rogers offered Lloyd's two basic alternative 'programme strategies': the more conservative of these involved first expanding the Room; the other was a crash programme that would mean first 'decanting' the 1925 building (still in use for many departments of the Lloyd's bureaucracy), pulling it down and going straight ahead with building a new Lloyd's on the 1925 site. This was, Rogers warned, the higher-risk option. It was nevertheless the one that Lloyd's finally chose. They might seem to be conservative in style, but they had after all been in the risk business all their lives.

Rogers' design met the original request that the Room should remain a unity. If the central Room is to be uninterrupted, then toilets, heating, elevators and the other services would have to be round the outside.

That consideration dictated an 'inside-out' design. 'To take advantage of the constraints,' Rogers says, 'that's the game.'

The site is irregular. Therefore there is room for what architects call the 'servant areas' in the spaces between the edge of the largest possible atrium and the outer limits of the site. That gives a very high net–gross ratio, which is to say, a high proportion of commercially usable space to the total volume of the building. 'And there is an "urban" reason too,' Rogers added. 'The buildings of the 1950s and 1960s have poor human relationships. You have to use technology and keep the richness of texture of older buildings.'

Rogers' solution, in its final form, is startling, yet organized by a compelling logic. In the centre, on the upper-ground-floor level, is a vast single underwriting Room, sixty-eight metres by forty-nine metres, the largest space that could be accommodated on the site. Above it, in the centre, is an atrium roofed in by a great glass vault shaped like half a barrel; wrapped around this central shaft of daylight are eleven storeys of offices. Below the Room, shops, restaurants and wine bars are open to the public. Around the Room and its encasing offices, the services – entrances, elevators, stairs, structure, air-conditioning and lavatories – are grouped in six irregularly spaced towers roughly the same height as the glass vault of the central atrium. These towers provide, as Rogers put it, 'a whole series of surprises and secret spaces that open up as the passer-by moves around the building'.

Richard Rogers thinks in bold flights and large conceptions. He is also fascinated by detail. When we talked, he kept reverting to the subject of lavatories. I asked him why.

'It turns out toilets are important at Lloyd's. There are ten times as many people in the Room as in the same space in an office building. Between 1,500 and 2,000 people leave Lloyd's in fifteen minutes between 12.30 and 12.45 every day, and return between 2.15 and 2.30. They all like to have a good lunch, and before they go back into the Room they all want to have a pee. If you're not careful, you've got the biggest *pissoir* in London. And don't forget the influence of class! They've got at least four or five kinds of toilets, besides male and female. Members have toilets, and you wouldn't want them to share with substitutes or subscribers!'

The story of how Lloyd's chose an architect and how he designed them a building is interesting in itself. It also suggests certain things about Lloyd's. Those who see in Lloyd's only a stuffy, conservative British institution must be surprised both by the way Lloyd's went about choosing a new home, and also by the substance of the choice.

They went for the least cautious of architects, and for his least cautious design. They were obviously psychologically prepared for change.

To a certain extent, perhaps, these attitudes are those of an elite at Lloyd's, even in some measure those of Courtenay Blackmore himself, who succeeded in converting first Ian Findlay, then other key members of the Committee to his own enthusiasm for modern architecture. Certainly there has been a fair amount of grumbling at Lloyd's about the new building. A more general reaction has been a mixture of puzzlement and pride: 'I must say it looks a funny sort of building to me, but isn't it nice that all the experts say we've chosen so well!'

Richard Rogers himself says that he found Lloyd's interesting as a client. 'The first amazing thing is that the Committee of Lloyd's itself deals with architects, not some middle-level bureaucrat, which is what you deal with in most big organizations. Then the tradition they have at Lloyd's is that you deal with a matter at *that* meeting.' A lifetime spent in the risk business has certain effects on people: it seems to give them a freedom from defensive habits, a willingness to take decisions swiftly and without hiding behind hierarchical or institutional defences. Above all, there is a pervasive sense that in order to survive, Lloyd's must change.

Architects like Richard Rogers make a fundamental assumption. Buildings, they believe, change people and the way they live their lives. For over a hundred years, Lloyd's has been consciously a closed society, exclusive and secretive. Its successive homes have reflected that instinct. Now comes Richard Rogers, trying to open Lloyd's up to the life of the City around it. But does Lloyd's want to be opened up? Will it not rather choose to be a sort of offshore island in the City of London, a ship whose interior life is protected from the wind and the waves outside?

CHAPTER 11

DRY DOCK

If he were
To be made honest by an Act of Parliament
I should not alter in my faith of him.

Ben Jonson,
The Devil Is an Ass

The progress of any bill through Parliament is a majestic business. It resembles not so much an obstacle course or a hurdle race as the passage of a great liner through the successive locks of a ship canal. Although both the British Parliament and the American Congress evolved from the same eighteenth-century model, they have become quite different. The legislative committees are far more powerful in Washington, for example, the parties more so at Westminster. Most of the proposed legislation that attracts public notice in Britain, therefore, is sponsored by the government, which by definition commands a majority in the House of Commons; the opposition can draw attention to its weaknesses in the House of Commons, and can sometimes modify it in committee. Even the House of Lords can sometimes change bills significantly, though it now rarely rejects an important bill altogether and constitutionally can only delay, not defeat, legislation. But for most of these 'public bills' the government can be sure of a majority in the end.

Private bills are a different matter. They originate as petitions that must be deposited, together with printed copies of the proposed bill, by 27 November each year. Like any other bill, it is 'read' by the House of Commons three times. (At each stage, the House may debate it and may 'divide', or vote, on a motion 'that the bill be now read'.) The bill is first presented to the House and read for the first time purely formally. Debate follows on the second reading, after which the bill is sent to a select committee, chosen ad hoc to consider this particular bill. The committee holds formal hearings at which both the promoters of the bill and any petitioners against it are represented by counsel, and then reports it, with any proposed amendments, back to the full House, which receives it and may amend it further at the 'report and consideration stage'. It is then read for a third time, after which it goes to the House of Lords.

The procedure in their Lordships' House is essentially the same. On a private bill, the second reading is usually taken without debate, but if the Chairman of Committees believes that opposition to it is such that he ought not to move the second reading without a debate, he will ask the promoters of the bill to find another peer to move it, and there may then be a debate on the motion that the bill be read a second time. The second reading also allows a member of the House of Lords to put down instructions to the committee to take special notice of some particular matter. If the bill is opposed, then it goes to a select committee for a formal hearing at which once again promoters and petitioners may be represented by their lawyers. The select committee can report that the bill should not proceed, or that it goes on with or without amendments. A bill reported from committee is then read for the third time; again, this is usually formal, but if the bill is controversial it may be debated.

Any amendments made by the House of Lords have to be agreed to by the Commons. Once this is done, the bill needs only the assent of the sovereign, signified in the ancient Norman-French formula *La reyne le veult* ('the queen wills it'). The royal assent has not been withheld from a bill passed by both Houses of Parliament since 1707, when Queen Anne refused to sign a bill establishing a militia in the Highlands of Scotland. In the extremely unlikely event of the queen refusing her assent, she would presumably use the equally venerable, if evasive, formula Queen Anne used on that occasion: *La reyne s'avisera* – the queen will take counsel.

Sir Peter Green and his allies faced a dilemma: any bill that compelled brokers to divest themselves of their underwriting agencies would be hard to get past the members of Lloyd's. Any bill that did not would be hard to get past the Members of Parliament. In the end, by a combination of good luck and good judgement, skill and serendipity, the thing was done. But it was a close-run thing. It was not done without a comedy of errors that nearly sank the whole bill. And not before an unlikely alliance, which bound together Ian Posgate and Kenneth Grob, Malcolm Pearson of the *Savonita* and Leon Boshoff of Sasse, had emerged from the Cave of Abdullam and done their best, with attendant heralds and trumpeters, to defeat one part or another of the bill and so in effect, if not in intention, to destroy it all.

Before the ship could sail, the captain had to secure the assent of his passengers. On 20 August 1981 Green wrote to all members of Lloyd's pointing out that before presenting a bill to Parliament Lloyd's would have to call an extraordinary general meeting at which not less than three-quarters of the members must vote in favour of the bill. He enclosed a questionnaire with just three questions: Do you intend to attend the meeting? Do you support the proposals to form a Council and to transfer power to it from the members in general, meeting by Act of Parliament? Any further comments?

The response was better than the Committee had dared hope, both quantitatively and qualitatively. There were 13,587 replies from some 18,000 members, and almost all of those, 13,124, said they favoured the Committee's proposed remedies. Of those who volunteered comment, the largest number, 603, urged that there should be some backstop veto to prevent the new Council's power from being absolute. (On the issue of brokers divesting themselves of underwriting syndicates, only 136 people – 1 per cent – bothered to write in that they were opposed to this, and they were outnumbered by 180 write-ins in favour of divestment.)

Even so, the Chairman and the Committee were taken aback by the margin of their eventual victory at the members' meeting at the Albert Hall in November 1980. It was a walkover. The Chairman spoke briefly, took questions from the floor and then put the bill to the vote. There were 13,219 votes in favour, and only 57 against. (More than 10,000 of the votes in favour were proxies. Even so, close to 3,000 members of Lloyd's had taken the trouble to turn up – an impressive demonstration of support for the Committee and the Chairman.)

So Lloyd's petition, with the draft bill attached, was duly deposited with the House of Commons on 26 November, and the bill was presented there and given its first reading on 22 January. There was a debate on the second reading on 24 March, and then the bill was sent to a committee of four. As a result of the unpredictable working of the House of Common's Committee of Selection, the chairman of that committee was Michael Meacher, MP, an owlish 45-year-old left-wing socialist who before being elected to Parliament was a university lecturer in social administration. The Meacher committee held its first hearings on the bill in May, and it was not until after those hearings that the pattern of opposition to it became clear.

Clear, indeed, is not the right word. The opposition focused on several distinct issues. Some who raised them did so out of specific concern, but others apparently wanted to destroy the Lloyd's bill altogether. The cost of sustaining a petition against a private bill before Parliament – including the cost of retaining solicitors, parliamentary agents, junior counsel and Queen's Counsel in silk gowns – runs into many tens of thousands of pounds. So there were shifting alliances, tactical alliances, even what some would consider unholy alliances. But the opposition to the Lloyd's bill was largely sustained by a handful of determined and wealthy people whose confidence in the way Lloyd's was run, and in the people who ran it, had been deeply bruised in the course of the three great Lloyd's rows. I have described two of those *causes célèbres* – Sasse and the *Savonita* – at length. The third was what might be called a subterranean scandal, generally referred to at Lloyd's in subdued tones as 'Posgate's problem'.

The Sasse affair provided the background to the first issue: the treatment of 'outside', non-working Names, and specifically the bill's proposal that they should form a separate electorate voting for six places on the Council, while the working Names voted for the sixteen places allotted to them. A number of outside Names, including many of those who had voted against the bill at the Wharncliffe meeting, joined a new Association of External Members, formed in January 1981. (It was significant that the association was chaired by Lady Middleton, wife of an army officer, who lived in Yorkshire and had been one of the Sasse Names.) The Association was to be plagued by internal dissension and never attracted more than a couple of hundred members. Still, it showed the concern that the Committee had not adequately protected outside Names in the course of the Sasse affair.

Two of the handful who voted against the Lloyd's bill, John Burrows and Nicholas Parker, were moved to petition against the bill on the grounds that it was wrong that the membership should be divided between working and outside Names at all. Their petition acquired more importance than it would perhaps have earned on its own because of a little-known point of parliamentary law. Members of a society like Lloyd's that was promoting a private bill could, under parliamentary standing orders, only petition against, if they had taken advantage of the opportunity to vote against the bill at the Wharncliffe meeting. Some of the bill's opponents, therefore, used the Burrows–Parker petition to hang their own cases on. It is reasonable to assume that they also contributed to the costs resulting from prolonging hearings on the petition.

One of Parker and Burrows' complaints was that outside members were under-represented on the Council, and Lloyd's was prepared to go some way to meet them on that. Sir Graham Page, M P, the respected

Conservative backbencher who had agreed to manage the bill on behalf of Lloyd's, gave an undertaking in the second reading debate that Lloyd's would increase the outside Names' representation on the Council from six to eight. Burrows and Parker, however, continued to press their petition on the point of principle. They wanted the Council chosen by the whole membership, working and non-working, voting as a single electorate.

A second strand of opposition, more noticeable in Parliament than at Lloyd's, was made up of those who had been influenced by Malcolm Pearson and by Jonathan Aitken's account of the *Savonita* affair in the adjournment debate of March 1978. This included several younger Conservative Members of Parliament, including Aitken, Archibald Hamilton and Robert Cecil, Viscount Cranborne. (As heir to the Marquis of Salisbury, he carries the standard of the most respected of all the Tory clans. The Cecils have been known as guardians of the Conservative conscience since the days of their ancestor the Marquis of Salisbury who was Queen Victoria's last prime minister.) These young Tory members of Parliament wanted something written into the bill to deal with fraud. The Committee agreed to cover the predicament of a broker, like Malcolm Pearson, who suspected fraud. But Pearson and this group of MPs were also concerned about Lloyd's immunity against suit, which was granted in Clause 11 of the bill. Several MPs, including the chief Labour spokesman, Stanley Clinton Davies, objected to this clause in the second reading debate, and MPs of various political stripes shared Pearson's doubts right through the parliamentary battle.

The immunity issue was essentially simple. Clause 10 of the bill gave the Committee of Lloyd's and its employees the same narrow protection against suit which a director or officer of a company enjoys under Section 488 of the British Companies Act where a court finds that he or she has acted honestly and reasonably. But if Lloyd's and its employees were effectively to police the market and investigate alleged infringements of the rules, the Committee were advised, they would need more protection than that. Clause 11 gave members of the Committee and their employees immunity against suits arising out of acts or omissions carried out in the course of their duties. It also, more questionably, gave Lloyd's as a society protection against being sued by individual members (like the Sasse Names) who had suffered underwriting losses. The broad question of public policy was whether this immunity against suit from members of the Lloyd's community (not from policy-holders or the general public) was necessary or justified.

Two other aspects of the immunity question deserve mention. First, Malcolm Pearson's solicitor, who called the shots in this dispute, and who on more than one occasion negotiated with Lloyd's over immunity, was none other than Leon Boshoff, the 'six feet four of South African granite' who won the fight against the Committee on behalf of the Sasse Names. The Committee was facing a veritable coalition of those it had been in conflict with on specific issues before. Second, the issue of immunity for Lloyd's became entangled in at least some MPs' minds with a far more embittered and contentious issue of British politics: the question of immunities for trade unions, which the Thatcher government, at that precise moment, was proposing to restrict by means of its employment bill. As the *Economist* commented in a sharp editorial: 'As some Labour Members of Parliament are aware, if Parliament does indeed grant Lloyd's the immunities it wants, the Conservative government may find it harder (or at least more embarrassing) to push through proposed legislation depriving British trade unions of some of their legal immunities.' The thought was indeed present both to some Conservative MPs who wanted the employment bill passed, and to Labour MPs who regarded it as anathema.

The issue was confused by Sir Graham Page, with the best intentions. In the second reading debate he proposed to meet objections to giving Lloyd's immunity against suit by taking the immunity clause out of the bill itself and burying it in a schedule – that is, a list of matters affected by bill, but with less legal force than the bill itself. Naturally this pleased no one. In the end the Meacher committee accepted that Clause 11 was a reasonable provision (though Meacher himself now confesses to doubts about it) and insisted that the clause be put back in the bill. And there, after months of parliamentary fire and fury, it remains.

Far more contentious still was the issue of brokers' divestment of underwriting syndicates. It helps to see it in two phases. In the first, promoters were faced with the most successful underwriter in the market, Ian Posgate, campaigning *for* divestment and against its being left up to the Council to carry it out five years after the passage of the bill. After several dramatic twists, he was successful: Michael Meacher and his committee insisted that mandatory divestment be written into the bill. That led to a second phase, in which the whole idea was furiously attacked, by none more furiously than Posgate's colleagues on the board of the Alexander Howden Group, Kenneth Grob and Ronald Comery. Each side to this strange internecine conflict within one of the half-dozen biggest firms of Lloyd's brokers had obvious financial motives, as well as motives derived from personal relations and past history. Only the chief actors can say which were the more important.

Ian Posgate had every interest in acquiring control, as a result of mandatory divestment, of the immensely profitable underwriting agencies that he had built up under the Alexander Howden aegis over ten years of spectacularly successful underwriting. Ken Grob and Ron Comery had an equally obvious interest in not being forced to lose those agencies. They accounted for one-fifth of the Howden Group's profits, and that was only a start. Out of almost 3,000 Names at that time on the Howden-owned Posgate syndicates, fewer than 600 were direct Howden Names; the odds were that those Names, and the commission on their underwriting, would drop into Posgate's lap like ripe fruit before very long, since all Posgate would have to buy was the agency business and the members would follow. Even that was not all. A substantial slice of Howden's *broking* income originated from Posgate's underwriting success. By 1979 the Posgate syndicates had a total premium income of some £80 million ($120 million). The Posgate syndicates ceded some £23 million in reinsurance premium, and more than half of that amount, £13 million, was placed by Alexander Howden brokers, three-quarters of it, almost £10 million, with in-surance companies owned by the Howden Group. Even that might not be the end of the chain, since Howden brokers might help place the reinsurance programmes for all or part of those companies' business. Posgate's success as an underwriter, in a word, generated a massive cash flow that had helped powerfully to build up the Howden Group as a whole, and the prospect of losing the first claim on that cash flow was not attractive to Grob and Comery.

Behind these obvious financial interests on either side lies the story of Posgate's problem. In the spring of 1970, Ian Posgate was an able and ambitious young underwriter who had just been given permission by the Committee of Lloyd's to run his own underwriting agency. Then, in May, the auditors for his syndicates raised certain questions about its accounts. The accountants Baker Sutton & Co. were called in, and in September their preliminary report drew attention to certain problems connected with reinsurance effected with a company called Reinsurance (Bermuda) Ltd. The Committee summoned Posgate to explain, but his explanation was not accepted. Baker Sutton were asked to carry out a second investigation. As a result of their second report, and after Posgate had been interviewed again by a sub-committee, the full Committee of Lloyd's decided to take disciplinary action against him because, the Committee found, he had misapplied money belonging to Syndicate 128/9 and failed to keep proper underwriting accounts.

Posgate was severely censured. He must cease to be a principal or a shareholder in any underwriting agency and to act as an underwriting agent, or to operate as a managing agent, responsible for a syndicate's accounts and trust funds. But the Committee withheld its ultimate sanction: Posgate was *not* banned from being an active underwriter. On 27 November 1970 the following notice was posted in the Room:

NOTICE

As from the 1st January, 1971, in accordance with the directions of the Committee of Lloyd's, Mr Ian Richard Posgate will cease to act as an Underwriting Agent at Lloyd's and will cease to be a Shareholder in or Director of any Company or a Partner in any Firm acting as an Underwriting Agent at Lloyd's.

Mr Posgate has been severely censured by the Committee for the way in which he has conducted the affairs of Syndicate 128/9.

Mr Posgate has given an undertaking not to underwrite for more than one Managing Agent, who would be approved by the Committee of Lloyd's.

Negotiations are proceeding which may enable a Managing Agent approved by the Committee to commence a new Syndicate as from the 1st January, 1971, with Mr Posgate as the Active Underwriter.

BY ORDER OF THE COMMITTEE

The solution the Committee had found was one that was intended to protect Names while allowing a talented and energetic underwriter to continue to attract business to the market, and at the same time avoiding public scandal. Posgate was to continue as the active underwriter for Alexander Howden (Underwriting) Ltd, under the supervision of Howden's managing director, Kenneth Grob.

The relationship with Posgate was to prove highly profitable for Kenneth Grob and for Howden's, but it was no sinecure. As we have seen, Posgate is an exceptionally shrewd, daring and professional underwriter. His characteristic innovation was to cut rates *after* a sharp rise. After heavy losses caused rates to jump, Posgate would come in and quote a rate well below what his competitors were asking, but well above what the market had been charging before the losses. By this method he attracted an enormous flood of business to his box. Both his syndicate's and his own personal account continued to grow rapidly. But his affairs continued to be brought periodically to the Committee's attention.

Posgate had great difficulty, through sheer energy and avidity for risks and the premium they bring in, in keeping himself within the premium income limit laid down by the Committee, even though at one time he had the highest personal limit in the history of Lloyd's. In February 1971 he increased his premium income limit to the then maximum of £350,000, in November of the same year to £450,000 and in March 1973 to the round £500,000. In spite of this high limit, in September 1974 the Committee learned that he had exceeded it again by £58,000. And in 1975, though his syndicate stayed inside its premium income limit of £30 million, this was achieved only by reinsuring more than half its premium income.

Late in 1974, Kenneth Grob was hauled over the coals by the Committee because of reports that Posgate was canvassing for new Names for his syndicate in the middle of the year, the implication being that he needed them to sop up excess premium income. Grob was informed that the Committee was satisfied that there was enough evidence to warrant removing Howden's from the register of approved underwriting agencies, but that he would be given one more chance to control Posgate.

Gradually, Posgate's premium income limit problems did come under control, though not without moments of near-panic at Howden's, and though the Committee from time to time expressed concern to them both over the volume of premium income flowing into the Posgate syndicates, and over the high proportion of it that was flowing out in reinsurance premium. As late as the summer of 1981, indeed, when Posgate was giving evidence to the Meacher committee, anxious letters were being exchanged between Howden and the Committee about the 'grave doubts' whether the syndicates' premium income could be kept within limits.

Step by step, meanwhile, Posgate was treading the road back to acceptance at Lloyd's as a reformed character. Early in 1974, Howden's asked the Committee if they could put him on their board of directors, but the Committee refused to set aside its 1970 decision. But in 1977 the Committee relented. Posgate joined the main board of Howden's and became chairman of the underwriting subsidiary. At the same time he was allowed to have a quarter of the shares in a new agency company, Posgate & Denby (Agencies) Ltd, under a formula by which he would increase his holding gradually, subject to approval by both Howden's and the Committee of Lloyd's, until he acquired full control in 1984. In 1981, he passed an even more significant milestone: he was elected to membership of the Committee of Lloyd's.

Posgate's keenness to see divestment made compulsory was no doubt motivated not only by the financial interest he had in gaining control of his own syndicates, but also by a burning wish to vindicate himself and to prove that he was as good as the Committee that censured him. When I asked him about the problems of Reinsurance (Bermuda) Ltd, he admitted that 'it was not a valid reinsurance', but went on in the same breath to say 'but everyone else was doing the same'.

Posgate is a self-made man. He does not come from an old Lloyd's family. I asked him whether he felt he had been persecuted out of jealousy, because he had been so successful. He replied, 'I was certainly persecuted.' He feels that he is an outsider. 'Lloyd's has a second-generation problem,' he says. He means that his great rivals in the market, Sir Peter Green and Stephen Merrett, are both the sons of famous and successful underwriters, but he is also thinking of Paul Dixey, chairman of the Committee that censured him in 1970. 'If I had known then what I know now,' he told me about that episode, 'I would have fought, and I would have won. I have always been bitter about the way I was treated, very bitter.'

I asked him about the Lloyd's bill, then still before the House of Commons. His answer was revealing of both his tactics and his feelings. 'There will be no Lloyd's bill without divestment,' he said shortly. 'Peter Green will not give way on immunity. So in the end he will come to me and say, "Ian, you must help us for the good of Lloyd's." '

The story of Ian Posgate's return from the very brink of the outer darkness to a position of great influence and reputation at Lloyd's does great credit both to his courage and to his determination. Some would say that Posgate's story also illustrates how self-regulation can work better than rigid regulation. On this view, the Committee of Lloyd's found a solution that enabled Ian Posgate to be rehabilitated and to become an outstandingly useful member of the Lloyd's community. Another view could be that Posgate drove a coach and four horses through the rules and got away with it, and that commercial considerations triumphed over the duty to enforce the rules. Certainly, the Committee's treatment of Posgate over the years is hard to explain. If he actually committed an offence serious enough to deserve 'severe censure', why did it progressively whittle away the penalties over the years? If his offence was venial, why was he severely censured and punished in the first place?

At any rate, with this history behind him, Posgate was determined to fight for compulsory divestment. He did not trust the Committee to carry out full divestment as quickly as he wanted to see it done. His original plan was to petition Parliament himself. But he found that he was barred from petitioning because he had voted for the bill at the Wharncliffe meeting. So he joined forces with John Burrows and Nick

Parker, who were already planning to petition on the narrow issue of classifying members into working and outside Names. He contributed part of the heavy legal costs of the Burrows–Parker petition on the understanding that it would include divestment. Malcolm Pearson, eager to fight the immunity issue, did the same.

A parliamentary committee hearing evidence from the promoters of a bill and from petitioners against it shows many of the best and worst things about Parliament. The atmosphere, in a panelled committee room in the Palace of Westminster, is non-partisan, patient, formal and courteous, more like that of a civil court trying a big commercial case than that of a political committee.

What is less impressive (and contrasts sharply with congressional practice in Washington) is the lack of staff support for the Members of Parliament who make up the committee. There were four of them on the committee hearing the Lloyd's bill, chosen more or less at random by the whim of the chairman of the Committee on Selection. They sounded oddly assorted but in fact got along amicably in a non-partisan mood. Michael Meacher, the chairman, belongs to the left wing of the Labour Party, and so does the other Labour man on the committee, Reg Race. Meacher is a considerable expert on the economy, but with no special interest in or knowledge of finance or insurance. The two Conservatives, on the other hand, came from sharply divergent wings of the party: Nicholas Scott from its liberal fringe, and John Biggs-Davison from the flags-and-drums right. (Scott was replaced by another Conservative, Michael Marshall, for the second committee hearings in the Commons.) None of them had any specialized staff to help them. The promoters and the petitioners of the Lloyd's bill sailed into the committee room with armadas of lawyers and staff at their back. The Members of Parliament sat alone, helped only by a single clerk. The consequence, in the case of the Lloyd's bill, was a comic muddle that delayed proceedings by many months, added many thousands of pounds to the parties' costs and almost destroyed the whole bill.

The hearings on the Lloyd's bill before the House of Commons committee alone lasted for thirteen days, and immense care was taken to get facts straight and to allow each witness to get his point across. Both the promoters and the petitioners were represented by counsel, with Peter Boydell, QC, leading for Lloyd's and Michael Mann, QC, for the petitioners. It all began peacefully enough on 12 May. 'This bill is concerned with the proper running of the coffee house,' said Boydell, and proceeded to take his time about explaining to the committee how Lloyd's works and what the bill was intended to do.

The bill as presented to the House of Commons contained no clause requiring brokers to get rid of their underwriting interests, only a suggestion in the 'schedule' that the new Council might, if it chose, make by-laws on this issue. In this, it followed the draft bill attached to the Fisher report – which, however, had *recommended* divestment. As early as 3 February, Sir Peter Green had given an assurance to Sir Graham Page that the separation of broking and underwriting interests would be required. But that, too, seemed to fall short of compulsory divestment. For Green, the issue was whether divestment should be in the Act itself and therefore compulsory, or in the schedule and therefore voluntary. But there had already been rumblings from Members of Parliament in the second reading debate that such an important issue ought not to be left to 'secondary legislation', but ought to be clearly stated as mandatory in the Act itself.

Even before Posgate gave his evidence on the third day of the hearing, claiming that various actual abuses did result from broker control of underwriting agencies, Sir Peter Green knew that he had what he called 'a credibility gap'. Michael Meacher was even more sceptical when he questioned Green:

> Do you really believe that it is right that this matter should be left to a Council which I would have thought it fair to expect will still be dominated by brokers? . . . Is it not a reasonable assumption that Lloyd's will remain under the control of brokers? If that is the case, is it really right for Parliament to be expected to leave to them a decision which so closely and immediately affects their interests?

It was clear enough that the credibility gap had not been bridged, and that the parliamentary committee might insist on compulsory divestment. That would put Green and his advisers in an awkward position. For the members had given their assent to what Fisher had proposed, and compulsory divestment was not in Fisher. If compulsory divestment was in the bill, then the members would have to be consulted again.

That was the way things were going.

Then came the comedy of errors. Or was it perhaps a stroke of forensic genius on the part of the petitioners' counsel, Michael Mann?

On the third day of the hearing, after Peter Miller and Ian Posgate had been examined as witnesses, Mann proposed three draft clauses that he wanted the committee to write into the bill. The first proposed compulsory divestment: brokers must get rid of managing agents, immediately. The second was uncontroversial, simply because it dealt with a rare situation: it said that any managing agents who owned brokers should get rid of them, too. The third was the cuckoo in the nest: it prohibited managing agents from acting as members' agents. This came to be known as 'divorce', to distinguish it from divestment.

This was something, as far as the bill's supporters were concerned, that had never been seriously considered. Not only had neither Cromer nor Fisher suggested it, but none of the individuals or groups who gave evidence to the two boards of inquiry had suggested it either. But, as Meacher pointed out more than once, the parliamentary committee was not bound to follow the Fisher report.

On 21 May, after deliberating in private with his fellow members of the committee, Meacher announced his decision: 'The bill ought to be amended so as to provide for complete divestment as between brokers and underwriters, and also precluding managing agents from acting as members' agents; and that this should be done within a period of five years of the bill receiving royal assent.'

'We retreated in some confusion,' said Irene Dick, the young lawyer who had acted as secretary to the Fisher inquiry and was now liaising on the bill between the Chairman of Lloyd's and the lawyers. She smiled like someone remembering a bad dream.

It was a nightmare for the Committee, which decided that it was prepared to go back to the members and ask them to endorse compulsory divestment, but not divorce. Even this would be no easy matter. There would have to be a postal ballot. That would require a new by-law under the 1871 Act. There would have to be not one but two extraordinary general meetings. The Recorder of London would have to give his permission. The ghostly lilt of a Gilbert and Sullivan overture could be heard from an imaginary orchestra. The danger was that, once the attention of the members and of the big brokers was concentrated on compulsory divestment, enough of them would change their minds for the Committee to lose its Wharncliffe three-to-one majority, and then the whole bill would be lost.

On 1 June, the parties came back before the parliamentary committee. Whether it was a coup by the petitioners' lawyers or, more likely, plain muddle, the Lloyd's people were caught by surprise, and for a vital moment no one knew what to do. The cat was now among the parliamentary pigeons.

Desperately, Peter Boydell repeated that his clients had already decided that they could not ask the members to support divorce. 'Is my learned friend saying on behalf of his clients that they would rather this bill failed than that it should go ahead on the basis we suggest?' Lloyd's had already conceded compulsory divestment. That was what Ian Posgate wanted, wasn't it? Was he going to put it at risk by insisting on divorce?

Mann refused to be drawn. If Lloyd's could not get the members to agree to divorce, then they would have to come back to the committee, and the petitioners would reconsider their position. And Meacher and his colleagues stuck to their guns. They thought that both divestment and divorce ought to be in the bill. If Lloyd's could consult the members on the one, they could consult them on the other. They were given until 20 July to come back with the answers.

Sir Peter Green and the Committee of Lloyd's were now faced with a serious prospect of losing the entire bill. If the whole effort to provide Lloyd's with a new constitution fell at this fence, it might never be possible to get it going again. Parliament had proved less amenable than expected. And there were signs that at Lloyd's, too, the seas were rising.

There was no time to be lost if the members were to be consulted in time to meet the parliamentary committee with a clear mandate by 20 July. On 5 June, the Chairman wrote to all members explaining the position, and the two extraordinary general meetings required if there was to be a postal ballot were duly held on 9 June and 17 June. On the second of those two dates, the Room was used for a meeting for the first time in 300 years. Trading stopped for about eighty minutes, and about 2,000 members stopped work to listen to the speeches. Sir Peter Green spoke earnestly in favour of divestment and against divorce, saying he had told the parliamentary committee the latter 'would greatly weaken the market and was not in the best interests of Lloyd's'. Ronald Comery of Alexander Howden spoke up against compulsory divestment, and Anthony Mitchley of the Association of External Names questioned Green about immunity. The resolution enabling a postal ballot to be held was carried with only twenty-six votes against.

The next day, the Chairman wrote to the members again, summarizing the arguments for and against both divestment and divorce. He told them that since Lloyd's had pledged to the parliamentary committee to seek the members' support for mandatory divestment, the Committee urged them to vote for that. On divorce, he left it to the members to make up their minds, though the balance of arguments for and against divorce in the letter left no doubt where the Chairman and the Committee stood.

The month between that second meeting and the meeting with the parliamentary committee on 20 July were the most dangerous in the whole history of the Lloyd's bill. The press had begun to scent a story. The passage of the bill would hardly be news, but its failure would be something else. On 8 July, for example, the London *Daily Telegraph* wrote: 'The bill is now in serious danger of foundering ... if this bill fails there is no chance of any future bill getting approval from both Lloyd's and Parliament.'

Meanwhile, inside Lloyd's, opposition to compulsory divestment was beginning to coalesce around the formidable personalities of the two men who had most to lose by it, Kenneth Grob and Ronald Comery. Comery in particular had been greatly irritated by Posgate's evidence before the parliamentary committee. With active support from Grob, Comery began to develop an intellectual case against divestment; to gather support in the market, especially from the heads of some of the other major brokers, for a fight against it; and to plan to petition against it when Parliament met for the 1981–2 session in November. As early as 26 June, the chairmen of two major broking groups, Minet and Stewart Wrightson, and the deputy chairman of another, Bain Dawes, together with half a dozen leading underwriters, turned up for a meeting with Grob and Comery.

Ron Comery was utterly convinced that the case the Fisher inquiry made in favour of divestment rested on fundamental misunderstandings of how Lloyd's works, and he put his arguments with great force. (These arguments were given added force by the resentment many brokers felt because they had not been invited to explain their point of view to Fisher's committee.) The theoretical conflict of interest between broker and underwriter is of no significance, he argued, because in reality they are interdependent. When Ian Posgate in his evidence said that 'the broker is not our friend, he should not be', Comery believed he was expressing a distorted view of how the market works. Secondly, he believed it was misleading to call companies like Howden or Bowring or Sedgwick 'brokers'. They may have started as brokers, but they are now integrated insurance and financial conglomerates, with broking no more important than many other activities. It follows that it was false to argue that the Committee of Lloyd's is broker-dominated; no one would call Sir

Peter Green a broker just because he is a director of Hogg Robinson.

In spite of these rumblings, the postal vote was another triumph for the Chairman and the Committee. More than 76 per cent of the membership voted, providing an overwhelming margin as Sir Peter Green had asked them to do: for compulsory divestment, by more than thirteen to one; and by 13,743 to 707, or almost twenty to one, against divorce. Once again they had demonstrated their willingness to trust the lead given by the Committee. And once again, it might be added, Green had shown both bold leadership and a sure sense of how the members would react.

How Members of Parliament, and Michael Meacher in particular, would react was another matter. But in the end, those in the press who had been predicting 'a major clash' between Lloyd's and Parliament were disappointed. The petitioners, having got what they really wanted – compulsory divestment – backed off graciously on divorce and expressed themselves willing to be satisfied by the Committee agreeing to make sure that two recommendations of the Fisher report, calling for agents to give their Names more information, should be carried out by the Council within two years. Meacher, once again showing himself to be not at all the left-wing ogre some people at Lloyd's had expected him to be, merely pointed out that Green himself had spoken of the need for a 'detailed examination' of the workings of the agency system, and asked that the Committee of Lloyd's promise to review the relationship between brokers and members' agencies. Counsel for Lloyd's duly gave such an undertaking, and Michael Meacher said that in that case the committee would allow the bill to proceed without divorce. There were sighs of relief all round, in which perhaps the members of the parliamentary committee surreptitiously joined. All that remained was for Meacher to propose that the bill be put into cold storage and carried over to the new session of the House of Commons in November.

In retrospect, it is clear that the opposition within Lloyd's to compulsory divestment reached its peak around the time of the postal votes, but that was by no means clear at the time. Throughout the summer, Ron Comery threw his considerable bulk into the fray with great energy – contacting Members of Parliament, arranging press interviews and organizing research. He even wrote a letter to the prime minister, which drew a non-committal reply. A Conservative Member of Parliament, Roger Moate, a director of Alexander Howden, was involved in the planning from an early stage, and Howden's retained one of the ablest lawyers at the London bar, Sir Frank Layfield, QC, to present their petition to the committee for them.

On 22 July Comery saw Sir Peter Green at the latter's request and left the Chairman in no doubt of Howden's determination to fight divestment. However, he reassured Green that Howden's would not use the compulsory divestment issue to defeat the bill. The high point of his campaign against divestment came at a meeting at Howden's offices the next day. Those who turned up included some heavyweights: John Wallrock, the chairman of Minet's; J. D. Rowland, chairman of Stewart Wrightson; Frank Holland, chairman of C. E. Heath; Sir Frederick Bolton, chairman of Bolton Ingham (Agency) Ltd; D. E. Coleridge, the chairman of the major underwriters, R. W. Sturge; and Colin Murray, the non-marine underwriter with the R. J. Kiln syndicate. At that point, Howden's were close to the kind of stampede among the old market hands that might have forced the Committee to give way, but the momentum died away. Some of those at the meeting declined to join a campaign. Others said they must consult their boards first. In the end, Howden's were left with a respectable, even – to borrow a word used of the petitioners by Michael Mann – a 'doughty' band of warriors, but not one that was likely to cause Green to lose much sleep. Not only had the membership voted overwhelmingly for compulsory divestment. None of the three great powers in the market, Sedgwick, Bowring and Willis Faber, had shown any sign of weakening.

On 17 November Alexander Howden duly put in their petition against the 'additional provision' for compulsory divestment. When the Meacher committee's hearings resumed on 14 December, there were therefore two petitions: one from Parker and Burrows, still represented by Michael Mann, and Howden's, represented by Sir Frank Layfield.

Peter Boydell, for Lloyd's, put up only two witnesses: Stephen Merrett, who could argue that divestment was both necessary and practicable; and Ronald Taylor, chairman of Willis Faber, who said he would have preferred to see divestment left to the new Council, but thought the parliamentary committee had done the right thing and was sure divestment would not drive business away from Lloyd's.

The hearings went on for another six days, making thirteen days in all. Layfield's star witnesses were the two broker barons Ken Grob of Howden's and John Wallrock of Minet. Perhaps their most telling counter-argument was that business *was* already leaving Lloyd's, and they produced Robert Corroon, chairman of Corroon & Black of New York City, the fifth-largest insurance broker in the United States and one of the first Americans to become a member of Lloyd's, to argue that overseas members, in particular, had confidence in the brokers they knew, not in an underwriter they could rarely if ever meet.

The main argument Layfield was trying to make was that the pressures on underwriters were due not to ownership, but to the marketplace, so there was no need to go beyond separation of management, which everyone accepted, to separation of ownership. This was ably done, and in the process Sir Frank drew from his witnesses a whole encyclopaedia of information about Lloyd's. But it was not enough. Meacher put his finger on a weakness even Layfield could not hide. Layfield argued that divestment did not need to be made compulsory in the bill, because if the Council delayed implementing it, Parliament could always step in. But that, Meacher saw, would not be easy. He preferred Parliament to act, now that it had the chance.

So compulsory divestment was in the bill that was reported back to the House of Commons, and there it stayed. In effect, Parliament had decided that it could not trust the Council of Lloyd's to carry it through.

There were still half a dozen more locks for the ship to pass, but now it was over the watershed. Back in the Commons, the emphasis of opposition shifted back to the matter of immunity from suit. Many Members of Parliament, on the left and on the right, were uneasy about giving such broad immunity to a private body. Predictably one left-wing Labour MP made the comparison with the trade unions. But it was a Conservative lawyer, Sir Charles Fletcher-Cooke, who asked the question in its pithiest form: 'Why should a body that has been negligent be protected from its own negligence?' Meacher had given his answer. Withhold immunity, he told the House, and 'it would expose the Corporation of Lloyd's in a manner which would severely restrict the effectiveness of its supervisory and regulatory powers'.

In the House of Commons, after many more hours of debate, that argument triumphed. The bill was finally given its third reading and went to the House of Lords on 3 March 1982. In the House of Lords debate on the second reading on 1 April, the same uneasy concern about immunity was expressed by many of their lordships. Two of them had strong personal reasons for concern: Lord Napier and Ettrick and Earl Fortescue, both members of the Sasse syndicate who had sued Lloyd's and won. Both pointed out with some force that under the new immunity clause in the Lloyd's bill they would no longer be able to sue. 'In a country governed by the rule of law,' said Lord Fortescue, 'an aggrieved party is surely entitled to go to court for redress.' 'I submit,' said Lord Napier, 'that there can be no genuine justification for it at all. I say to Lloyd's: "Have you no faith in the courts? If you have done your job properly, what have you to fear?" '

One of the peculiarities of the House of Lords is that their lordships' sonorous, feudal-sounding titles sometimes conceal a vast amount of experience of the workaday world. Among those who spoke in the Lloyd's debate, for example, Lord O'Brien was once Governor of the Bank of England, Lord Windlesham was a television executive, Lord Strathalmond was an employee of a Lloyd's underwriting agency, and Lord Strathcona was a former naval officer with an interest in engineering and other enterprises. Perhaps the most thoughtful speech was made by Lord Mishcon, who as Victor Mishcon was a highly successful commercial solicitor until he was ennobled by the Labour government. It was, he admitted, 'a very innovatory and, possibly, a wrongly innovatory provision to have written into a statute an immunity from suit for anyone or any institution'. On the other hand, Lloyd's could be terribly damaged if they were under the temptation to give into blackmail exercised through the threat of litigation. It was, he concluded, 'a question of balance'. In the end, the balance came down on the side of granting to the reformed Society of Lloyd's this vast, innovative privilege of immunity from civil suit.

It was not until the summer of 1982 that the bill was read for the third time by the House of Lords and duly received the royal assent. It had taken four years to equip Lloyd's with a new constitution. The hazardous voyage that had begun with the storms and perils of the late 1970s was over at last. The ship was back in port, and with new articles for its further ventures.

CHAPTER 12

ICEBERGS!

And now there came both mist and snow,
And it grew wondrous cold:
And ice, mast-high, came floating by,
As green as emerald.

Samuel Taylor Coleridge,
'The Rime of the Ancient Mariner'

The Rolls-Royce slides silently up to the door of J. H. Minet's elegant
new office building. A broker emerges and marches into the building,
puffing slightly, for it is after lunch. His suit is admirably cut, his wide-
striped shirt too loud only to the chastest of tastes. A Concorde tag
hangs from the handle of his briefcase. The chauffeur waits, well-
trained patience written in the line of his shoulders. Nearby, two
derelicts watch impassively. They must be about the broker's age,
though they look twenty years older. Their faces betray envy, even
anger, not surprise. Yet ten years ago any such visitation of opulence
would have been unthinkable in Leman Street, in the East End of
London.

London may have been moving to the west for centuries: now the
Lloyd's community is defying that gravitational pull and expanding
eastwards, out of the traditional financial district, over the boundary
of that self-governing businessman's sanctuary, the City of London,
into what is now officially known as the borough of Tower Hamlets,
but still answers to its traditional name: the East End.

It is not only Lloyd's as a whole that is getting ready to move house.
Half a dozen of the first eleven brokers – Minet, Heath, Hogg Robinson, Bain Dawes, and Sedgwick among them – either have recently
moved into large new office buildings on the eastern fringe of the City,
or are getting ready to do so. These blocks in one current idiom or
another – some with curved brick cladding over their steel frames, some
with reflecting glass – are springing up in what used to be a dingy
wilderness of sooty warehouses and sweatshops. A highly visible

prosperity is invading what has been for more than a hundred and fifty years a classic slum. This is Whitechapel, where Jack the Ripper stalked his prostitute victims in the fog. The brokers' Rollses, Ferraris and Jaguars are parked within a stone's throw of Cable Street: this is the heart of the harsh reception area, just inland from the docks, where one wave of immigrants after another has got its first taste of England. From the 1880s on, this was the ghetto where Russian and Polish Jews congregated, refugees from the pogroms of the Pale. In this new home they were protected from extinction, but not from discrimination or insult. In the 1930s, Cable Street was the scene of fierce rioting when Sir Oswald Mosley's British Union of Fascists marched through. By the 1950s, it had become the reception area for new waves of migrants from the Mediterranean, the Caribbean, West Africa, the Far East and the Indian subcontinent. On the shopfronts of the wholesale clothing factories and the rag-trade sweatshops, Patel is replacing Goldberg, Khan taking over from Kahn.

These contrasts throw into high relief how awkwardly, in many respects, Lloyd's fits into modern Britain. It is an enclave of wealth in an inner London that is in economic decline; a community of confident, upper-middle-class people, virtually all of them white, in an inner city that is increasingly poor and black; a luxury liner in a sea full of boat people. In one sense, Lloyd's resembles not so much a ship as an offshore island. It is isolated both by specific privileges (tax arrangements, for example) and by its links with multinational business from a society that has had a long experience of economic failure; whose egalitarianism is sincere and passionate, but largely negative; where equality often implies resentment of conspicuous success rather than any commitment to giving everyone a chance to make it; where the standard response to the sight of a man in a Rolls-Royce is not that he must have given proof of superior abilities, but that he must either have inherited the money or stolen it.

In this society, where envy and impoverishment are widespread, Lloyd's is an enclave of conspicuous affluence and conspicuous privilege. It is possible to succeed at Lloyd's if your family did not have a great deal of capital, but it is neither easy nor especially common. In any case, whatever the actual socio-economic origins of Lloyd's people (and these are, as I have suggested, rather more varied and more modest than either Lloyd's or its critics would have us believe), once you are at Lloyd's, wherever you came from, you inhabit what is culturally speaking a self-consciously upper-class world. There are few manual workers there, and they occupy clearly demarcated roles as virtual servants. There are conspicuously few non-whites (though no evidence that anyone consciously discriminates against blacks). The accents, the clothes, the naval and yacht club ties all reinforce the same impression: this is the world of the officers' mess, the wardroom, the club, the enclosed world of the English public school boys who ran the British Empire.

What has such historical symbolism to do with the humdrum, if sometimes lucrative, business of insurance and reinsurance? In a country as sharply divided in class and ideological terms as Britain, the answer has to be: 'intrinsically nothing, emotionally everything'. Lloyd's indeed is a potent symbol of a world some in Britain would love to eradicate without mercy, and others would like to restore. It seems hard for both its defenders and its detractors to see it as anything else.

To its detractors on the left, Lloyd's is anathema as a bastion of privilege, a relic of imperialism, a device for preserving inequality. The view was forthrightly expressed in July 1979 by an editorial in the socialist weekly the *New Statesman*: Lloyd's, it said, was nothing more than 'a mob of upper-class bookies with a mild talent for PR'. The opposite view is, if anything, even more rigid. It starts from the assumption that the institution is either so perfect in itself, or so valuable to Britain as an earner of foreign exchange, that it ought to be completely immune from criticism.

The argument that Lloyd's deserves special consideration because its foreign earnings prop up the British pound was always suspect and is now more dubious than ever. Lloyd's publishes yearly figures showing its contribution to Britain's 'invisible earnings' (earnings from banking, shipping and insurance), from which the inference is often drawn that without Lloyd's the nation's economy would be in even more parlous shape and the pound even lower. But those figures are deceptive. The total is inflated because it includes reinsurance, and when comparisons are drawn between Lloyd's on the one hand and manufacturing industry on the other, they are often presented in a way that exaggerates Lloyd's contribution to Britain's foreign-exchange earnings. The gross premium income of Lloyd's underwriters is compared to the net earnings of, say, the aircraft or car industries, where the fair comparison would be between gross and gross, or net and net. In any case since the development of the North Sea oilfields has made Britain self-sufficient in oil and natural gas, the balance of payments has been rather consistently in surplus. An institution can no longer claim special consideration merely because it contributes to that surplus.

For some, though, the arguments about the balance of payments are not the real source of prejudice in favour of Lloyd's. There are many who count among Lloyd's virtues the very traditionalism and elitism that others find so offensive. A Conservative Member of Parliament, himself a Name, spent half an hour one day at lunch telling me of his bitter hostility to the Committee and all its works, and then added as he left, 'But you won't write anything to damage Lloyd's, will you?' It was almost an appeal to my patriotism.

As a result, Lloyd's has almost always been discussed in one or the other of two modes, the denunciatory or the deferential. Neither is appropriate for the questions that remain to be answered. Will Lloyd's continue to thrive? What lessons have been drawn from the recent crisis? Will the improved system of self-regulation installed by the Lloyd's Act of 1982 eradicate dangers and abuses? Will Lloyd's continue to thrive in a world of intensified competition?

Much of the press coverage of Lloyd's from 1977 to 1982 was like a party game. The winner was the player who could dream up the supreme catastrophe that would bankrupt Lloyd's. What if two jumbo jets collide over Manhattan? Or how about an earthquake in Tokyo Bay? As estimates of the aggregate losses in the computer leasing affair mounted, many reports were written as if the losses had only to reach a certain figure and Lloyd's would be bankrupt.

That betrayed a fundamental misunderstanding of both the principle of insurance and its practice. The principle is that insurance means spreading the risk. Underwriters are at least as clever as journalists at imagining the ultimate in catastrophic losses, so they accept no greater net exposure than they think they can afford. And they reinsure, so that if they get their sums right no conceivable loss, not even any imaginable aggregation of loss, can wipe them out. Of course underwriters are fallible. They can get it wrong. Sometimes a large part of the whole market gets something wrong. That was what happened with offshore drilling in the mid-1960s, with computer leasing and again with product liability for asbestos. It could happen again. If, for example, existing designs for deep-water drilling platforms prove unable to withstand a freak North Sea storm; if the market writes insurance for satellites which perform dramatically worse than they are expected to do; if some product that has been universally distributed in supermarkets turns out to be toxic: then the accumulated losses could shake the market to its roots.

Is the liner ploughing through the northern ocean unaware of some gigantic unsuspected iceberg in its path? It is possible. It is far more likely, though, that danger will come from inside the ship, either from a serious fault in its design, or from indiscipline and sloppy behaviour on the part of the crew or officers.

A prolonged error in the market's method of underwriting would, for a start, be far more dangerous to international insurance than any likely aggregation of loss. The danger is not so much that underwriters may miscalculate the chances of some particular kind of casualty occurring, as that they might run their own business on unsound lines for a prolonged period. One danger arises from the overcapacity in world insurance markets, which has meant that for some years now it has been hard for underwriters, at Lloyd's and elsewhere, to charge the rates of premium they need to balance their books in strictly underwriting terms. Increasingly they have relied on investment income. With interest rates at historically high levels, that was all right. Now that interest rates have fallen, underwriters are squeezed.

Thoughtful people at Lloyd's are not too alarmed by this prospect, however. Present low rates of premium, they argue, are the result of the excess capacity drawn into the insurance industry during the fat years of the cycle. A sharp decline in interest rates should reduce capacity, as capital is withdrawn from insurance and invested in other sectors of the world economy. The period of adjustment may be painful, but ultimately rates of premium will rise again in the self-correcting insurance cycle. For two reasons, Lloyd's is better poised to survive this kind of crisis in the world insurance industry than most of its competitors, or so many people at Lloyd's believe. The first is that the sheer capacity of Lloyd's is very great and perhaps more easily expandable than that of most of its competitors, because it is relatively easy to call on the Names for more money. The second is that much of the present overcapacity in world insurance markets comes from competitors who can withdraw if they wish, because insurance is not their main business. This, Lloyd's men argue, applies to the Arab and Far Eastern capital that has recently ventured into insurance. It also applies to the Bermuda 'captives' owned by multinational industrial companies, and even to the big composite insurance companies in the United States, Western Europe and Japan, which have recently strayed from their own traditional markets into the international insurance and reinsurance markets in which Lloyd's has long been involved. If a substantial share of this new money were to be withdrawn, many analysts at Lloyd's told me, then, by a self-adjusting mechanism, capacity would once again be brought into line with profitability. Lloyd's and the other survivors would then be able to raise rates of premium to more 'realistic' levels and move to the profitable segment of the insurance cycle. In this argument there is, I fear, more than a trace of a complacent assumption that Lloyd's deserves to hold on to a certain share of the international insurance market by divine prescription, and that there is something abnormal about new competitors coming into those long-hallowed preserves.

The fact is, Lloyd's share of the international insurance market has been declining steadily for many years. In part, this decline has been inevitable, the arithmetical consequence of losing a near-monopoly in certain fields. Once, for example, Lloyd's did have a virtual monopoly of marine insurance. As soon as strong competitors, like the oil companies with their captive insurance subsidiaries, entered the field, Lloyd's market share was bound to drop dramatically. The same applies in other fields, such as treaty reinsurance, where Lloyd's also enjoyed a near-monopoly in the past. Again, the rise of national, and often nationalistic, insurance industries in countries such as France, West Germany and Japan, all of which largely exclude Lloyd's from their domestic markets, is a fact of economic history that no amount of shrewdness or energy could have changed.

Still, the impression persists that Lloyd's market share has declined more than can be explained away by these factors outside Lloyd's control. You can attribute this decline to a lack of business talent, to the atrophying of the entrepreneurial spirit or to the growth of the 'cartel mentality'. There is some truth in each of those charges. Perhaps more to the point, a large number of people have been able to make very large incomes without unduly exhausting themselves under the existing system during the past thirty years: why should they have worried if their collective share of the world market was shrinking? Life was very good to them.

Yet in spite of everything there is a good deal of evidence that Lloyd's has remained a place where innovation and inventiveness can thrive. In the United States it is the custom to describe Lloyd's as a 'venerable' institution, as 'staid old Lloyd's of London', as *Barron's* magazine put it in 1982 in a headline over an article describing activities that could be called anything but staid. But those who think of Lloyd's as merely old-fashioned and fuddy-duddy must explain why, in that case, Lloyd's has grown so fast; why it has been so profitable over the past fifteen years; why American brokers have been so eager to buy in. Indeed, much American reporting about Lloyd's has been rather glaringly inconsistent. In the same breath it portrays Lloyd's as an ultra-respectable, traditionalist institution, and as an unregulated casino teeming with hustlers and get-rich-quick artists.

The truth is that the danger to Lloyd's comes not from the fact that it is so different from the American insurance industry so much as from the fact that it is closely attached to it. Lloyd's is so quintessentially British in style that it is easy to miss how heavily it relies on the American connection. Lloyd's is vitally dependent on the goodwill and business strategies of the big American brokers. Long before Marsh & McLennan bought Bowring, they already possessed a decisive measure of control because of the share they produced of Bowring's most profitable business. In greater or lesser degree, the same applied to the other big Lloyd's brokers. They are not colonial dependencies of the American brokers – not even when they are wholly owned subsidiaries. But even when they are not American-owned, they are and have been for years integral component parts of an international system that is dominated by American brokers and American business – rather as Wimbledon or the British Open golf championship are not truly independent, but are part of international commercial systems controlled from the United States.

It has long been true that the big American insurance brokers could decide for any one of a dozen reasons, good or bad, to cut off, or merely to cut back, the flow of insurance business they send through Lloyd's brokers to the Lloyd's market. For the time being, the new American insurance exchanges are potential, rather than actual, competitors for Lloyd's, but that could change if American brokers were ever to feel that they would get better services or cheaper rates of premium at home. Again, for any number of reasons, including tax, big American multinationals might decide to give more of their insurance business to their own captives in Bermuda or elsewhere. The domestic American reinsurance market could grow to the point where it absorbed most of the reinsurance of American companies that now goes to Lloyd's.

Lloyd's would be highly vulnerable to any such adverse trends. But no such abrupt shift in American business is likely to take place all of a sudden so that the grass will begin to grow through the floor of Richard Rogers' new building – except on one hypothesis. The one thing Lloyd's has to fear is scandal.

That is why the Committee of Lloyd's was so sensitive to the series of rows that troubled the market in the late 1970s. Even more than most institutions, an insurance market depends on its reputation. The goods that are exchanged there are not fish or vegetables, not even gold bars or stock certificates. They are financial obligations to be met in certain contingencies at some uncertain time in the future. Everything depends on trust. And that unquestioning trust in the 'utmost good faith' of anyone to be met with in the Lloyd's marketplace, once damaged, is not easily repaired.

That is why, as the row over the *Savonita* reached the press and the House of Commons, and as the full extent of the Sasse mess became known, the Committee of Lloyd's grasped that at any cost the market's reputation must be protected. It had a second instinct, almost equally strong: that whatever happened, Lloyd's must continue to regulate itself. And so, to protect the market's reputation and at the same time to ward off intervention from Parliament or the government, the Committee called in the Fisher working party. It was convinced that any price was worth paying to protect the market's good name; it was even prepared to swallow divestment, against the interests and better judgement of some of its own members. That was why the Committee was determined – and surely representing the great majority of the Lloyd's community, which voted overwhelmingly time and again for its proposals – to make sure that a Lloyd's bill providing for effective self-regulation became law.

The market's reputation is all-important. But it is not something mystical and unassailable, like the good name of a Victorian maiden. It is, of course, highly desirable that people of all kinds throughout the world should hold a good opinion of Lloyd's. But three relationships, for a market like Lloyd's, are vital, in the sense that any serious damage to them could swiftly bring the market as a whole into mortal danger.

The most fundamental of these is drummed into everyone connected with Lloyd's from the first day they set foot in Lime Street. It is the sanctity of the Lloyd's policy. 'It can justifiably be claimed,' wrote an enthusiast in 1937, 'that the security behind every Lloyd's policy is unassailable and in keeping with the outstanding position which Lloyd's occupies in the Fields of Insurance,' making them sound like the fields of Elysium. It is vital to everyone at Lloyd's, brokers and underwriters alike, that anyone, anywhere in the world, who holds or is contemplating acquiring a Lloyd's policy should be free from the slightest doubt that, in any of the contingencies provided for in that policy, underwriters at Lloyd's will pay valid claims promptly and in full.

This basic confidence remains essentially unassailed. From time to time there has been grumbling that underwriters are slow to pay (an important point in a period of unprecedentedly high interest rates). When Lloyd's underwriters found themselves disputing tens of millions of dollars of claims in American courts, as they did over computer leasing, it was not the best kind of publicity for the idea that the spirit of C. E. Heath lives on. Yet notwithstanding this and other litigation, the security of the Lloyd's policy is not in question.

The second vital relationship is between the Names and the market. Names must go on making their personal fortunes available as working capital for their active underwriters. That was what made the Sasse affair so serious: for the first time on such a scale, Names rebelled against the Committee of Lloyd's, and forced it to admit that they had grounds for complaint about the way the market had risked their money, and about the way the Committee had enforced its rules. It is significant that for the first time for more than a decade the rate of growth in the number of Names braked sharply after the Sasse affair. If ever Names in general were seriously worried about how their money was being used and about the risks they were being exposed to, Names might begin to resign, as they did after the exceptional losses of the mid-1960s.

Third, it is vital that the American brokers who bring in the lion's share of the premium should go on believing that they can repose absolute trust in the people they deal with at Lloyd's. For the American business is literally irreplaceable. Without it, Lloyd's would soon wither into a minor monument of the insurance industry's past, stagnant and unprofitable. There is no reason to fear, however, that the American brokers will suddenly lose confidence in Lloyd's. They have given evidence of how useful they have found the market in the past.

That is why the reputation of Lloyd's is vital in the most specific, hard-headed financial calculations. In the summer of 1982, when the queen signed the Lloyd's bill into law, the Committee of Lloyd's, and Sir Peter Green in particular, had every reason to heave a sigh of relief. The market's reputation now looked safe. A system had been put in place that equipped the new Council with the powers to regulate the market in an efficient and convincing fashion. The danger of continuing scandal, and therefore of continuing pressure for outside interference, seemed to be at an end.

There were, in point of fact, a number of ominous clues lying about in the summer of 1982 that might have warned an astute or suspicious tracker in the Lime Street woods that all was not well. What surprised everyone, however well informed or ill disposed, was that in the interval between the Lloyd's Act receiving the royal assent in July 1982 and its coming into full effect on 1 January 1983, not one but a whole series of scandals came to light, a whole closetful of skeletons. These raised more damaging questions about the prevailing ethics at Lloyd's, and the prospects of self-regulation being effective, than everything that had happened in the long years that led to the passage of the Act.

Not everything that bubbled to the surface in that extraordinary series of revelations can be taken as proven truth. Some of the more disturbing allegations may prove unfounded. Equally, many transactions may still remain unrevealed which, if known, would suggest that certain questionable practices were widespread at Lloyd's in the past. Not the least of Lloyd's difficulties is that the Society itself and several of its most prominent members are now caught in a spider's web of litigation, and it will be a long time before all the charges and counter-charges can be sorted out.

Two circumstances, however, make it impossible to dismiss these revelations. The first is that some of the most important and powerful people at Lloyd's are involved, and no one can argue that the problems are caused by a peripheral handful of 'bad apples'. Even more serious, those problems touched the two points of Lloyd's greatest vulnerability. If a malign conspirator of infinite cunning had sat down to devise the worst damage that could be inflicted on Lloyd's, he would have come up with two devilish stratagems: he would have sought to shake the confidence of the Names in the way their money was being handled by their active underwriters; and he would have tried to shake the confidence of the American brokers in the integrity of their partners at Lloyd's. Without any help from external or diabolical agencies, those were precisely the two feats that eminent members of the Lloyd's community succeeded in performing by themselves.

During the very months when they were locked in battle with Ian Posgate over the Lloyd's bill, Kenneth Grob and Ronald Comery were pushing through a deal they had been thinking about for twenty years: they were selling out to the huge American firm Alexander & Alexander. The two partners had in fact been talking about merging with Alexander & Alexander even before they won control of Alexander Howden in 1966. Plans for a merger were far advanced in 1974 when the London stock market nosedived and upset the equilibrium between the two companies, which had previously been close to one another in size. There were further talks in 1978, but once again Howden backed out. Only then did Alexander & Alexander begin to talk about a merger with Sedgwick. When those talks in turn broke down after two years in July 1981, Alexander & Alexander, now under the leadership of a New Yorker named John Bogardus, turned back to the girl next door.

This time the courtship was uneventful. Bogardus moved with great speed. He telephoned only two days after the news that talks with Sedgwick had broken down to ask Ken Grob, 'Are you for sale?' That night, twelve copies of Howden's accounts were flown to New York by special courier, and within six weeks the deal was done. The question has to be asked whether Bogardus and his advisers really studied those accounts or, if they did, whether they understood them. In any case, in September 1981 Alexander & Alexander announced that it had acquired the Alexander Howden Group for £150 million in cash and shares.

The Alexander Howden Group had started life as the firm of Howden & Bellamy in 1821, and Alexander Howden, shipbroker, shipowner and insurance broker, became a member of Lloyd's in 1844. In the 1960s, the group was well established in underwriting at Lloyd's; it controlled the Gilbert and Aubrey syndicates, which Grob and Comery put together with several other underwriting agencies. Then, in 1970, the fateful association with Ian Posgate began.

Probably only Kenneth Grob, Ronald Comery and Ian Posgate fully understand the history of their strange adversary partnership. None of them is very forthcoming on the subject, and since all three are deeply involved in litigation, none is likely to be for a long time to come.

The essential facts of the relationship can be sketched out, however. In late 1970, as we have seen, Ian Posgate came within a whisker of being banned from underwriting altogether as a result of the transactions described in Chapter 11. He was severely censured, and the Committee seriously considered sending the papers in the case to the Director of Public Prosecutions to decide whether a criminal prosecution should be initiated. Instead, the Committee decided to allow Posgate to continue as an active underwriter, on condition that he was put under the tutelage of an underwriting agency approved by the Committee. The agency the Committee approved was Alexander Howden.

Throughout the 1970s the partnership prospered. A spectacularly successful underwriter, Posgate led the unofficial league table of his rivals in terms of the profits he earned for his Names year after year. Names fought to get on to his syndicates, which grew and grew. He himself says he wrote for twenty-eight Names in 1965, 3,612 in 1982. Counting the Howden and Posgate & Denby syndicates together, Posgate was by 1982 writing for some 6,000 Names, or more than a quarter of all the Names at Lloyd's, and a conservative estimate is that he was underwriting $7\frac{1}{2}$ per cent of all the premium written at Lloyd's.

In spite of the rapid growth of his syndicates, and therefore of their aggregate premium income limits, Posgate continually had difficulty in keeping within those limits. Both in 1976 and in 1977 Kenneth Grob, as chairman of Alexander Howden, was summoned by the Chairman of Lloyd's and warned that if Posgate continued to overwrite, the Committee would have to consider whether or not Alexander Howden Underwriters could be allowed to remain a managing agent at Lloyd's. But that was perhaps already an empty threat. Posgate was already known to the market as Goldfinger, and Kenneth Grob was coming to be called the Grobfather. The syndicates owned by Howden and written for by Posgate were already so big and so profitable that to have suspended them would have caused a major rebellion. What was later called before the parliamentary committee the 'incestuous relationship' between Posgate and Howden was making both of them rich.

Kenneth Grob is an urbane man, but his urbanity hides great entrepreneurial energy. During the 1970s, he and his friend Ron Comery expanded Howden by means of an aggressive policy of acquisitions. Between 1969 and 1977, it grew at an average annual rate of 40 per cent a year.

From the start, Grob and Comery had seen that the future lay in expanding an insurance brokerage into a diversified insurance supermarket, offering all kinds of insurance services to international corporate clients. First they had three operations: underwriting; broking to Lloyd's; and broking to the London companies market. Then they took over an insurance company, the Sphere. The next development was that the American tax authorities demanded that the Bermuda-based captive insurance companies owned by American oil and other multinationals could not claim certain tax advantages unless they could show they were receiving insurance business from the open market. At the same time, insurance companies from all over the world were keen to start writing international reinsurance business in the London market. So Howden ended up owning a string of reinsurance companies in London, Bermuda, and around the world. Swann & Everett, the first firm Grob and Comery took over in the early 1960s, had been a reinsurance specialist. Alexander Howden continued to specialize in what was now the fastest-growing class of insurance business worldwide.

A situation was coming into existence that was at once profitable, dangerous and tempting. Here was Alexander Howden, the owner of a cluster of fast-growing underwriting syndicates with a constant need to keep their premium income below the limit set by the Committee.

The best way to do that was to arrange, in addition to such more conventional reinsurances as Posgate might feel he needed to protect him against catastrophic loss and so on, large 'premium stripping' quota-share reinsurances. (A quota-share reinsurance is one where an underwriter simply hands to the reinsurer a certain fraction of his whole account, of course paying a reinsurance premium for the privilege.) At the same time, Howden was a leading reinsurance broker – and, by a happy chance, owned a whole string of reinsurance companies.

Howden was far more dependent on its underwriting subsidiaries than any other major broking group. But in addition to the 20 per cent of its income that came directly from Ian Posgate's underwriting, the group depended much more than the casual observer could suspect on indirect income from that golden rain. In the 1982 parliamentary hearings, counsel for Lloyd's, Peter Boydell, QC, pressed Kenneth Grob about this. Boydell first got Grob to agree that in 1978 Howden took out £50 million in reinsurance premiums and placed it in other markets, as against £74 million in premium placed at Lloyd's – a very high proportion.

MR BOYDELL: Very well. In so far as £50 million is taken out of the Lloyd's market in reinsurance it is directed, is it not, to a great extent to your own subsidiaries, which are not in the Lloyd's market?
MR GROB: No, sir. That is not the significance of those figures at all, if I may respectfully say so. I am perfectly prepared to explain what they mean.
Q: I am not at the moment asking you what they mean – I am asking you whether it is not true.
A: It is not true.
Q: Not true?
A: No.
Q: Not to any extent at all?
A: Not to any extent at all.
Q: To your own subsidiaries?
A: No.

Boydell then quoted to Grob a document disclosed to the Securities and Exchange Commission in Washington by Alexander & Alexander, stating that Howden broking subsidiaries dealt with approximately 40 per cent of the reinsurance business placed by the Howden syndicates at Lloyd's. Eventually, after Grob had shown a surprising degree of ignorance of the details of the Posgate syndicates' reinsurance arrangements, and had been given time to acquire more accurate information, Boydell dragged the figures out of him.

'When we first started reinsuring the Posgate syndicate,' Grob admitted, 'a quota-share reinsurance treaty was always necessary because there were always problems with premium limits, and one method of reducing the premium written by the syndicate is to arrange a reinsurance on a proportional basis.' In 1979, he went on, the Posgate syndicate's premium income was about £80 million, of which no less than £23 million was paid in reinsurance premium. Of that, £13 million, or 56 per cent, was placed by Alexander Howden brokers and £9 million went to reinsurance companies owned by Alexander Howden. So Alexander Howden would receive the underwriting profit on the full £80 million, plus brokerage commission on £13 million, plus underwriting profit on £9 million, and the profit would be likely to be high on these reinsurances, since few claims could be expected.

No wonder Grob and Howden were fighting divestment tooth and nail. No wonder Ian Posgate was fighting just as hard to free himself. Posgate had been elected to the main Howden board in 1977. But relations between the wayward genius and his minder were not easy. And they seem to have deteriorated still further over the period of the sale to Alexander & Alexander. Throughout this period the two men were bitter opponents in the struggle over the Lloyd's bill. Each spent a fortune to beat the other, hiring Queen's Counsel at fees of many tens of thousands of pounds the way anyone else would hire a jobbing gardener.

In mid-March 1982, the relationship was exacerbated by a bizarre market row. For thirty years the well-known brokers Bain Dawes had placed fleet cover and legal liability insurance for the Australian airline Qantas. It was a tasty piece of business: premium was $5·5 million annually for three years. On 15 February a top Howden broker, Peter Brewis, fired off a telex to Qantas saying Howden could place the business for $500,000 less than the Bain Dawes quotation. Finally it was shown to Posgate, who wrote 15 per cent of it. Even then it proved impossible for Howden to complete the risk (that is, to get underwriters to take all 100 per cent of it). In the end the risk was led by the Orion company, outside Lloyd's, for a premium of $5·5 million, and Howden had to make up the difference. Even so, the aviation underwriters were furious. They were annoyed that Howden had reduced the premium in order to win the business away from Bain Dawes; lower premium means less money for underwriters. And in this case the last straw was that such a juicy slice of the premium went outside the normal aviation market to Posgate, who was Howden's own man. They thought the whole transaction was unfair. They complained to the Committee of

Lloyd's, which eventually upheld their complaints, at least to the extent that Peter Brewis was found guilty of discreditable conduct and suspended for a year.

The real significance of the affair was that, at the very moment when Howden was attempting to persuade Parliament that big brokers did not use their influence on the underwriting syndicates they control, the Qantas affair seemed to show that Howden had used its control of the Posgate syndicate to seize a valuable piece of brokerage commission from Bain Dawes.

On 16 March Posgate resigned from the Howden board, and a general reorganization followed. Alexander & Alexander were moving in. Posgate's reason for resigning had nothing to do with the Qantas affair, though he claimed he was unhappy about the way the Qantas slip had been broked to him. He was angry, he explained later, because he had not been included in the takeover negotiations in spite of the fact that he was the group's major profit-earner and a major shareholder.

Once Alexander & Alexander were in control, it took their accountants a long time to find anything amiss. But in early summer attention began to focus on two insurance companies owned by Howden in London, the Sphere and the Drake (they later merged into one). The company filed accounts with the British Department of Trade, signed by accountants Arthur Young McLelland Moores on 30 June, which made no mention of a reinsurance deficiency in its accounts. But this was strange, because on 13 June the Alexander & Alexander report said that Alexander Howden had injected £10 million of additional money into the reserves of Sphere Drake. Why did Sphere Drake need that money?

Lloyd's has always been a rumour mill. This is inevitable when several thousand people meet almost daily to talk about often secret transactions involving many millions of pounds and dollars. But no one at Lloyd's can remember a time of more insistent, crazy-sounding, yet increasingly plausible rumours than July 1982. There was historical irony about the timing. As the bill that was supposed to regulate the market once and forever moved serenely through the final ceremonial stages towards receiving Her Majesty's signature on 23 July, Lloyd's was alive with rumours about Howden's and the two men who had taken the lead on opposite sides in the fight over the bill. There were rumours that locks in some offices might be being changed. As early as 2 July one of the most powerful members' agents, R. W. Sturge, advised its Names to leave the Howden-managed syndicates, citing nothing more concrete than the facts about Howden that had come out in the parliamentary hearings six months before. More surprising, Howden's underwriting company sent out a letter to all the Names on the Posgate syndicates saying they had stopped writing new business because of the danger of overwriting. 'Funny,' said the Captain's Room cynics. 'That never stopped them in the past.'

Early in July Alexander & Alexander took a drastic step. John Bogardus put in a heavyweight firm of accountants, Deloitte Haskins & Sells, to carry out a 'fair value' audit. Deloitte discovered something more disturbing than unexpectedly large losses at Sphere Drake. They found an enormous hole down which some tens of millions of Howden's money – of what ought now to be Alexander & Alexander's money – had disappeared.

And it was far worse than that. For who should the accountants find sitting at the bottom of that hole, with their buckets ready to catch the falling stream of gold, but Messrs Grob and Comery, together with two of their fellow Howden executives, Allan Page and John Carpenter?

Two months later, Alexander & Alexander reported the gist of Deloitte's discoveries to the Securities and Exchange Commission in Washington. By that time Howden was a subsidiary of Alexander & Alexander Services Inc., itself a subsidiary of Alexander & Alexander, and it was this intermediary that filed the information with the SEC and is therefore referred to in the document, known as the '8-K', as 'the Registrant':

On 20 September 1982 the Registrant filed suit in the United Kingdom against these four individuals, K. V. Grob, R. C. Comery, A. J. Page and J. H. Carpenter, seeking remedies for breach of fiduciary duty and misrepresentation stemming from transactions occurring up to May 1982 and from the acquisition of Howden and for breach of the settlement agreement.

The Registrant has also brought suit, in the same proceeding, against I. R. Posgate ... The Registrant's claims against Mr Posgate also involve allegations of misrepresentation and breach of fiduciary duty ...

The suit against the four former officers and Mr Posgate alleges that, through a series of Lichtenstein [sic] trusts and Panamanian corporations, the four former officers and directors named above own Southern International RE Company SA ('SIR'), a Panamanian company not licensed to engage in the re-insurance business, and that they owned Southern Reinsurance AG ('SRAG'), a Lichtenstein [sic] corporation engaged in the insurance business. Also, the four individuals, along with Mr Posgate, owned interests in New Southern RE Company SA ('NSR'), a Panamanian corporation.

Beginning as early as 1975, funds totalling approximately $55 million, including payments purporting to be insurance and reinsurance premiums from

Howden insurance companies and quota-share premiums from Howden-managed insurance underwriting syndicates of which Mr Posgate was the underwriter, were paid to SRAG and SIR, with SIR paying approximately $7 million to NSR. The monies taken in by these entities were used in part for the personal benefit of the four individuals and Mr Posgate. The benefits included works of art received by Mr Posgate.

... The funds paid by SIR to NSR were used on behalf of the four and Mr Posgate to purchase a substantial interest in the Banque du Rhône et de la Tamise SA from Howden at a time when they and Mr Posgate were directors of Howden. Neither the four nor Mr Posgate disclosed their interests to Howden. These interests were held in Liechtenstein trusts. Additionally, information developed by the Registrant during its inquiry indicates that certain bank loans to Mr Posgate, totalling approximately $2·5 million, were partially guaranteed by SIR.

The implications of these revelations could hardly have been more devastating. For a start, if things turned out to be as his company's lawyers had reported them to the SEC, then Bogardus had just paid $300 million for a company that might turn out to be worth far less. (At one point Deloitte's are said to have thought that as much as $90 million might be missing.) He had poured Dom Pérignon champagne with Ken Grob to celebrate acquiring control of what he thought was one of the solidest insurance businesses in London, the final jewel in a crown of Alexander & Alexander subsidiaries that circled the world. Now Bogardus found himself the proud owner of a wriggling nest of rumours, audits, investigations and lawsuits. No doubt it would be possible to rescue Howden, given time. But would there be time? On top of his other troubles, Bogardus could easily be swamped with stockholder suits demanding that he justify the Howden acquisition.

For Lloyd's the situation was equally grave. Eleven days before the Lloyd's Act received the royal assent on 23 July, Sir Peter Green got back from holiday to learn from his deputy chairmen that Bogardus had put Deloitte's into Howden to do a 'fair value' audit. Publicly, as late as mid-August, he was still saying that Lloyd's had no plans to look into the affairs of the Howden group, since only the underwriting and Lloyd's broking activities of the group fell under Lloyd's jurisdiction.

In the meantime, the Committee and the Chairman were, not for the first time, talking to Grob and Posgate about the latter's overwriting. The Committee put in Ernst & Whinney, the leading London investigative accountants, to check Posgate's projections of premium income. In the course of these inquiries, Ernst & Whinney found that Posgate's syndicate had a quota-share reinsurance of its whole account with, among others, Southern International Reinsurance Company SA, a firm unknown to Ernst & Whinney. Whatever it was, it was siphoning off a certain proportion of the stream of premiums that Posgate was writing. The Chairman asked Posgate about it, and Posgate told him that Ken Grob had said it was a company within the Howden group. Posgate told Green he had asked Grob to replace it with Sphere Drake, and this had been done.

Then on 1 September came the bombshell. Alexander & Alexander announced that it had discovered, in the course of the Deloitte's audit, that there was a deficiency of 'not more than $25 million', and that some companies in the Howden group had arranged reinsurance with companies secretly owned by Grob, Comery, Page and Carpenter. At the Committee meeting on 8 September, it was decided to put in Ernst & Whinney again. The following week the Committee set up a three-man committee, consisting of the two deputy chairmen, Tim Brennan and Murray Lawrence, and Henry Chester, to supervise the inquiry.

On 16 September Bogardus telephoned to say that he wanted to see Sir Peter urgently about a new development. He came round that afternoon with Roderick Hills, chairman of Alexander & Alexander's audit committee, which is specially charged with protecting the interests of Alexander & Alexander's shareholders. (Hills is also a former chairman of the SEC.) They had hot news. Alexander & Alexander had come to the conclusion, as a result of fresh evidence, that Posgate, too, had been involved. The next afternoon, Bogardus and Hills came back and met Sir Peter and Brennan with some Lloyd's staff people. Bogardus and Hills said that as a matter of American law (this was subsequently challenged by Posgate's lawyers), Alexander & Alexander would have no alternative but to file the facts of the case with the SEC at ten o'clock on the following Monday, 20 September, at which point they would become public knowledge.

That Friday evening, Sir Peter therefore summoned a special meeting of the Committee of Lloyd's for Monday morning. When Ian Posgate arrived at the meeting he was asked to leave, since the purpose of the meeting was to discuss his personal position. This he at first refused to do. After a brief argument, he left under protest and went over to a board meeting of the Howden underwriting subsidiary a few streets away. It was not his day. Shortly after noon, a letter arrived from Lloyd's announcing that the Committee had suspended him from all his syndicates and ordering his removal from the board of the Howden underwriting company. At first the board agreed to suspend but not dismiss him. Bogardus then executed a manoeuvre that caused Posgate, for the second time that morning, to leave under protest, and he was duly removed from the board.

Sir Peter Green realized as clearly as anyone that Lloyd's was now in the middle of the gravest crisis in its history. All that had been achieved by the long campaign for the Lloyd's Act now seemed to be at risk. That same day, 20 September, the Department of Trade announced it was investigating Howden's affairs under Section 165 of the Companies Act. It was also reported in the press that the City of London Fraud Squad had been called in. Each new day brought headlines about Lloyd's affairs in the press, and a week earlier Michael Meacher, the Labour member of Parliament who had been so helpful in the parliamentary hearings, wrote to the Secretary of State for Trade calling urgently for a full inquiry.

Behind all these immediate problems there loomed the spectre of permanent damage to the two vital relationships with the Names and with the American insurance industry. There were concerned rumblings from powerful members' agents. Within two days of the first revelations about Deloitte's discoveries, Albert Lewis, New York State superintendent of insurance, made a sharp statement criticizing Lloyd's for incompetent regulation. That was not easy to rebut.

Yet, as September passed into October, it became apparent that things were not so simple, and that Lloyd's had not got an open-and-shut case. For one thing, Grob, Comery, Page and Carpenter, and quite separately Posgate, denied all allegations of impropriety and announced that they were determined to counter-sue. The solicitors to the 'Gang of Four', as they were inevitably known, stated in mid-October that their clients 'have answers to each and every allegation which has been made against them', answers they would produce at the proper place and at the proper time – that was, to the Department of Trade's inspectors and in court in their defence of the action brought by Alexander & Alexander.

Posgate sounded even more confident. He put out a statement saying that not only would he firmly resist the Alexander & Alexander action, but he was also starting proceedings against Alexander Howden Underwriting Ltd, in respect of his 'purported dismissal'; and, thirdly, that he was applying for a judicial review to declare that Lloyd's had acted beyond its powers in suspending him. On 11 January Mr Justice O'Connor, in the Queen's Bench divisional court, found that the Committee had no power to require Alexander Howden Underwriting Ltd or Posgate's other employer, Posgate & Denby, to suspend him in such a manner as would amount to suspending him as a member of

Lloyd's. The court pointed out that the Committee did have the power
to take another action conveyed in the same letter – namely, to require
that all underwriting on behalf of the syndicates managed by the two
companies be suspended until the Committee was satisfied; and that
would have had the same effect. Still, with many hearings to come and
many issues to be decided, it was clear that Posgate was going to defend
himself with determination.

Less than a week after Posgate's suspension and the 8-K filing with
the SEC on 20 September, the London *Sunday Times* Insight team of
investigative reporters published a long article about the affair. Not
only was it sauced with tantalizing details of the opulent lifestyle of
Kenneth Grob and his friends, but it also brought out a previously
unknown fact that seemed to complicate the simple picture of secret
wrongdoing, righteously brought to light: *after* discovering that Grob
and his colleagues had been paying large sums in purported reinsurance
to companies secretly owned by themselves, but *before* going public
with this knowledge on 1 September, Bogardus had made a deal with
the Gang of Four.

The deal was this. With the money that had passed through SIR,
SRAG and NSR, the four men had bought a bewildering array of
assets. These included a block of one million shares in a company called
L. Texas Petroleum, so called after an eponymous entrepreneur called
Les Texas, and several hundreds of thousands of dollars' worth of
paintings, including two by the Impressionist master Camille Pissarro
and one by an almost equally illustrious master, Odile Redon. The style
in which the operations were carried out is suggested by the fact that
when the four friends were asked by Bogardus to list their 'material'
assets, 'material' was defined to mean assets worth more than
£300,000. The total assets belonging to the four men involved in the
deal, allegedly bought out of funds diverted from Howden, was about
£6 million, according to the Insight report.

The most romantic of this portfolio of assets belonged to Kenneth
Grob personally. It was a house, not incomparably smaller than
Buckingham Palace, in one of the most desirable corners of the Côte
d'Azur. (Grob also owns a scarcely less magnificent house in the
ostentatious splendour of the Nash terraces surrounding Regent's Park
in London's West End. Truly, Lloyd's brokers had become the last
heirs of the carefree magnificoes of Victorian England.) Grob's house
in the south of France, known as the Villa Olivula, was valued in the
agreement at just under £2 million. Even the hardbitten reporter from
the *Sunday Times* sent to view it waxed lyrical: 'Neighbouring houses

belong to Europe's titled and wealthy, and the house is appropriately guarded by electronically controlled gates, a pack of fearsome Dobermann pinschers and an equally fearsome concierge. It is set in spacious grounds full of French pines, olive groves, mimosa and bougainvillea, and has a staggering view of Cap Ferrat.'

The most intriguing of the list of assets, however, more significant and no doubt also more desirable even than Impressionist pictures, oil shares or Riviera villas, was the controlling interest in the Fabulous Four's own Swiss bank. This was the Banque du Rhône et de la Tamise SA in Geneva, the coyly named Bank of the Rhône and Thames. It had belonged to Howden until as recently as 1980, when it was sold to a syndicate of investors. This included Mario Benbassat and Eliahou Zylkha (cousin of Selim Zylkha of the Mothercare chain of stores), who ran the bank; Grob, Comery, Page and Carpenter; two others whom we shall meet before very long; and Ian Posgate.

Posgate acknowledges that, at Kenneth Grob's suggestion, he agreed to form what he understood to be a Swiss trust called the Hereford Settlement, of which he was to be the beneficiary, and which was to buy shares in the Banque du Rhône. The money to buy them was to be borrowed from the bank, and the shares in return pledged with it as security for the loan. All these arrangements, Posgate contends, were left in the hands of Grob and Page, and he, Posgate, never received any share certificates, transfers or any other documents, or any money from the transaction. Furthermore, he denies any knowledge that the shares had been bought by money from SIR or NSR.

The deal offered by Bogardus was simply that Grob and his friends would hand over this imposing list of assets, in return for which the four would be given a promise of immunity from civil suit and a cash pay-off into the bargain. Bogardus, in other words, wanted above all to get Howden's money back. To do so, he was prepared to turn a blind eye to the public implications of the affair.

The deal seems to have broken down, after Grob, Comery, Carpenter and Page had accepted it, for two reasons. First, Alexander & Alexander had a hard time recovering the assets covered by the agreement. It turned out that the Villa Olivula was owned by a Liechtenstein *anstalt* (a special kind of corporate entity available for investors in search of discretion in that sympathetic principality). If it were sold, half the proceeds would be consumed in French taxes. Alexander & Alexander claim that the other assets were similarly worth less than they had hoped. One of the two Pissarros was worth less than at first appeared. The other was in Posgate's possession, and Posgate claimed it was a gift from Grob; he was prepared to hand it over, but only if Alexander & Alexander could first establish who it belonged to.

The second reason why the deal did not stick was Posgate himself. Bogardus tried to bring him into the agreement, but he protested that he knew little or nothing of what Grob and the others might have done. He knew none of the details of the way he had become a shareholder in the Banque du Rhône, he said, and while he admitted that he had steered almost £30 million in reinsurance premium to the Panamanian company, SIR, he maintained that he had all along believed it to be a subsidiary of Howden, registered not in Panama but in Bermuda.

Immediately after signing the agreement with Grob and the other three, Bogardus set forth to tackle Posgate. Flanked by another Howden executive and by one of the top men from Deloitte's, he drove down to have lunch with Posgate at his country home, Badgemore Grange, near Henley-on-Thames, a white-stuccoed Victorian house in ample grounds. In New York style, Bogardus came quickly to the point. He asked Posgate if he was a shareholder in the Banque du Rhône. Posgate answered that Grob had offered him a shareholding, but that he had received neither share certificates nor dividends.

At that lunch, and at later meetings in London, Bogardus pressed Posgate about certain 'roll-over' policies. Roll-over funds are widely used by Lloyd's underwriters. What happens is that an underwriter pays whatever may be the excess of his profits in a given year as the premium for a reinsurance, with the understanding that he can claim on it when he needs to. A roll-over policy can be used as a way of squirrelling away money from good years against the danger of high claims in the future – in effect, as an insurance against under-reserving. It can be used to smooth out a syndicate's profits and to avoid sharp fluctuations between years of account for the Names. Or it can be a device for reducing taxable profits.

Posgate claimed that he had almost £19 million of his syndicates' money in a 'pot' of roll-over funds with Sphere Drake. He had already told Sphere Drake, or its owners, Howden, that he would be making claims for £4 million, £2 million and £1 million for the years 1980, 1981 and 1982 respectively. He had also recently claimed some of his syndicates' substantial computer leasing losses from Sphere Drake under his reinsurances, and these had been paid.

Alexander & Alexander, of course, have a totally different view of the matter. Their case is, as they put it to the SEC, that when Deloitte's audited Howden, they found a massive deficiency in the Sphere Drake assets; that $55 million had been paid by Sphere Drake in reinsurance premiums to companies secretly owned by Grob, Comery, Page and Carpenter; that Posgate had an interest in New Southern Re (NSR); and that $7 million was paid from SIR to NSR, part of which was used to buy Posgate a shareholding in the Banque du Rhône et de la Tamise.

By late October 1982, the first shock of all these revelations had begun to subside. The Lloyd's community, and an increasingly fascinated general public, were settling down to wait for a whole series of investigations and lawsuits. Virtually every well-known firm of solicitors in the City of London was busy working for one party or another. It was clearly going to be many months before the truth of the Howden affair could be finally established.

In the meantime there were other dramas at Lloyd's to attract people's attention. There were new beginnings and endings of old stories. At the end of September Christopher Moran and Reid Wilson were both found guilty by the umpire in the arbitration procedure laid down in the 1871 Act of 'acts and defaults discreditable'; it was up to the members to decide what their punishment should be. On 5 October there was a ceremony to commemorate the beginning of work on the underwriting floor of the new Lloyd's building, which was starting to rise across Lime Street.

On 25 and 26 October, the Committee heard the Qantas case and found Peter Brewis guilty of discreditable conduct, and the next day saw the final act in the Moran saga. At an extraordinary general meeting held in the Room the vote was 957 to 610 on the exclusion of Wilson; since an 80 per cent vote is needed to exclude a member under the 1871 Act, that meant that Wilson stayed a member. The voting against Moran, on the other hand, was overwhelming: 1,708 to exclude, against 113. At thirty-four Moran's meteoric career at Lloyd's was over. Life, however, was not all black for him. He and his wife, a 24-year-old model and former holder of the Miss Thames TV title, had just bought 47,000 acres of mountain and grouse moor in the north of Scotland for £1 million, and told reporters they were looking forward to spending a lot of their time there.

Then, without warning, in the midst of these various distractions, another revelation crashed through the Room like a brick through a window. It was as startling and as serious in its implications for Lloyd's as the Howden discoveries that Deloitte's had made in July. Indeed, in one way it sprang from those earlier discoveries.

On 29 October representatives of Alexander & Alexander met Sir Peter Green and told him about the latest fruits of their explorations at Howden. On 2 November Lloyd's issued a brief statement to the effect that 'The Committee of Lloyd's has received from Alexander Howden Insurance Brokers Ltd certain information concerning Quota Share Reinsurances placed by P. C. W. Underwriting Agencies Ltd, and W. M. D. Underwriting Agencies Ltd, on behalf of the syndicates under their management.' The statement went on to say that Peter Dixon, chairman of PCW and WMD, had voluntarily suspended himself from his duties while Ernst & Whinney carried out a full inquiry on behalf of the Committee of Lloyd's.

What Howden had discovered was that the two underwriting agencies, both owned by the major Lloyd's broking firm, Minet Holdings, had paid a total of $40 million in quota-share reinsurance premium on their marine account to offshore companies, at least some of which seemed to be controlled by insiders. This reinsurance was said to have generated some $25 million in profit over five years – profit, that is, that would otherwise have accrued to the Names on the PCW and WMD syndicates if it had not been skimmed off in this way. The money was paid to a number of reinsurance companies in such places as Liechtenstein, the Isle of Man, Guernsey and Gibraltar, not previously known for their thriving reinsurance markets. That was not all. The reinsurances had been placed by two broking firms called Zephyr and APEG. According to *The Times* of London, Zephyr was owned by Kenneth Grob and his friends from Howden. And APEG was owned by Peter Dixon, the chairman of the two underwriting agencies and Peter Cameron-Webb, PCW himself.

That was not the only connection between Grob and his confederates on the one hand, and Peter Cameron-Webb and Peter Dixon on the other. The remarkable fact was that until only two weeks earlier Cameron-Webb and Dixon had owned 15 per cent of the Banque du Rhône et de la Tamise between them. It was the discovery of that fact, apparently, that led the Howden investigators to unearth the other connections between the two cases.

The chairman of Minet was a bluff seadog called John Wallrock, who liked to tell all comers that he had been thirty years at sea as both a master mariner in the merchant marine and a Royal Navy officer. He was one of Grob's and Comery's staunchest champions in their fight against divestment. He was loud in his insistence that the danger of conflicts of interest between brokers and underwriters under their control did not arise. He appeared as a witness before the parliamentary committee and came out strongly for more discipline. 'What we want,' he said, 'and what the Committee of Lloyd's has been sorely lacking in is disciplinary powers. It is the half or quarter per cent in any market writing $2 billion worth of premium per year who will not abide by the rules, and unfortunately as the whole thing got bigger and bigger the rules have got inadequate. I am in favour of every disciplinary rule that Sir Henry Fisher laid down in his report.'

The reaction of this stern upholder of the ancient virtues to the news of what had been going on in the two agency companies of which he was a director was perhaps surprising. Wallrock, the respected *Guardian* City editor Hamish McRae reported, 'spent the best part of a day trying to persuade the Department of Trade inspectors that an investigation was not necessary'. The company then issued a statement claiming that the investigation was 'completely unjustified', and that the two agency companies represented only a small part of Minet's business. Exactly two weeks later, Wallrock admitted that for the past eight years he had himself had a secret personal interest in the PCW and WMD reinsurance arrangements. His interest, he pointed out, was quite small: only 5 per cent, worth no more than $2 million. Indeed, Wallrock did not seem to see what the fuss was all about. 'The matter which is the subject of criticism,' as he termed it, 'arose some eight years ago when I was offered a minor percentage stake in what I was informed was to be part of the PCW syndicate's very complicated reinsurance programme. I wish to emphasize that this proposal had been approved by both lawyers and accountants possessing knowledge of Lloyd's practice.'

That was an unfortunate way of putting it. For now not just the insurance community, but the whole of the City of London was in an uproar. And what was bothering people was precisely the question of what Lloyd's practice was. If top executives at both Howden and Minet, two of the biggest broking firms, whose collective influence was said to have become dominant at Lloyd's, were involved in what looked like insider dealing at the expense of outside Names, to put it no more strongly than that, then who else might turn out to be doing the same?

For a few days, the Room was awash with rumours of other investigations under way at other major brokers. None of them has so far been substantiated. But Frank Holland, the chief executive of C. E. Heath, went to the lengths of issuing a public statement denying rumours of problems at his own august group.

The Minet revelations were a specially hard blow for Sir Peter Green personally. For one thing, both Peter Cameron-Webb and Peter Dixon had been associates of his father, Toby Green, at the family box, Janson Green. And only a year earlier, Peter Cameron-Webb had been at the centre of another Lloyd's investigation which, most unusually, the Chairman had decided to carry out himself.

Once again it was an international reinsurance arrangement that had given rise to controversy. This particular contract was a quota-share reinsurance of a certain proportion of the PCW syndicate's whole account (and PCW is a substantial marine syndicate, with premium income in 1982 of £42 million). The broker was Seascope, a well-known middle-sized Lloyd's broker now owned by the Ansbacher merchant bank. A company specially set up for the purpose called Unimar Monaco was involved as an 'intermediary'. Apart from a 10 per cent holding owned by Seascope, Unimar Monaco was owned by Unimar Panama, and that in turn was owned by a London banker called John Nash, who is a director of the Swiss subsidiary of the eminent London banking house S. G. Warburg, and partly by a property investor called Willy de Bruyne.

The story going round Lloyd's, in some circumstantial detail, was that, in addition to the normal 2·5 per cent brokerage commission to Seascope, an 'override commission' of another 10 per cent was to have been paid to the Names on the PCW syndicate, but that the arrangement was altered at the behest of Peter Cameron-Webb, and the money sent to a bank in Switzerland.

The Chairman investigated personally and satisfied himself that though there had been carelessness and 'sloppiness', no one was being dishonest. Apparently, Cameron-Webb had dreamed up what was later called by the Chairman 'a plan of business development which was original in its conception [but] was made to look unnatural in its implementation'. The override commission seems to have been conceived as a way of rewarding those whose services were needed to set up a sort of 'reciprocal international reinsurance pool'. Peter Dixon later explained in a letter to the PCW Names that 'if all expectations had been fulfilled, Unimar could have earned at the rate of £130,000 a year for producing very substantial additional premium income for the syndicates'. This unfortunately did not happen. Dixon went on to explain that 'the documents prepared by Seascope evidencing the contract contained errors which most regrettably were perpetuated throughout the lifetime of the contract' – that is, for four years. On 26 January 1982, Peter Cameron-Webb and Peter Dixon jointly signed a letter, formally requested by the Chairman, confirming that 'the books of PCW Underwriting Agencies Ltd properly recorded the Unimar transactions'. The letter admitted that there had been 'an error of description originating in the office of the placing broker and perpetuated in our reinsurance department', with the result that the documents 'did not at first reflect the true intent of the parties'. Although Cameron-Webb said he had given instructions to correct this regrettable error in 1979, it was not until January 1982 that the necessary telexes were sent out. Most, though not all, of the money – some £400,000 – was repaid to the Names. At about this time Cameron-Webb, whose second marriage was in the process of breaking up in some tumult, retired from underwriting. He now spends much of his time on his yacht in the West Indies.

The gossip at Lloyd's inevitably suggested that if the Chairman had dug deeper in his investigation of PCW in this specific episode, he might have uncovered the transactions that were to be revealed later in the year. That was not the only matter in connection with which the Chairman now found himself the subject of embarrassing gossip. Many years ago his father, Toby Green, had set up an insurance venture in Nassau, in the Bahamas, jointly with two American railroad operators. The initial purpose of the Imperial Insurance Company was to insure American railroads against the cost of strikes. The Hogg Robinson group, of which Sir Peter is a director and a major shareholder, still has 20 per cent of the shares in Imperial. Later the registration of the company was moved to the Cayman Islands.

It was generally known at Lloyd's that Sir Peter had once had a shareholding in Imperial but had sold it when he became Chairman. What was the subject of much discussion and even innuendo was the nature of the continuing relationship between Imperial and the Janson Green syndicates, for which Sir Peter was the active underwriter. Eventually, at the first meeting of the new Lloyd's Council, Sir Peter made a lengthy personal statement about the Imperial connection. He explained that Imperial did reinsure some of the risks accepted by his syndicates. The intention was to create a 'roll-over' catastrophe fund in a tax haven. The reserves were built up out of the syndicates' untaxed income. Sir Peter gave his fellow members of the Council an example. He placed an excess-of-loss reinsurance covering the syndicates' exposure on oil rigs with Imperial and another, unconnected, company. The interest earned, and the money that accumulated in Imperial, were paid back to the syndicates at a fair rate of interest.

Sir Peter explained that when he became Chairman of Lloyd's in 1980 he tried to sell his shareholding in Imperial. No buyer was found, however, and instead a discretionary charitable trust was formed to hold the shares. Under the terms of the trust, neither Sir Peter nor his wife may benefit, and they have no children. However, a single-partnership farm company owned by Sir Peter may benefit.

It is a small but telling measure of how Lloyd's had become swamped with rumours, gossip and suspicion in the wake of the Howden and Minet revelations that Sir Peter had to take up some considerable part of the first Council meeting, which might naturally have been something of a celebration of his two years' efforts to put the Fisher report into effect, by explaining his own affairs. But in the last weeks of 1982, the reputation of Lloyd's was being battered from every direction.

There was the Brookgate affair, for example. Raymond Brooks and Terence Dooley are the underwriters of Lloyd's marine Syndicate 89, owned by a holding company called Brookgate. Members of the syndicate discovered in late 1982 that Brooks and Dooley were connected with the Fidentia Marine Insurance Company in Bermuda. Fidentia was set up with £12,500 in share capital contributed from Brookgate, later boosted with another £25,000. In 1974 the company, unusually for an outfit specializing in marine hull insurance, bought residential property in Cyprus and also set up a subsidiary in Panama. By 1976 its assets were £9·4 million, £1·5 million more than the claims against it. The next year the company seemed to melt away. There was an outflow of nearly £1 million in fees to unnamed brokers. Quoted investments fell by another million. There were heavy loans to unnamed companies. And finally the company was sold to a buyer, also unnamed, for just under £900,000 in cash.

The links between this interesting company, which experienced such mysterious good fortune and sudden decline, and the underwriters of Syndicate 89 were never revealed to that syndicate's members.

Just before Christmas 1982, the Committee of Lloyd's set up an official inquiry into Fidentia. The name, incidentally, is simply the motto of Lloyd's. It is the Latin for 'utmost good faith'.*

In the first week of April 1982, a struggling insurance company in Chicago filed its annual statement with the Illinois Department of Insurance.

The Kenilworth had a small office in the Time/Life building in Chicago. For some years it had been declining slowly towards insolvency by one of the best-tried roads: writing sub-standard automobile insurance. Its president and majority stockholder, Chester Mitchell, was prepared to resort to desperate measures to stave off its

---

* Strictly speaking, 'utmost good faith' is a translation of the Latin phrase *uberrima fides*, or 'good faith overflowing'. *Fidentia* means 'trust', or 'good faith', without the superlative.

collapse. Just how desperate, the insurance department already suspected. Soon the investigators had proof.

When the department's examiners looked at Kenilworth's annual statement, they saw that the company's health had taken a sudden turn for the better. It showed international business reflecting $3·1 million in direct premiums written, and $2·2 million in premiums earned without any losses incurred. There was also an amount due of some $5·5 million from an insurer not admitted in the state of Illinois called Universal Casualty & Surety.

On 14 April the Illinois insurance director met Chester Mitchell and his treasurer. Since Kenilworth's surplus was just $3·6 million, without those two entries it was insolvent. Were they pennies from heaven? What about the $2·2 million in international earned premium?

The director was presented by the investigators with a telex from a company called B. F. G. Toomey & Associates in London. It listed fifteen risks supposedly written for Kenilworth in the London market; the premium totalled $2·2 million. At the bottom of the telex were the accommodating words: 'If you need more, please let me know.'

There was a mysterious break-in at the Kenilworth's offices over the weekend after this first interview with the insurance department. The investigators found no documents missing at that stage, but they did find an elaborate taping system by means of which every telephone call in the Kenilworth offices could be listened to from the president's office. They also learned that in order to generate some commercial business, Mitchell had entered into a managing-agency agreement with a company called Robco Worldwide Facilities, run by one Robert Patterson. They also discovered that, impoverished as it was, Kenilworth had paid out $60,000 for improvements to a luxury apartment a few blocks away, on the sixty-first floor of the Lake Point tower. What was more striking about it, when the investigators got in, was the fact that strewn on the floors, shelves and furniture were hundreds of Kenilworth policy files. A young lady was sitting at a typewriter preparing invoices to brokers who had produced new business for Kenilworth. And sitting at the dining-room table with her own set of account books was none other than Joyce Splendoria, the constant companion of Alan Assael and book-keeper to Jack Goepfert. Goepfert owned Universal Casualty & Surety; his footprints were all over the operation.

During the very months when the Howden revelations were shaking Lloyd's to the foundations, justice was catching up with John Valentine Goepfert and some – by no means all – of his confederates. Goepfert

pleaded guilty in federal court in New York and he, Assael, Dennis
Harrison and Mamarella were all convicted of various offences committed in the process of diverting well over $1 million that should have
gone to the Sasse syndicate into numerous companies controlled by
Goepfert and into secret bank accounts in Curaçao. On 19 October
1982, he started serving a ten-year prison sentence, to run concurrently
with another five-year sentence passed on conviction for another insurance fraud by a federal court in Philadelphia. Assael was sentenced
to one year in prison, Dennis Harrison to three, and Mamarella to five
years' probation, during which time he was not to engage in any
insurance activity.

Even while he was under indictment in the Sasse case, however,
Goepfert was milking Kenilworth of millions of dollars. Indeed, when
the Illinois investigators got access to Kenilworth's telephone bills, they
found that the company were paying for Assael to call the FBI long-
distance to check in with them. Cooperating with insurance authorities
in New York and California, they discovered what many people had
long suspected: that the Sasse affair was only one incident in a long
campaign of fraud stretching back over many years. 'For nearly twenty
years,' the *Wall Street Journal* reported in December 1982, 'Mr Goepfert and a vast array of corporate alter egos and cohorts have fleeced
insurance companies here and abroad of as much as $200 million,
Albert Lewis, New York's state superintendent of insurance, estimates.'

Goepfert's method was to move in on an unsuspecting or near-
insolvent insurance company, somehow get control of it and then fill
it as full of premium as a Strasbourg goose. The premium came from
a 'special book' of business, most of it low-quality commercial fire and
casualty business from the less salubrious parts of the United States.
He seems to have been able to produce some $30 million almost
instantaneously. Then the premium was skimmed by a thousand cunning devices. In one case, the Kenilworth was paying 112·5 per cent in
commission for its premium!

In 1973, Goepfert moved in on the Argonaut Insurance Company in
Los Angeles. When he was removed by new management in 1975, it
was estimated that he had cost the company some $20 million. The
company alleged in court documents that Goepfert diverted money
from it towards the purchase of his 200-acre estate at Wall Township,
in suburban New Jersey, and 'to pay his horse trainer, stable hands,
mistress and others'.

In the mid-1970s Goepfert had discovered Lloyd's – a fateful encounter. He had also discovered the attractions of the international reinsurance market, much of it run from Lloyd's or from London, but through conveniently secret offshore companies. This is no place to follow the ramifications in any detail. But on 1 December 1982, at a special meeting of the National Association of Insurance Commissioners in Dallas, William Allen, a consultant to the Illinois insurance department, spelled out some of them in mind-boggling complexity in a 153-page paper illustrated with numerous diagrams showing the connections between dozens of insurance companies, some of them fraudulent, others victims.

Yet although John Valentine Goepfert was at the centre of a vast web of fraudulent insurance operations for many years, it does not follow that he was the head of the loose organization responsible for the frauds. Specifically, American investigators believe there are links between the Kenilworth case and Promotora Occidente SA of Panama (POSA), the international reinsurance firm now being investigated by New York insurance authorities. As we saw in Chapter 9, a key figure in the POSA case is Raymond E. Karlinsky, with whom Goepfert was once associated. Karlinsky was also a race-going acquaintance of Tim Sasse and Charles St George, whose Oakeley Vaughan firm was the subject of a Lloyd's inquiry in 1981.

There are many connections between the Kenilworth case and the London reinsurance market, including Lloyd's brokers. In December 1982 the London *Sunday Times* reported that Barry Toomey of B. F. G. Toomey and Associates, the obliging firm that sent the telex asking how much premium Kenilworth needed, had produced about $40 million of reinsurance business for Kenilworth from Lloyd's. The Kenilworth investigators say that Howden was a major producer of reinsurance business for Kenilworth. A spokesman for Alexander & Alexander was quoted by the *Wall Street Journal* as commenting that the company could find no record of a current relationship between Howden and Kenilworth, though he added, 'It's possible Howden did some isolated broking for Kenilworth in the past.'

American insurance regulators and their investigators are now bitterly critical of Lloyd's failure to regulate the market effectively. 'Kenilworth is just the tip of the iceberg,' William Allen told the assembled American regulators. 'The recent publicity related to Alexander Howden and Minet Holdings is just the beginning, because they are all interrelated and, once one fails, the others will come after. In my opinion,' he went on, 'Lloyd's and the Department of Trade in London need to realize the crisis of credibility they are facing and take steps towards coming into the twentieth century with respect to the transaction of the insurance business. All of these people we have mentioned are known by those men who walk the floor of Lloyd's and who represent Lloyd's in the real world, but for some reason as yet unexplained, they are still more than willing to deal with them in the London market.'

The New York insurance superintendent, Al Lewis, has been even more outspoken. He once described Lloyd's as a 'pirates' cove'. A more measured assessment by Lewis was cited in the newsletter *World Insurance Report*, owned by the *Financial Times* of London: 'An insurance market with the prestige of London's, which handles a significant share of international insurance business, is expected by its customers to have internal security and accounting systems to ensure the proper use of funds. The absence of such safeguards has severely damaged London's credibility, Lewis maintains. If the UK authorities do not act quickly both to protect the market and to restore international confidence, the USA could eventually insist that business remains in the domestic market rather than being placed in London, he warns. Almost 50 per cent of Lloyd's business comes from the USA.'

This stark prediction could be dismissed, as such criticisms by American observers frequently are at Lloyd's, as competitively motivated, though in fairness to Lewis his interest has been in regulating insurance business in New York, not in promoting it. But the same thought was tersely put by a Lloyd's insider, David D'Ambrumenil, the son of a Chairman of Lloyd's and a director of the brokers Seascope: 'This will destroy the market if it goes on,' he said, 'because Lloyd's exists on good faith and trust. The only people to gain will be the Americans.'

The log has recorded fire, storms and many other incidents alarming and comical. A mutiny among the first-class passengers proved to be too resolute to be put down, and had to be settled by an accommodation that may prove in the long term to have weakened the authority of the bridge. There have been many predictions that there are icebergs across her course ahead. The greater danger in all probability could still come from indiscipline among the crew, and even from pirates who have smuggled their way on board.

Still, even over the last troubled years, the balance sheet has not been negative: far from it. The number of passengers has grown steadily, and if when the seas were rough there may have been a little pilfering by the stewards from the cabins, it is noticeable how few of the passengers

*have complained. The captain and his officers have met all problems
with great resolution, and now there is a highly qualified new first mate
at the captain's side. A thorough survey was carried out, and new ship's
articles give the captain the authority he needs to run his command.
A comprehensive physical refit has been ordered, and is going ahead
on schedule. Trading may be less profitable for the next few years than
in the recent past, but even that is not certain. Most of the passengers
do not have to rely on the results of the ship's trading to pay their fare;
they find the comfort of the familiar ship and its Blue Riband style
reassuring. As long as the passengers are willing to pay their fare, and
the native traders keep pulling alongside with their lighters and bum-
boats piled high with trade goods, then the voyage will go on.*

Up until the passage of the Lloyd's Act in the summer of 1982, and
the subsequent explosion of revelations, it was possible to interpret the
problems of the years 1977–82 in some such cheerful and healthy-
minded way. This is probably the way most people who spend their lives
at Lloyd's think about its problems, even if their optimism is tempered
with cynicism and gallows humour as one scandal succeeds another.

Practical people have an instinct to avert their eyes from the more
remote and the deeper-lying causes of possible danger. If their ship hits
a reef, they patch it and sail on. Up to a point, it is a healthy instinct.
By late 1982, though, those who thought about Lloyd's in something
more than a day-to-day way found it harder and harder to be complacent about its problems. Sir Peter Green, though temperamentally
a pragmatic and cheerful man, was far from dismissive of the problems.
On 29 November – just seven days after John Wallrock's forced
resignation from Minet – he gave a thoughtful talk at the Insurance
Institute of London. All he could say about Howden and PCW in the
circumstances was that these things could hardly have happened at a
worse time, because the new Lloyd's Council would not assume its
powers until 5 January 1983. As a result, 'a situation which is potentially damaging to the worldwide reputation of Lloyd's and of the
London insurance market generally is having to be dealt with by a
system which was recognized as being totally deficient but cannot yet
be discarded'.

The implication was that once the machinery set up by the new Act
for policing the market came into operation, and once the Council was
seen to be capable of enforcing the rules, then all would be well. There
were many who doubted that. The very day after the Insurance Institute
talk, Sir Peter met the Secretary of State at the Department of Trade,

the government minister ultimately responsible for overseeing business, who expressed, as the official communiqué put it, 'the government's anxiety at recent events at Lloyd's'. Sir Peter, according to the same stilted source, 'informed the Secretary of State of Lloyd's determination to implement with the utmost vigour the powers of self-regulation granted by the Lloyd's Act, which cannot, however, become effective until the first meetings of the Council of Lloyd's on 5 January 1983'.

In other words, the Conservative government, with something over a fifth of its supporters in the House of Commons members of Lloyd's, was furious at the news from Lloyd's and putting pressure on Sir Peter to get the animals back in their cages. Even more effective pressure was coming from another source. The Governor of the Bank of England has no statutory authority over Lloyd's, but in the world of the City, where much is done informally, and where tradition may be more powerful than statute, the Governor's opinion is not lightly ignored. The then Governor, the merchant banker Gordon Richardson, was nearing the end of a long and successful tenure. (He was shortly to be made Lord Richardson.) He was beginning to be concerned about the effect the revelations at Lloyd's, and their underlying causes, might have on the reputation not just of Lloyd's, but of the City as a whole, and consequently on Britain's vast earnings from banking, insurance, securities, commodity and futures trading, and the rest of the City's financial and commercial activities.

Richardson determined that the City must put its own house in order so as to forestall outside regulation by the government. The case for government intervention was being heard again. On 9 November 1982, the London papers reported that John Smith, the Labour MP from Scotland who is the opposition's spokesman on trade and insurance matters, had demanded formally of the minister, Lord Cockfield, that the government take 'direct powers of supervision over Lloyd's'. Such powers, Smith wrote, were now 'necessary to protect both the public interest and public confidence'. The newspapers were getting restive, too. Several financial editors wrote in scathing terms of Lloyd's failure to regulate its members. After the Minet revelations the *Guardian*'s headline was: 'External regulation of Lloyd's took another step closer'. The *Observer* called it bluntly: 'The great Lloyd's whitewash'.

This was just what both Green and Richardson wanted to avoid. Sir Peter was clear about where he stood on government intervention; it would be, he said, 'the ultimate confession of failure'. He was well enough aware of how deadly perilous the situation had become. So he accepted, without too much difficulty, the two recommendations that

Richardson pressed on him: he announced a new inquiry into Lloyd's audit standards, under the very able Ian Hay Davison, London head of accountants Arthur Andersen; and shortly afterwards he announced that Davison was being hired, at £120,000 a year, as Lloyd's first-ever chief executive.

Most people at Lloyd's – like most businessmen generally, in Britain as in the United States – have an instinctive aversion to all forms of government regulation and interference. Like the City of London as a whole, Lloyd's believes in self-regulation. Though in many respects the businessmen of the City of London inhabit a society that is far less friendly to business enterprise than the United States, they have traditionally enjoyed an enviable freedom from government regulation. The American businessman might justifiably mutter that that is nice work if you can get it.

So when things began to go wrong at Lloyd's in the late 1970s, the first local reaction was to say: 'Right, the traditional arrangements whereby the Committee of Lloyd's regulates the market haven't been working very well. So let's bring them up to date.' That was what the Fisher reform exercise was about. The Fisher working party duly reported; the Committee accepted its proposals – with, as we have seen, a certain reservation over the most controversial of these, divestment – and won massive support from Lloyd's membership; and after a long and sometimes doubtful struggle, Parliament provided Lloyd's with a new Council, armed with tougher, modernized police powers.

No sooner had the queen signed the new Lloyd's Act into law, however, than the Howden and Minet affairs broke. It was in the ensuing concern that the Committee appointed Ian Hay Davison as their new chief executive. With the Committee's backing, he set about a new round of reform, rationalizing accounting practices and enforcing tighter accounting practices. The majority view at Lloyd's, therefore, remains the same: that government interference is to be shunned at all costs. What is needed is more self-regulation. Most members of Lloyd's believe that the Lloyd's Act, with the new Council, the new chief executive and the new rules, will take care of any problems that have arisen or that may arise in the future. The constitution of Lloyd's was archaic. The old Committee lacked the power to deal with those few offenders there will always be, even in a society specially chosen to exclude all but decent chaps. Very well – so goes this prevailing view – but now the constitution has been reformed. The Council and the chief executive have got the powers they need. So all will be well ...

This optimistic view is predicated upon very different assumptions from those that govern both American businessmen and their regulators. Regulation as a political and legal philosophy in the United States which goes back to the Progressive Era, was a response to the unimpeded depredations of the Robber Barons. When, in the high noon of nineteenth-century capitalist expansion, businessmen enriched themselves so ruthlessly and succeeded in concentrating such a dangerous amount of social and economic power in their hands, the European response was socialism. The American answer was regulation: let democratically elected legislatures prescribe where the public interest lay; then let the professional regulators, armed with proper sanctions, make sure that businessmen did not trespass on the public interest so defined. And as for the rest, where neither law nor regulation fenced them in, the businessmen were free to ride the range as they wished.

Businessmen never liked regulation, though they might have preferred it to socialism. But for the greater part of the first three-quarters of the twentieth century they accepted that regulation was a fact of life. In the past decade the pendulum has swung away from the regulators. Deregulation is all the rage. The prevailing philosophy is not that the public needs no protection from business, but that the frontier of the zone that should be left free for business's legitimate activity needs withdrawing, so as to reduce the regulators' power to interfere with enterprise and the operations of the free market.

Both these alternative American approaches to the problem of regulating business to protect the public interest are very different indeed from the assumptions behind the City of London's traditional claim to the privilege of self-regulation. In the American tradition, it is taken for granted that the businessman is a free spirit who can be counted on to take every advantage for himself that he can. The only difference between the Progressive of the Teddy Roosevelt–Woodrow Wilson era and the modern Reagan Republican is that the latter thinks that on balance the damage done by regulation when it impedes the natural working of the market far exceeds the harm done by free enterprise, whereas the old Progressives thought that, desirable as free enterprise was, there were spheres in which it had to be restrained to protect the public.

The tradition of the City of London is very different. It is that the gentlemen who are admitted to practise as bankers, or stockbrokers, or insurance underwriters, or whatever else it may be, can be counted on – because of the way they have been winnowed and sifted before being allowed into the club – not to be greedy. It follows that the best people to regulate the various clubs, or guilds, that practise the arcane mysteries of finance capitalism are the most trusted members of those guilds. There are contradictions in this attitude, to be sure. On the one hand, Lloyd's men are apt to argue that Lloyd's should be left alone because its activities are so much in the public interest; it earns so much foreign exchange, for example. On the other hand, they instinctively believe that what they do is nobody's business but their own. In either case, the deep hostility at Lloyd's to government interference owes nothing to the sort of political ideology that motivates deregulation in the United States. At bottom, Lloyd's perpetuates the ideology of the medieval guild, whose masters and freemen regulated its business to avert scandal and to protect its reputation. Such a tradition hates the idea of government interference, but sees nothing wrong with a little benign interference by the masters themselves to keep things running smoothly.

There is an even sharper distinction. Americans tend to assume that most businessmen will get away with whatever they are not effectively prevented from doing, if it is in their interest. The City of London assumes that, if suitable precautions are taken to prevent 'the wrong sort' getting into the club, then it can be taken for granted that the great majority will behave honestly. The problem will be limited to dealing with a handful of 'bad apples'. If they can be prevented from contaminating the others, then natural honesty and the fear of being ostracized by the club will take care of the rest. That belief, as the Lloyd's market has discovered over the past five years, rests on a dangerous half-truth. It is true that the great majority of underwriters and brokers at Lloyd's, like the great majority of businessmen in California or Cameroon, are reasonably honest when it is clearly defined what honesty implies and what the consequences of breaking the rules will be. But that has not been the case at Lloyd's over the past twenty years. Lloyd's has operated in a climate of privilege and secrecy that has left many fundamentally honest people who work there genuinely confused about many specific questions of what is and what is not acceptable business conduct.

Many factors have worked together for many years to produce this unsatisfactory and in some respects unwholesome atmosphere. Perhaps the most important of these is taxation. The men who control Lloyd's underwriting syndicates and Lloyd's brokers are very wealthy men. They have grown up in a society that since 1945 has taxed those with large investment incomes very heavily. (Until 1979, the top rate of tax on investment income was for some years 98 per cent!) Many of them also have fiduciary responsibilities towards Names who are also wealthy, one of whose motivations for becoming members of Lloyd's may well have been to minimize the impact of taxation on themselves. Add to this the fact that high taxation in Britain since 1945 has essentially been imposed not to raise income, but with the intention of diminishing inequalities in a country where, before 1939, those with investment income and those without were virtually two nations. For those who set the tone at Lloyd's (with the exception of a few individualists like Paul Dixey, the Chairman who was a fox-hunter and a socialist!), minimizing the impact of taxes on oneself and on one's Names was more than good business practice: it was a sacred duty.

Then add the fact that increasingly, in the 1950s and 1960s, Lloyd's brokers and underwriters inhabited an offshore world. There were several reasons for this. Their business was international. Much of it was marine, and the maritime industry was rapidly taking itself offshore in those years as British and American shipowners sought to free themselves from taxes, government regulation and union demands in order to compete with the Greek- and Chinese-owned fleets, many of them already registered offshore. The non-marine market and Lloyd's brokers also lived in symbiosis with big multinational corporations whose executives were catching on to the numerous advantages offered by offshore tax havens, not only for tax reasons, but because of the general freedom from interference and regulation to be found in Bermuda and the Bahamas, Luxemburg and Liechtenstein, Curaçao and the Cayman Islands, not to speak of wilder shores like Tortola and Belize.

A third factor was the growth of capital flight from Britain during the years of unfriendly socialist governments, high taxation and inflation. From the Second World War until the Thatcher government scrapped them in 1979, strict exchange controls prevented British residents exporting their capital from the United Kingdom except in rare circumstances. One of the exceptions to the exchange control regulations exempted insurance premiums (partly because Parliament was persuaded of the vital importance of the London international insurance market). There is no means of knowing how much capital was exported by means of bogus insurance schemes. But the thing was easy to do. The exchange control authorities had little chance of proving that a large premium was not genuinely related to an insurable risk, or of preventing the insured who had paid a fat premium in sterling in Britain claiming on his policy in dollars, or Swiss francs, or krugerrands. Certainly, the thing was done sometimes. Perhaps it was done rather often. In any case, the anxiety of many wealthy families in Britain to ship at least part of their money out of the country added to the toleration that was accorded to secretive and questionable arrangements in outlandish corners of the earth.

The most scrupulous and puritanical underwriter could hardly fail to notice the opportunities such places offered for increasing their Names' fortunes and for protecting them from unnecessary taxation, while incidentally enriching and protecting themselves at the same time. To an older generation of Lloyd's people, the knowledge that a man had registered a string of private companies in Nassau or Liechtenstein would have enhanced that man's reputation about as much as a propensity for wearing blue suede shoes in the Room. Suddenly, not to be offshore was to risk being thought fuddy-duddy.

By the late 1960s, growing overcapacity in international insurance markets and, consequently, growing competition drove down premium rates. Underwriters everywhere found it harder and harder to make money on underwriting itself, at the very moment when historically high interest rates increased the temptation to write for premium and not care too much if there was no underwriting profit at the end of the day, so long as you could get your hands on the largest possible cash flow and invest it at 15 per cent or more. The dilemma was how to maximize premium income without breaching Lloyd's strict premium income limits. An answer was ready: reinsurance.

There are perfectly sound insurance reasons for the spectacular growth of the international reinsurance market in the past quarter-century. The growth in insured values for risks like nuclear power plants, supertankers, jumbo jets and other products of high technology meant that exposures simply had to be split and spread around by ever more elaborate programmes of reinsurance. Even the strongest insurers needed to protect themselves. Newly independent Third World countries were reluctant to see insurance premiums leaving their boundaries, though the capacity of their own domestic insurance industries was inadequate to the demand for commercial insurance. The answer again was reinsurance: direct insurance was largely kept in national markets, whose capacity was in effect increased by international reinsurance. But there is no way of deciding whether a given reinsurance is 'sound' or not, either at the time or, except in extreme circumstances, afterwards. Brokers offered reinsurance. And reinsurance underwriters, who like most businessmen like to increase their turnover, especially if they think the business is profitable, were in no mood to turn the contracts down.

A substantial proportion of the growth in reinsurance in the Lloyd's market, however, was motivated primarily by the need to keep premium income down below strict premium income limits. This 'premium stripper' type of reinsurance, usually taking the form of a quota-share reinsurance of a syndicate's whole account, was the first step down a primrose path of temptation. Such contracts, where most of the exposure in a book of business was already covered by excess-of-loss, facultative or catastrophic insurances, often yielded, or could be manipulated to yield, high and almost guaranteed profits.

The temptation to take those profits offshore, in order to shield them against what was generally thought to be outrageously high taxation, was only one of many temptations. Among others, one was to funnel the most profitable of this almost risk-free business into 'baby syndicates', justified as a way to reward the efforts of the professional 'working Name' (a distinction that had been sharpened by the rapid rise in membership). There was a subtle disingenuousness in excluding the ordinary Names, without their knowledge, from more profitable parts of the business. And always there was the temptation to cross what was becoming a more and more invisible line and arrange re-insurances with companies secretly owned by the men who paid the premiums, so that the premium was simply siphoned from the Names' trust funds, where it belonged, to the private pockets of those who were supposed to hold those funds on trust.

In such a climate of privilege, secrecy and temptation, self-regulation at Lloyd's became increasingly difficult. The point is that the old, clear standards of what was right and what was wrong had been blurred in this new world of offshore registration, tax avoidance and secrecy.

Moreover, the gap between the practices and attitudes of the market and those of the outside world was widening. It might be the most normal thing in the world, inside Lloyd's, to hold your family's assets in a trust in the Bahamas. But to most ordinary people, that sounds suspect, to say the least. And so the secrecy that had been traditional at Lloyd's in the days when people normally minded their own business now became touchier, more defensive. No doubt the unmentionable, not-a-word-to-a-soul transactions were only a fraction of the business that went through Lloyd's. Meanwhile, Lloyd's was busy providing a valuable service to hundreds of thousands of people in shipping, aviation, industry and business as a whole. But the murky fringe was not quite so exceptional as to be negligible.

Supporters of self-regulation argue on its behalf that, as Ian Hay Davison puts it, 'the rules are drafted by those who know the game'. That has its advantages. It also has very serious disadvantages. Self-regulation requires men who have grown up in the values and practices of a marketplace to pass judgement on those values and practices. There will be some behaviour that is obviously wrong by their own standards, and such behaviour is easy to condemn. But there will be other things that are not obviously wrong, that are in fact quite common practice in the market, and yet may be very harmful to its reputation and therefore to its future. Indeed, the failure of self-regulation at Lloyd's was a catalogue of just such instances.

Self-regulation asks the regulators to choose between enforcing the rules and defending commercial interests. That is a real conflict of interest. There is, or there certainly ought to be, no difficulty about asking people to choose between doing their duty by enforcing the rules and following their *own* commercial interests. The system has always rightly assumed that the rewards and punishments of peer reputation would see to that. The difficulty arises when the Committee of Lloyd's has to choose between enforcing its rules and defending the commercial interests of Lloyd's as a whole. It has not always taken the right decision in such dilemmas. The thing can be simply put: you do not ask the grocers' trade association to enforce the weights and measures legislation. Why ask the insurers to protect the public (not to mention their own investors) from the possible malpractice of insurers? It is only because Lloyd's has succeeded in wrapping itself in such a rich velvet cloak of mystery, grandeur and ancientry that it does not seem so incontrovertible as that.

Of course the solution is not massive, obtrusive government interference. It is, rather, to support and help the process of self-regulation by establishing an independent regulatory body, set up by Parliament and with the power, as the old phrase has it, 'to send for persons and papers'. The function of this body would be not to regulate the market, but to regulate the regulators. It would check the effectiveness of what they were doing. It could also be an authority of last resort to which the Chairman and the Committee could turn in time of perplexity. There have been times when recent Chairmen would have been, or should have been, grateful for that possibility. The argument that this would impose an unbearable burden of additional record-keeping does not stand up. Underwriters and brokers ought to be recording and storing for their own purposes just the sort of information that a regulatory body would need. In an age of microprocessing, it would be simple to give the regulators access to data. The modest cost, even some slight inhibition of the market, would be infinitely less damaging than the buffeting administered by the *Savonita* and Sasse, Howden and Minet.

Lloyd's is rightly proud of its reputation, and of its ideal that it is a marketplace where men and women can place and accept great risks 'in utmost good faith'. But reputation, like money, can be inherited; however, it cannot be kept without attention and prudence. You have to work to keep what you have. Good faith is not a commodity that can be given to some, withheld from others. It cannot be guaranteed to the Lloyd's policy-holder and refused to the American broker who buys a Lloyd's broker, or to the Names who entrust their underwriter with everything they possess. If the men and women who will shortly move across Lime Street to the new Lloyd's are to look forward to a collective future as prosperous and as glorious as the past, they will be right to put the preservation of their collective good name first. And in that task they ought not to be too proud to accept some help.

It would be wrong to end this story with talk of misbehaviour and regulation. It is important, of course, that the ship should be properly conducted. But what has caught the imagination of the world is that Lloyd's is a collective venture of some daring. The ship's fabric has been refitted. The new articles have been drawn up and explained to the crew. She is slipping down the tide again, and it is time for us to wave our handkerchiefs and wonder what the next voyage will bring.

EPILOGUE

Late in 1983, Sir Peter Green made an unexpected decision to retire as Chairman at the end of the year with his second term incomplete. Shortly before, he had been able to announce that total profits for all Lloyd's syndicates were up from $242 million to $368 million. But only $22 million of that came from actual underwriting profit. The rest was investment income or capital appreciation of syndicate funds. A few days later, press reports revealed that Sir Peter had written to Names on his syndicates about £34 million ($49 million) in 'special reinsurance' in the form of 'somewhat esoteric policies' taken out by Imperial Insurance in the Cayman Islands. The problem, Sir Peter explained to his Names, was to justify to the British tax authorities that the scheme did not constitute tax avoidance.

He was succeeded on 1 January 1984 by his close friend Peter Miller. Both he and Ian Hay Davison were confident that Lloyd's was dealing with its problems. 'When I came here at the end of 1983,' Davison said, 'we had just seen the end of a holocaust. The air was full of the sound of skeletons falling out of cupboards, and nobody knew how many skeletons there were, or how many cupboards.' Davison pinned his faith in disclosure, and moved rapidly to make Lloyd's a more open and more accountable institution. 'Every week,' he said, 'there is further evidence that Lloyd's can and will deal with the miscreants. There is no evidence of further plunder. Steps are being taken. We are not sweeping our problems under the carpet.' The new Chairman, too, said he could not believe that 'the shameful behaviour of a very few people is representative'.

As for John Bogardus, chairman of Alexander & Alexander, while he waited for his litigation against Ian Posgate, Kenneth Grob and the others to come to court, he too put his trust in Lloyd's capacity for self-regulation. 'I feel Lloyd's ought to have a chance to put their own house in order.'

How long did he think they had? he was asked.

He smiled.

'I think they've got a couple of years,' he said.

In Rudyard Kipling's words, he seemed to be saying, if the gentlemen from Lloyd's had had no end of a lesson, it would do them no end of good.

INDEX

accident insurance   86, 109
accounting
   Lloyd's   106–8, 354
   net   260
   see also audit
Acker, Ray Allen   234–5
Acland, Brigadier Peter   274
Adam Brothers   126–7, 223–5, 227–228, 233–5
Adams-Dale, Simon   92, 95
Additional Underwriting Agencies Ltd (AUA)   276
Admiralty lawyers   171
Agnelli family   200–201, 204–6, 212, 217
Aitken, Jonathan   36, 43–4, 212–14, 305
Albahaa B   191
Alder, K. F.   96
Alder, Mrs Margaret   127
Alexander & Alexander   37, 124, 140, 142, 149–50, 329–30, 332–8, 340–43, 350, 362
Alexander, Robert   279–80
Alexandros K   178, 186, 187
Algeria   161–2
Allen, William   350
all-risks insurance   64
American Nuclear Insurers (ANI)   16–18, 21
American Public Power Association   16
Amery, Cecil   78
Amoco Cadiz   35, 165–70
amusement insurance   269–70
Angerstein, John Julius   53–4, 56
Angola   178–80
Annivas, Andreas   191
Ansbacher, Henry   126
APEG   343

arbitration   42–3, 275–6
Archibald, Hon. Mrs Liliana   126–7, 224
architects   295–6
Argentine kidnapping   88–90
Argonaut Insurance Company   253, 257, 349
Aristoteles   176–7
Arnold, Robert   195, 197–8, 217
arson   36, 255
Arthur Young McLelland Moores   334
Arup Associates   295–6
asbestosis   99, 107–8, 323
Ashby & Co.   276
Assael, Alan   257–8, 260, 348–9
assurance Act of 1601   48
Atkins, Humphrey   214
Atlantic Empress   155
Atlantic Saga   8
Attar, Dr Wahib   189
Atzori, Luigi   196, 197
audit
   certificate of   109
   Lloyd's   108–9, 269, 272–3, 275, 354; underwriters'   70–72, 74, 269
Austin, Jack   188–9
aviation insurance   29, 75, 83, 85, 98, 126–7, 152–3, 252, 333
Avondale   162–3

Bache Insurance Services   126
Bahamas   346, 359
Bahrain   38
Bain Dawes   124, 315, 320, 333–4
Baker, Desmond   208–9, 211, 213, 219
Baker-Harber, Michael   182
Baker Sutton & Co.   307

bank guarantee insurance   226–7
Bank of England   353
bankers' indemnity insurance   87
banking crisis of 1974   142
bankruptcy   60
Banque du Rhône et de la Tamise
   340–43
Bantry Bay oil terminal   35
Barbon, Nicholas   62
Bardari, Captain   170–71
Barebones, Praise-God   62
Bari, Aladin Hasan   191
Baring, Sir Francis   55
Barling, David   77–8
barratry   181–2
Barrett, Jim   136
Bastion company   201–2
Bathurst, Andrew   80
Beaverbrook, Lord   213
Bedford, Peter   18
Bell, Judith   127
Benbassat, Mario   340
Benge Vanga   155–6
Benjamin, Joe   270–71
Bennett, John   55, 56
Bentley-Buckle, Anthony   267
Bermuda   159–60, 169, 341, 347
Berry, John F.   221
Betelgeuse   35, 154
Betty   177–8
Biggs-Davison, John   311
Bilbrough, A., & Co.   169–70
Bill Crosbie   7–9, 11–14
Binney, Ivor   147
Bishop, Robert   199, 203–6, 208, 262
Blackmore, Courtenay   295–6, 300
Bland Payne   146, 239
Bland Welch   129, 131–2
'blocking and trapping' risk   81
bodyguards   93
Bogardus, John   140, 329–30, 335–7,
   339–41, 362
Bolton Ingham (Agency) Ltd   317
Bondi, Andrea   128
Born brothers   89
Boshoff, Leon   269–70, 272–7, 281–
   282, 302, 306
bottomry   47–8
Boulton Sidney   69–71
Bowring, Benjamin   133, 137

Bowring, C.T.   85, 120, 133–4, 137,
   315, 317
   Marsh & McLennan and   18, 20,
   37, 124, 135–6, 142–3, 146–50,
   326
Bowring, Clive   149
Bowring, Edgar   142–3
Bowring, Peter   148
'box', underwriter's   12, 25, 76–9
Boydell, Peter   311–14, 317, 332
Brazilian State reinsurance company
   (IRB)   245, 253, 260, 262–3, 265
Brennan, Tim   337
Brentnall Beard   245, 250, 252, 258–
   261, 265–6, 277, 282
Brewis, Peter   333–4, 342
bribery   175, 235
Brilliant   187
British Insurance Brokers Association
   149
British insurance industry   141–2
British Petroleum   132–3
British Trident   186–7, 193
Broadley, Robin   40, 285–6
brokers   21, 25–6, 50, 104, 119, 126,
   215–217, 256
   American   37–8, 43, 122–4, 131–2,
   134–6, 328–9, 140–41, 317, 326;
   British firms and   123, 129,
   138–9, 142–50, 289, 326, 329
   company of   48
   control of underwriting syndicates
   289–94, 302–3, 309–10, 312–
   318, 334
   diversification by   120, 122, 124
   divestment issue   292–4, 302–3,
   306, 309–10, 312–18, 327, 333
   incomes   124
   international   123, 129–32, 137,
   142–3
   liability of   42
   Lloyd's   21–2, 28–31, 58, 61, 77,
   81–2, 84, 97–8, 115, 119–21,
   124–6, 130–41, 144–50, 163,
   195, 200, 223–5, 252, 326
   mergers   37, 121–2, 129, 131, 138,
   143–4
   numbers of   121
   premium income   122–3
   registration   144

brokers–*cont.*
  suspended 38
  takeovers 146–50
  women 126–8
Brookgate affair 347
Brooks, Raymond 347
Brown, Shipley 125
bugging devices 234
bullion shipments 88
Bunge & Born 89
burglary insurance 63–4
Burnand, Percy G. C. 70, 72, 74
Burnett, David 80
Burrows, John 304–5, 310–11, 317
butter mountain case 42–3
Buxton, Sydney 69

Cabot, Godfrey L. 161
Cameron-Webb, Peter 85, 343–6
Canada 135, 252, 265–6, 270, 275
Candler, Richard 48
capital
  exports 357–9
  gains 27, 110
  transfer tax 110
cargo
  frauds 175–6, 184–5
  reinsurance 196, 198–200, 203–4,
    206–7, 219
  shifting 8
Carpenter, Guy 134–5, 146, 148
Carpenter, John 335, 337–8, 340–42
Carter-Ruck, Peter 218
Cassidy & Davis 88, 90, 93–5
Cassidy, Tony 88–91
Casualty and Indemnity 254
catastrophic reinsurance 96, 98, 359
Cayman Islands 346, 362
Cecil, Robert, Viscount Cranborne
  305
charter fraud 175–7
Chatham 295
Cheeseman, Reggie 131
Chemical Bank 234
Cheney, Richard 148
Chester, Henry 8, 11–13, 42, 85,
    183, 337
Chimo Shipping 11, 13
Chinese, overseas 153, 185
Chiomenti, Pasquale 207

Christopher, Charles S. 221–4, 228,
    231–5
Churchill, Sir Winston 66
c.i.f. system 172–3
City of London 24–5, 30
claims 99–102, 106–8, 161, 167–71,
    203–19, 327–8
  computer leasing 38–9, 220, 222,
    237–9, 328
  fraudulent 184, 193, 219;
    suspicion of 200, 203–4, 208,
    212, 214–19, 262–3
  salvage loss 209
Clarkson, Puckle 125
class prejudice 248
Clifford-Turner 276–7, 279
Clutterbuck, Dr Richard 92
coffee house 46–7
  Lloyd's 49–53, 58
Coles, Lambert 144
Collins, Frank 129
Comery, Ronald 150, 306–7, 314–
    317, 329–31, 335, 337–8, 340–43
Commonwealth Leasing 234, 236,
    239
Company Act, Gladstone's 61
competition 159, 184
computer leasing 230–32, 236, 240,
    266
  claims 38–9, 220, 222, 237–9, 266,
    323, 341
  insurance 227, 232–3, 235–7, 243
computer peripherals 223–4, 231–2,
    235, 237
Computer Weekly 220
computerrs 67, 77, 80, 94, 97, 286
Conch International Methane Ltd
  161
Conch LNG, Inc. 162–3
Conoco 161
constructive total loss 12, 163–4,
    204, 208
contingency insurance 224–8, 233
contractual penalties 226
Control Data 229, 231
Control Risks Ltd 91–5
convenience flags 153, 157, 171–2
Convention on Civil Liability (CLC)
  168
Conway, Barbara 177

Cooke, Gilbert 146, 148
Cool Girl 178–9
Corroon, Robert 317
cotton 135
county families 267
credit insurance 72–3
crew fatigue 155
Cripps, Sir Stafford 110
Cromer, Lord 113–14
 report 287, 289, 313
Crosbie & Co. Ltd 7–8, 11–13
Cullen, Terence 271–3
Curaçao 258
Cyprus 175–7

Daily Express 221
Daily Telegraph 315
D'Ambrumenil, David 126, 351
Danson, J. T. 61, 66
Dashwood Underwriting Agencies
 104
Davies, Bill 88
Davies, Paddy 268–73, 280
 group 268–9, 271, 275, 281–2
Davis, Stanley Clinton 214, 305
Davison, Ian Hay 354, 359, 362
de Bruyne, Willy 345
defamation, law of 36
Delbourgo, Ralph 201–2
Deloitte Haskins & Sells 335–6, 341
Delta Sigma Pi 183
Delwind 180
demurrage fiddles 174–5
Den-Har binder 244–5, 251, 253,
 258–63, 265, 271, 275, 277–8,
 280–81
Denby, Mark 79–80
de Rougemont, G. C., & Others 87
Deslauriers Wilkins & Associates,
 Inc. (DWI) 252, 265–6
Dew, Leslie 261–2, 277
Diana 53
Dick, Irene 128, 285, 313
direct insurance 96, 358
disability cover 226
'divorce' (managing agents) 313–16
Dixey, Paul 310, 357
Dixon, Peter 343–5
Dooley, Terence 347
Dotoli firm 203–8

Dow-Jones 136
Drewry, H. P. 156–7
Drilling Rig Committee 130–31
drilling rig line slip 131
 see also oil-drilling rigs
duelling 69
Dumas & Wylie 138
Dunne, John 146

Eagle Star 201
Earle, Roger 18–20
earthquake insurance 64–5
East End 320–21
Economist 71, 218, 306
Edison companies 16
Edmunds, Basil 250, 263
Edwards, Gordon 203–4, 206, 210
El Paso Company 162–5, 222
El Paso Paul Kayser 165
Ellen, Eric 174
Elsbury, Stanley 251
equipment leasing 228–30, 232–3,
 236
 see also computer leasing
Ernst & Whinney 336–7, 343
errors and ommissions insurance
 21, 276, 281
ethical standards 42–3, 116, 219, 244,
 278–9, 329, 356, 358–60
European Economic Community
 (EEC) 42, 147
Evangelides, Vassilios 187
excess-of-loss cover 65, 96–8, 169,
 251, 346, 359
exchange control 357
exports, invisible 30, 322

facultative reinsurance 96, 359
Fadi Shipping Group 191
Far East 276
Far Eastern Regional Investigation
 Team (FERIT) 184
Federal Leasing 220, 222, 233, 236,
 239
Fenchurch International Group 19–
 21, 125
Ferrigno, Pietro 204–5, 208–9, 219
Fiat 195–6, 198, 200–201, 204–7,
 215, 217, 219

Fidentia Marine Insurance Company 347
fiduciary duty, breach of 335
Fielding, Thomas 52
financial guarantee insurance 227–8
Financial Times 38, 218, 220
Findlay, Ian 42–3, 144, 213, 214–15, 218, 264, 270, 272, 280–81, 291, 294–5
fire at sea 198–9, 203–19
fire insurance 62–4, 134, 266
First National Bank of Boston (FNBS) 238–9
Fisher, Sir Henry 40, 284–5, 288, 291
  inquiry 41, 44, 150, 195, 219, 283, 287, 327
  report 285–6, 287–93, 312–13, 315–16, 344
Fletcher-Cooke, Sir Charles 318
f.o.b. system 172
Foden-Pattinson, Peter 261
Follows, John 202, 249–51
Follows, Welley-Poley 249–50, 265
Follwell, Inc. 265
Forbes, T. W. 129
foreign trade 67, 322
Fortescue, 7th earl 242, 243–4, 268, 318
Forwood, A. B. 60, 74
Foster Associates 295
Fox, Geoff 234
France 166–9
fraud 57–60, 72–5, 253–8, 305, 349–350
  charges 252
  charter 175–7
  marine 35, 37, 39, 43, 50, 151–2, 172–94, 200, 203–4, 208; suspected 200, 203–4, 208, 212, 214–19
  property insurance 257–60
  underwriters' 72–5, 243–4
  see also under claims
Frizzell 125
Furness Holder 125

Gaddafi, Colonel 227
Galbraith Wrightson 190
Gallagher, Eddie 89

gambling 52
Gardner Mountain & Capel-Cure 124
Gaze & Sons 70
General Public Utilities Corporation (GPU) 16–18
George I, King 51
Georgoulis, Dimitrios 178, 186–7, 191–2
Geyer, Richard 234
Gibb, Charles 272
Gibraltar 343
Giffin, L. K. 131
Gill & Duffus 125
Gladstone, W. E. 61
Glanvill Enthoven 126
Goddard, Ken 110–11
Goepfert, John Valentine 116, 253–260, 263, 277, 348–50
Gold Sky 181–2
Gordon, Bob 87
Gordon, Murray 270–71, 281
government regulation 286–7, 353–355, 360
Graham, Gordon 295
Graham Miller 200, 204
grammar schools 248
Gray, Bruce 261, 284
Greece 157, 175, 177–8
Green, Sir Peter 41, 79, 85, 91, 159–160, 272, 281–2
  Chairman of Lloyd's 291, 293, 302–3, 312, 336–8, 345–7, 352–353, 362
  Lloyd's reform and 314–17, 328
  underwriting interests 85, 124, 127, 183, 227, 310, 344
Green, Toby 344, 346
Greenberg, Maurice 'Hank' 145–6
Grigalunas, Thomas 169
Grob, Kenneth 150, 302, 306–9, 315, 317, 329–33, 335–43, 362
Gross, Christopher 92
Guardian 353
Guernsey 343
guerrillas 88–90

Hall, Frank B. 18, 19, 37, 124, 142–143, 147, 163
Hamilton, Archibald 305

Hanseatic merchants   47–8
Hargreaves, Walter   134
Harrison, Dennis   345, 253, 257–8, 260, 262, 277, 280, 349
   see also Den-Har binder
Harrison fraud case   58, 116, 227
Harrison, Stanley B. K.   72–3
Harvey Bowring & Others   20
Hattrick, Ian   273, 279–81
Haven International   188–9, 191–2
Hawkes, John   170
Hazell, Dick   19, 21, 85
Heath, Cuthbert Eden   62–5, 70–71, 84–5, 98, 239, 317, 320, 328, 344
Heath, Edward   114
Hereford settlement   340
Heritage Insurance Company   253
Higgins, Alec   261, 277
Hill, Roy   203–6, 209–12, 217
Hill Samuel   125
Hills, Roderick   337
hire-purchase finance   72
Hirtenturm   8, 13
Hodge, Julian   250
Hogg Robinson   85, 91–2, 120, 124, 291, 316, 320
Holland, Frank   344
Hollerith, Herman   228
Holmwood & Crawford   8, 11, 125
Holsteinson   72
Hong Kong   153, 160, 185
Horsey, Sylvia   127–8
Howard, George   156
Howden, Alexander   37, 79, 81, 124, 142, 150, 306–9, 314–17, 329–34, 350
   funds diverted from   335–42, 352
Howell, John   253
Hozier, Henry   66–9
Hudson, Sir Havelock   40, 42, 205–206, 217, 294
Hudson syndicate   88
Hurrican Betsy   35, 113, 131, 145
hurricanes   97
Hurst, Margery   127
Hutton, Gordon   284

immigrants   321
Imperial Insurance Company   346, 362

Ince & Co.   210
Inchcape, earl of   124
income tax   109–12, 114
Indepenta   155
Indonesia   264
Industrial & Commercial Finance Corporation   125
Industrial Guarantee Corporation   72
inert-gas safety systems   156
inflation   160–61, 168
Insurance Company of Africa v. SCOR   203
intelligence department, Lloyd's   9, 77–8
Intercap   234–5
interest rates   243, 327
Intergovernmental Maritime Consultative Organization (IMCO)   154, 168
International Business Machines (IBM)   220, 223, 228–31, 235–238, 240–41
International Group Pool   169
international insurance market   121–3
   overcapacity   358
IntraGlobal   245, 253
invisible earnings   30, 322
IRA   89
Iran   173–4
Irving Birch   11
Isle of Man   343
Italian kidnapping   89–90
Itel   235–6, 238–9

'J' forms   227
Jackson, Robin   85
James, Fred S.   125, 150
James, Len   76
Janson Green   124, 163, 224, 291, 344, 346
Japan   153, 185
Jardine group   126
Jenner, Michael   149
jewellery insurance   64, 87
Johnson & Higgins   138–9, 148, 150
Judd, Kate Sliwinska   80

Kaiser Aluminium   162–3

Kalamiropoulos, Antonios 192
Kameteros, Costas 176–7
Karlinsky, Raymond E. 256, 276, 350
Keeni-Meeni Services (KMS) 93
Kenilworth insurance company 347–50
Kentridge, Sidney 279
Kershaw, R. F. 104
kidnapping and ransom (K & R) 23, 88–95
Kiln, R. J. 85, 317
Kiln, Robert 34–5, 292
King, General Sir Frank 92
King, Peter 245
Kintore, 12th earl of 267
Kissinger, Henry 139–40
Kitchin, Harcourt 71
Komiseris, Stylianos E. 181–2
Kramer, Donald 145

Langton, Thomas 284
Larner, David 39
Latin American kidnapping 88–9, 90–91, 95
Lawrence, Murray 20–21, 238, 240, 337
Lawrence, Sir Thomas 53–4
Layfield, Sir Frank 317–18
Lease Financing Corporation 233
Leasco 230–31
leasing, equipment 228–30, 232–3, 236
see also computer leasing
Lebanon 176–8
LeBoeuf, Lamb, Leiby & Macrae 258–60, 263, 269, 277
legal costs 226, 265, 279
leisure insurance 269–70
Leslie & Godwin 37, 124, 143–4, 147
Lewis, Albert 145–6, 338, 349, 351
liability
    aggregation of 165
    brokers' 42
    Names' 105, 270–73
    oil pollution 168–9
    underwriters' 64–5, 73, 99, 270–271
    unlimited 243–4, 270–71, 278, 282; hedge against 116

Liberia 57, 169, 192
Liechtenstein 335–6, 340, 343
Lima Navigation 179
line slip 225
liquid natural gas (LNG) carriers 154, 161–5, 222
Lloyd, Edward 49–50
Lloyd's 141, 164, 172, 321–2
    accounting system 106–8, 354
    Act (1871) 56, 60, 80, 244; (1911) 62; (1982) 319, 323, 328, 354
    agents 65–6
    American takeover bid 149
    anchor mark 61
    audit 108–9, 269, 272–3; inquiry 354
    buildings 24–5, 53–8, 76–7, 294–300
    Caller 77
    coffee-house 49–53, 58
    Committee 40, 53, 116, 300, 307, 309–10, 337; American insurance market control fears 37–8, 43, 144–5, 147, 149–50; constitutional reform and 40, 287, 291–294, 316; criticism of 36, 39, 56, 214; Den-Har and Sasse losses and 258–9, 262–5, 269, 272, 275, 280–83; powers 55, 57, 59–60, 71, 227, 244
    competitors 159, 184
    confidence in 327–9, 350–52
    constitutional reform 284, 287–294, 302–6, 310–19
    Council 288, 292–3, 303–6, 312, 318, 328, 346–7, 354
    criticism of 36, 38–40, 44, 56, 61, 214, 218, 222, 239–41, 258–9, 263, 322, 338, 350–51, 353
    earnings 30, 322
    employees 29–30, 76
    foreign business 96–7, 129, 135, 138–9, 141–2, 146–8
    general meetings 288, 303, 313–314
    immunity against suit 305–6, 310, 314, 318–19
    intelligence department 9, 77–8
    List 65–6

Lloyd's–*cont.*
  market   22, 25, 62–3, 75, 159
  members   26–8, 30–31, 38, 56–8,
    74, 99, 112, 288–9; agents   28,
    103–5, 281, 313, 316; Association
    of External Members   304, 314;
    expulsion of   60, 252; numbers
    113–16, 288; postal vote   316
  Merchants' Room subscription
    58–9
  non-marine role   22
  'open form'   13, 170–71
  policies   227
  Policy Signing Office (LPSO)   29,
    80, 94, 134, 261–3, 266, 277, 280,
    295
  private bill   292–3, 302–3, 302–6,
    310–19
  prosperity   30–32, 35, 114
  radio licence, withdrawn   69
  Register   65–6
  Room   76–84, 294, 298–9
  rules, breach of   244, 261–2, 270–
    271, 273–4, 278, 280, 310
  Savonita inquiry   215–19, 287
  scandals   72–4, 152, 227, 326–9,
    342, 344, 346–7, 350, 352
  self-regulation   285–7, 323, 327,
    329, 353–6, 359–60
  services provided by   9–10, 61–7,
    75, 153
  sued by Names   274, 276–80
  tradition   45–6, 323, 325
  Trust Deed   56–7
  Underwriters Claims & Recoveries
    Office (LUCRO)   12–13
  women in   126–8
  world market share, declining   325
  see also brokers; mergers; take-
    overs;   underwriters;   under-
    writing
Locks, Thomas Jurgen   190, 192
London Association   169
London Assurance   51
London, business migrations in   23–
  25, 320–21
Lord, Bissell & Brook   259
Lord Byron   180–81
loss
  clerk   77–8

constructive total   12, 163–4, 204,
  208
  excess of   65, 96–8, 169, 251, 346,
    359
loss-of-profits insurance   63, 98
losses   36, 113, 323
  carrying forward   252, 265, 270
  computer leasing   220, 222, 238–
    239, 266, 323, 341
  gas carriers   162–5
  marine   33–5, 39, 42, 54, 159–61,
    181–3, 198–9, 210–11
  property insurance   243, 263–4,
    266
  repaid by government   111
  Sasse syndicate   243–4, 263–4,
    266, 268–71, 274, 282, 349; legal
    proceedings   273–4,   274–80;
    negotiated settlement   281–3;
    revolt against   243–4, 270–83,
    328
  satellites   136–7
  tankers   35, 154–9, 165–9, 185–94
  see also fraud; premium, skim-
    ming, stripping; scuttling
Lowes, Roger   7, 165
Lowndes, Lambert   125
Ludwig, Daniel K.   159
Lutine   33, 78
Lutine bell   33–4, 78
Lyon de Falbe   42

Macaulay, Lord   47
Macaulay, Zachary   55
Maclean, Alexander   129
McCrindle, Robert, QC   279
McRae, Hamish   344
Maitland, Bill   163
Makrygiorgos, Gregorios   187
Malik, Rex   221
Mamarella, Richard   257–8, 349
managing agents   290–92, 294, 313–
  316, 348, 331
  see also brokers, divestment issue
Mance, Sir Henry   127
Mann, Michael, QC   311–14, 317
Marconi   68–9
Maria Alejandra   155–6
marine insurance   10–11, 14, 29, 47–

marine insurance–*cont.*
  52, 61, 69, 75, 135, 151–4, 159–
  160, 171, 325, 357
  see also losses
Mark, Sir Robert 92
Marryat, Joseph 56
Marsh & McLennan 18, 20, 37–8,
  122, 124, 135–6, 140, 142–3, 146–
  150, 239, 326
Marshall, Michael 311
Marson, Giorgio Ajmone 201
Marten, Frederick William 62, 75
Mathew, John 205, 213, 215–17
Mattarelli, Dr 205, 208
Matthew Wrightson 137
Maynard, Leslie 170
Meacher, Michael 311–12, 316, 318,
  338
  committee 303, 306, 309, 311, 314
Meak, Raimondo 219
Mendelsohn, Martin 270–72, 276,
  279–80
Mercers' Hall men 51
Merchants' Room subscription 58–
  59
mergers 37, 121–2, 129, 131, 138,
  143–4, 329, 334
Merrett Dixey 264, 269, 273–4
Merrett, Roy 264
Merrett, Stephen 79, 83, 84–5, 224,
  264–6, 268–9, 272, 274, 276, 310,
  317
Methane Pioneer 161
Mexico, Gulf of 35
Michael 181, 182–3
Michalopoulos, Captain 180–81
Miller, Peter 156, 170, 312, 362
Miller, Thomas R. 125
Millett, Richard 208, 213, 218
Mills & Allen 125
Mills, Neil 150
Minet Holdings 343–4, 352
Minet, J. H. 85, 124, 315, 317, 321
Mishcon, Lord 319
misrepresentation 335
Mitakis, Nikolaos 186, 190–91
Mitchell, Chester 347–8
Mitchell, Parry 223, 240
Mitchley, Anthony 314
Mitolo, Giorgio 116, 196–7, 203–5,

  207, 209, 211, 215, 217, 219
Moate, Roger 316
monopoly *v.* private individuals 51
Moran, Christopher 38, 251–2, 342
motor insurance 29, 75, 85, 99, 107,
  141, 249, 347
multinational corporations 90–91,
  95, 123, 129, 137, 143, 173–4,
  324, 326, 331

Names 99, 103–6, 112–18, 243, 267,
  290, 328–9, 359
  audit 108–9, 273, 275
  deficiencies 263–4, 266
  liability 105, 270–73
  Lloyd's reform and 304–5, 311,
    318
  Lloyd's sued by 274, 276–80
  premium income limit 105–6, 108
  taxation 109–12
  women 126–7
  see also Sasse syndicate
Napier, Nigel, 14th baron Napier &
  Ettrick 242–3, 268, 318
Nash, John 345
Nasi, Giovanni 206, 217
national reinsurance companies 96–
  97
nationalist insurance industries 325
natural gas, liquefied (LNG) 161–5
Nelson, Ted 96–8
Nerité 132
'net line' underwriting 15, 19
New Southern RE Company (NSR)
  335–6, 339–40, 342
New Statesman 322
New York insurance exchange 38,
  145
New Zealand 38, 276
Newfoundland 11, 135
Newman, John 245–6, 248–53,
  257–61, 265–6, 282
news media 22–3, 123
Nigeria 174–5, 176
non-marine insurance 21, 29, 61, 69,
  75, 82–4, 95–6, 134–5
Northern Ireland 89, 98
Northern Ships Agency 188–9
Nottage, Peter 228, 233–4, 237,
  240–41

Nuclear Mutual Ltd (NML)   16, 18, 21
Nuclear   Regulatory   Commission   17, 18, 20
nuclear risk insurance   14–22
   pools for   15–16

Oakeley Vaughan   247, 350
O'Brien, Lord   319
Observer   353
Ogden Corporation   162
oil
   cargo owners' liability   168
   companies   84
   drilling rigs   10, 35, 82, 130, 323, 346
   pollution   22, 166–9
   revenues   174
   tankers   35, 67, 153–4; losses   35, 154–9, 165–9, 185–94; premiums   156, 159
O'May, Donald   158
O'Neill, Terry   269–72
'open form', Lloyd's   13, 170–71
Organization of Petroleum Exporting Countries (OPEC)   187
Outhwaite, Dick   85
overdue market   78, 134
Oxford Shipping   189

Page, Allan   335, 337–8, 340–42
Page, Sir Graham   304–6, 312
paintings, insurance of   87–8
Palmer, Rita   145
Panama   172, 175, 185, 256, 335, 341
Pao, Sir Y. K.   153
Parker,   Nicholas   304–5,   310–11, 317
Parliament   43–4, 51, 56, 195, 213
   Lloyd's   members   in   Commons   213–14, 353
   regulation of Lloyd's by, danger of   287
   Savonita affair in   213–15, 305
   see also Lloyd's Act
Parliamentary bills, private   292–3, 300–301
   Lloyd's   302–6, 310–19
Patterson, Robert   348
Paul Bradford   125

Payne, E. W.   129
PCW   124, 224, 343–5, 352
   see also Cameron-Webb, Peter
Peace, Charles   63
Pearson,   Malcolm   39,   116,   195, 197–8, 200–208, 210–19, 302, 305–6, 311
Pearson   Webb   Springbett   (PWS)   195–203, 205, 206, 208, 211, 216
Pei, I. M.   295–6
Pepys, Samuel   56
Pero Shipping Company   177
Persian Gulf   23, 38, 81–2
personal accident insurance   86
Peterson, Roger   157
Peyton-Jones, Jeremy   104
Phillips, Nicholas, QC   279
Phoenix Trust Ltd   254
Piano & Rogers   295–6
Pickering, Murray   277
Pierrakos, Nestor   182
Pilcher, Anthony   84
Pimmerton Shipping   188–9
piracy   35, 151, 175, 177, 187
Pires, Manuel José   178–80
Platt, Adrian   163
Poland syndicate   84, 125
policies   11, 227
Policy Signing Office, Lloyd's   29, 80, 94, 134, 261–3, 266, 277, 280, 295
political risks   91, 93, 95, 226–7
Pompidou Centre   296–7
Posgate, Ian   78–84, 108, 124, 137, 256, 302, 306–10, 312, 314–15, 330–38, 340–41, 362
   dismissal by Howden's   338
   problem of   304, 307–9, 330
   suspension   337–9
   syndicates   307, 330–32, 336
Posgate & Denby   79, 81, 309, 330
premium   78–9, 84–5, 88–9, 96, 99, 103, 159–61, 324–5, 358
   capital exported as   357
   income   122–3, 307; limits   105, 108, 260, 263, 276, 308–9, 331, 333, 358–9; world   121–2
   skimming   255, 257–8, 260, 343, 349
   stripping   332, 337, 359

premium–*cont.*
  trust fund 71–2, 105, 359
  underwriting for 101, 160, 358
Prentice, John 138, 196–7, 207–11, 213, 217–18
Price, Charles 129
Price–Anderson Act, 1956 (US) 16–17
Price Forbes 249
product liability insurance 99
profit-sharing 147
profits 27, 58, 114
  underwriting 27, 100–102, 106–7
Promotora de Occidente SA (POSA) 256, 276, 350
property insurance 243, 253–4, 260–62, 270
  'Fair Plan' 255
  fraudulent 257–60
  losses 243, 263–4, 266
proportional reinsurance 96
Protection and Indemnity (P & I) Clubs 169
Pryke, John 20–21
public schools 41, 248, 322

Qantas airline 333–4
quota-share reinsurance 96, 332–3, 336–7, 343–5, 359

Radcliffe, Julian 91–2
radio communications 68–9
Raw, Charles 250
Reed Stenhouse 124–5
Regan, John 38, 140, 142–4, 146–9
registration abroad 357
Reidel, Anton 186, 187–9, 191–2
reinsurance 10, 15, 19–21, 29–30, 65, 80–84, 95–8, 135, 141–2, 170, 197, 202, 250–51, 324–5, 350
  American 38, 96–7, 107, 145, 326
  cargo 196, 198–200, 203–4, 206–207, 219
  catastrophe 96, 98, 359
  facultative 96, 359
  premium income limits and 309, 331, 358–9
  property 243, 253, 260–62, 270
  quota-share 96, 332–3, 336–7, 343–5, 359

Third World 256, 358
  to close 106–7
Reinsurance (Bermuda) Ltd 307, 310
Remington Rand 229
Renton, Timothy 214
reserves, underwriting 27, 100, 105–108
  tax relief on 110–11
Resources Insurance Company 253
Reyner, Pedro 256
Rheingold syndicate 246–7, 252
Richardson, Gordon 353–4
risks, taking 300
Robco Worldwide Facilities 348
Robinson, George Richard 58
Rogers, Richard 296–300
Rogowski, Mario 178–9
Rokeby-Johnson, Ralph 85, 224
roll-over policy 341, 346
Roscoe, John 139
Rosina, Enzo 205, 219
Rothschild Investment Trust 147
royal assent 302
Royal Exchange 51, 54, 58
Royle, Tim 91–2
Rugg, Sir Percy 218
Rutherford, Richard 161, 163

St George, Charles A. B. 247, 257, 350
Salaroli, Benedetto 206–7
Salek 204
Salem 185–94
Salenrederierna 188
salvage
  agreement 13, 170–71
  loss claims 209
Salvage Association 13, 66, 154, 156
Samuel, Marcus 132, 133–4
San Francisco earthquake 64–5
Sasol 191, 193
Sasse, F. H. ('Tim') 243–8, 251–3, 257–62, 264–6, 268, 277–8, 280, 282, 304, 350
  syndicate 36, 41, 58, 267–8, 277, 304–5, 327–8
  legal proceedings 273–83
  losses 112–14, 243–4, 263–4, 266, 268–71, 274, 282, 349; revolt

Sasse, F. H.–*cont.*
    against 243–4, 270–83, 328
    suspended 263–4
Sasse Turnbull 264–5
satellite insurance 136–7
Saudi Arabia 177–8, 191
Savonita affair 36–7, 39, 43, 195,
    198–9, 203–19, 304, 327
    Lloyd's inquiry into 215–19, 287
scandals 72–4, 152, 227, 326–9, 342,
    344, 346–7, 350, 352
Scott, Nicholas 311
scuttling 35, 153, 157–8, 176, 181–5,
    193–4, 204
Seascope 126, 345, 351
Secret Service 23, 93
Secretan marine syndicate 84–5
Sedgwick Group 18, 37, 85, 129–32,
    149–50, 163, 239, 315, 317, 320
semaphore 68
Serete 295
Serrati, Gian Carlo 205, 208
Shell Oil 132, 159, 161, 167, 186,
    190, 191–3
Shipomex 190
shipping
    intelligence 61, 65–7, 77
    recession 152
    turnround delays 174
Shorrock, Jim 188–9
signal stations 66–8
'slip', broker's 11–12, 25–6, 81, 225
Small, Michael 18–19
Smith, Fred 267, 282
Smith, John 353
Smith, Ted 245, 253, 260, 262
Società Assicuratrice Industriale
    (SAI) 196, 202, 206–7, 217
Società Italiana Assicurazioni Tras-
    porti (SIAT) 196–200, 202–6,
    208–11, 215–17, 219
solicitors 268
Somalia 180–81
Soudan, Frederick Ed 188–9, 191–2
South Africa 186–94
South Sea Bubble 50–51
Southern International RE Company
    SA (SIR) 335–7, 339–42
Southern Marine and Aviation
    Underwriters, Inc. 131–2

Southern Reinsurance AG (SRAG)
    335–6, 339
Special Air Service (SAS) 88, 92–3
Special Branch 93
Sphere Drake 334–7, 341–2
Splendoria, Joyce 348
Springbett, David 201–2, 206
Standard Oil 169
Starter 183–4
State Fire and Casualty (Florida)
    256–7
Steele, Michael 188
Steele, Richard 49
Stein, Bert 190–91
Steinberg, Saul 230–31
Stewart Smith 131
Stewart Wrightson 315, 317
Stock Exchange 114, 124, 142
Stoddart, Peter 149
'stop loss' policy 108–9
Strathalmond, Lord 319
Strathcona, Lord 319
Stratton, Bert 86–7
Street-Porter, Cecil 233, 237–8
Sturge, Arthur Lloyd 73–4, 85
Sturge, R. W., & Co. 85, 317, 334–5
Sunday Telegraph 39–40, 157, 218
Sunday Times 339–40, 350
supertankers 35, 67, 154–5, 158–9
Surety Leasing Inc. 223–4, 231, 234
Swage, Mrs Maureen 127
Swann & Everett 331
syndicates 12–14, 26–7, 61–2, 711–
    712, 75, 79–81, 84, 96, 99, 104–6,
    109, 115, 120, 267
    expenses 290
    management 103, 111–12

takeovers 146–50, 326, 331, 333–4,
    345
Tanker Owners Voluntary Agree-
    ment concerning Liability for Oil
    Pollution (TOVALOP) 168
tax
    avoidance 356–7, 359
    capital gains 110–11
    income 109–12, 114
    relief 108–12, 120
Taylor, Ronald 213, 317
tea 46

Telex, Inc. 231
terrorism 92–4
Texas, Les 339
Third World 30, 152, 226
  reinsurance 256, 358
Thomas Organization 125
Thornton, Dicky 55
Three Mile Island reactor accident
  14, 16–21
Three Quays agency 85
Times, The 71
Titanic 134
'tonner' policy 251
Toomey, Barry 350
Toomey, B. F. G., & Associates 348,
  350
Toplis & Harding 238–9
Torinita 206
Torrey Canyon 156, 166, 168
toxic chemicals 108
Trade Department 338, 350
  insurance division 109, 286
trade union immunity 306
tradition 45–6, 323, 325
Transamerica 125
Transworld Underwriters 245, 253
Triandafilou, Andrew 189
Tung, C. Y. 153, 155
Tunstall, Jeremy 123
Turle, Arish' 92, 93, 95
Turnbull, Thomas 245
Tyler Navigation 183

uberrima fides 26, 347n.
underwriters 12, 21, 76, 96, 255–6,
  356, 358
  accounts 308; auditing of 70–
  72, 74, 269
  active 25, 28, 85–6, 98
  American 146
  fraud by 72–5, 243–4
  insolvency 57–9, 70–74
  liability 64–5, 73, 99, 270–71
  Lloyd's 25–31, 51, 54–6, 60–61,
  77–85, 98–9, 158–9, 163, 184,
  203, 209–17, 219, 323; binding
  authority 244–5, 247, 251–3,
  257–62, 271, 273, 275–6, 278,
  280; Claims and Recoveries

Office (LUCRO) 161, 163,
  203–4; in default 269; suspended 78, 334, 337–9; tri-
  bunalizing 262, 271; *see also*
  Savonita affair
  salary 103
  trust deed 59
  trust fund 70–72, 74
  v. companies 51–2, 54, 61
  women 126–8
underwriting
  account, certificate of 273, 275
  agent 28
  broker-controlled 289–94, 302–3,
  306, 309–10, 312–18, 334
  commission 103
  error 324
  for premium 101, 160, 358
  see also claims; losses; Names;
  premium; profits; reserves
Unimar Monaco 345
United Leasing 240
United States of America
  anti-trust suits 228–9
  banks 221, 223, 232–4, 236, 238–9
  brokers 37–8, 43, 122–4, 131–2,
  134–6, 140–41, 317, 326;
  British firms and 123, 129,
  138–9, 142–50, 289, 326, 329
  Congress 301, 311
  criticism of Lloyd's 350–51
  Federal Maritime Administration
  163
  gas imports 162
  insurance exchanges 38, 145–6,
  326
  insurance market 10, 140, 142,
  259, 326, 328
  oil pollution claims in 167–9
  protectionism 141
  regulation of business in 355–6
  reinsurance 38, 96–7, 107, 145,
  326
  Securities and Exchange Commission (SEC) 332, 335, 337,
  339, 341
  signal stations 68
  underwriters 146
Universal Casualty and Surety 348
Universal Oil Trade 173

unlimited liability 243–4, 270–71, 278, 282
  hedge against 116
U.S. Excess 257–8, 260
'utmost good faith' 26, 34, 37, 42, 219, 241, 244, 327, 347, 361

Vansittart 50
Vehicle & General Insurance Company (V & G) 249–51
Venezuelan 60
Vernon, Rutherford 88
Vestey family 104

Wall Street Journal 349–50
Wallrock, John 317, 343–4, 352
Waltham, Brian 210
Waltons & Morse 272–3, 277–8
war 35, 54–6
War Risk Exclusion Agreement 227
war risks 23, 38, 54, 81–2
Washington Post 221, 224, 232
Watson, Brook 55
Watson, Thomas J., Jr 230, 240
Watt, David 40, 285
Webb, John 197, 201–2
Webb Zerafa Menkes Housden Partnership 295

Webster, Peter 273
Weller-Poley, J. H. 250
Weller-Poley, John 104, 247, 249–51
White, F. A. 71
Whitechapel 321
Wigham Poland 143–4, 146, 150
Wilcox, Alec 74–5
Wilde, Oscar 221
Williams, E. F. 224, 237
Willis Faber 37, 39, 82, 97, 120, 127, 137–9, 148, 150, 317
  Savonita affair and 195–8, 206–8, 210–13, 217–18
Willis, Henry 137
Wilson, Reid 342
Windlesham, Lord 319
W M D Underwriting Agencies Ltd 343–4
women at Lloyd's 126–8
Wood, Charles D. 132
workmen's compensation 98
world insurance market
  Lloyd's share of 325
  overcapacity 324

Zephyr 343
Zylkha, Eliahou 340